THE MASTER MUSICIANS

VAUGHAN WILLIAMS

SERIES EDITED BY R. LORRY TODD

THE MASTER MUSICIANS

Titles Available in Paperback

Bach • Malcolm Boyd

Bartók • Malcolm Gillies

Berlioz • Hugh Macdonald

Beethoven • Barry Cooper

Brahms • Malcolm MacDonald

Britten • Michael Kennedy

Bruckner • Derek Watson

Chopin • Jim Samson

Grieg • John Horton

Handel • Donald Burrows

Liszt • Derek Watson

Mahler • Michael Kennedy

Mendelssohn • Philip Radcliffe

Monteverdi • Denis Arnold

Mozart • Julian Rushton

Musorgsky • David Brown

Puccini • Julian Budden

Purcell • J. A. Westrup

Rachmaninoff • Geoffrey Norris

Rossini • Richard Osborne

Schoenberg • Malcolm MacDonald

Schubert • John Reed

Schumann • Eric Frederick Jensen

Sibelius • Robert Layton

Richard Strauss • Michael Kennedy

Tchaikovsky • Edward Garden

Vaughan Williams • James Day

Verdi • Julian Budden

Vivaldi • Michael Talbot

Wagner • Barry Millington

Titles Available in Hardcover

Bach • David Schulenberg

Beethoven • Barry Cooper

Berg • Bryan R. Simms and Charlotte Erwin

Bizet • Hugh Macdonald

Byrd • Kerry McCarthy

Carter • David Schiff

Chopin • Jim Samson

Debussy • Eric Frederick Jensen

Schubert • John Reed

Elgar • Robert Anderson

Handel • Donald Burrows

Liszt • Derek Watson

MacDowell • E. Douglas Bomberger

Mozart • Julian Rushton

Musorgsky • David Brown

Puccini • Julian Budden

Rossini • Richard Osborne

Schoenberg • Malcolm MacDonald

Schumann • Eric Frederick Jensen

Schütz • Basil Smallman

Richard Strauss • Michael Kennedy

Strauss • Laurenz Lütteken

Stravinsky • Paul Griffiths

Tallis • Kerry McCarthy

Tchaikovsky • Roland John Wiley

Vaughan Williams • Eric Saylor

Verdi • Julian Budden

THE MASTER MUSICIANS

VAUGHAN WILLIAMS

ERIC SAYLOR

OXFORD

UNIVERSITY PRESS

OXFORD
UNIVERSITY PRESS

Oxford University Press is a department of the University of Oxford. It furthers
the University's objective of excellence in research, scholarship, and education
by publishing worldwide. Oxford is a registered trade mark of Oxford University
Press in the UK and certain other countries.

Published in the United States of America by Oxford University Press
198 Madison Avenue, New York, NY 10016, United States of America.

© Oxford University Press 2022

Library of Congress Cataloging-in-Publication Data
Names: Saylor, Eric, author.
Title: Vaughan Williams / Eric Saylor.
Description: New York : Oxford University Press, 2022. |
Series: Master musicians series | Includes bibliographical references and index.
Identifiers: LCCN 2021058960 (print) | LCCN 2021058961 (ebook) |
ISBN 9780190918569 (hardback) | ISBN 9780190918583 (epub)
Subjects: LCSH: Vaughan Williams, Ralph, 1872-1958. |
Composers—England—Biography. | Vaughan Williams, Ralph,
1872-1958—Criticism and interpretation. | Music—England—20th century—
History and criticism.
Classification: LCC ML410.V3 S18 2022 (print) | LCC ML410.V3 (ebook) |
DDC 780.92 [B]—dc23
LC record available at https://lccn.loc.gov/2021058960
LC ebook record available at https://lccn.loc.gov/2021058961

DOI: 10.1093/oso/9780190918569.001.0001

1 3 5 7 9 8 6 4 2
Printed by Sheridan Books, Inc., United States of America

For my family

Contents

Guide to Abbreviations and Editorial Methods

Several of the most regularly cited sources by or about Vaughan Williams used in this book have been abbreviated as follows (full citations are available in the bibliography):

CCVW   Alain Frogley and Aidan J. Thomson, eds., *The Cambridge Companion to Vaughan Williams*

CVW   Michael Kennedy, *A Catalogue of the Works of Ralph Vaughan Williams* (2d ed.)

HR   Ursula Vaughan Williams and Imogen Holst, eds., *Heirs and Rebels*

NME   Ralph Vaughan Williams, *National Music and Other Essays* (2nd ed.)

RVW   Ursula Vaughan Williams, *RVW: A Biography of Ralph Vaughan Williams*

TSR   Stephen Connock, ed., *Toward the Sun Rising: Ralph Vaughan Williams Remembered*

VWD   Celia Newbery, ed., *Vaughan Williams in Dorking*

VWE   Byron Adams and Robin Wells, eds., *Vaughan Williams Essays*

VWL   Hugh Cobbe, Katharine Hogg, and Colin Coleman, eds., *The Letters of Ralph Vaughan Williams* (online database, http://vaughanwilliams.uk). Citations of this source will feature the abbreviated title followed by the number of the relevant letter (e.g., *VWL* 234). Note that the online numbering system differs from that of the original print version of this source (ed. Hugh Cobbe, OUP, 2008)

VWM   David Manning, ed., *Vaughan Williams on Music*

VWP   Lewis Foreman, ed., *Ralph Vaughan Williams in Perspective*

VWS   Alain Frogley, ed., *Vaughan Williams Studies*
VWW   Jon Ceander Mitchell, *Ralph Vaughan Williams'*
            Wind Works
WVW   Michael Kennedy, *The Works of Ralph Vaughan Williams*
            (2d ed.)

Additionally, citations of any compositions, articles, or essays written by Vaughan Williams (including those published in *NME* or *VWM*), and any correspondence involving Vaughan Williams's participation, will employ the unitalicized "RVW" in place of his full or last names.

Abbreviations employed for regularly recurring archives and journals are as follows:

BL   The British Library
JRMA   *Journal of the Royal Musical Association*
ML   *Music & Letters*
MQ   *The Musical Quarterly*
MT   *The Musical Times*
RCMM   *The RCM Magazine*
VWJ   *Ralph Vaughan Williams Society Journal*

Dates associated with compositions refer to the year of first performance unless otherwise indicated.

Preface

James day, in the preface to the third edition (1998) of his Vaughan Williams biography belonging to the present series, excitedly alluded to the recent release of "a number of new works on the composer."[1] A generous assessment of his claim tallies four new books published between 1988 and 1998 (and some notable revised editions), along with a few dissertations and a handful of journal articles—a small harvest, though some of its fruits have proven exceedingly nourishing. In the quarter-century since, however, that scholarly bounty has grown beyond all expectations, encompassing compilations of Vaughan Williams's correspondence and prose writings; detailed analytical and interpretive studies of his symphonies, wind music, and stage works; memoirs and reminiscences; guides to research; new and revised editions of scores; myriad professional recordings and documentaries; and multiple essay collections, journal articles, and book chapters. The sheer volume of material reflects the revival of interest in Vaughan Williams's life and music among twenty-first-century scholars, performers, and audiences—not just in the British Isles, but in continental Europe and North America as well. That the present life-and-works biography is the first one written by an American author indicates the degree to which Vaughan Williams's music, though inspired by many English cultural influences, has transcended narrowly nationalistic creative goals and interpretations.

Given these circumstances, I have begun entirely afresh with this biography, examining the documents that Vaughan Williams and his contemporaries left behind and poring over the wealth of secondary sources now available, all of which illuminate a far more wide-ranging and complex portrait of the composer than the one historically presented. Yet I must also acknowledge my very great debt to the pioneering work of Ursula Vaughan Williams and Michael Kennedy, whose respective authorized biography (*RVW: A Biography of Ralph Vaughan Williams*) and works study (*The Works of Ralph Vaughan Williams*) have withstood the test of time since their initial publication in 1964. Writing a volume covering both biographical and musical topics that is less than half the length of theirs combined means sacrificing a certain level of detail, and their unique relationships to the composer provided them with insights inaccessible to me. Although I have made some corrections and emendations to their accounts in my own, I enthusiastically direct readers seeking further information on the composer and his music to their aforementioned volumes as a first port of call.

With that said, I have had the opportunity to study and listen to many of Vaughan Williams's early works to which Kennedy's access was limited or nonexistent, the freedom to address certain biographical topics that may have been awkward or insensitive to raise in the past, and the ability to review sources and analyses that did not exist in the mid-1960s. Additionally, the passage of time has had profound effects on the methodologies, perspectives, and ideological treatment applied to the biographical study of composers in general, and particularly for a figure as paradoxical and contradictory as Vaughan Williams. Here is someone who felt that cultural nationalism could facilitate international understanding and cooperation; who mentored, collaborated with, and facilitated professional opportunities for women throughout his life, while also embarking on an extended affair with the woman who would become his second wife; whose dedicated work ethic and fastidious attention to detail never quite banished his fears of failure and incompetency; whose contributions to sacred music reveal a powerful understanding of and respect for religious faith despite his own lack of belief; whose establishment credentials belied a strong disruptive streak. His musical legacy has proven no less in need of reconsideration. The outdated assumption that his musical influences began and ended with English folk song has been replaced by a far more nuanced understanding of his idiom. Folk song is indeed a part of that, but so too is post-Wagnerian chromaticism, French impressionism, Tudor-era ecclesiastical music, neoclassicism, eighteenth-century counterpoint, Beethovenian symphonism, and so much more. These combine to form a complex and highly adaptable admixture of stylistic traditions and scalar languages—tonal, modal, pentatonic, whole-tone, hexatonic, octatonic—resulting in a harmonic lexicon "no less progressive than that employed by Bartók, Stravinsky, Prokofiev, or Shostakovich."[2] Moreover, the sheer range of Vaughan Williams's contributions to music over a six-decade period—from hymn tunes to operas, keyboard etudes to solo concerti, wind-band music for amateurs to what is arguably the finest symphonic cycle by any twentieth-century composer—reflects levels of talent and skill as rare as they are impressive, stemming from his rock-solid belief that music should be part of everyone's life, whether to entertain, educate, or inspire.

This need to address such profound shifts in the treatment of Vaughan Williams's life and music has led me to make such a split in this book. The odd-numbered chapters are largely biographical in their scope, focusing on people, places, and events, with significant compositions alluded to but generally not addressed in detail. Such treatment is reserved for the even-numbered chapters, each of which considers more closely the musical works mentioned in the chapter immediately preceding. While space limitations preclude extensive coverage or close analytical detail, I have attempted to extend particular focus to compositions that have hitherto lacked much discussion in the secondary literature, especially those from the early part of the composer's career.

I owe an immense debt to many, many people and institutions for their assistance over the course of writing this book. My employer, Drake University, helped fund two extended sabbatical visits to England in 2018 and 2019, and so I must thank the Provost's Office, the College of Arts and Sciences, the International Center, and particularly Drake University's Center for the Humanities for allowing me to serve as the 2018–2021 Humanities Center Research Scholar; I must also extend my appreciation to my colleagues and students in the Department of Music for their encouragement over the years. Further generous financial aid came from the Vaughan Williams Charitable Trust and its Director, Hugh Cobbe—whose kindness in giving me my first professional break will, I hope, be partly repaid within these pages—and from the Visiting Research Fellowship awarded by Merton College, Oxford, with gracious thanks to Daniel Grimley and Tiffany Stern for encouraging me to apply, and for their scholarly insights, thoughtful assistance, and warm friendship.

This book has benefited from the assistance of librarians, archivists, historians, and musicologists across Britain and North America. I have drawn most heavily upon the holdings at the British Library, especially the Papers of Ralph and Ursula Vaughan Williams, and am very grateful for the patient consideration and unflagging efforts of Steve Cork, Chris

Scobie, and the staff in the Rare Books and Music Reading Room. I would also like to thank my colleagues at Drake University's Cowles Library (particularly Hope Bibens, Laura Krossner, and Kris Mogle), as well as the librarians and archivists at the Cambridge University Library, the Fitzwilliam Museum, and Trinity College, Cambridge (with special thanks to Nicolas Bell); the Shakespeare Birthplace Trust Library and Archives in Stratford-upon-Avon; Catherine Smith at the Charterhouse School Library; Peter Linnitt, Michael Mullen, and the library staff at the Royal College of Music, London; the archivists at the Dorking and District Museum, especially Jane le Cluse; and multiple librarians at Oxford University, including Martin Holmes at the Bodleian Library, Amanda Saville and Michael Riordan at the Queen's College, and Robin Darwall-Smith at University College. I also received unexpected assistance from Helen Upcraft at the Imperial War Museum and Elizabeth Yardeni at the English National Opera, who provided me with hard-to-find historical film and performance recordings. Rosie Johnson, with the RVW Trust, was tremendously helpful in helping me locate and source many of the photographs; additional thanks in this regard to Katie Buehner, Stephen Connock, John Francis, Peter Linnitt, Patrick Russill, and Robert Weedon. Last, but certainly not least, I cannot adequately express my gratitude to Katharine Hogg and Colin Coleman, editors of *The Letters of Ralph Vaughan Williams* online database (and to Hugh Cobbe, who started it all). Without their colossal efforts transcribing and annotating Vaughan Williams's correspondence into a digitally accessible format, this volume simply would not exist.

I am enormously indebted to Jenna Harmon—once the student, now the master—for her assistance with translations and for her thoughtful, perceptive, and honest feedback on several early chapter drafts, which crucially shaped the focus and structure of this book. Later evaluations and suggestions from Kaitlyn Aberson, Charles McGuire, Jennifer Oates, Aidan Thomson, and Paul Watt were no less valuable, and my appreciation for their time and talents just as heartfelt. Special thanks in particular to John Francis, with much gratitude for his patience, enthusiasm, laser-like focus on historical minutiae, facility with scanning technology, and seemingly endless file of old newspaper cuttings. Many other people have generously shared their knowledge and resources over the course of this project, including Byron Adams, Paul Andrews, Robin Barber,

Ian Beckett, Joanna Bullivant, Michael Burden, Jonathan Clinch, Peter Doubleday, Stewart Duncan, Alain Frogley, Peter Gilliver, Deborah Heckert, Laura Kennedy, Brooks Kuykendall, Sherry Lee, David Manning, Andrew McCrea, Michelle Meinhart, Julian Onderdonk, Ceri Owen, Marcía Porter, Nicholas Roth, Phil Rupprecht, Roger Savage, Christopher Scheer, Tom Stone, Amanda Eubanks Winkler, David Wright, and many members of the North American British Music Studies Association; most affectionate thanks as well to Dr. Annabel Brown, for her boundless hospitality and friendship. I appreciate Larry Todd's confidence in recruiting me to take on the formidable task of rebooting this particular line in the Master Musicians series, and to Norm Hirschy and the editorial staff at Oxford University Press—especially Leslie Safford for her conscientious proofreading, Ponneelan and the production team at Newgen, and the external reader assigned to this manuscript, whose thoughtful and extended comments were extremely helpful—for seeing this book through to its conclusion. Everyone previously mentioned has done all they can to enhance my competence and disguise my shortcomings; any remaining errors and failings are entirely my own.

Finally, I cannot say enough for the patience and support of Amy, Lee, and Tamsin, who inspire me every day. I love you all, and promise to come up from the basement now.

Urbandale, Iowa
November 2021

"This Desperate Attempt to Get a Living" (1872–1901)

R ALPH VAUGHAN WILLIAMS'S GREAT-GRANDFATHER WAS JOHN Williams (1757–1810), an Oxford-educated Welshman called to the bar in 1784, who rose through the legal ranks as serjeant-at-law and king's serjeant. His second son, Edward Vaughan Williams (1797–1875), ascended even higher in the field, becoming a judge of the common pleas in 1846. He was knighted the year after, having earned a reputation for fairness, concision, and meticulous accuracy. After marrying Jane Bagot in 1826, Sir Edward passed on his middle name to his children, creating the double-barreled surname used by subsequent generations. Though they lived in London, the family also rented Tanhurst, a country house attractively situated among the Surrey Hills, about thirty miles south of the city.

Their Tanhurst neighbors were the Wedgwoods, who lived upslope at Leith Hill Place. It was an old and sizable house, if not quite a stately home; its patriarch was Josiah Wedgwood III (1795–1880), grandson of the pottery magnate. In 1837, he married Caroline Darwin—his first cousin, and older sister to naturalist Charles Darwin—and the couple had three surviving daughters: Katherine Elizabeth (known as "Sophy," 1842–1911), Margaret Susan (1843–1937), and Lucy Caroline (1846–1919).

The Wedgwoods and Vaughan Williamses knew one another well, so it was no surprise when romance later kindled between Margaret and Arthur Charles Vaughan Williams (1834–1875), Sir Edward's third son, who broke with family tradition to take up a career in the church. He attended Christ Church, Oxford, taking his BA in 1857 and receiving the MA in 1860, the same year he was ordained as Deacon. His first appointment was near Salisbury in Bemerton, former parish of cleric and poet George Herbert, where Arthur flourished; he was subsequently assigned to parishes in Lancashire and closer to home in Hampshire, at which point his relationship with Margaret blossomed. To the pleasure of both families, they married in 1868, immediately after which Arthur was named vicar of All Saints Church in the tiny Gloucestershire village of Down Ampney (pronounced "AMM-nee"). They had three children: Hervey (1869–1945), Margaret (known as "Meggie," 1870–1931), and Ralph—pronounced "Rayf"—born 12 October 1872 in the Down Ampney Vicarage.[1]

Clearly, Vaughan Williams came from privilege, but of an unusual sort. His ancestors' money, education, and status were built upon accomplishments in commercial artisanship, the church, the judiciary, and the government; while comfortable with the gentry, they were not of it. Many occupied positions outside the usual class boundaries of British society, providing a certain latitude in their beliefs and behavior that might otherwise be considered socially unacceptable. Branches of the Vaughan Williams, Wedgwood, and Darwin family trees intertwined radical nonconformists, artists, and abolitionists with jurists, businessmen, and intellectuals, an unusual union of many different perspectives and experiences. As a result, "these members of the social establishment were uniquely positioned to challenge the nineteenth century's new industrial plutocracy through the authority of the state and the civil service, attempting to unite rationality with altruism to build a fairer society."[2] Some relatives, however, gained notoriety for their challenges to the social order. Around the age of six, Vaughan Williams asked his mother about the significance of *On the Origin of Species*, her Uncle Charles being a regular visitor to Leith Hill Place. She responded, "The Bible says that God made the world in six days, Great Uncle Charles thinks it took longer: but we need not worry about it, for it is equally wonderful either way."[3] While a child's answer, it is also a thoughtful one, leaving multiple paths open for young Ralph to consider, and with the promise of joy in discovering the truth of either one.

Tragically, Vaughan Williams never got to know his father, for Arthur died after a short illness in February 1875. Following his death, Margaret and the children moved to Leith Hill Place, where her parents and sister Sophy still lived, so young Ralph grew up surrounded by his extended family, including many aunts, uncles, and cousins. He was closer with Meggie than with Hervey, both in his youth and in adulthood. Like Ralph, she was musically inclined, conducting the Coldharbour Village Choir and later serving as Honorary Secretary for the Leith Hill Musical Competition (LHMC); she also shared her younger brother's propensity for self-deprecation, though to a more damaging degree. Hervey went on to become a barrister and enjoyed a life of quiet middle-class respectability; he sang in the Bach Choir when Ralph was its conductor, and the brothers remained amicable if distant throughout their adulthood.

Life at Leith Hill Place was comfortable, with a staff of a dozen servants to manage the running of the house and some four acres of gardens, lawns, and orchards. Vaughan Williams was particularly fond of his nursemaid, Sarah Wager (affectionately calling her "a complete red"), who shared her radical politics with the children while instilling respect for good manners, and the children enjoyed adventures throughout the house and grounds.[4] It was also here that Vaughan Williams had his formative musical experiences. His Aunt Sophy gave him his first lessons in piano—later augmented by the Goodchild family in nearby Ockley—and in music theory, working with him through Dorothy Kilner's *A Child's Introduction to Thorough Bass* (1819) and John Stainer's *Harmony* (1871) before he undertook a correspondence course in music theory through Edinburgh University at the age of eight. (Sophy was allowed to dictate his answers because his penmanship was appalling; naturally left-handed, he conformed to the Victorian practice of obliging right-hand dominance.) He also exchanged letters about orchestration methods with Wager's brother, Henry, an organist and teacher, and began taking violin lessons when he was about seven from one Mr. Cramer, a German music teacher in Eastbourne. Vaughan Williams called the instrument "my musical salvation" (though he later switched to viola), preferring it and singing to playing keyboard instruments, though he regularly performed piano duets with his siblings, and an organ was installed at Leith Hill

Place for his use.[5] He also began writing short compositions, most either for piano or "operatic" pieces for toy theater productions, none of which evinces a professional composer in the offing.

Just before his eleventh birthday, Vaughan Williams was sent to Field House, a prep school in the village of Rottingdean (near Brighton) where Hervey was already boarding. During his three years at the school, which was run by brothers James and William Hewitt, Vaughan Williams enjoyed a thorough education, if somewhat spartan living conditions. He received particularly good teaching in mathematics and foreign languages, especially Latin and Greek, developing notable proficiency at the latter.[6] He also benefited from extensive musical training, taking violin lessons from William Michael Quirke, an Irish-born musician based in Brighton, and studying piano with a visiting teacher, Charles T. West, who introduced him to the music of Bach. The Hewitts themselves were quite musical. Vaughan Williams remembered James taking him to see Hans Richter conduct works by Wagner, Beethoven, and Weber in Brighton, and there were annual school and community concerts in Rottingdean for which the schoolboys would perform popular songs and tunes adapted from French light operas.

In 1887, Vaughan Williams left Rottingdean for Charterhouse, one of England's leading public schools, and where Hervey had once again preceded him. Founded in 1611, the school, originally established in London's Smithfield district, had relocated to the Surrey market town of Godalming in 1872. The headmaster at the time, William Haig Brown, was a formidable yet reform-minded administrator dedicated to raising educational standards and expectations, making Charterhouse an unusually enlightened institution among Victorian public schools. Vaughan Williams was an average student, maintaining his aptitude for classics and foreign language while struggling at mathematics, and served as head of Robinites house for five terms. Although there were no academic classes in music, he sang in the choir and played viola in the orchestra, practiced on the chapel organ, and occasionally performed concerti grossi with a select group of boys led by one of the housemasters, Frederick "Duck" Girdlestone. The high point of his musical tenure came in 1888 when he and a friend, H. Vivian Hamilton, received special dispensation from Haig Brown to use the Hall for a concert that included some of their own compositions. Vaughan Williams's contribution was the single-movement Pianoforte Trio in G Major, after the performance of which the maths professor, James Noon, "said in that sepulchral voice which Carthusians of my day knew so well, 'Very good, Williams, you must go on.' I treasured this as one of the few words of encouragement I ever received in my life!"[7]

Vaughan Williams's cousin (and fellow Carthusian) Stephen Massingberd played the cello in that trio performance, and changed the course of Ralph's life by introducing him to Hubert Parry's *Studies of Great Composers* (1886). Vaughan Williams remembered being struck by Parry's declaration "that a composer must write music as his musical conscience demands," which was "quite a new idea to me, the loyalty of the artist to his art."[8] This epiphany led him to seek out some of Parry's compositions, including *The Glories of Our Blood and State* (1883), *Judith* (1888), and *Blest Pair of Sirens* (1887), that last of which he later called "my favourite piece of music written by an Englishman."[9] Inspired by both Parry's music and aesthetic philosophy—and despite his family's objections—Vaughan Williams determined to study with him at the Royal College of Music (RCM), aiming to become a composer himself, and took his first class there on 25 September 1890, a month after leaving Charterhouse. Following two terms working under Francis Gladstone—during which time Vaughan Williams completed every exercise in George A. Macfarren's *Harmony*, a standard text of the era—he earned a Grade V (the highest level) on the College's Harmony and Counterpoint exams, which qualified him to enter Parry's studio for private composition studies. He did so for six terms between 1891 and 1893, including two after enrolling at Trinity College, Cambridge, in autumn 1892. He took two degrees while there, a MusB in 1894 and a BA (second class) in History the following year. As music was not a Tripos subject at Cambridge until 1948—that is, a program of study leading to the awarding of a BA—Vaughan Williams was obliged under university guidelines to take it as a second degree, and so (perhaps apocryphally) chose History as his first degree in part because the lectures did not conflict with Parry's teaching schedule.

In a eulogy to his mentor that was published in 1918, Vaughan Williams stated that "Parry taught music as a part of life," by which he meant that "there was no distinction for him between a moral and an artistic problem."[10] Parry's tutelage blended utilitarian compositional experience with the historian's breadth of literary and theoretical knowledge, a combination that would later define Vaughan Williams's own career. Above all, Vaughan Williams valued Parry's musical idealism, expressed in his oft-quoted exhortation to "write choral music as befits an Englishman and a democrat."[11] In this regard, Parry's influence on Vaughan Williams was less about developing his pupil's musical voice than shaping his ideological worldview, firing his creative imagination, and modeling composition as a vocation. Gustav Holst later dismissed "that healthy vigorous beefsteak optimism of Parry" to his friend as "a delusion that blinds one to the real difficulties in the way" of achieving a musical career.[12] But by expanding Vaughan Williams's knowledge of musical repertory, by inspiring him with his enthusiasm and eloquence, and above all, by taking his fledgling compositional efforts seriously in a spirit of "broad-minded sympathy," Parry inducted his pupil into a world undreamed of at Leith Hill Place or Charterhouse.[13]

Fortunately, Vaughan Williams received a sound foundational technique elsewhere. In addition to his work with Gladstone, he studied counterpoint at Cambridge with Charles Wood, who taught harmony and counterpoint at Gonville and Caius College. Vaughan Williams called Wood "the finest technical instructor I have ever known," but unlike Parry, Wood "was rather prone to laugh at artistic ideals and would lead one to suppose that composing music was a trick anyone might learn if he took the trouble."[14] Practical application of these lessons came at the organ bench, under the supervision of Walter Parratt at the RCM and Alan Gray at Cambridge. Vaughan Williams described himself as "the world's worst organist" and "the only pupil who entirely baffled Sir Walter Parratt,"[15] but was in fact more competent than he claimed. He scored a respectable III/1 on the RCM's Organ examination in 1896, and went on to pass the demanding exam for the Fellowship of the Royal College of Organists (FRCO) in 1898—without, despite his colleague Hugh Allen's running joke, having bribed the examiners—thus opening doors for gainful employment as a church musician.

Upon completing his Cambridge degrees in 1895, Vaughan Williams returned to the RCM for further compositional study. However, Parry had been appointed the new Director following George Grove's retirement in 1894, so Vaughan Williams transferred to the studio of Charles Villiers Stanford. Vaughan Williams worked with Stanford for four terms between 1895 and 1896, but with considerably less bonhomie than under Parry. Although one of England's leading composers and an excellent musical craftsman, Stanford was choleric, demanding, and blunt to the point of abusiveness. He regularly rejected his students' efforts as "all rot" or "damnably ugly," judgments countenancing no argument or appeal. He once accused Vaughan Williams of committing "all the crudities in [the music of John] Blow mentioned in Burney's History," and "would sometimes sigh deeply when I brought him my week's work and say he was hoping against hope!"[16] Having spent the previous five years diligently learning his craft, Vaughan Williams regularly challenged Stanford's comments. He later placed much of the blame for their fraught relationship on himself ("Stanford was a great teacher, but I believe I was unteachable"), though he noted that "Stanford never displayed great enthusiasm for my work," and was disinclined to meet his pupil halfway.[17]

To Stanford's credit, his treatment of Vaughan Williams improved once the latter had graduated from the RCM, and he endorsed, rehearsed, and conducted several of Vaughan Williams's works between 1899 and 1910. However, Stanford was not alone in his pessimistic assessment of his student's prospects. Alan Gray believed that despite demonstrating "considerable knowledge and taste on organ and music matters generally," Vaughan Williams was "hopelessly unhandy" at the organ and his professional future "seems to me somewhat hopeless,"[18] while Charles Wood confessed "that he had no hope for him as a composer."[19] Such comments came even from members of his own family. His cousin Gwen Raverat remembered a relative dismissing "'that foolish young man, Ralph Vaughan Williams,' who *would* go on working at music when 'he was so hopelessly bad at it.'"[20]

Happily, Vaughan Williams found more sympathy among his fellow students, even though he remembered feeling "at a certain disadvantage with these companions: they were all so competent and I felt such an amateur."[21] He was not yet the gregarious and sociable figure of later years, but "reserved in manner and did not make friends readily," though he formed close bonds with those he did befriend.[22] One of the first was Richard Walthew, a fellow Parry student and later Professor of Music at the Queen's College, Oxford, with whom he played piano duets ("or rather, he played and I stumbled behind him as best I could"); he recalled having his musical snobbishness deflated after seeing *Carmen* at Walthew's insistence.[23] At Cambridge, he made friends through the University Musical Club. One member, George McCleary, remembered Vaughan Williams as physically imposing, and "though he was not co-pious or fluent in talk, what he said was worth hearing. He gave an impression of latent power and a capable and original personality. Even in those early days he was evidently Somebody."[24] Vaughan Williams would have scoffed at this description, but might have applied it to Sidney "S. P." Waddington. An outstanding composition student, and later a faculty member at the RCM, Vaughan Williams deemed Waddington "one of the best informed minds on all subjects that I have ever met," and eagerly sought out his advice, criticism, and artistic insight.[25]

The University Musical Club's vitality stemmed partly from the man who took it over in 1892: Hugh Allen, the new organ scholar at Christ's College, whose vigorous leadership presaged similar efforts as Director of the RCM. Allen made them rehearse demanding music by the likes of Brahms, Schumann, and Schubert, but also programmed comic songs and new works by the group's members. These last included a vocal quartet by Vaughan Williams—possibly a setting of "Music, When Soft Voices Die" from 1891—the poor performance of which Allen attempted to mitigate by arranging an error-free encore (although the composer claimed that "the audience disliked it the second time even more than the first").[26]

Beyond the University Musical Club, Vaughan Williams met several people at Cambridge through Frederic Maitland, who held the Chair of the Laws of England at Downing College. His wife, Florence, was the eldest daughter of Herbert William Fisher, who had befriended Arthur Vaughan Williams at Christ Church, a connection facilitating Ralph's admittance to the Maitlands' social circle. Maitland regularly hosted chamber music performances at West Lodge, his Downing residence, through which Vaughan Williams got to know Nicholas and Ivor Gatty, Yorkshire-born brothers and aspiring musicians whose other siblings (René and Margot) Vaughan Williams later befriended.

Vaughan Williams was also active in multiple social and professional spheres at the RCM, most famously the college's Literary and Debating Society. This group originated among Stanford's pupils in 1895, but soon drew (male) participants from across the college, including Gustav Holst, John Ireland, Thomas Dunhill, Martin Shaw, Nicholas Gatty, William Hurlstone, Keith Falkner, H. C. Colles, Fritz Hart, and Evlyn Howard

Jones. Their regular Saturday meetings included readings and debates— Vaughan Williams "read papers on Purcell and Bayreuth and opened a debate on the motion 'That the Moderate Man Is Contemptible,'" while Ireland recalled him expounding on *Jude the Obscure*—and sessions closed with members retiring to Wilkins Tea Shop on Kensington High Street for refreshments and arguing.[27] And although he never pursued a career as a solo performer, Vaughan Williams sang in the chorus for the RCM's revival of Purcell's *Dido and Aeneas* in 1895 and took the triangle part with the RCM orchestra for at least one concert in March 1896.

Two contemporaries stand out during his college and university years. The first was Ralph Wedgwood, Vaughan Williams's maternal second cousin, invariably called "Randolph." They attended Trinity College together in 1892, and although he was two years younger than Vaughan Williams, surviving letters give the impression that Wedgwood was the senior figure in the relationship. Vaughan Williams expresses almost desperate eagerness to arrange meetings with Wedgwood for concerts, cycling tours, or reading parties with friends. Guests at these last events included G. E. Moore, George Trevelyan, Crompton Llewellyn Davies, and Maurice Amos—an impressive group, with three future Order of Merit (OM) recipients among them—and in whose company, Vaughan Williams confessed to Wedgwood, he felt a little self-conscious. "How splendidly you used to bear with my indecent or otherwise low remarks, or amazingly silly things I used to do & say, how you ever bore it I don't know."[28] Such diffidence, displayed in many of his youthful relationships, suggests that Vaughan Williams envied the talents and easy confidence of these men, and craved their approval. He implied as much to Wedgwood, admitting "how much being with you kept me up to the mark. I am naturally of a bestial, lazy, sensual, earthly devilish nature but when I was with you a lot of that used to disappear, it was entirely your example that made me do what little work I did do."[29]

Vaughan Williams's other great friendship, of course, was with Gustav Holst. They met in 1895 at the RCM; Vaughan Williams remembered that Holst "started the ball by quoting Sheridan's *Critic*. This, for some reason, broke the ice and seemed to seal our friendship, and almost from that time onwards we used to meet at frequent intervals and give each other composition lessons."[30] As both men belonged to Stanford's studio, these critical exchanges—expanding into what they later called "field days"—presumably stemmed from their shared dissatisfaction with Stanford's methods. For Vaughan Williams, this relationship differed from those with Walthew or Waddington, in that he and Holst came to it as equals. Holst clearly felt the same: "When under a master I instinctively try to please him whereas our business is to learn to please ourselves which is far more difficult as it is so hard to find out what we want."[31] Their shared quest to find their creative voices forged a deep and lasting connection, as recalled by Holst's former student Claire Mackail. "They understood each other and inspired each other. One can still see them so clearly, as complete a contrast in appearance as could possibly be imagined, and yet so profoundly united in heart."[32]

Whatever personal doubts Vaughan Williams still harbored about his own abilities upon returning to the RCM in 1895 failed to impede his professional aspirations. Having conducted a small choral society at Cambridge and assisted Alan Gray in organ performances, Vaughan Williams felt qualified to accept an organist appointment at the Church of St. Barnabas in South Lambeth. In addition to rehearsing the choir and boys' choir, he directed and performed for Wednesday and Sunday services, the monthly children's service, and choral communion; he also founded choral and orchestral societies ("both of them pretty bad," he admitted) and gave occasional organ recitals.[33] Although he disliked the position—claiming it largely involved "playing hymns & swearing at choir boys"—it paid £50 per year (a bit over $7800 in 2020) and provided several auxiliary benefits.[34] Not only could he gain "some of the practical knowledge of music which is so essential to a composer's make-up," but it also provided an excuse to acquire rooms in London—initially near the church at 2 St. Barnabas Villas, and later in Westminster and Pimlico between 1895 and 1897.[35] It further proved that he could support himself in a musical career—even if his earnings were augmented by a small family allowance—burnishing his credentials as both a respectable professional and prospective spouse.

Vaughan Williams's thoughts were likely turned in this direction by his burgeoning relationship with Adeline Maria Fisher (1870–1951). The fifth of eleven children born to Herbert William Fisher and Mary Louisa Fisher (née Jackson), Adeline grew up in the New Forest village of Brockenhurst. She was exceptionally attractive and capable, her quiet demeanor belying a sharp wit and discriminating intelligence. Vaughan

Williams first met her at the Maitland musicales—Florence Maitland was Adeline's older sister—at which she would play cello or piano. In addition to her musical abilities, she had an aptitude for languages (she spoke conversational German and passable French, and studied Russian and Czech), was a dedicated amateur photographer, and had a knack for dramatic readings, especially to children, with whom she had a natural rapport. Adeline also had a strong practical streak and sense of familial duty that made her indispensable to her mother's management of the close-knit family's affairs; she was the first to respond in a crisis and the last to consider her own needs. Her surviving letters from this era reveal a lively, observant, and thoughtful correspondent, with occasional flashes of naughty humor. Margot Gatty remembered Adeline's hair of "burnished gold—wonderful colouring and blue eyes," and that she "always wore distinctive and artistic clothes."[36]

While all these virtues made Adeline a desirable match, they may have intimidated some potential suitors—but not Ralph. Some of the elder Fishers "found it odd that [Adeline] should prefer this awkward silent fellow, younger than herself and without a proper profession, to his more presentable rivals."[37] Yet prefer him she did, accepting his proposal of marriage in June 1897. Unfortunately, a cloud hung over their engagement after the sudden death of Adeline's cousin (and Virginia Woolf's half-sister) Stella Duckworth on 19 July. Duckworth died from complications of peritonitis barely three months after her own wedding, a huge blow to the Fisher family, particularly Adeline, whose grief nearly caused her to call off her own engagement. However, the solicitousness of the Fishers and Vaughan Williamses helped her manage the situation, and so she and Ralph were married in a quiet ceremony on 9 October at Hove, three days before Vaughan Williams's twenty-fifth birthday.[38] Guests were limited to family members, with Ralph Wedgwood serving as best man, and Adeline's nieces, Fredegond and Ermengard Maitland, as bridesmaids.

Although Ralph had regularly visited the Fishers in Hove, he evidently found the clannishness of Adeline's relatives somewhat trying, and so shrewdly decided to pursue "a few months' study and experience abroad" with his new wife.[39] Rejecting Stanford's suggested destination of Italy, Vaughan Williams chose Berlin, acquiring a letter of introduction to Heinrich von Herzogenberg, who recommended him to Max Bruch. Thus the Vaughan Williamses' honeymoon site seamlessly transitioned into their temporary home, where they remained into the following year. Berlin was made more welcoming by the presence of Nicholas and Ivor Gatty's younger brother, René, an aspiring poet and amateur musician, who soon became close friends with the couple.

Bruch turned out to be an excellent match. Vaughan Williams said that he "worked hard and enthusiastically" while in Berlin, and "Bruch encouraged me, and I had never had much encouragement before."[40] With the possible exception of Parry, not since James Noon's exhortation at Charterhouse had anyone in a position of authority, it seems, told Vaughan Williams that he was not wasting his time with music, so this validation from such a distinguished source must have provided a huge boost to his confidence. Posterity has not preserved many details about Bruch's teaching, other than that he may have encouraged his pupil to rely less on rules and more on results—less "Augen-musik" and more "Ohren-musik."[41] Bruch provided him with a testimonial near the end of their time together, in which he called Vaughan Williams "ein sehr guter Musiker und ein talentvoller Componist."[42]

The Vaughan Williamses returned to England in April 1898. The vicar at St. Barnabas had been willing to hold Vaughan Williams's position for him—John Ireland deputized for him during his absence—and so the couple once again looked for London accommodations.[43] By the end of May, they had moved into a furnished flat at 5 Cowley Street, in the heart of Westminster, and Ralph was soon hard at work. He was sharpening his keyboard skills both for the difficult FRCO examination in July and for rehearsals of Stanford's *The Revenge* at St. Barnabas, and heard a play-through of his new String Quartet in C Minor at the RCM in late June.

Early that summer, Vaughan Williams told Ralph Wedgwood that he had "thoughts of going in for my Mus: Doc: in January—but this must be a secret in case I fail."[44] Those thoughts turned to deeds the following spring, when he took his doctoral counterpoint exam and viva (the final oral exam required to complete the doctorate) at Cambridge between 8 and 10 March 1899. Shortly thereafter, he received his ARCM (Associate of the Royal College of Music) diploma in Theory and Composition, and then spent most of the summer revising his Serenade in A Minor and writing his doctoral degree exercise (the so-called *Cambridge Mass*), which he submitted in October. Although he was approved for the doctorate by December, his inability to pay the required fees meant that he did not take it until May 1901.[45]

After completing the Mass, he and Adeline took a short holiday to Berlin and Prague, but not before he quit his position at St. Barnabas and signed a six-year lease for a house at 10 Barton Street, Westminster, barely a block away from their Cowley Street residence. They took possession on 29 December 1899, and moved in shortly thereafter.[46] The house needed significant maintenance (Adeline wrote about workers' presence as late as February 1900) and "there was no bathroom, so hot water had to be carried from the kitchen to fill a brown tin bath, and the lavatory was in the back yard."[47] On the other hand, it was quite spacious— Vaughan Williams used the ground-floor drawing room as an office, and regularly invited Ralph Wedgwood and the Gattys to stay in their spare room—and the location, practically in the shadow of Westminster Abbey, was enviable.

In 1900, Vaughan Williams completed the *Bucolic Suite* and a setting of *Dover Beach* (now lost), and began drafting the *Heroic Elegy and Triumphal Epilogue*; he witnessed performances of its first movement (as well as of his Quintet in D Major and Serenade in A Minor) in 1901. Several new non-compositional opportunities were also occupying his time. Most significant in the short term was an invitation from the Purcell Society to edit two volumes of *Welcome Songs* for that composer's forthcoming complete edition. Although unpaid for his efforts, Vaughan Williams found the project congenial, not least because it let him work with rare manuscripts at the British Museum and Buckingham Palace (though his initial failure to show up appropriately attired at the palace meant that he had to enter and leave through the kitchens). He had also begun writing articles about music. His earliest, inspired by the death of Brahms ("The Romantic Movement and Its Results"), appeared in an 1897 issue of *The Musician*, and another was accepted in April 1900 by a weekly magazine called *The Londoner*, though the title is unknown, and it is possible that it was unsigned. However, he told Ralph Wedgwood in February of that year that several other "trivial but brilliant essays" had been rejected:

> 1. How to play Brahms 2. A school of English music 3. The soporific finale 4. Bach & Schumann. I am now writing a longer and more solid one on "The Words of a Musical Drama." [. . .] I am also going to write two more

on "Palestrina & Beethoven" and "A precursor of Wagner." Then I am going to get an introduction to the reader of Smith Elder and send him the lot as a small book—when he returns it I shall send it round to several others, and having finally failed in this desperate attempt to get a living I shall take to composing symphonies.[48]

As it happened, all of these (except "A Precursor of Wagner") were accepted in 1902 by a new periodical, *The Vocalist*, which also published several of Vaughan Williams's early songs.[49] He also undertook additional scholarly work around this time, writing two entries ("Conducting" and "Fugue") for the second edition of *Grove's Dictionary of Music and Musicians* (1904) with assistance from Holst and Henry Wood.[50] The "Fugue" entry is the more staid of the two, its commentary limited to technical and historical details. "Conducting," by contrast, engages with issues of taste and aesthetics, and many details reflect Vaughan Williams's own opinions, such as his disdain for showboating and his preference for collaborative rather than dictatorial podium manners.[51] Other projects came in fits and starts: he taught music lessons at multiple schools, undertook some local university extension lectures, unsuccessfully attempted to organize a concert series, and briefly took voice lessons. Part of the reason he took on so many tasks was because Adeline was frequently staying with her family in Hove and Lymington. Her older brother Arthur (known as Jack) was fighting in the Boer War, and her younger brother Hervey suffered from psychological and physical disabilities that left him an invalid. Her parents relied on her to mitigate these difficult circumstances, which obliged regular absences from Barton Street. However, she and Ralph took as many opportunities as they could to visit each other, including several short holidays together and with friends.

Despite a recurring attack of sciatica, 1901 ended promisingly for Vaughan Williams. On 27 December, Adeline reported that he "sold 2 songs the other day [to *The Vocalist*] for £2.12.6! the first money he has earned in that way. Two more are coming out shortly."[52] Neither she nor her husband would have imagined that the publication of those modest settings—"Linden Lea" and "Blackmwore by the Stour"—were only the first in a career that would span more than half a century and transform Britain's musical culture.

Early Works (1890–1901)

T HE STANDARD NARRATIVE ARC OF VAUGHAN WILLIAMS'S EARLY CA-
reer parallels the one he outlined in "A Musical Autobiography"
(1950). After chronicling his work at the RCM and Cambridge, and with
Bruch, he vaguely alludes to his activities in London around the turn of
the century, and then suddenly cuts to his discovery of folk song, editing
the *English Hymnal*, his period of study with Ravel, and reminiscences
about friends and colleagues. Engaging though his recollections are,
references to his own compositional activities are conspicuously absent,
and his memoir leaves the impression that these events laid the ground-
work for the "real" portion of his career—which, by his definition, did
not begin until after his time with Ravel.

Vaughan Williams's marginalization of his early compositions—and
self-deprecating references to his abilities as a young composer—has led
many biographers and researchers to do the same. For reasons that remain
obscure, Vaughan Williams withdrew many early works, destroying some
and stemming the circulation of others. Several pieces completed between
1898 and 1908 therefore received only a handful of performances (if any),
and most were not published or recorded until the twenty-first century.
The historiographical record thus emphasizes Vaughan Williams's non-
compositional activities during these years alongside the factors shaping
his extended apprenticeship, formal or otherwise. This focus has created
the erroneous impression that, with a handful of exceptions, he spent
most of a decade passively assimilating elements from post-Wagnerian

tonality, English folk song, Anglican hymnody, Tudor church music, and French impressionism rather than actively composing, or deliberately limited himself only to small-scale genres like songs and hymn tunes. Such an approach makes it seem as though works like *On Wenlock Edge*, *A Sea Symphony*, and the *Fantasia on a Theme by Thomas Tallis* had appeared unprompted and met with completely unexpected success, providing little indication of the extensive compositional experience and effort preceding them.

In fact, about half of Vaughan Williams's immediate post-collegiate works (i.e., those written between late 1897 and 1902) belong to large-scale choral and instrumental genres, not to the body of art songs, hymns, and folk-tune arrangements that has traditionally defined the scope of his early career. Several of these compositions demonstrate impressive technical facility and creative depth, as do many of his other recently rediscovered or long-suppressed orchestral, choral, and chamber works written before 1908. Their recovery provides the opportunity to appraise Vaughan Williams anew, replacing the standard narrative of a clumsy compositional trajectory of unexceptional achievement with one that more accurately details his ambitious goals and high standards.[1]

With that said, little in Vaughan Williams's juvenilia portends what was to come. His earliest surviving composition was a four-bar piano piece entitled "The Robin's Nest" ("heaven knows why," mused the composer) written when he was six; several other minor chamber, piano, and dramatic works of varying length and quality followed between 1882 and 1889, including the Pianoforte Trio in G performed at Charterhouse.[2] His first significant works emerged while he was studying under Parry and Stanford, though many are more interesting for what they reveal about his interests and influences than for their intrinsic qualities. Solo and part songs dominate this period, the earliest surviving example of which is "Summum Bonum" (1891), a setting of Robert Browning's eponymous poem. Vaughan Williams described it as based on "a passage out of the third act of *Siegfried*," which he heard performed under Mahler and for which Parry had lent him the score.[3] Vaughan Williams harbored strongly pro-Wagnerian sympathies during this time. He heard a transformative Munich performance of *Die Walküre* in 1890, and George McCleary recalled him being so deeply moved by *Tristan und Isolde* that he could "remember not being able to sleep after a performance of it."[4]

That passionate intensity is fully displayed in "Summum Bonum" (although the waltz-like opening sounds more like Chopin than Wagner), enhanced by octave doublings, a leaping bassline, and triplet figurations, while applied chords and other chromatic alterations saturate the harmony. The vocal line requires the exertions of a heldentenor both for its range and unabashedly romantic passion, which quickly peters out at the end. He tapped this particular expressive vein in only one other student song, "Wishes" (1893), which demonstrates a similarly thick accompaniment, strongly declamatory rhythmic profile, and flexible, through-composed melody.

Most of the solo songs from the 1890s are more restrained, such as two drafts of Tennyson's "Crossing the Bar" (1892), which provide a rare look at Vaughan Williams's early revision processes. Both feature ABAC form and demonstrate effective accompanimental contrast between the verses, but the melody of the revised version is better designed and the C section more proportionally appropriate; it also employs a more effective climax and avoids excessive repetition within the final quatrain. "To Daffodils" (1895) demonstrates a similarly graceful quality inviting comparisons to the songs of Robert Schumann, as does the beautiful and delicate setting of Swinburne's "Rondel" (or "Kissing Her Hair," 1896), in which a deceptive cadence sets off the final couplet. Finally, the *Three Settings from "Rumpelstiltskin"* stand out from others from this period. The texts come from Lady Florence Bell's *Fairy Tale Plays and How to Act Them* (1896), the first and third of which are set to short tunes evoking the quality of nursery rhymes. The intervening "Spinning Song" is strikingly different—not only from the others in this set, but also from this period more generally, as the undulating pentatonic opening and long-breathed, ethereal melody strongly suggest awareness of Debussy's piano music.[5]

Part songs also dominate the composer's early catalogue, many of which emphasize Palestrinian part-writing conventions, suggesting that they were likely written either as bespoke exercises for his teachers or as practical applications of recently acquired techniques. This explanation was evidently the case for one of the *Three Elizabethan Songs*, "The Willow Song," for which Vaughan Williams jocularly claimed Parry wrote the last two bars (which, if true, would likely situate its date of composition around 1892 or 1893). Unlike with many of his student works, Vaughan Williams returned to this collection later in life. For example, "O Mistress Mine" debuted and was published in 1913 (with a Tonic Solfa edition following in 1924); furthermore, there is evidence that he encouraged Adrian Boult to program "Sweet Day" around 1920, and responded positively to a correspondent in 1955 who said he was making a recorder arrangement of it.[6] As a body, the ensemble songs from this era are attractive and competent, ranging in complexity from three light and airy "vocal valses" set to texts from Tennyson's *Window* (1896) to the rich and evocative madrigalisms for double chorus in *Echo's Lament of Narcissus* (ca. 1896). Tennyson's poems are the odd ones out, as most of the texts claim Elizabethan authorship from the likes of Ben Jonson, George Herbert, and especially Shakespeare, a favorite of Vaughan Williams even at this early date.

Vaughan Williams's most extended undergraduate work is *Vexilla Regis* (1894) for solo soprano, mixed chorus, string orchestra, and organ, written as his Cambridge MusB graduation exercise, and meant to display facility with the conventions of eighteenth-century polyphony. Vaughan Williams felt very comfortable employing fugue and counterpoint, crediting not only Charles Wood but also Sir Frederick Bridge, his tutor in the subject at the RCM, and so the work includes myriad contrapuntal devices. The first movement alone features a strict canon at the second between violin and soprano, a double canon, and free imitation, while later movements include fugues, free imitation, and extended fugal imitation. Conservatively designed and executed, the work closely hews to Handelian practices and thus precludes much individuality, but shows that Vaughan Williams's time "learning his stodge" was not misspent.

The preceding compositions were written before Vaughan Williams's study with Bruch, and when he returned from Germany he was ready to pursue an entirely new musical agenda. Bruch's support boosted his self-confidence, and the post-Berlin works shift abruptly from solo vocal music and part songs to more audacious chamber, orchestral, and choral-instrumental pieces, the earliest of which was the String Quartet in C Minor. He began working on it under Bruch in 1897, and while the official debut took place much later (1904), he and Adeline attended a read-though of it at the RCM in June 1898.[7] The overwhelming influence is that of Brahms, particularly in the first movement, but the work is full of ideas, almost to its detriment. The first two movements sprawl, introducing numerous themes in quick succession but with little development, the structural coherence suffering as a result. The opening Allegro is held together by little more than the relentless rhythm of the opening motive, while the Andantino whipsaws from a gorgeous lyric melody led by the viola to a bold second theme group that sounds as though it were inspired by *Carmen*. By contrast, the contrapuntal frameworks of the Intermezzo and the closing Variazione con finale fugato discipline the motivic material and improve the movements' formal clarity. This comes at the expense of the earlier melodic spaciousness, but both movements progress with ease and assurance.

Vaughan Williams evidently found chamber music congenial, as the next piece he wrote was the Quintet in D Major for the unusual combination of clarinet, horn, violin, cello, and piano. It shares several traits with the earlier quartet: he completed it in 1898, several years passed before its first performance (1901), and it demonstrates many of the same musical virtues and shortcomings. Strong evocations of Dvořák and Brahms predominate—the third movement alludes to the slow movement of Brahms's Fourth Symphony—along with conspicuous displays of melodic lyricism and counterpoint, and many opportunities for individual instruments to shine. The piece's increased length occasionally wears (as with the repetitive horn figure in the third movement, for instance, or the Finale's extended coda), and the formal schemes are not always entirely effective, but its ambition and imagination demonstrate a fresh vitality characterizing many of his post-Berlin works.

1899 turned out to be Vaughan Williams's most productive year yet. If the C Minor Quartet and the D Major Quintet were the first fruits of his studies with Bruch, the ripest still awaited harvesting: the Serenade for Small Orchestra in A Minor (1901). Vaughan Williams likely composed this work, originally titled Suite for Orchestra, during the winter of 1897–1898, but was still working on it in 1899, presumably making revisions that Stanford had recommended: "we agreed that if I <u>added</u> a short movement in E major in the middle & altered the Coda the thing might stand—I had already got an extra movement in E major which I had cut out!"[8] Stanford described the Serenade as "a most poetical and remarkable piece of work" to a member of the Leeds Festival Committee, and led three rehearsals of it by December 1899.[9] However, he then "threw it up for no apparent reason," leading Vaughan Williams to submit it (evidently unsuccessfully) for consideration to the Crystal

Palace before it finally received its first performance in Bournemouth in 1901.[10]

Nineteenth-century approaches to the orchestral serenade varied considerably, but they typically featured three to five movements that were shorter and lighter than those of a symphony, and eschewed sonata-allegro form. The movements in Vaughan Williams's contribution exhibit fairly restrained approaches to harmony and form, with an emphasis on melodic continuity and textural clarity appropriate for the genre.[11] As in the chamber works, the Serenade draws upon models from other composers (notably Beethoven, Brahms, and Dvořák), but there are also hints of works yet to come from his own pen. For instance, the Prelude—loosely organized as a series of short variations—starts with a rising figure in the cellos that presages the opening gesture from *Five Variants of "Dives and Lazarus."*[12] Other allusions are more general, such as the trochaic rhythms dominating the Scherzo, a pattern that Vaughan Williams regularly adopted in works evoking or associated with folk song. The Intermezzo and Trio—the later addition in E major, as Stanford recommended—exude a dignified stateliness throughout that effectively contrasts with the other movements' alternation between lyricism and rhythmic buoyancy.

The fourth movement ("Romance") is the most daring, exhibiting a degree of formal intricacy and expressive power not heard elsewhere in the work; this is particularly audible at the climax, which anticipates a similar effect that Vaughan Williams would employ in the Romanza from the Fifth Symphony. It displays an underlying tension throughout between the strings' long-breathed, rhythmically steady phrases and irregular, highly ornamented lines in the upper winds, and adopts a subtle and complex fantasia-like form not typical of this genre or Vaughan Williams's early pieces. But it was the extensively revised Finale that proved the most difficult for the composer, even though the rondo theme's martial confidence and the tranquil ease of the intervening episodes suggest otherwise.[13]

The highest stakes of 1899, however, rested on Vaughan Williams's final student composition: a partial setting of the Mass submitted as his Cambridge doctoral degree exercise. It has come to be known as *A Cambridge Mass*, to distinguish it from the later and better-known Mass in G Minor, even though Vaughan Williams never referred to the earlier work by that name. The Cambridge authorities required the doctoral exercise to meet several criteria. It had to comprise "some considerable portion for a chorus of eight real parts" with a smaller portion for one or more soloists, include examples of canon and fugue, feature an entirely instrumental movement in sonata-allegro form, employ a full instrumental ensemble for the entire work (a single a cappella movement was allowable), and last between forty and sixty minutes.[14] Vaughan Williams worked steadily on the composition over summer and early autumn 1899—alongside the revisions to the Serenade in A Minor—before formally submitting it on 16 October.

He told Ralph Wedgwood about his plans around June 1899 ("I'm going to write a mass—they're such fine words and you get such good climaxes out of them.")[15] His comment, however, should not be read as an endorsement of Christian belief. Stories about his religious iconoclasm during this period are well known: skipping chapel prayers at Trinity, disrupting Hall by announcing, "Who believes in God nowadays, I should like to know?" or forgoing communion at St. Barnabas, where he passed time in the organ loft by reading French novels.[16] Yet while he had little interest in dogma and doctrine, he was a humanist who respected the church's emphasis on beauty as a means of enriching the spirit, while the ritual and tradition embodied in the Latin text of the Mass would have appealed to his aesthetic sensibilities. There should be no reason, as he later argued, why an atheist could not write a good Mass—or at least one capable of satisfying the members of Cambridge's Music Exam Board.[17]

A Cambridge Mass comprises only the Credo and Sanctus (including the Hosanna and Benedictus) separated by an instrumental Offertorium, and its vigorous expression and technical complexity counter traditionally tepid assessments of Vaughan Williams's early music. The Credo demonstrates several impressive effects; it is difficult to hear the initial brass fanfare and choral entrance, for instance, as anything but a harbinger of the opening from *A Sea Symphony*. Other elements presage Vaughan Williams's more mature style, such as the predilection for running eighth notes in the bassline, the cross-relation at the final statement of "Et expecto," or the music accompanying "Deum de Deo, lumen de lumine," which could have been plucked directly from *Dona Nobis Pacem*. There are also echoes of several other composers throughout the work, including Dvořák and Parry, while Vaughan Williams's admiration of Verdi's *Requiem* comes through in his sudden contrast of the lyrical "et homo factus est" with the agonized wail of "Crucifixus." The Credo's closing "Amen" takes up about a third of the movement, shifting the emphasis from text expression to technical display as it cycles through six expositions while demonstrating a host of fugal techniques (including stretto, augmentation, and inversion). While necessary, given the circumstances of its creation, the successive false endings make it less effective in performance, a criticism that Vaughan Williams would also level at certain works by Dvořák.

The Offertorium fulfills the requirement for an instrumental movement, the main theme of which is based on the "Et resurrexit" motive from the Credo; straightforward and genial, it could stand alone as its own work. The concluding Sanctus once again employs various imitative devices. The opening pits two four-part antiphonal choirs in strict canon before giving way to a double fugue at the "Hosanna," and then a single fugue for the four vocal soloists at the Benedictus, the tune for which Vaughan Williams revisited in the analogous movement of the Mass in G Minor. He must have been disappointed not to have had heard it performed; not until 2011 did it receive its premiere.

The third major work of 1899 was *The Garden of Proserpine*, a choral-orchestral work featuring text by Algernon Swinburne. Vaughan Williams informed Holst around autumn 1898 that he had completed the first sketch "to music for chorus & orchestra with lots of trombones and things," a fitting description of this piece, and scored it after completing his doctoral exams the following March.[18] Mysteriously, however, Vaughan Williams seemed to lose interest in it after this point—he may have been focused on finishing *A Cambridge Mass* or revising the Serenade—and for whatever reason, it too went unperformed and unpublished until 2011. The symbolist text and chromatically saturated musical language distinguish it from the contrapuntal intricacy of *A Cambridge Mass* or the Serenade's urbanity, but its aesthetic aligns with the popular fin-de-siècle image of Vaughan Williams as a dashing figure aligned with the slightly overheated prose, decadent beauty, and world-weariness of the pre-Raphaelites.

As in the other works from 1899, *The Garden of Proserpine* demonstrates remarkable confidence and control in its design and expression. Like the

Example 2.1   *The Garden of Proserpine* (orchestral reduction), mm. 9–14

later oratorio *Sancta Civitas, Proserpine* consists of a single continuous movement, its multiple subsections unified by a recurring figure from the beginning of the piece (Example 2.1).

The choral forces skillfully balance freely imitative passages and antiphonal canons with extended soprano solos and unexpectedly austere four-part chorales. One wonders to what degree Vaughan Williams later scavenged this piece for ideas when he was crafting *A Sea Symphony*: the choral blocks set against the undulating bassline starting at rehearsal mark **B** sound like a dry run for sections of "The Waves," while the monotonous recitation of the final stanza foreshadows a similar effect at the words "down from the gardens of Asia descending" in "The Explorers." In *Proserpine*, however, the vocal tedium is broken by the exquisitely timed return of the opening orchestral gesture at the poem's closing words, softening the stark text as the piece gently drifts to a hushed conclusion. While Vaughan Williams had not yet adopted his preferred marking of *niente* for such situations, the effect is unmistakable.

Only one piece of music from 1900 survives, the *Bucolic Suite*, which Vaughan Williams described as "rather blousy in its nature. I'm not sure that I shan't call it 'Tom Jones' or perhaps 'Jan Steen' would be better."[19] The references to the novel and the Dutch painter, both of which unsentimentally captured the complexities of rural people and communities, suggest that Vaughan Williams was less concerned about portraying a landscape than responding to cultural tropes associated with the countryside. Regardless of this subtext, the *Bucolic Suite* is still comparatively light—it lacks the weighty introspection typical of the late Romantic symphony—but carefully crafted. It employs a larger ensemble than that of the Serenade (adding two more horns, three trombones, tuba, harp, and a small battery of percussion), and features various extended techniques and devices such as mutes and col legno strings. This instrumentation enables some striking sonic effects recalling Rimsky-Korsakov's *Capriccio espagnol* and *Sheherazade*, which Adeline may have had in mind when she suggested that her husband was "entering on a new phase of composition and is getting 'complicated' like the Russians."[20] The brass is particularly well showcased in this regard, as in the series of staggered entries in the Finale (mm. 101–141), the dissonances of which consistently resolve to chorale-like cadential figures. The rhythmic scope of this work is also more expansive than that of the Serenade, eschewing the filigreed arabesques and stately patterns of the earlier work in favor of propulsive lines and fast repetitive figures—particularly in the low strings—supporting long-breathed melodic contours above. Vaughan Williams also occasionally employs simple and compound time signatures simultaneously while maintaining the same tempo and grouping (e.g., setting $\frac{9}{8}$ against $\frac{3}{4}$, as from mm. 176–185 in the first movement), so that conductors do not have to modify their beat and instrumentalists do not have to view extended passages of borrowed rhythms.

Despite these innovations, the *Bucolic Suite* owes less to the symphonic examples of Strauss or Mahler than to concert overtures and suites by Dvořák, Rimsky-Korsakov, Sibelius, and, perhaps most significantly, Elgar. Vaughan Williams approached Elgar for lessons around the time he was writing the *Bucolic Suite*, and was gently rebuffed. "But although Elgar would not teach me personally," he later recalled, "I spent several hours at the British Museum studying the full scores of the [Enigma] Variations and *Gerontius*."[21] He was later astonished "to find on looking back on my own earlier works how much I cribbed from him," pointing to passages from the *Sea* and *London Symphony* drawn from *Gerontius*.[22] In the *Bucolic Suite*, however, he evidently turned to the *Enigma Variations,* for m. 9 of the Andante replicates the opening of Variation V (R.P.A.) note for note. Some of Vaughan Williams's other homages are more surprising. For example, the third movement was clearly inspired by Dvořák's *Slavonic Dances*, both in its overarching ternary form and—in the first A section—the orchestration, particularly in the deployment of auxiliary percussion. However, the B section replaces the expected trio with a series of short variations in the style of Glinka or Musorgsky, but with a more Elgarian approach to orchestration. The return of A also deviates from the Dvořákian model: rather than simply repeating the section, Vaughan

Williams truncates and reorchestrates it for a more delicate and subdued reprise, similar to the approach employed in the second movement of his Quintet in D Major.

While the *Bucolic Suite* does not quite match up to Vaughan Williams's more mature symphonic output—though there are hints of future pieces, such as the Overture to *The Wasps* near the end of the Finale—it reveals an increasingly confident composer learning how to transform the models he admired. This process continued in his next major symphonic work, the *Heroic Elegy and Triumphal Epilogue* (1901–2). In a letter plausibly dated 1901, Vaughan Williams told Holst about all of his recent work: "I've finished my 'Bucolic Suite' and written a song and made a rough copy of the score of the Trombone thing and finished a volume of Purcell and am starting another thing called a 'Sentimental Romance.'"[23] This latter piece might have been a forerunner of the now-destroyed *Symphonic Rhapsody* (1904), and the manuscript title pages for the *Heroic Elegy* and the *Triumphal Epilogue* reveal that they were "originally conceived as Parts II and III of a work entitled *Symphonic Rhapsody in Three Parts*."[24] If so, then the "Trombone thing" could refer to the *Heroic Elegy*, in which that instrument features prominently, and which he finished on 22 January 1901.[25] The *Triumphal Epilogue* was completed about almost ten months later, received its first performance on 11 July 1902, and was further revised between August and September. At some point, Vaughan Williams renumbered both movements as Parts I and II for the nascent *Symphonic Rhapsody*, but ultimately decided to pair them as an independent two-movement work.

The *Heroic Elegy and Triumphal Epilogue* extends the practices begun in the Serenade and continued in the *Bucolic Suite*, particularly the expansion of the orchestra and the dimensions of the individual movements. This is the most stylistically varied of the three early orchestral works, but also arguably the one in which Vaughan Williams's own voice is least audible. The two formal sections of the *Heroic Elegy* present studies in contrast: the A section's ceaseless ostinato and starkly soaring melody evoke Sibelius, while Tchaikovsky's influence permeates the B section's mediant relationships, delicate scoring, and arpeggiated triplet accompaniment. The *Elegy's* primary theme returns in the *Triumphal Epilogue*, but brass-heavy and richly chromatic passages dominate. While some of these recollect examples from Wagner (such as the brass fanfares at

E), they intensify to Straussian heights in their scope and sound, particularly after **K**. Despite these pervasive evocations of other composers, there are occasional flashes of gestures that would become idiomatic to Vaughan Williams. Extended passages of quartal and quintal harmonies regularly recur, while cadential cross-relations sound throughout the first section of the *Triumphal Epilogue*. Those gestures support a melody that anticipates a significant theme from the first movement of *A Sea Symphony*, a work further invoked by the *Epilogue*'s sweeping displays of orchestral brilliance.[26]

Critical responses to the composition were uniformly positive. Edwin Evans praised it in a profile of Vaughan Williams written in 1903, while the *Daily Graphic* called the *Elegy* "a work of exceptional power and beauty. Short as it is, it is distinguished by remarkable breadth and dignity of thought, and by a vein of deep yet restrained emotion, rare enough at any time, and particularly in the work of so young a composer. Mr. Williams [sic] is a man to be reckoned with."[27] Yet Vaughan Williams was never satisfied with the piece. He felt that "a good deal of the last movement does not 'come off,'" and fifty years later called it "a horrible amateurish business now happily lost—it so happened that its style fitted in for the moment with [Stanford's] prejudices."[28] John Ireland, however, attended the *Heroic Elegy*'s first rehearsal and remembered Stanford telling him, "That's better than anything you could write, me bhoy [sic]."[29]

Given that there is nothing in this piece (or elsewhere in contemporaneous works) supporting Vaughan Williams's claims of amateurishness, we should consider his demurral more carefully, particularly since he so frequently returns to it.[30] Two readings of this trope dominate the critical literature: the first takes his claim at face value, inferring that Vaughan Williams lacked technical competency, which is nonsense. Even if his academic credentials did not indicate otherwise, his meticulous craftsmanship and devotion to professional development would; the most cursory assessment of his output refutes any charge of clumsiness or incompetency. The second reading, more generously, assumes that this is good-natured self-deprecation—an obviously false claim made with a wink to the sympathetic reader. Again, this assumption seems implausible, given that Vaughan Williams was an intensely serious and self-critical composer, especially as a young man, and did not like talking about his music except to his closest friends. By all accounts, he was either embarrassed or genuinely humbled by praise of his work; he neither fished for nor expected compliments from others, in no small part because he often found it difficult to validate his own efforts as worthwhile.

Vaughan Williams's actual implication is therefore subtler and more poignant. He held himself to an extraordinarily high artistic standard, and rarely felt he had attained it. Moreover, at this early point in his career, he must have felt that his progress was intolerably slow. He had invested tremendous effort into becoming a professional musician, and had little to show for it as he approached his thirtieth birthday: a few certificates and diplomas, a handful of performances at the RCM and provincial halls, and some conducting and organ experience, but no steady job, no published works, no commissions, no obvious prospects. His assets consisted of a modest family allowance, steadfast support from a small group of intimates—most notably Adeline, Ralph Wedgwood, the Gattys, and Holst—and the unwavering desire to communicate in sound what he would later call "a partial revelation of that which is beyond human senses and human faculties."[31] And each composition further seasoned the whetstone of experience on which he sharpened his technique, honing an edge keen enough to strike "the perfect balance between inspiration and realization" of his expressive aims.[32] He knew, better than any critic, when his reach exceeded his grasp (even if he could not yet fully grasp how or why), of yearning to conjure beauty but always falling frustratingly short. Surely, if and when Vaughan Williams reflected on those years of struggle and insecurity, he must have vividly remembered feeling like the amateur his credentials and fellowships and doctorate insisted he was not. Perversely, this sense of inferiority drove him to improve his skills and refine his craft, but it also seems as though he had grappled with imposter syndrome for much of his life, always wary that his skills might fail and his inspiration dry up. That this never happened stands as testament to the wide-ranging study, conscientious work habits, and dogged persistence instilled during these years of apprenticeship.

"I Think I Am Improving" (1902–1908)

HE CONTRACT VAUGHAN WILLIAMS RECEIVED FROM *The Vocalist* AT the end of 1901 could not have been more opportune, professionally or financially. It granted the magazine exclusive rights to publish his songs for the next five years; after appearing in *The Vocalist*, they were released individually for a shilling apiece, the composer receiving one-and-a-half pence per copy sold ("so you see I'm on the high road to a fortune," he wryly told Wedgwood).[1] Additionally, *The Vocalist* provided Vaughan Williams a platform for essays he had written over the last several years, publishing eight in 1902 alone, and revealing him as a prose stylist of no mean skill.[2]

The first, "A School of English Music," represents his initial printed engagement with folk song. While Vaughan Williams credited collectors of English folk songs for their preservationist efforts, he argued that composers who based their own works on them were appropriating a tradition they did not truly understand—a locally derived equivalent of secondhand Strauss or watered-down Brahms, and as expressively insincere. "The national English style must be modelled on the personal style of English musicians. Until our composers will be content to write the music that they like best, without an ulterior thought, not till then shall we have a true school of English music."[3] A few months later, however, he was exhorting English amateur singers to perform songs from "our own dazzling treasury of British folk-tunes. Here we find all those qualities which are so painfully absent from the 'ballad-concert' song—sincerity, depth of emotion, simplicity of expression, and, above all, beautiful melody."[4]

If Vaughan Williams's attitude toward folk song seems inconsistent, it may be because almost all of his knowledge about it had been indirectly acquired.[5] He was familiar with collections like Lucy Broadwood and J. A. Fuller Maitland's *English County Songs* (1893) and John Broadwood's *Sussex Songs* (rev. ed. 1889), and had connected with members of the Folk-Song Society, such as Frank Kidson and Sabine Baring-Gould. But he was not yet an active member of this group, whose activities concentrated more on archival study than fieldwork. Nevertheless, by October 1902, he was leading a series of Oxford University extension lectures on English folk song at the Technical School in Pokesdown, near Bournemouth. Their enthusiastic reception led to further engagements in Gloucester and Brentwood (Essex) in early 1903, heralding major repercussions for his own understanding of the subject.[6]

All of this writing and lecturing took place against unsettled personal circumstances, for Adeline's brother Jack had returned from the Boer War traumatized from his experience. In an attempt to help her parents, already burdened with caring for Hervey, Adeline brought Jack to stay at Barton Street; however, a display of suicidal tendencies led to his institutionalization soon thereafter, followed by his death from appendicitis complications in March 1902. Adeline's father, Herbert, died the following January, after which point Adeline was often away from Barton Street. Not only was she visiting her mother in Hove almost daily, but she also expanded her role as mediator and facilitator for the extended Fisher clan, and took on additional responsibility for Hervey's medical needs.

With Adeline frequently absent, Vaughan Williams filled the time with his usual wide-ranging activities. He completed a *Fantasia for Piano and Orchestra* that had been occupying him since 1896, and attended the debuts of his *Bucolic Suite* in Bournemouth (paired with Holst's *Cotswold Symphony*) on 10 March 1902, and a new part song ("Rest," to words by Christina Rossetti) two months later at St. James's Hall, London. Thanks to *The Vocalist*, his songs were being taken up for public performance. "Linden Lea" and "Blackmwore by the Stour" premiered on a Hooton Roberts Musical Union concert in September, the latter also sung by Campbell McInnes alongside first performances of "Whither Must I Wander?" and an arrangement of "Entlaubet ist der Walde" in

November. Three other vocal works ("Tears, Idle Tears," "Silent Noon," and *Willow-Wood*) enjoyed first performances in February and March 1903. *Willow-Wood* had not yet been orchestrated, so the piano accompaniment must have sounded rather dense and complicated, but one critic stated that "the originality of the conception and the definite value of the musical ideas are beyond question. Mr. Williams [sic] is a composer who has something to say and must be allowed to say it in his own way."[7]

Vaughan Williams, however, remained unconvinced. Even when his music was successful, he often responded by bemoaning his lack of inspiration, a tendency Holst observed as early as 1903. "I really cannot feel concerned about your fears that all your invention is gone. [. . .] You got into the same state of mind just before you wrote the Heroic Elegy so that I look on it as a good sign and quite expect to hear that you have struck oil when you write again." He added the following admonishment:

> You have never lost your invention but it has not developed enough. Your best—your most original and beautiful style or "atmosphere" is an indescribable sort of feeling as if one was listening to very lovely lyrical poetry. I may be wrong but I think this (what I call to myself the real RVW) is more original than you think.
>
> But when you are not in this strain, you either write "second class goods" or you have a devil of a bother to write anything at all. The latter state of mind may seem bad while it lasts but it is what you want to make yourself do for however much I like your best style it must be broadened. And probably it is so each time you get into a hopeless mess.[8]

Only through struggle, Holst argued, would either of them find their artistic path, so even discomfort and frustration were preferable to simply being "good enough," as he addressed elsewhere. "I think we are 'all right' in a mild sort of way. But then mildness is the very devil. So something must happen and we must make it happen."[9]

And clearly, things were happening by 1903. In addition to all of the publications and premieres of recent months, Vaughan Williams had joined the Bach Choir, had completed the Quintet in C Minor (for piano, violin, viola, cello, and double bass) and two orchestral impressions,[10] had nearly finished his *Symphonic Rhapsody*, and had seen five further songs performed by April. All this activity attracted the attention of the critic

Edwin Evans. In a perceptive and sympathetic profile for the *Musical Standard*, he wrote that Vaughan Williams "belongs to the more level-headed of our young writers, and I am convinced of the absolute conscientiousness of his work. Of this I feel that the best has still to come. That sounds a little trite, as it is said of so many; but in this instance I feel persuaded that it *will* come. His future career depends rather more on his own self-confidence than on any very startling development. He has the ideas, the method and the manner, but wants to be a little more autocratic with each of them."[11]

Evans's assessment was spot on, with one exception: there was still a very startling development in the works, and it began with an invitation to a vicarage tea. Sisters Florence and Georgina Heatley had attended Vaughan Williams's lecture series in Brentwood; they were from the Essex village of Ingrave, where their father was the vicar. As the rectory was holding a party for elderly residents, the Heatleys invited Vaughan Williams to see if any guests knew the folk songs about which he had been lecturing, or might have others to share. He accepted, and upon arriving, was introduced to Charles Potiphar, a local laborer; though not comfortable singing at that occasion, Potiphar asked Vaughan Williams to return the next day. So he did, and the first tune that Potiphar sang was "Bushes and Briars," a rendition that changed the course of both Vaughan Williams's life and English musical scholarship. He became an avid collector of English folk songs, transcribing more than 800 over the next decade, and more than a quarter of that number in 1904 alone. He was not, of course, the only person engaged in such work. In addition to members of the Folk-Song Society and later personal collaborators (including George Butterworth and Ella Mary Leather), the most prominent of his fellow devotees was Cecil Sharp, a schoolteacher and former choral conductor who had begun collecting songs in Somerset a few months before Vaughan Williams had in Essex.

Like Vaughan Williams, Sharp wanted to preserve as many songs as possible before their singers died out. Yet Sharp sought to establish "definitive" versions of tunes (eliminating variants that he felt were corruptions of a perfected original), linking them to social reform movements meant to counter what he considered the moral and physical degradation of urban life. Vaughan Williams was not so ideologically driven (at least, not in this particular manner), and recognized that folk song was a living tradition subject to reinterpretation and transformation. He was not immune to idealizing his subjects or the tunes he collected, and his recording and preservation methodologies could be inconsistent, but he valued folk songs as significant artworks, respected their performers' creativity, and promoted them as integral parts of England's musical heritage.

This last point is crucial, particularly given Vaughan Williams's later reputation as an advocate of "national music." He defined this not as a particular musical style but as the *totality* of styles woven through a nation's cultural fabric, whether from traditional, cultivated, or vernacular genres. Above all, he believed that national music grew out of the needs and desires of those who made it, reflecting the history, customs, and institutions to which they belonged. As a result, national music was not some monolithic construct imposed upon a people, but a network of voices that encompassed and undergirded many different aspects of a nation. The people of England were rural and urban, rich and poor, radical and conservative, educated and unlettered, industrial and pastoral, aristocratic and untitled. Just as no single group defined what it was to be English, no individual musical style captured all of these experiences; only a chorus of different voices could represent England as a whole.

In some cases, however, Vaughan Williams challenged musical traditions when he believed they were unworthy of the nation they purportedly represented. For instance, his fifth lecture at Pokesdown, "Religious Folk Songs," took aim at *Hymns Ancient and Modern* (1861). Simply put, Vaughan Williams was not an admirer of the collection. He allowed that "the original intention of the compilers of these hymns was not wholly bad," but believed that they had capitulated to popular taste at the expense of musical—even moral—quality. He castigated the editors' proclivity for

> exotic and languorous tunes which could be nothing but enervating to those who sang and heard them; and in later editions the element of maudlin sentiment has grown alarmingly until at last the bad has almost driven out the good. National music should represent the people. Will anyone dare to say that the effusions of the [Joseph] Barnby school represent the English people?[12]

Such opinions may explain why, in late 1904, he was approached by Percy Dearmer—the socialist and reformist vicar of St. Mary's, Primrose Hill, London—to serve as the music editor for *The English Hymnal* (1906), a collection meant to supplant *Hymns Ancient and Modern*. Dearmer told Vaughan Williams that both Sharp and Canon Henry Scott Holland had recommended him; if he declined, the position would be offered to the devoutly religious Henry Walford Davies. As Vaughan Williams cordially detested both Davies's music and his liturgical opinions, he accepted Dearmer's request. While it took time away from composing, he admitted that "two years of close association with some of the best (as well as some of the worst) tunes in the world was a better musical education than any amount of sonatas and fugues."[13]

If Vaughan Williams's activities with folk song could be described as preservationist and promotional, then his efforts with hymnody constituted a reforming and revivalist approach to national music. (That his work for both was unpaid—in fact, he allegedly incurred £250 in clerical expenses while working on *The English Hymnal*, though this sum may be exaggerated—reveals his dedication to the principles that underlay them.) For while Vaughan Williams may not have been religious, he took its practice very seriously. He understood that by engaging in the mystery and beauty of ancient ritual, individuals could transcend the mundanities of daily life, much as he did when composing. In commemorating the fiftieth anniversary of the composer's death, Archbishop of Canterbury Rowan Williams praised this attitude:

> He wanted to do justice to the humanity gathered in a church or a cathedral, even if he wasn't very sure about the divinity. He wanted to recognise that to worship in a church is to enter a larger world, to inhabit a mysterious, challenging and almost unbelievingly exhilarating as well as sobering environment, from which you emerge with a sense of yourself and your environment transfigured. That is what he believed church ought to be like [. . .] In other words, he had higher expectations and higher hopes of church worship than a great many cheerful, or not so cheerful, believers. . . . He knew that it mattered for human beings to accept the invitation to celebrate, to be joyful, and to be transfigured by beauty.[14]

In the case of the hymnal, Vaughan Williams expanded the stylistic, geographic, and temporal range of the literature on offer, largely at the expense of the Victorians who dominated *Hymns Ancient and Modern*.[15] He was unable to eliminate all of the tunes he disliked, as the music committee felt several were too popular to remove, so in a compromise, "the worst offenders were confined in an appendix at the end of the book which we nicknamed the 'Chamber of Horrors.'"[16] He replaced the melodies he cut with tunes from British and continental psalters; sacred compositions by Tudor and Restoration-era composers such as Thomas Tallis, Orlando Gibbons, and Henry Purcell; new hymns commissioned from British composers, including Holst, Nicholas Gatty, Thomas Dunhill, W. H. Bell, and himself; songs of foreign provenance from Germany, France, Italy, Holland, Spain, and the United States; and, perhaps most significantly, arrangements or adaptations of folk songs. The result was an imaginative and stylistically varied compilation that, by the 1920s, had largely overshadowed *Hymns Ancient and Modern*.[17]

Fieldwork and editing meant that Vaughan Williams's compositional progress slowed by mid-decade. Still, Francis Harford programmed three of his fifteenth-century French song arrangements in February 1904, about a month before the premiere of the *Symphonic Rhapsody* in Bournemouth, and just two months before Vaughan Williams completed his first draft of *In the Fen Country*. He also arranged a program for London's Bechstein Hall that December, consisting entirely of his works and Holst's. Reviews mostly focused on Vaughan Williams's contributions; the *Manchester Courier*'s critic was particularly enthusiastic, praising the composer's "unusual gift for inventing beautiful melody," and claiming that his songs were "enough to give him a high place among our younger composers, and we may legitimately expect much excellent work from him in future."[18]

Not mentioned was that the program spanned the better part of a decade. Although it marked the premieres of two song cycles (*Songs of Travel* and *The House of Life*), a song from each had been performed previously ("Whither Must I Wander" in 1902 and "Silent Noon" in 1903), while two stand-alone songs debuting that evening ("Claribel" and "Orpheus with his Lute") had been composed in 1897 and 1902. A further pair of vocal duets on the program ("The Last Invocation" and "The Love-Song of the Birds"), first performed in Reading two months earlier, marked Vaughan Williams's earliest settings of poems by Walt Whitman, whose visionary worldview profoundly affected his own. He had completed the songs in Yorkshire earlier that summer, where he also wrote a short *Andante Sostenuto* for Adeline's birthday, and made significant headway on the orchestral impression *Harnham Down* and a choral symphony he had been working on since 1903. Sporting the working title *The Ocean* and also featuring texts by Whitman, the work had a long gestation because of the composer's other obligations and the piece's sheer scale.

Clearly, Vaughan Williams was increasingly comfortable managing many responsibilities and working to deadlines, sometimes on very short notice. These talents were put to the test in March 1905 when he was asked to write the music for *Pan's Anniversary*. This masque by Ben Jonson, last performed at King James I's court in 1625, was to be included as part of the Shakespeare birthday celebrations in Stratford on 24 April, and required both newly composed music and arrangements of folk and traditional tunes, some of which he subcontracted to Holst.[19] Vaughan Williams's letters to the organizers reveal both his alarm at the short deadline and his eagerness to control as many details of the work as possible, a tendency marking many of his future stage collaborations.[20] The performance garnered unanimous praise; the reviewer for the *Birmingham Weekly Mercury* called Vaughan Williams's music "exceedingly graceful and tuneful, and peculiarly appropriate to the spirit of the masque."[21]

Hard on the heels of *Pan's Anniversary* came another auspicious debut for Vaughan Williams: directing the combined choirs for the inaugural Leith Hill Musical Competition. He had been invited to serve in this capacity by his sister, Meggie, co-founder of the LHMC with Evangeline, Lady Farrer, of Abinger Hall. The two women had been friends for some years—but had not met through Ralph, even though he and Lady Farrer had overlapped as Parry's pupils at the RCM—and established a Festival Committee by August 1904, with Lady Farrer serving as President and Meggie as Honorary Secretary.[22] Soon after, they asked Vaughan Williams if he would serve on the Musical Committee (which was responsible for repertory selection) and conduct the inaugural concert on 10 May 1905, an invitation he accepted. This was the first of thirty-seven consecutive LHMC choirs that he directed over the next forty-eight years, during which time the Festival increasingly reflected his own idealistic aims for amateur music-making. In 1955, Vaughan Williams fondly recalled the early years of the LHMC:

Those who only heard the finished result knew little of the preparation period when week after week a devoted band of singers would meet in a cold but stuffy school room, half lit by two smelly oil lamps, accompanied by an astonishing machine which had once been a pianoforte. Here the hierophants struggled with music which was often in an idiom new to them, and sometimes at first incomprehensible. Occasionally the leading soprano lost her voice and could not sing, or one of the only two tenors, being the local doctor, was called out in the middle of a practice to assist at one of the joyful occasions that are so frequent in our village; leaving Mr. Smith of Kosikot to wrestle with Bach's difficult intervals or Handel's runs alone. And so it went on for the first few weeks. Then suddenly, as by a miracle, the music came alive and we sang on full of hope waiting for the great climax of the spring. At last it arrived. What had been a set of disintegrated units became one whole.[23]

He was abetted by the extraordinary women who succeeded his sister as Honorary Secretary after she stepped down in 1914: Cicely Tatham (who served from 1919 to 1923), Frances "Fanny" Farrer (1923–1939), and Margery Cullen (1939–1964). As the demands on Vaughan Williams's time increased over the years, the Honorary Secretaries ensured the smooth management of the Festival while liaising between its eminent conductor and the various committees to which he theoretically deferred, and he never failed to acknowledge the scope and significance of their contributions.

As the lease expired on 10 Barton Street at the end of 1905, the Vaughan Williamses moved to 13 Cheyne Walk, a spacious six-floor corner terrace on the Chelsea Embankment, conveniently close to where Adeline's mother now lived with Hervey. Vaughan Williams wrote excitedly to Wedgwood about their new residence, with its magnificent view of the Thames and Battersea Park: "I've got a grand study in the attic with a grand view of the river and a bridge and 3 great electric light chimneys and a sunset[.] Then I've also got a roll top desk a writing table & a new piano so I ought to do!"[24] It was a lively and convivial household. During the early 1920s, R. O. Morris and his wife, Jane—the nickname of Emmeline Fisher, Adeline's older sister, who married Morris in 1915—and Arthur Bliss all lived at Cheyne Walk for a time, and the house was a popular destination for many friends and colleagues, some of whom (like Holst, Martin Shaw, and the young Margot Gatty) became regular fixtures.

Vaughan Williams spent the first half of 1906 finishing the *English Hymnal*, interspersed with brief collecting excursions to Sussex and Essex. The spacious study at Cheyne Walk evidently stimulated his imagination, as he completed the *Norfolk Rhapsody No. 1 in E Minor*, began composing two additional pieces intended as part of a projected (but unrealized) three-movement *Norfolk Symphony*, and had scored the second movement of *The Ocean* by July.[25] He also accepted the invitation of Joanna Hadley, manager of theatrical entertainments in the Surrey market town of Reigate, to provide music for twelve scenes from John Bunyan's *The Pilgrim's Progress* (1678) as adapted by Evelyn Ouless. Vaughan Williams turned to folk songs and *The English Hymnal* for suitable material to accompany the scenic tableaux dominating the story's production, which, although modest in scope, took a deep hold on his imagination.

Vaughan Williams made an unexpected journey to the Canary Islands in January 1907, as his brother-in-law and former Cambridge colleague Frederic Maitland had died from pneumonia just before Christmas while there with his family. As none of Adeline's brothers could make the journey to help Maitland's widow, Florence (their eldest sister), and her daughters, Ermengard and Fredegond, with the preparations to return home, the responsibility fell to Ralph. He remained in Las Palmas for a few weeks to assist the Maitlands (and scale some volcanic outcroppings), but made it back to Britain in time to conduct the *Bucolic Suite* in Cardiff on 30 January. Soon after, he read the manuscript of Cecil Sharp's *English Folk-Song: Some Conclusions* (1907), offering copious suggestions and corrections to curtail its more polemical tendencies.

While in Las Palmas, Vaughan Williams also finished *Toward the Unknown Region*, which he dedicated to Florence Maitland. It spun off from a friendly competition with Holst, in which each set text from Whitman's "Whispers of Heavenly Death" to see who could do it better ("The prize was awarded by us to me," Vaughan Williams later told Imogen Holst).[26] His winning effort was the unison song "Darest Thou Now, O Soul"—not published until 1925—but he was apparently inspired to attempt a more expansive treatment of the text for chorus and orchestra. He led its hugely successful first performance at the Leeds Festival on 10 October 1907, his highest-profile debut yet, and was cautiously pleased about the result. He told Wedgwood that the performers were magnificent, but "conducting was like 1000 years of purgatory. [. . .] the audience seemed to like it—but that may have been to encourage me—But after all it's only a step & I've got to do something really big some-time—I think I am improving—it 'came off' better than my earlier things used to."[27] Certainly the performers thought so. Waiting at a hotel after early rehearsals, he told Wedgwood, "I suddenly heard 'Hello Master Williams' and found myself clapped on the back by two burly Yorkshiremen—they turned out to be members of the chorus—they insisted on standing me drinks and one of them wanted to take me home with him—promising me a spare bed and a 'Yorkshire steak' cooked by his wife!"[28]

Such anecdotes suggest that the diffidence that Vaughan Williams's Cambridge colleagues had observed was beginning to diminish, perhaps exorcised by regular engagement with strangers during his song-collecting expeditions. If nothing else, he had developed an easygoing demeanor that enabled him to navigate an array of social situations, which would have served him well upon asking Frederick Delius to look at the recently completed draft of *The Ocean*. Vaughan Williams was clearly embarrassed upon recalling the meeting many years later. "Poor fellow! How he must have hated it. But he was very courteous and contented himself with saying 'Vraiment il n'est pas mesquin,'" faint praise indeed.[29] Unhelpful though this meeting may have been, it hints at what Vaughan Williams later described as his "lumpy and stodgy" compositional language, which he felt "had come to a dead-end."[30] He was as yet unable to resolve the conflicts between his conservatory training and the vernacular traditions he had come to admire, so decided to find someone who could.

Against all reasonable expectations, Maurice Ravel turned out to be that person. This "tiny, rouged, Baudelairean dandy of a composer," five-time loser of the *Prix de Rome*, and two-and-a-half years Vaughan Williams's junior, was an incredible choice as a tutor—both in that Michel-Dimitri Calvocoressi's recommendation of him was highly surprising, and that the outcome was so successful as to defy belief.[31] After finalizing arrangements for his studies, Vaughan Williams arrived in Paris on 12 December 1907, and stayed for slightly over two months. As Adeline did not accompany him (though she did visit), he took a room at the inclusively named Hôtel de l'Univers et du Portugal, located near the Louvre on the rue Croix du Petits Champs.

Several details from Vaughan Williams's account of his Parisian studies, however delightful, likely constitute exercises in selective memory or historical embellishment.[32] What is clear is that after Calvocoressi accompanied him to his first lesson to facilitate the formal introductions, Vaughan Williams got down to some serious work. Within days, he knew that Ravel was "exactly what I was looking for. As far as I know my own faults he hit on them all exactly."[33] Ravel primarily instructed him on orchestration, although Vaughan Williams absorbed more than that during his four or five lessons a week, which he knew were excessive: "I hope it doesn't worry him too much—only I feel that 10 years w^d not teach me all I want."[34] For his part, Ravel provided positive reinforcement à la Bruch, but in the spirit of a discussion between peers rather than as a master validating an apprentice; indeed, Ravel complimented Vaughan Williams as the only one of his students who "n'écrit pas de ma musique."[35] Ravel also gave him the courage to put greater trust in his own instincts. "[Ravel] is telling me to do exactly what I half feel in my mind I ought to do—but it just wanted saying."[36]

Despite the expense of lessons and lodging, Vaughan Williams was able to provide some financial assistance to Holst. His friend hit a low ebb in January 1908, exhausted from neuritis, overwork from his job as Musical Director at Morley College, and parental stress (his daughter, Imogen, had been born the previous April). The last straw came when his opera *Sita* narrowly failed to win the prestigious Ricordi Prize, denying him a performance and £500.[37] Knowing this, when Vaughan Williams learned that Holst's doctor had advised him to holiday in a warm climate, he sent his cash-strapped friend £50—nearly $7100 in 2020—to do so, a typically generous act. Again and again, he used his resources to provide other people with the opportunities, financial or otherwise, that he had enjoyed. Stories abound of his generosity: the "anonymous donor" who always ensured that the LHMC musicians had meals available, the Morley College students who discovered that their lesson fees had been mysteriously covered, the performing ensemble that received an unexpected donation. (Vaughan Williams later jokingly referred to such contributions as coming from the "Cheeseworth Trust.") Vaughan Williams was aware of his inherited privilege, and although he wore it lightly, his moral compass was guided by a combination of noblesse oblige and principles of

Morrisonian socialism reflecting his commitment to fair play, equal opportunity, and communal responsibility.

After returning to London in early 1908, Vaughan Williams resumed collecting folk songs (tabulating over 110 that year, primarily in Norfolk, Herefordshire, Surrey, and Sussex) and published *Folk Songs from the Eastern Counties* with Cecil Sharp. He also led a series of extension lectures at Morley College, conducted *Toward the Unknown Region* at Cambridge, and completed a handful of songs. His most important work, however, was going on behind the scenes, and its impact would reverberate for years to come.

The Music of 1902–1908

VAUGHAN WILLIAMS'S CREATIVE EFFORTS WERE ENRICHED, DIRECTLY and tangentially, by his engagement with musical styles, traditions, and performance practices beyond the academic curriculum and concert-hall repertory of his training, including those of the Anglican church, the Purcell Society, and amateur choristers. None, however, had a greater long-term impact than English folk music. Vaughan Williams's devotion to the collection and dissemination of folk songs stemmed from his belief that they represented "an art which grows straight out of the needs of a people and for which a fitting and perfect form, albeit on a small scale, has been found by those people; an art which is indigenous and owes nothing to anything outside itself, and above all an art which to us today has something to say—a true art which has beauty and vitality now in the twentieth century."[1] In other words, these tunes were not just beautiful, but also represented individual creative expressions of shared cultural experiences—qualities that he sought in his own music, and among other English composers. Moreover, they arose within communities whose engagement with music seemed unself-conscious, natural, and open to all, the kind of culture he hoped to foster in Britain more generally. Finally, he was less interested in imitating English folk songs than in absorbing "the musical coherence and structural tautness that he perceived" in them, an approach that might catalyze a response suitable to his needs and the expectations of the concert hall.[2]

Although Vaughan Williams focused his collecting efforts in East Anglia and the southeast of England, he went as far afield as Northumberland, Herefordshire, and Dorset, and even collected tunes in London.[3] His primary interest was accurately transcribing melodies, usually by aural transcription, though he very occasionally used recording equipment. He took pains to preserve tunes exactly as they were sung, even (sometimes particularly) if they deviated from theoretically "correct" practices, but he allowed his own taste and judgment to guide certain editorial decisions when he was preparing songs for publication.[4] He was often less interested in the texts, especially when he had to record both words and music. In some cases, he provided only the first verse for strophic tunes, leaving them out entirely in others. He would then either collect the words for additional verses from the singer at another time, or append a reference to a broadside featuring a text for the tune, even when it wasn't performed by the singer from whom he had collected the song. He sometimes made textual omissions to avoid publishing indelicate language, but typically recorded it in full in his notes.[5]

While folk songs consumed much of his time and energy, they were not his sole focus in the early 1900s. Vocal music—including solo songs, duets, part songs, and a cantata—accounted for seventeen of Vaughan Williams's twenty-one works published or first performed between 1902 and 1903. Commentators often inaccurately claim the influence of English folk song on these early melodies, a misapprehension likely stemming from the popularity of three settings of Dorset dialect verses by William Barnes ("Linden Lea," "Blackmwore by the Stour," and "The Winter's Willow"), all published by *The Vocalist* in 1902.[6] That inaccuracy does not mean that modal inflections were absent, as the flattened seventh in "Blackmwore by the Stour" and the natural minor melody of "Boy Johnny" demonstrate, but their supporting harmonies anchor them within a diatonic key. Furthermore, Vaughan Williams had not yet begun collecting English folk songs when these pieces were written, and still considered folk idioms an ineffective means of cultivating an individual style.

Most of these early songs gravitate toward melodic and harmonic diatonicism, with simple accompaniments (which, if strophic, often transform by the third verse), repetitive rhythms, comfortable ranges, and a pronounced absence of virtuosity. This accessibility made songs like "Blackmwore by the Stour" and "Whither Must I Wander?"—the latter subsequently incorporated into the *Songs of Travel*—suitable for amateur performers, while professionals could indulge more dramatic realizations. There are a few exceptions to this trend; for instance, the thick texture, flexible declamation, pervasive chromaticism, and plaintive text by Tennyson place "Tears, Idle Tears" more in line with the songs of the 1890s. Other contributions from this period include arrangements of German and French folk songs and three part songs, two of which ("Rest" and "Sound Sleep") feature lyrics by Christina Rossetti.

A more audacious effort appears in the luxuriantly pre-Raphaelite cantata *Willow-Wood* (1903). An interconnected set of four sonnets from Dante Gabriel Rossetti's collection *The House of Life*—and composed at the same time as the song cycle of that name—*Willow-Wood* was originally written for baritone and piano, though some reviews suggested that the accompaniment seemed better suited for orchestra. Vaughan Williams took this critique to heart, orchestrating the work shortly after, and revised it further between 1908 and 1909 by adding a wordless women's chorus. This version premiered in September 1909, but the composer deemed it a "complete flop," leaving it to languish in obscurity until the early twenty-first century.[7] This neglect is unfortunate, as the work demonstrates some of his first extended applications of triadic oscillations, consecutive semitone alterations, and mutable fluctuations among diatonic, modal, chromatic, and whole-tone sets.[8] Its expanded dimensions and musical language set it apart from other solo songs of this period, both in Vaughan Williams's own oeuvre and among English composers more generally, although the emphasis on a single emotional state is somewhat monotonous.

The six songs in *The House of Life* form a more conventional cycle than those of *Willow-Wood*. Despite retaining the latter's poetic archness, *The House of Life* responds to Rossetti's verses with greater expressive and musical variety. As with the earlier work, several critics questioned the sonnet form's suitability for lyric treatment, though it seems that the songs' length, musical language, and formal unpredictability rankled more than their poetic design.[9] In fact, Vaughan Williams responded to the textual challenges with careful consideration. For example, the opening song ("Love-Sight") splits the opening poetic octave into two diatonic quatrains, which are set off from the chromatically unstable sestet that follows—a musical shift correlating with the narrative arc rejoicing in love's presence before brooding upon its inevitable loss in death.[10] These thematic contrasts, however, are mitigated by undulating eighth notes and beautifully naturalistic declamation, which impose a strong sense of continuity. The next song ("Silent Noon") divides into two stylistically opposing pairs of quatrains and tercets, but recalls the music of the first quatrain in the second tercet. The resulting ABCA' form thus balances the thematic contrasts and chains of mediant modulations in the central sections, generating unity within an otherwise episodic composition.

The emotional range displayed in *The House of Life* expanded even further in the *Songs of Travel*, which has a strong claim as Vaughan Williams's first major success. Its nine poems came from Robert Louis Stevenson's *Songs of Travel and Other Verses* (1896), which Rufus Hallmark calls "refreshingly varied in structure, direct in sentiment, plain in diction, and often quite singable," arguing that they would have "provided [Vaughan Williams] with excellent material for his intertwined cultural imperatives" of raising contemporary songwriting standards while showcasing the best of British literature.[11] The cycle focuses on the experiences and reflections of the nameless Vagabond, "who stands on the edge of society, dips his bread in the river, makes palaces in the wild, has dreams, rises in the night to see the stars, and transmutes his experience into art."[12] (Its unabashedly masculine tone also mollified critics "trying to find an escape from . . . the hothouse femininity" of *The House of Life*.[13]) It played to the Edwardian vogue for recreational country walking as an alternative to the city's stifling conformity, and captures the era's sense of confident vitality and idealization of a hearty wayfaring life.[14]

The fact that all nine *Songs of Travel* were not published together until 1960 (following the posthumous discovery of "I Have Trod the Upward and the Downward Slope") has not affected the cycle's popularity or its thematic and musical cohesion.[15] That said, its range of styles and techniques is exceptionally wide, even though individual songs tend to concentrate on one at a time. As in *Willow-Wood*, though to different effect, nonfunctional triadic relationships and unfamiliar pitch collections emerge throughout the cycle, the former most conspicuously in "Bright Is the Ring of Words" and the latter in the brief pentatonic passage from "Youth and Love," the B section of which alludes to both "The Vagabond" and "The Roadside Fire." This treatment further suggests that the songs were conceived as a unified whole from the outset, even though the publishers emphasized the cycle's alternation between extroverted and introspective texts by releasing it in two collections.[16]

Both *The House of Life* and *Songs of Travel* debuted on the same concert in 1904, alongside the Whitman-texted duets "The Last Invocation" and "The Love-Song of the Birds." These received short shrift from critics, although "Crescendo" in *The Star* thought that the second was "perhaps the most effective of all the songs" performed that evening.[17] Whitman's poetry had recently captured Vaughan Williams's attention, and these two texts combine Rossetti's linguistic sensuality with the visionary freshness of Stevenson. They also employ a violin obbligato, the first example of Vaughan Williams's later tendency to augment or replace the piano in his songs with other instruments.[18]

One last song category remains: hymn tunes, the composition of which Vaughan Williams approached very differently from that of art songs. His frequent references to hymnody's moral impact indicate that he connected it with issues of musical suitability, and that improvement to one obliged adjusting the other. He wrote to Martin Shaw about the challenge in striking such a balance:

> The great difficulty about church music at present seems to be this—it is obviously useless to produce mere weak imitations of the old style—and yet it is equally obvious that the highly coloured sensational music which we usually hear in churches, even if it were good in its self, w^d be quite unsuitable to a service which is based on immemorial custom and of which the very language is that of the 17th century.[19]

The solution he pursued as music editor of *The English Hymnal* was to connect "the music of the hymn book to the cultural roots of England through a commitment to an explicitly revivalist agenda and a determined quest for musical excellence."[20] Although Vaughan Williams contributed only four original compositions to the first edition of *The English Hymnal* (DOWN AMPNEY, RANDOLPH, SALVE FESTA DIES, and the oft-quoted SINE NOMINE), he arranged another sixty-three tunes that he attributed "to my old friend, Mr. Anon."[21] English folk tunes, many of which he had collected, constituted more than half of those arrangements, but reflect a different conception of folk song than the one he privileged when collecting. In the latter context, Vaughan Williams focused on recording a tune's performance as accurately as possible, emphasizing its distinctive and idiosyncratic qualities. When adapting these melodies for the hymnal, however, he had to consider the limitations of often untrained prospective singers, while also being "sensitive to the constrictions of vocal range and clear part-writing" that typified Anglican hymnody.[22] This consideration led him to alter pitches, rhythms, and phrasing to create versions suitable for congregational singing, yet he also eschewed the plodding, repetitive patterns of *Hymns Ancient and Modern* in favor of the harmonic and rhythmic variety of Bach's chorale arrangements. A steady walking bass, for instance, might underpin a more flexible rhythm in the tenor or soprano, the melody for which could be enlivened with suspensions or passing tones—practices audible in both SALVE FESTA DIES and SINE NOMINE—all well within the capacity of small congregations or amateur organists, and engaging to hear and sing.

One unexpected result of Vaughan Williams's work with folk songs and hymns was the opportunity to apply them within Ben Jonson's masque *Pan's Anniversary* (1905) and the Scenes Adapted from Bunyan's *The Pilgrim's Progress* (1906). His decision—as music director for both productions—to link the distinctively national traditions of English folk song and Anglican hymnody with similarly illustrious examples from England's literary past seems intuitive. *Pan's Anniversary* "marks the intersection of many Edwardian movements and trends," including "the concern of masque as a form, the vogue for recreating elements of Jacobethan culture, the cult of 'Merrie England,' the campaign to make Stratford a national artistic centre . . . the revival of English folk-dance, [and] the increasing integration of folk-elements in Vaughan Williams's musical style."[23] One could easily overlook, however, just how diverse the music actually was. Sixteenth-century dance tunes, English folk songs, ceremonial fanfares, newly composed choral-orchestral hymns, and Morris music all appeared, although the historical fidelity of their application was tenuous at best.[24]

As in *Pan's Anniversary*, Vaughan Williams arranged six folk songs for the *Pilgrim's Progress* scenes—in fact, he reused both "Sellenger's Round" and "The Lost Lady" from the earlier masque—but also employed tunes from *The English Hymnal*, including YORK (No. 472, associated with the play's character of Bunyan), MONK'S GATE (No. 402, adapted from the English folk tune "Our Captain Calls" and setting lyrics by Bunyan himself), and most famously, Thomas Tallis's Third Mode Melody (No. 92), which characterized Christian's "anguished yearning for salvation."[25] Vaughan Williams also wrote new musical numbers, most significantly the Angel's Song heard after Apollyon's defeat in scene 5, which he later recast in *The Shepherds of the Delectable Mountains* (1922).[26]

Beyond the musical possibilities Vaughan Williams found in Bunyan's text, Evelyn Ouless's stage adaptation—balancing dialogue-heavy scenes with wordless tableaux vivants—coincided with his own dramaturgical preferences. A few years later, when beginning to write *Hugh the Drover*, he argued that "slow—long tableaux—or long dramatic pauses are always good, as the music takes a long time to speak, much longer than words by themselves—in fact, one wants purely musical effects in an opera just as one wants purely poetical effects in a drama," an idea that he came to via Wagnerian music drama.[27] The absence of dialogue in the tableaux enabled him to convey their inherent drama through purely musical means that, while arguably a sensible decision for this amateur production, remained a problematic idée fixe in his later treatments of the work.[28] Nevertheless, the production was warmly received, despite—or perhaps because of—the unorthodox casting of sisters Ruth and Rachel Charrington in the traditionally male roles of Faithful and Hopeful.

While many of Vaughan Williams's early songs and hymns remain repertory staples, the same cannot be said of his contemporaneous orchestral and chamber music, with the exceptions of *In the Fen Country* and the *Norfolk Rhapsody No. 1*. One of the most remarkable of these compositions is the *Fantasia for Piano and Orchestra*, which Vaughan Williams began composing in October 1896, completed in February 1902, and then revised twice in 1904. There is no record of it receiving a performance, but even before he had completed the revisions, Vaughan Williams called it one of his "most important works."[29] At 527 measures, it was certainly one of his longest, exceeded only by the multi-movement *Bucolic Suite*. The *Fantasia*, by contrast, is a single movement with six unequal subsections, inviting comparison with the *Fantasia (quasi variazione) on the Old 104th Psalm Tune* (1949) for piano, mixed chorus, and orchestra, not least because of the recurring pseudo-chorale first heard in m. 15 (Example 4.1).

Unusually for Vaughan Williams, the solo piano part includes several floridly virtuosic passages, but these serve an accompanimental role

Example 4.1   *Fantasia for Piano and Orchestra* (lower strings only), mm. 15–30

just as often as they showcase the soloist. In this respect, the concerti of Brahms, Grieg, and (particularly) Rachmaninoff appear to be the most influential models, evinced by the thick orchestral textures, sweeping passagework, and thorough use of various contrapuntal devices, especially fugal writing. For a composer whose piano works are often criticized as awkward, the *Fantasia* exudes astonishing confidence and assuredness, all the more surprising given its early compositional date. His decision to abandon it is therefore baffling, especially since he would revisit many of the technical effects and structural ideas it explored.

Vaughan Williams's other orchestral efforts from this period exclusively comprise single-movement impressions or rhapsodies: brief, lightly programmatic concert overtures with titular geographic allusions. These include the three *Norfolk Rhapsodies*, the "symphonic impression" *In the Fen Country*, and four orchestral impressions associated with a proposed collection called *In the New Forest*, a designation that requires some parsing. In 1903, Vaughan Williams completed *Burley Heath* and *The Solent*, allegedly the first "of a projected *Four Impressions for Orchestra* to be called *In the New Forest*."[30] There is no evidence that *Burley Heath* was ever performed, but *The Solent* received a hearing on 19 June 1903, likely a private performance. Two further works, *Harnham Down* and *Boldre Wood*, were completed by 1907 and performed at the Queen's Hall that November, though the score for the latter has been lost.[31] It seems likely that these pieces belong with *Burley Heath* and *The Solent* as part of a larger New Forest quartet: Boldre Wood and Burley Heath both lie within the boundaries of the New Forest, while the Solent lies offshore to the southeast and Harnham is situated just a few miles to the north— well within reason to consider them parts of a geographic whole. They also reflect some of Vaughan Williams's literary interests, since all but *Burley Heath* possess a textual epigraph. The others are preceded by poetical excerpts from Philip Marston ("To Cicely Narney Marson," in *The Solent*), Matthew Arnold ("The Scholar Gypsy," in *Harnham Down*) and George Meredith, whose Dantean phrase "Enter these enchanted woods / You who dare" is the only surviving detail associated with *Boldre Wood*.

The New Forest impressions display some of the shortcomings found in Vaughan Williams's previous orchestral efforts, particularly undigested allusions to other composers' styles or works. These evocations occur most conspicuously—but also most interestingly—in *The Solent*, portions of which Vaughan Williams later incorporated into at least four other works: *A Sea Symphony* (1910), the film score for *The England of Elizabeth* (1957), *Variations for Brass Band* (1958), and the Ninth Symphony (1958).[32] The opening theme group invokes a gesture that would later typify his approach to thematic extension: a long-breathed melody sounds in a single solo instrument or instrumental group, and then repeats in an ensemble setting—often strings, as employed here—with a minor-oriented but tonally ambiguous harmonization (or within a minor-inflected mode) before closing on a Picardy third (Example 4.2).

The second theme group favors a brass-heavy tune set against chromatically undulating figures in the strings, recalling the "Magic Sleep" passage from *Die Walküre*. (Wagner's music is similarly invoked in *Harnham Down* with references to *Tristan und Isolde*, a fitting allusion, given its pervasive harmonic ambiguity.[33]) This theme is followed by a new melody for the oboe (m. 62) recalling the rhapsodic Romance from the *Serenade*

Example 4.2   *The Solent*, mm. 1–13

of 1899. In short, while these themes are effectively conceived and executed, little binds them together. More internally consistent is *Burley Heath*, thanks to the motives' gradual introduction and transformation. It balances the evocation of familiar musical idioms—particularly that of Dvořák—with lighter, more folk-like material that may have been a byproduct of Vaughan Williams's recent fieldwork, building tension though textural and dynamic changes rather than conventional thematic development.[34]

The three *Norfolk Rhapsodies* have a similarly convoluted history. Following an extraordinarily fruitful folk-song collecting expedition around the Norfolk town of King's Lynn in January 1905, Vaughan Williams composed a series of orchestral rhapsodies based on several of the melodies he recorded. His original aim of combining them into a three-movement *Norfolk Symphony* went unfulfilled. As the manuscript for the third *Rhapsody* is lost—presumably destroyed—and the second remained incomplete and unpublished until 2014, the first *Rhapsody* is the only one to survive in the repertory, but it underwent considerable revision following its debut in 1906. Vaughan Williams reduced the number of folk tunes quoted from five to three, rewrote the introduction, and changed the rousing and brilliantly scored conclusion to a reprise of the introduction ending *niente*, the first published instance of the marking that would later characterize most of his major symphonic works.

Of the three tunes employed in the *Norfolk Rhapsody No. 1*, "The Captain's Apprentice" is the most pervasive. First introduced by a solo viola ("freely as if improvising," according to the score), it is immediately harmonized and repeated in the strings and oboe before being succeeded by the second tune, "A Bold Young Sailor." This is carried primarily by the winds until "The Captain's Apprentice" returns in a full orchestral statement, giving way to a jauntier central section featuring "On Board a Ninety-Eight." This passes through many different pitch centers and timbral guises before the truncated A section brings the work to an understated close.

The second *Rhapsody* provides an interesting comparison with its predecessor. It also features three melodies ("Young Henry the Poacher," "All on Spurn Point," and "The Saucy Bold Robber"), but they are not so deftly handled. "The Saucy Bold Robber" is too repetitive, the strings' flowing accompaniment nearly overwhelms the horn statement of "All on Spurn Point," and the closing *molto tranquillo* section goes on too long without a clear sense of direction. Overall, the folk elements are less effectively treated than in the first *Rhapsody*, but their comparison reveals the impact of Ravel's tutelage and the passage of time upon Vaughan Williams's approach to folk materials, as the revised version of the first *Rhapsody* demonstrates.[35]

The last of the early orchestral works, *In the Fen Country*, was completed in 1904 but not performed for another five years, and underwent multiple revisions in the interim (and further changes to the orchestration in 1935). The opening theme resembles "Searching for Lambs," a song Cecil Sharp had recently collected in Somerset and to which Vaughan Williams would repeatedly return over his lifetime.[36] That tune, however, is subjected to more conventional development than those of the later *Norfolk Rhapsodies*. Despite the modally ambiguous opening, *In the Fen Country* gravitates toward a highly chromatic idiom, its density and complexity mitigated by the recurring brass chorales and string responses first heard four measures before **C**. These combine with "fleeting echoes of Debussy, and fresher modal perspectives" foreshadowing not just Vaughan Williams's later work, but also that of composers like Stravinsky in *The Firebird*, though "at times it relies too heavily on imitation or strained modulations to generate momentum from contemplative musical material."[37] The result is a piece in which the structural and harmonic intricacy of post-Wagnerian chromatic tonality collides with unorthodox diatonic schemes drawn from folk, liturgical, or non-Teutonic sources, and so looks simultaneously forward and back along Vaughan Williams's stylistic timeline.

Once the songs and orchestral music from this period have been accounted for, only a handful of other compositions remain. The Quintet in C Minor (1905) extends many practices associated with the previous century's chamber works—the influence of Brahms and Dvořák is once again evident, augmented by that of Schubert—but appears to have taken longer to write than its predecessors. Vaughan Williams completed it in 1903, but revised it in 1904 and 1905. It received "a capital performance" at its debut, according to *The Times* (London), which deemed it "a work of very great beauty and originality, closely knit on themes of strong individuality and well written for the instruments."[38] Like *The Solent*, the Quintet went unpublished, but Vaughan Williams later employed the finale's main theme in his Sonata for Violin and Piano (1954).

One further cluster of chamber works deserves mention. In 1904, Vaughan Williams completed his *Ballade and Scherzo* for two violins, two violas, and cello. He substantially revised it in 1906, cutting ninety measures from the *Ballade*, retitling it *Nocturne: By the Bivouac's Fitful Flame*, and composed an entirely new Scherzo for it.[39] He also prepared an even shorter unaccompanied choral version of the *Nocturne*, long erroneously listed as the second movement of the *Three Nocturnes* (1908).[40] None of these received a public performance during Vaughan Williams's lifetime, nor were any published until the twenty-first century.[41] The *Scherzo* of 1904 is a giddily energetic movement evoking the liveliness of Schubert's quartets, with multiple stretches of elaborate imitation and, in an unusual display of extended techniques, a ghostly passage featuring harmonics. The *Nocturne and Scherzo* (1906) occupies a different expressive sphere altogether: the *Scherzo*'s delicately motoric ostinati, percussive pizzicato motives, and extended lyrical melodies—loosely based on the folk tune "As I Walked Out" (a.k.a. "The Old Garden Gate"), which Vaughan Williams collected in Essex in 1903—invite comparisons to Ravel's String Quartet, though Vaughan Williams wrote this movement before his studies in France.[42] The *Nocturne* is contrastingly introspective, its extensive chromaticism and complex interplay of lines conjuring a far more mysterious soundscape.

The *Nocturne and Scherzo*'s implicit tribute to Whitman became explicit the following year in *Toward the Unknown Region* (1907), one of Vaughan Williams's first large-scale pieces to secure a place in the standard repertory. Given the composer's personal ambivalence to statements of Christian faith—expressions of which had dominated English choral music over the last century—Whitman's poetry provided an attractive alternative, "a kind of liberal-humanist *purgatorio* and *paradiso* for the progress of the soul in death."[43] The opening measures imply A Phrygian as the primary collection, but D minor is confirmed by m. 20—an initial tonal ambiguity appropriate for the text's allusions to terrain "where neither ground is for the feet nor any path to follow." Vaughan Williams cannily balances textural shifts over the next two stanzas, which move from monophony to chromatic free counterpoint to compact homophony, systematically building and releasing tension as the motivic material spins out over increasingly spacious dimensions.[44] The fourth stanza thins the instrumental forces, setting them against a comparatively fast contrapuntal declamation of the text, intensifying the dramatic anticipation before the final stanza bursts forth "in a peroration that contains elements reminiscent of a march, a hymn [Sine Nomine], and an anthem."[45] This confident, optimistic music celebrates the vision of a hitherto inaccessible land, the joy in discovery casting off fears and uncertainty. Reviewers unanimously praised the work, most agreeing with *The Musical Times* that it "exhibits power to maintain due perspective on a large canvas, and to invest musical ideas with deep and impressive significance."[46] The critical consensus advanced Vaughan Williams to the front line of younger British composers, and the high expectations for his creative potential would soon be rewarded.

"The Best Thing I Have Done" (1909–1914)

TO THE CASUAL OBSERVER, THE YEAR AND A HALF FOLLOWING Vaughan Williams's return from Paris looks somewhat anticlimactic. In addition to all of his work with folk songs, he was leading an extension lecture series ("From Haydn to Wagner") at Morley College, serving on an advisory committee for *The English Church Pageant*,[1] and conducting both the LHMC ensembles and the St. Valentine's Orchestra. Although the latter lasted for only about two years, the repertory selections and his own comments about the ensemble's playing suggest a high standard of performance.[2] He completed a few songs in 1908 ("Buonaparty," "The Sky above the Roof," and "Is My Team Ploughing?"), but left several larger works unfinished, including three nocturnes on poems by Whitman, a setting of Matthew Arnold's *The Future* (for soprano, chorus, and orchestra) and a sketch of Whitman's *Aethiopia Saluting the Colours* for narrator and chorus.[3] However, it seems that Vaughan Williams abandoned these pieces because he was increasingly consumed by ones that he thought were even better.

Around 2 March 1909, Adeline contracted influenza. Her mother had a fall at about the same time, and experienced some health relapses during her convalescence. Despite objections from Ralph and her sisters Emmie and Cordelia, who were looking after Mary without difficulty, Adeline traveled daily from London to Hove to check on her. Their concerns were prescient, for Adeline's own illness persisted for almost three weeks, and Ralph and Cordelia became convinced that her subsequent struggle with rheumatoid arthritis stemmed from this episode. They had no idea at the time; in fact, by late March, Adeline had recovered enough to go with Ralph to Weymouth for a brief holiday.[4] However, symptoms soon emerged—mainly body aches that led her to start visiting a masseuse regularly—and her mobility and range of movement gradually diminished. Always rather shy, she withdrew socially as her disease advanced, since it became difficult for her to travel, hike, bicycle, play instruments, or dance, all activities she had previously enjoyed. Her apparent aloofness was reinforced by her austere tastes and emotional reticence stemming from her Victorian upbringing.

Her mind, however, was unaffected, and she retained "a lovely spirit with warm features," but she "had a domineering spirit," remembered Gerald Finzi's son, Nigel. "She was realistic—what she had, she had to accept."[5] Vaughan Williams relied on her formidable intelligence and discerning ear to judge works in development, and many years later, when she could no longer attend rehearsals or concerts, she reported on radio performances of his music. Remarkably, her ability to write was unaffected, so Ralph regularly dictated letters to her (particularly for recipients unfamiliar with his "cacography," as he described his handwriting), and she helped copy and correct his music.[6] Her niece Mary Bennett said this aligned with family practice: "In the Fisher tradition women were dark stars, reflecting the glory of their men [. . .] They grew up to feel that they must provide support to their husbands. That was their job which they did with great efficiency."[7] Yet Vaughan Williams also attended conscientiously to Adeline's needs, even as they grew increasingly onerous for them both.

Much of 1909, however, was sociable and pleasant. Ravel visited in the spring, and had a delightful time sightseeing (he was particularly interested in the Wallace Collection's artworks) and partaking of English cuisine. Ralph and Adeline holidayed in Paris, Italy, and Woodhall Spa (Lincolnshire), and visited Liverpool in September to hear the revised version of *Willow-Wood*. Perhaps the most exciting development, however, was the vocal-score publication of *The Ocean*—now renamed *A Sea Symphony*. Vaughan Williams dedicated it to Ralph Wedgwood, informing him that "it c^d have no better fate" than to bear his initials.[8]

November proved exceptionally busy. On the 8th, the Schwiller Quartet premiered Vaughan Williams's new String Quartet in G Minor at a meeting of the Society of British Composers; one week later, it debuted in London alongside the new song cycle *On Wenlock Edge.* Between these performances, Vaughan Williams completed incidental music for the Cambridge Greek Play production of Aristophanes's *The Wasps*, which opened on 26 November. This organization had produced ancient Greek plays in the original language since 1882, featuring music by such distinguished figures as Parry, Stanford, and Charles Wood.[9] Vaughan Williams's schoolboy proficiency in Greek endured two decades on, as the manuscript score indicates he wrote in that language as easily as (and more legibly than) English. The limited rehearsal time posed a challenge, but chorister L. W. Batten remembered that one of the producers "thought there was too much music and put blue pencil through whole pages of the score, whereupon the chorus—led, I think, by [William] Denis Browne and Stuart [sic] Wilson—said it would strike if any more were cut. None was."[10]

As this work, *Pan's Anniversary*, and the *Pilgrim's Progress* scenes indicate, Vaughan Williams was increasingly interested in composing for the stage, and by summer 1910, his earlier assumption that "he was not made to write opera" finally fell by the wayside.[11] Composing an opera was a daunting prospect, both in terms of the technical challenges and because British composers with such aspirations faced a lack of resources and a surfeit of critical snobbishness. He teamed up with an equally inexperienced librettist—author, critic, and journalist Harold Child—and was pessimistic about their chances of success: "If our scheme ever comes to anything then it will never get past pen on paper, for I see hardly any chance of an opera by an English composer ever being produced, at all events in our lifetime," a somewhat hyperbolic claim.[12] Covent Garden may have been out of reach for most British composers—foreign composers and music dominated there, as at most British opera houses, and serious opera sung in English remained rare—but many other theatres, student groups, and touring companies regularly produced British works ranging from light musical comedies to grand opera. Still, Child and Vaughan Williams's detailed correspondence reveals the many difficulties they faced in writing the work that became *Hugh the Drover.* Their efforts bore early fruit with the *Fantasia on English Folk Song*, the score for which has not survived despite its high-profile premiere at one of Henry Wood's Promenade Concerts in September 1910.

While this *Fantasia* has disappeared from the repertory, another that debuted the same month met a very different fate. The *Fantasia on a Theme by Thomas Tallis* was the first work the Three Choirs Festival commissioned from Vaughan Williams, and was performed inside Gloucester Cathedral itself—only the second time in the Festival's history an instrumental work had been so honored.[13] Although now widely considered Vaughan Williams's first masterpiece, early critical responses were surprisingly cool.[14] J. A. Fuller Maitland, writing in *The Times*, was among the few who immediately perceived its transcendent beauty. "The work is wonderful because it seems to lift one into some unknown region of musical thought and feeling. Throughout its course one is never quite sure whether one is listening to something very old or very new . . . it cannot be assigned to a time or a school, but it is full of the visions which have haunted the seers of all times."[15] A satisfied Vaughan Williams called the *Tallis Fantasia* "the best thing I have done," though he revised it in 1913 and 1919.[16]

Herbert Howells remembered attending the performance with Ivor Gurney, and how they wandered Gloucester's streets afterwards, dazed by the *Fantasia*'s impact; Howells later called the *Tallis Fantasia* "a supreme commentary by one great composer upon another."[17] They were not the only younger British musicians who had come to admire Vaughan Williams. Foremost among them was George Butterworth, a peripatetic Oxford graduate who had worked under Fuller Maitland at *The Times*, taught music at Radley College, and studied briefly at the RCM. He found his salvation in the study of English folk song and dance, and cinched his reputation through his musical responses to A. E. Housman's poetry. Vaughan Williams thought highly of his compositions, calling him "one of our rising lights," and they were close friends by 1910.[18] Two of Butterworth's Oxford contemporaries, organist Henry Ley and composer and pedagogue R. O. Morris, both entered Vaughan Williams's social circle around the same time, as did musicologist and composer E. J. Dent. Dent was a longtime Fellow of King's College and eventually Professor of Music at Cambridge, while Ley and Morris would serve as faculty at the RCM with Vaughan Williams. Morris also, upon marrying Adeline's sister Emmeline, became Vaughan Williams's brother-in-law in 1915.

Ties to the RCM also facilitated Vaughan Williams's contact with younger musicians, including Ernest Farrar—a promising composer and organist—and Rebecca Clarke. Clarke played viola for the Schwiller Quartet's premiere performances of the Quartet in G Minor and *On Wenlock Edge*, her first professional engagements, and got on well with Vaughan Williams in rehearsals. Some months later, she and her friend Beryl Reeves asked if he would lead a group of RCM students and recent graduates learning to sing Palestrina's music. "We were a motley crowd," Clarke later recalled. "It must have sounded pretty awful."[19] To their surprise, Vaughan Williams accepted but, as he wrote to Reeves, "you must not think that I am an expert on [Palestrina] or that I know very much of his work or the traditions as to how he ought to be sung— If after this confession you would still like me to conduct you I should be delighted to do so—perhaps we can make up a tradition of our own!"[20] His presence on the Palestrina Society's podium meant that friends like Butterworth and Steuart Wilson occasionally dropped in to fill out the tenors, while Vaughan Williams and Holst took advantage of a captive ensemble to occasionally rehearse their own new pieces.

A higher-profile conducting engagement came at the 1910 Leeds Festival, where Vaughan Williams directed the premiere of *A Sea Symphony* on his thirty-eighth birthday. Though he and the choir had nearly a week to prepare, and Stanford (the Festival's principal conductor) was on hand to assist, Vaughan Williams was intensely nervous when he mounted the podium for the performance, having barely eaten or slept for days, wondering if his seven years' labor had been worth it. Judging by the response in the hall, it was. From the fanfare heralding the sea itself to the soul's final voyage into the trackless distance, the Leeds audience was captivated by the grandeur, scope, and "poetical grasp with which Mr. Vaughan Williams has handled his subject, bringing ever richer and richer musical treasures forth as the words inspire him,"[21] which led critic Samuel Langford to call Vaughan Williams "a new figure in the first rank of our English composers."[22] Hugh Allen immediately began planning a second performance at Oxford, while a third was conducted by Arnold Barter, director of the Bristol New Philharmonic Society and Chorus, and an early promoter of Vaughan Williams's music.[23]

Characteristically, Vaughan Williams did not rest on his laurels following *A Sea Symphony*'s initial success. A considerable amount of work lay ahead in 1911, including the Three Choirs Festival's commission of the *Five Mystical Songs*, a collection of metaphysical verses by George Herbert (1593–1633). Vaughan Williams conducted it on 14 September, but had very little rehearsal time, and his nerves were so frayed by the concert that he thought he imagined seeing Fritz Kreisler—there to perform Elgar's Violin Concerto—playing at the back of the violins. It was no hallucination: Kreisler had broken a string and wanted to play in its replacement before his performance, but the only way he could without being heard was to sit in with the orchestra and sight-read the piece.

Earlier that summer, the coronation of George V inspired a host of activities, among the most spectacular of which was *The Pageant of London*. This massive open-air performance, staged on the Crystal Palace grounds, was a highlight of the Festival of Empire held in conjunction with the coronation that June. Its music director, W. H. Bell, asked Vaughan Williams to arrange a series of folk and traditional tunes for a scene entitled "The London of Merrie England: May Day Revels in the Days of Henry VIII." Vaughan Williams disliked the nostalgia-laced Merrie England movement ("it seems to my mind to be connected with . . . all the worst kind of obscurantism," he grumbled), but ever the professional, he completed the requested numbers and handed them off to his colleague Cecil Forsyth to orchestrate.[24] Held concurrently with the *Pageant* was Morley College's revival of Purcell's *The Fairy Queen*, enjoying its fullest realization in over two centuries.[25] Holst led the concert at the Victoria Hall, and Vaughan Williams, whose extensive lecturing experience put him at ease in front of audiences, introduced the various scenes. Even more anticipated was the engagement of the Ballets Russes at Covent Garden in July, an event that led to an unusual meeting. Actor and stage designer Gordon Craig had recently made Vaughan Williams's acquaintance, and proposed a balletic collaboration on the story of Cupid and Psyche. To that end, Craig arranged a breakfast and a lunch at the Savoy with Sergei Diaghilev, Vaclav Nijinsky, and Vaughan Williams to discuss it further. However, Vaughan Williams did not warm to the subject, disliked Diaghilev's proposal (originally Craig's) that Nijinsky dance both title roles, and refused to produce a score for Craig without first seeing a scenario. Craig insisted otherwise, and so the idea foundered.[26]

While not fond of the Ballets Russes' productions, Vaughan Williams's interest in dance paid dividends elsewhere. Having taken part in various folk-dancing events for some years (if with more enthusiasm than skill), he was elected to the committee of the newly founded English Folk Dance Society (EFDS) in 1911. He also got to know American dancer and choreographer Isadora Duncan, possibly through their mutual friend Martin Shaw, but more likely via Gilbert Murray, Regius Professor of Greek at Oxford.[27] Duncan had approached Murray about collaborating on a large-scale production of Greek plays, and it appears that all three met in October to discuss how such a project might proceed. Duncan was flirtatious and bohemian; her unconventional and naturalistic choreographic style resonated with the composer, and he began setting a passage from Euripides's *The Bacchae* for her as part of a proposed choral ballet. Unfortunately, Duncan evidently lost interest and broke off communication, but not before Vaughan Williams had completed several choruses for *Electra*, *Iphigenia in Tauris*, and *The Bacchae*.

Brief though these engagements with Craig, Duncan, and Murray were, they reveal that people outside Vaughan Williams's immediate sphere were increasingly aware of his music and his growing reputation.[28] Arthur Bliss, for example, remembered that "the *Songs of Travel* were on all pianos" at Cambridge between 1910 and 1913; additionally, *The Times* was promoting his music to a broad readership—first by Fuller Maitland, then by his successor, H. C. Colles.[29] The Leith Hill Festival continued going strong as well. Parry adjudicated in 1911, and told Meggie Vaughan Williams how pleased he was "to see your generous activity producing such wonderful results—and to see your brother devoting his abilities to such good purpose."[30] Ravel also arranged a Paris performance of *On Wenlock Edge* in early 1912, which Vaughan Williams attended; Ravel later reported that "in everyone's opinion your lyrical settings were a revelation."[31]

Closer to home, Vaughan Williams was gratified to see some of the folk songs he had collected taken up by his friends. Siblings Robert ("Bobby") and Margaret Longman—scions of the Longman publishing family—who grew up near Leith Hill Place, wrote and mounted folk-oriented plays on its grounds for neighboring families and friends in the summers. The Vaughan Williamses occasionally came down to watch, and the composer was so delighted with the results that he later employed

Margaret to sing the musical illustrations for his folk-song lectures.[32] Sometime during the summer of 1911, Ralph introduced Bobby to Dorothy Fletcher, a talented young violinist he had worked with in the LHMC and the St. Valentine's Orchestra, which ultimately led to their marriage in 1915. In later years, he enjoyed going on long hikes with them, often with Fanny Farrer in tow.

Despite elevated public interest in his music, it was at this time that Vaughan Williams wrote perhaps the most polemical article of his career, "Who Wants the English Composer?" (1912). In it, he argued that young English composers—one senses he still counted himself among them—were "unappreciated at home and unknown abroad," mostly due to their own shortcomings. English musicians, he asserted, were too apt "to think of composition as a series of clever tricks which can be learnt and imitated," particularly if those tricks were of foreign provenance. Audiences, meanwhile, had been enculturated to believe that music was best when it was foreign, because nothing of comparable quality allegedly existed at home. Vaughan Williams found this attitude untenable. "So long then as our composers are content to write operas which only equal Wagner in length, symphonies made up of scraps of Brahms at his dullest, or pianoforte pieces which are merely crumbs from Debussy's table, we can hardly blame the amateur for preferring the genuine article to the shoddy imitation."[33]

The solution, he suggested, was for English composers to take more interest in what was happening domestically—not just music performed in concert halls, but music-hall choruses, barrel-organ tunes, Salvation Army hymns, choral festivals, football chants, street cries, and factory girls' sentimental songs. Such a milieu could arise nowhere else but England, and to dismiss it was to deny one's birthright:

> Have all these nothing to say to us? Have we not in England occasions crying out for music? Do not all our great pageants of human beings, whether they take the form of a coronation or a syndicalist demonstration, require music for their full expression? We must cultivate a sense of musical citizenship; why should not the musician be the servant of the State and build national monuments like the painter, the writer, or the architect? . . . The composer must not shut himself up and think about art, he must live with his fellows and make his art an expression of the whole life of the community—if we seek for art we shall not find it.[34]

While Vaughan Williams allowed that such a goal would be difficult to achieve, he was convinced that native music and musicians would be welcomed in new and unconventional settings.[35] But his larger point— that British music could and should thrive without relying on foreign influences—met with skepticism from the musical establishment. Parry dismissed the article as "jokey" and "mostly chaff," but the thin-skinned Stanford took it as a rebuke of his teaching and music, and showed little interest in or sympathy for Vaughan Williams's works from that point forward.[36]

English music was on Vaughan Williams's mind when this article was published, for most of his output in 1912 and 1913 comprised arrangements and editions of folk songs, carols, dances, and hymns.[37] Two of the largest such works were the *Fantasia on Christmas Carols* (1912) for baritone, chorus, and orchestra—his third commission from the Three Choirs Festival in as many years—and the *Five English Folk Songs* (1914) for unaccompanied mixed chorus. One of the few exceptions to this trend was the *Phantasy Quintet* for two violins, two violas, and cello, completed in 1912 but first performed in March 1914 at an F. B. Ellis chamber concert.[38] Vaughan Williams wrote these comparatively minor works while engaged with other projects, musical and otherwise. One example of the latter was his service as Treasurer for the Russian Famine Relief Fund, likely at Percy Dearmer's request, which raised about £1700 ($228,290.65 in 2020).[39] On the professional side, *A Sea Symphony* and the *Tallis Fantasia* enjoyed their London debuts in February 1913, while *Hugh the Drover* continued simmering away; he had shared portions of it with Butterworth, Allen, Ley, and almost certainly Holst. But he realized that his limited stage experience was a drawback, so he accepted an invitation to serve as the Shakespeare Memorial Theatre Festival's music director for the autumn 1912 and spring 1913 seasons in Stratford. He was initially engaged to "conduct the Theatre orchestra, to rearrange music for *Richard the Second* and *Henry the Fifth*, and eventually to reconsider music for all the Histories."[40] This final request went unfulfilled, not only because it was unrealistic, but also because Frank Benson, the festival's long-standing manager and lead actor, was uninterested. However, Vaughan Williams wrote music for the two named plays, as well as for *The Merry Wives of Windsor, Henry IV Part 2, Richard III, Much Ado about Nothing*, and G. B. Shaw's *The Devil's Disciple*. He also conducted existing scores for several other productions mounted between April and May, receiving a "silver-mounted baton of ebony and ivory" as thanks from some venerable festival patrons.[41]

Following a brief holiday with Adeline in Cornwall, he accepted commissions from the London Church Choir Association for an anthem (*O Praise the Lord of Heaven*) and for incidental music to accompany Maurice Maeterlinck's plays *The Blue Bird* and *The Death of Tintagiles*. Vaughan Williams put the fee from the latter toward a holiday in Austria that July, the first of several trips that year. In September, he took an Irish walking holiday with Wedgwood, and spent much of the winter on the Italian Riviera with Adeline, Mary, Emmeline, and Hervey Fisher. While there, he maintained a steady stream of correspondence with Child about *Hugh the Drover*—nearly finished by mid-February 1914—and was completing a similarly audacious project: his first fully orchestral symphony. He credited Butterworth with the idea:

> We were talking together one day when he said in his gruff, abrupt manner: "You know, you ought to write a symphony." I answered, if I remember aright, that I never had written a symphony and never intended to. This was not strictly true, for I had in earlier years sketched three movements of one symphony and the first movement of another, all now happily lost. I supposed that Butterworth's words stung me and, anyhow, I looked out [sic] some sketches I had made for what I believe was going to have been a symphonic poem (!) about London and decided to throw it into symphonic form. Butterworth assiduously saw me through my trouble.[42]

The result was *A London Symphony* (1914), although Vaughan Williams stated that "Symphony by a Londoner" would be more accurate;[43] either way, the work was "an unqualified triumph" at its Queen's Hall premiere—another F. B. Ellis concert—on 27 March.[44] *The Sunday Times* praised it in openly nationalistic terms: "it pictures the magnitude and majesty of the great city, its diversity of life, its pleasures, its sorrows, and struggles . . . It is, in short, a work that can be claimed without demur as genuinely British."[45] His friends were equally enthusiastic. Butterworth said, "You have at last achieved something worthy of your gifts," Dent called it "real deep and moving stuff from beginning to end," and Steuart Wilson wrote that "not one of us is worthy to sit in the same room as you in this world, or to black your boots in the next."[46] Most gratifying must have been Holst's praise: "You have really done it this time. Not only have you reached the heights but you have taken your audience with you. [. . .] I wish I could tell you how I and everyone else was carried away on Friday. However, it is unnecessary as I expect you know it already."[47]

Vaughan Williams was humbled by his friends' responses. "I am <u>very</u> glad you like it," he told Dent, "I feel my self [sic] that I am perhaps beginning to emerge from the fogs at last."[48] He remained busy as ever through the early summer, having been appointed advisor to the music department at Borough Polytechnic in London, and the Leith Hill Musical Festival celebrated its tenth anniversary with performances of his *Fantasia on Christmas Carols* ("the best performance I have heard") and selections from Gluck's *Orfeo ed Euridice*.[49] In July, he and Adeline spent a week with Dent in Cambridge (Adeline was visiting a specialist about her rheumatism), where he continued revising *Hugh the Drover*; he was also writing a new piece for violin and orchestra, and reviewing proofs for a hymn set intended for the Three Choirs Festival that autumn. However, that year's festival did not take place. Vaughan Williams may have felt the mists of self-doubt finally lifting, but they were replaced, as for so many of his contemporaries, by the fog of war.

The Music of 1909–1914

B Y 1914, VAUGHAN WILLIAMS'S CONTRIBUTIONS TO MYRIAD GENRES—
large and small, vocal and instrumental, ensemble and solo—
demonstrated the breadth of his musical abilities. Performers and
conductors were increasingly taking up his works, his critical cachet was
rising, and he was writing several pieces between 1909 and 1914 that
would find homes within the standard repertory, including two of his
most celebrated: the *Tallis Fantasia* and *A London Symphony*. However,
while these compositions demonstrate new levels of technical facility
and expressive individuality, the immediate post-Paris years are better
thought of as a transitional stage between his period of apprenticeship
and his postwar career. As a whole, works from this era are stylistically
inconsistent, but evince the development of a compelling and idiomatic
compositional voice. Most conspicuously, pentatonicism, modes, whole-
tone scales, and octatonicism increasingly augment or replace the fin-de
siècle chromatic tonality that had dominated Vaughan Williams's music
up to that point, sometimes extending practices drawn from English folk
song or hymnody, contemporary French music, and Tudor-era works
(real or imagined). Some of his early compositions engage with such
materials and practices, but usually in brief or isolated contexts; the works
completed after 1909 more thoroughly integrate them into their underlying design, suggesting a fundamental reconsideration of their potential
function.[1] An offhand remark Vaughan Williams made in 1914 hints at
this: "The so-called 'modal' harmony of the Palestrina school is not truly

modal at all—its character and beauty depend largely from the fact there is a half-way house between modal and major-minor,"[2] and in that house were many mansions in which Vaughan Williams would later dwell.

Perhaps the most important stylistic influences shaping Vaughan Williams's musical language during this time came from France. Despite the Edwardian era's entente cordiale, practices associated with contemporary French music often inspired skeptical responses from English musicians—but not from Vaughan Williams, who embraced the potential of impressionism's harmonic oscillations, exotic scalar materials, and parallel triads.[3] These were especially prominent in a cluster of works first performed in November 1909: the String Quartet in G Minor, *On Wenlock Edge*, and the music for *The Wasps*. The French influence in the Quartet was immediately apparent to wags who dubbed it "L'après-midi d'un Vaughan," one of the kinder responses to the piece.[4] *The Musical Times* said it "represented the extreme development of modernism" and pushed the boundaries of musical acceptability, *Musical News* found it "discordantly chaotic," while *The Times* deemed it a largely unsuccessful experiment with "harmonic progressions that often torture the ear."[5] Such criticism disappointed Vaughan Williams ("I must confess that hardly <u>anyone</u> but me likes it," he told Dent), leading him to revise it in 1921.[6]

As no score for the original Quartet survives, such vitriolic responses suggest either that its critics had unusually conservative tastes, or that it must have been considerably stranger than the revised version we know today. Despite the designation of "G Minor," all four movements are modally organized. Vaughan Williams undermines the key signature by consistently modifying pitches (e.g., the beginning of the first movement changes E♭ to E♮, resulting in G Dorian) or eliding them—for example, using G–A–B♭–C–D–F to imply G minor and G Dorian simultaneously. The application of parallel triads three measures before **H** also obfuscates the underlying tonality, as do triadic successions encompassing non-standard pitch collections (such as the set E–F♯–G♯–A–B–C–D three measures before **L**) and extended passages employing octatonicism or whole-tone scales.[7] The first and third movements emphasize such harmonic ambiguities most strongly; the second and fourth, by contrast, focus instead on rhythmic vivacity and an almost folkish melodic ebullience to propel them forward.

On Wenlock Edge garnered better press than the Quartet, with which it was paired at its debut, and their harmonic resemblance strongly suggests that Vaughan Williams looked to the former when revising the latter. *On Wenlock Edge*'s unconventional performing forces—tenor, piano, and string quartet—complemented familiar poems from Housman's *A Shropshire Lad*, which divide broadly into two categories: meditations on the timeless English countryside, and laments on lost loves (some more sincere than others). Housman generally disliked musical settings of his poems, and *On Wenlock Edge* especially got under his skin, not least because the composer cut a stanza from "Is My Team Ploughing?"[8] Vaughan Williams had no compunction about modifying texts from any author or source—Bunyan, Shakespeare, Whitman, the Bible—to better suit his musical aims.[9] He argued that "the composer has a perfect right artistically to set any portion of a poem he chooses provided he does not actually alter the sense"; indeed, considering the lines he cut, he felt he was doing Housman a favor.[10]

As a whole, *On Wenlock Edge* reveals the lessons Vaughan Williams learned from Ravel: light and transparent scoring, elegant and ingenious harmonic schemes, and beautifully naturalistic text setting, though this last was equally informed by his work with folk songs and hymns.[11] Just as important, though, is his intuitive grasp of how his music could elevate Housman's texts. In Vaughan Williams's hands, the staid quatrains of "Is My Team Ploughing" become an anguished, guilt-ridden confession; the gale that plies the saplings double in the title song whips through the ensemble's tremolos, trills, and arpeggiations, amplifying the narrator's uneasy spirit; the successions of rippling triads opening "From Far, from Eve and Morning" embody the mysticism only hinted at in the text.[12] Additionally, the restrictions obliged by Housman's short, epigrammatic poems effectively tamed Vaughan Williams's expansive tendencies, reaching a charming apotheosis in the twenty-four bars of "Oh When I Was in Love with You." The one exception is the penultimate song, "Bredon Hill," the emotional heart of the cycle and the one that draws most upon impressionistic techniques. Parallelisms abound: fourths, fifths, and stacks of seventh chords alternate between languid and icy effects, with carefully placed dissonances eliciting the same tintinnabulations as Ravel's "La vallée de cloches" from *Miroirs* (1904–1905).[13] Bell sounds linger in the final song ("Clun") alongside oscillating triads and sudden modulations between modal and pentatonic sets, but the mood shifts from heartbroken resignation to clear-eyed acceptance of one's ultimate destiny.

The last premiere of November 1909 was that of the music for *The Wasps*. This satire of the Athenian legal system, pitting the bigoted Philocleon against his smarmy son, Bdelycleon, was last produced at Cambridge in 1897 with music by T. Tertius Noble, the Savoy-like lightness of which was now evidently unfashionable—hence the commissioning of new music from Vaughan Williams. *The Times* praised the score's "remarkable strength and beauty," aside from the "uncouth and jarring intervals preferred by the new French school" that opened the overture.[14] That theme's rhythmic vivacity and whole-tone orientation sounds a world away from its expansively lyrical F-major closing melody—used later in the work to signify reconciliation between father and son—yet the two ingeniously unite at the overture's end.

Besides the overture, *The Wasps* included nine choruses, a dance scene, an extended Parabasis—essentially, a reflective choral *scena* addressed to the audience—and numerous entr'actes and melodramas. It is a particularly allusive score, in which Vaughan Williams pays homage to the musicians and traditions that shaped him by quoting music of Parry (*The Birds*) and Debussy (*L'après-midi d'un faun*), and English folk song (the Cambridgeshire tune "The Lady Looked Out," collected the previous year).[15] Similarly evocative passages occur throughout the work, such as the Nocturne (no. 2) depicting Philocleon's disturbed sleep in a manner recalling Don Quixote's attack on the sheep in Strauss's eponymous tone poem, and a hymnlike tune in the Parabasis later included as no. 302 in *Songs of Praise* (MARATHON). Elsewhere, pentatonic and modal collections connote both impressionistic and folkish qualities, depending on their arrangement. The composer excerpted passages from the music to form an *Aristophanic Suite in Five Movements* (1912), and the Overture itself remains a popular curtain raiser, but it is the rarely performed full score that most accurately captures the potential of Vaughan Williams's burgeoning abilities.

Those reached an early peak in the *Fantasia on a Theme by Thomas Tallis*, "the first work in which Vaughan Williams fully realized the individual stylistic synthesis that would form the basis of his mature compositional output."[16] The fantasia is an unusually inclusive genre, valued most for composers' display of technical skill and imagination, regardless of the methods employed in doing so.[17] The genre flourished between the late sixteenth and mid-seventeenth centuries, an era widely considered England's musical golden age. Vaughan Williams's titular invocation of Tallis—and, by implication, other distinguished predecessors like Byrd, Gibbons, Thomas Morley, and Thomas Tomkins—thus forged a conspicuous link with the nation's musical past, strengthening his own claims to its inheritance and extension.

The *Fantasia* was based upon the Third Mode Melody from Tallis's Psalter for Archbishop Parker (1567), previously featured in *The English Hymnal* and the Reigate scenes from *The Pilgrim's Progress*. Scored for double string orchestra and string quartet, the *Tallis Fantasia* features formal spaciousness, luminous orchestration, and triadic modal harmonies that elevate practices first heard in the Quartet in G Minor and *On Wenlock Edge* to new heights of nuance and sophistication.[18] Ecclesiastical traditions, both musical and architectural, are often invoked in descriptions of this piece, if with varying levels of accuracy. Still, the antiphonal exchanges between the imbalanced ensembles, not to mention the organ-like sonorities coming from the muted, closely spaced lines in the second orchestra starting three measures before **F**, make such associations difficult to avoid.[19] Perhaps in response to early critiques about its length and apparent fragmentary design, the composer cut thirty-three measures over the course of two revisions, yet the work still took some time to catch on. It was performed at only one Queen's Hall Promenade concert between 1910 and 1933; however, it received seventeen Proms performances between 1934 and Vaughan Williams's death in 1958, reflecting its steady rise in both critical and popular acclaim.[20] With the benefit of hindsight, we can see the *Tallis Fantasia* for the achievement that it is: a union of past and present, sacred and secular, institution and aspiration. It speaks with Vaughan Williams's voice, but echoes with the inflections and accents of his mentors, collaborators, and colleagues, their collective sound resolving years of creative dissonance and development in tones of crystalline triadic beauty.

Barely one month after the *Tallis Fantasia's* premiere came the auspicious debut of *A Sea Symphony*, Vaughan Williams's most audacious work to date, and an expression of maximalist Romanticism "fabricated . . . from an assortment of ideas which the composer willed

into a coherent statement" over the course of seven years.[21] If that coherence is occasionally strained, it seems an unavoidable consequence of
the piece's extended growth and revision, the copious drafts of which
reveal complicated transformations and excisions (including the deletion
of a fifth movement called "The Steersman" that preceded the finale).[22]
In the end, however, its vibrancy and visionary power carry the day,
resulting in a compelling creative achievement that displays "an almost
palpable sense . . . of an artist discovering the full extent of his powers for
the first time."[23]

Like Whitman, the *Sea Symphony* contains multitudes and contradicts
itself. In one sense, it is no symphony at all, but a multi-movement cantata that "looked back to an aesthetic predicated on the Handelian and
Mendelssohnian oratorio" passed down through choral works by Parry,
Stanford, Elgar, and Delius.[24] Vaughan Williams claimed that he used
"Symphony" in the title "because the treatment of the words is symphonic rather than dramatic . . . the words are used as a basis on which
to build up a decorative musical scheme."[25] Yet it is the work's vast scale,
massive instrumentation, and passages of post-Wagnerian chromaticism
that engage the broad rhetorical qualities of the late Romantic symphony,
notwithstanding its sometimes unorthodox approach to motivic development and formal organization (especially in the sprawling and episodic finale). Like *In the Fen Country* and *Toward the Unknown Region*, the
Sea Symphony's shifts between modal and tonal pitch collections—especially in ways that emphasize hexatonic and/or mediant relationships—
present imaginative alternatives to the increasingly tottery tonal system.[26]
As Daniel Grimley has pointed out, "these techniques enable [Vaughan
Williams] to compose chains of diatonic root-position triads that operate
within a non-diatonic (usually modal) harmonic context," now an increasingly standard part of his expressive lexicon.[27] The brilliant opening
fanfare juxtaposing B♭ minor and D major is but the most memorable example, a simple gesture that somehow becomes shockingly new, as bracing
and powerful as the seascape it invokes. Similarly, Vaughan Williams's textual choices deftly situate Whitman's vision of international brotherhood
and cooperation "within the ideology of English nationalism," if one that
engaged more with the sea's symbolic and metaphorical aspects than its
place in British imperial culture.[28] But it does not so much start a new
chapter in Vaughan Williams's career as end one, its expressive dynamism

and sonic boldness not quite able to disguise its essentially Romantic language and spirit. In this way, it elegantly inverts the *Tallis Fantasia*, a work beneath whose ancient veneer beats a revolutionary heart.

Nearly all the original compositions Vaughan Williams completed between 1911 and 1914 align with a genre he employed between 1909 and 1910 (songs, incidental music, choral music, fantasias, chamber music, and/or symphonies), while the visionary spirit permeating both *A Sea Symphony* and the *Tallis Fantasia* persisted, if more concisely, in the *Five Mystical Songs* (1911). Written for solo baritone, chorus, and orchestra, the songs maintain the lyricism of *On Wenlock Edge* while their flexible formal schemes parallel similarly inventive approaches from *The House of Life*, applied here to stanzas rather than sonnets. Four of the songs set three-verse poems, but none features strophic form. "I Got Me Flowers" and "The Call" employ bar form, while "Easter" adopts a loose ternary in which the second A section reprises only the first line. The remarkable third song ("Love Bade Me Welcome") is essentially through-composed, and certain motives and harmonic effects—most notably, the modulation from E minor to E major before the final couplet, as the wordless chorus intones the antiphon "O sacrum convivium"—anticipate those later explored in the *Pastoral Symphony*. The closing "Antiphon" is also through-composed, but imposes unity through the recurring couplet "Let all the world in ev'ry corner sing / My God and King," forming a joyous choral conclusion to the cycle.

Not long after the *Five Mystical Songs'* premiere, Vaughan Williams renewed his engagement with Hellenic drama by setting choruses from three plays of Euripides: *The Bacchae*, *Iphigenia in Tauris*, and *Electra*. Though the choral ballets for which they were originally intended never came to fruition, the choruses were performed on 31 May 1912 at the Royal Court Theatre. A press release for the concert reassured readers that the composer "is not experimenting in styles, but rather seeking inspiration from the idiom and sentiment of the poet's phrases."[29] Vaughan Williams struggled to find the most effective musical approach in setting Gilbert Murray's translations, ranging from unaccompanied chant to "other parts in a more operatic method."[30] In the end, he alternated between homorhythmic choruses, rhythmically flexible passages for solo soprano (often with minimal or no accompaniment), and spoken monologues. Vaughan Williams's use of naturalistic declamation in all three scores was undoubtedly influenced by his study of English narrative balladry, although there is nothing folkish about the resulting sound. Octatonic, whole-tone, and pentatonic sets are employed and modified to create unusual and often striking triadic successions, but the careful voice leading preserves strong musical continuity throughout.

Although the Euripidean choruses are not incidental music in the conventional sense, Vaughan Williams did compose and arrange a large amount of such music just before the Great War, primarily for seven of the twelve plays mounted during the Shakespeare Memorial Theatre Festival's spring 1913 season. While these scores contain some original passages, they largely comprise arrangements of folk songs, dance tunes, popular melodies, hymns, and other vernacular musics. Most are short, designed to cover scene changes or mark entr'actes, though there are a few songs and choruses intended for diegetic use.[31] More elaborate were two newly composed scores for Maeterlinck plays (*The Death of Tintagiles* and *The Blue Bird*) written that same year. *The Death of Tintagiles* was commissioned by Philip Sassoon—whom Vaughan Williams called "the Millionaire in Park Lane"—for a private performance, but Maeterlinck's fatalistic story ill-suited the vapid London society audience, resulting in a disastrous debut.[32] This is a shame, as Vaughan Williams's starkly brooding music complements the symbolist theme, hinting at similar veins that he would later tap in *A London Symphony* and *Riders to the Sea*. The music for *The Blue Bird* differs considerably, though the only surviving numbers come from the end of Act I, where fairy magic enchants a collection of household objects to cavort in a charming series of *Nutcracker*-like dances.

Equally attractive and varied are two fantasias based on folk materials: the *Fantasia on English Folk Song* (1910) and the *Fantasia on Christmas Carols* (1912), which resemble earlier folk-inspired works like the *Norfolk Rhapsodies*. While folk song's musical and expressive elements informed Vaughan Williams's musical voice for many years to come, he stopped collecting them in 1913; nevertheless, his efforts had transformed the field. He published or contributed to several folk-music compilations during this period, including *Folk Songs for Schools* and *Folk Songs from Sussex* (both 1912), and released several folk-song arrangements for unaccompanied choir—most notably, *Five English Folk Songs* (1913)—as well as for solo voice with piano, and choir with orchestra; he also arranged a series of traditional and folk tunes for a scene in *The Pageant of London* (1911).[33]

We know little about the now-lost *Fantasia on English Folk Song* other than it was an orchestral byproduct of ongoing efforts with *Hugh the Drover*. Subtitled "Studies for an English Ballad Opera," it opened with a quotation of "Seventeen Come Sunday" and featured a "slow middle section" that functioned as "a sort of study for what I sh[d] like my love scene" in Act II of *Hugh* to be like, closing with "a short finale of a *scherzando* nature" that recalled the previous melodies at the end.[34] The *Fantasia on Christmas Carols* took a similar approach, but within a choral–orchestral context. Vaughan Williams was particularly fond of carols, contributing several to the *Journal of the Folk-Song Society* and later co-editing *The Oxford Book of Carols* (1928).[35] The *Fantasia* features carols from Somerset ("Come All You Worthy Gentlemen"), Sussex ("On Christmas Night") and two from Herefordshire, "The Truth Sent from Above" and "There Is a Fountain," which both strongly resemble "Searching for Lambs," and which he collected near Weobley, Herefordshire, with folklorist Ella Mary Leather in 1909.[36] The response to the *Carol Fantasia* was somewhat muted, perhaps because the subject was unusual for a September concert, while *The Times* expressed disappointment "that a composer who has so much that is interesting to say should refrain from saying it, and should devote his efforts to the arrangement of other people's tunes."[37] Nevertheless, the arrangements come off well, enhanced by harmonic shifts heralding each new carol and by the choir's effective use of vocables, humming, and closed-lipped singing.

As the title implies, the *Phantasy Quintet* occupies a slightly different niche from that of this era's other fantasias. W. W. Cobbett, a wealthy businessman and enthusiastic amateur musician, founded a competition in 1905 to encourage the composition of short, single-movement works for string quartet. He used the term "Phantasy" to describe such pieces, but specified no parameters beyond "different sections varying in *tempi* and rhythms."[38] In 1910, he commissioned twelve phantasies representing the potential instrumental combinations on a chamber program, including one from Vaughan Williams—hence the unusual instrumentation of two violins, two violas, and cello.[39] While the *Fantasia on Christmas Carols* aligned more closely with Cobbett's original conceit of the phantasy (i.e., a single movement with contrasting subsections), the compact *Phantasy*

Quintet featured four clearly delineated movements played without breaks, though material from the opening prelude returns throughout. At its premiere in March 1914, *The Times* noted the "infinite content which the composer finds in successions of common chords," comparing it favorably to the *Tallis Fantasia*.[40] Certainly the Prelude recalls that work's coloristic and harmonic effects, but the Scherzo's combination of melodiousness and a giddily propulsive $\frac{7}{4}$ meter evokes Bartók's approach to recasting folk influences in a wholly idiomatic and original manner. The closing Burlesca draws the piece to a satisfying conclusion, alternating between graceful counterpoint and rollicking homophony, the whole drawn together by a consistent lyricism that anticipates the spaciousness and linear continuity of *The Lark Ascending*.

A London Symphony closes out the prewar works, and represents a more conventional approach to the genre than its predecessor. It is no less ambitious in its size and expressive breadth, however, despite being the first original multi-movement orchestral work Vaughan Williams had completed since the *Bucolic Suite*. A vast range of pictorial and musical references emerge over the course of its four movements. Some are quite specific, like the Westminster chimes that strike in the first and fourth movements, or the Lavender Cry in the second movement, while others evoke broader associations with extramusical phenomena.[41] The gently flowing rhythmic figures in the introductory *Lento* and closing Epilogue, for instance, invite comparisons to the Thames as it enters and exits the great city, whose battering din threatens to overwhelm the listener. Sounds of hansom cabs and harmonicas, trains and traffic, street cries and steamships echo through the score, capturing all the oppressive magnificence and churning tumult of the great metropolis, and revealing heights of stylistic inclusivity and pictorial variety more typically associated with Mahler or Ives.

Curiously, however, Vaughan Williams insisted that the symphony be judged as absolute music, nonsensically claiming that any obvious musical allusions were "accidents, not essentials of the music."[42] He clarified his position to the critic Olin Downes after denouncing a program that the conductor Albert Coates used in conjunction with the symphony:

> I want the symphony to express the <u>spirit</u> of London. If my music does not do so, it will not help to say that a certain bit "means" the Thames or Bloomsbury, etc—if it <u>does</u> represent the <u>spirit</u> then the detail can be left

to the hearer's own imagination—the eternal peace which surrounds the turmoil I have tried to express in the music—to some the river may give that—to another not. [. . .] What I hope is that people who know London will recognise in my music the same emotion which London gives them, and those who do not know London will get an emotional picture of what London means to some people.[43]

Vaughan Williams quite often *did* have specific considerations in mind when writing his symphonies, but was reluctant to reveal them, believing that a piece should be able to "make itself understood as music without any tributary explanation."[44] (This may reflect Parry's influence, as his mentor expressed similar antipathy about French composers' recourse to programs.) Still, Vaughan Williams publicly linked the symphony's second movement with "Bloomsbury Square on a November afternoon" and the Scherzo with "Westminster Embankment at night,"[45] and privately stated that anyone looking for the finale's "actual coda" should "see end of [H. G.] Wells' *Tono-Bungay*," a literary connection that may have sparked the whole work.[46] However, the symphony is not merely a bricolage of impressionistic portraits cobbled together over four movements. Its cyclical themes and formal clarity represent a real advance in structural control at such a scale, making it a far more cohesive work than *A Sea Symphony*.[47] It also employs a coherent tonal plan oriented around G major—the primacy of which is challenged at various points by the now-familiar mélange of rival tonalities, modalities, pentatonic sets, and symmetrically organized pitch collections—but here they are more effectively integrated into the overall harmonic fabric than in the past. Beyond articulating the structure, these competing sonic forces also expressively highlight the city's internal diversity and its contrast with the natural world.[48] Still, impressive as *A London Symphony's* expansive vision and scale proved to be, Vaughan Williams's multiple revisions and cuts indicate an awareness of his occasional proclivity for the grandiose gesture and a growing desire to bring it under control, a skill he would soon acquire in a world transformed by war.

"Beyond Powers of Expression" (1914–1922)

THE OUTBREAK OF WAR LED VAUGHAN WILLIAMS TO IMMEDIATELY enroll in the Special Constabulary, a part-time volunteer police force, and he was promoted to sergeant by the end of August. One of the Specials' main tasks was to protect water supplies, so Vaughan Williams remained in Chelsea to supervise the London County Council pumping station and sewer works. This assignment enabled him to continue his work with both Borough Polytechnic and Morley College while overseeing the reconstruction of *A London Symphony*, the score of which had been sent to Germany (and, as it would turn out, lost).[1] A plan emerged to create a new copy of the score from the individual parts, which were still in London. Armed with them and a short score prepared some months earlier, Vaughan Williams, Adeline, Dent, and William Denis Browne managed to produce a new score in time for a performance in Edinburgh on 30 November.

Vaughan Williams's Special Constabulary activities did not satisfy his desire to serve his country, and so on 31 December 1914, he enlisted in the Territorial Forces as Private no. 2033 (later reassigned as no. 534386)—even though, at forty-two, he was over the age of conscription (which is perhaps why his medical form lists his age as thirty-nine). He was assigned to the 4th London (Reserve) Field Ambulance unit, later the 2/4th London Field Ambulance, Royal Army Medical Corps (RAMC), the headquarters for which was based at the Duke of York's School in Chelsea. However, the 2/4th relocated to Dorking at the beginning of

January 1915, and so Vaughan Williams could easily stay either at Cheyne Walk or Leith Hill Place when he was granted leave. The training was difficult, especially in that winter's frigid conditions, and included lectures, long marches—round trips to Guildford were not unheard of—extensive stretcher drills, and first aid training, including a month of practical work at Guy's Hospital in London. The unit left Dorking once spring had arrived, first for Watford, then Saffron Walden by mid-May, where they remained until spring 1916.

By this point, Vaughan Williams was bored with the endless drill, dismayed by the Territorials' dubious reputation, and frustrated by the lack of action.[2] The more tedious aspects of military comportment annoyed him deeply, particularly appropriate dress (such as proper cap angle and correctly wrapped puttees).[3] Some of this frustration was mitigated by his fellow private, Harry Steggles. Twenty years Vaughan Williams's junior and from the other end of the social spectrum, Steggles instantly got on with "Bob," as he called the composer ("for I couldn't call him Williams and R.V.W. seemed impertinent"), taking it upon himself to help him manage the mundanities of enlisted life.[4] Vaughan Williams was grateful, and valued Harry's abilities as both a soldier and a musician. For as usual, he had turned to music to provide purpose for himself and others. While at Saffron Walden, he organized a band of dubious quality, played organ at a local church (with Steggles blowing the bellows), and directed the RAMC Choral Society, performing an organ rendition of "The Mummers' Carol" for a Christmas concert in 1915. He was also fortunate to be placed with the Machray family in nearby Bishop's Stortford, who had specifically requested billeters interested in music. He and Steggles regularly participated in the family's musicales, Vaughan Williams on piano or viola, and Steggles singing, playing the harmonica, and even once assembling a makeshift drum kit.

In early 1916, the unit moved to Sutton Veny Camp near Warminster. Mobilization orders came through on 15 June, and exactly one week later, the 2/4th sailed to Le Havre before setting out for Écoivres, a small village near Arras where they relieved the 51st Highland Division. The complicated trench system where the Field Ambulance was stationed for the next four months was called the Labyrinth: support branches snaked from the main line to a series of advance aid posts. As described by unit member H. P. Chipperfield, "our work was to evacuate the wounded from the Regimental aid posts, which were close by, back to our advanced dressing station, which necessitated carrying for two twenty minute spells—no light task—especially as it was usually done in the dark and over duck-boards from which many struts were missing."[5]

Hard though the work was, Vaughan Williams preferred it to parading and drill. "I am very well and enjoy my work . . . I am 'wagon orderly' and go up the line every night to bring back wounded and sick on a motor ambulance—this all takes place at night—except an occasional day journey for urgent cases."[6] His light tone belies the appalling conditions. Lice, flies, and rats by the millions infested the trenches, and the waterlogged muck of northern France was a constant obstacle. Portions of the Labyrinth had been hastily dug to hold gains made in frantic advances, which meant that soldiers regularly encountered limbs and bones protruding from the earthen walls, their putrefying stench unaffected by the liberal spreading of corrosive chlorate of lime. The German lines were only a few hundred yards away, so the sound of artillery constantly accompanied the sixteen-hour shifts spent transporting the wounded and maintaining the trench infrastructure. Incredibly, even under these conditions, Vaughan Williams kept up the choir formed at Saffron Walden, having brought a box of music from which the men could perform, and even mounted occasional informal concerts. He and Steggles also shared lighter moments, such as sneaking into a local tavern to drink champagne, or glimpsing the German trenches from the ruined Abbey window at Mount St. Eloi, just over the ridge from Écoivres. Even in the midst of war's horror and desolation, Vaughan Williams could still find beauty in a sunset glimpsed while he was transporting the wounded from the ridge near Écoivres, a vision that would later inform one of his most sublime compositions.

In October, the unit was relieved and sent to Eaucourt-sur-Somme, near Abbeville, where gas drills and the assignation of protective gear led many of the men to believe they would soon be bound for the ongoing slaughter of the Somme. Instead, the 2/4th boarded HMT *Transylvania* with the rest of the 179th Brigade on 19 November for an eleven-day voyage to Salonika, Greece, in order to reinforce troops fighting the Bulgarians. From there, they departed for the town of Katerini, about fifteen miles northeast of Mount Olympus, where they arrived on 15 December. Harry Steggles fondly remembered Vaughan Williams leading the RAMC choir in Christmas carols within sight of the vast peak, and gathering dance tunes while they sampled local wines at a village cafe.

Overall, the conditions were less fraught and the demands less difficult than in Écoivres—though the endless damp was replaced by freezing cold—but Vaughan Williams grew increasingly restive. More than anything, he wanted to directly contribute to the war effort, a desire that his assignment in the backwaters of Salonika left unfulfilled. Some of his frustration may have come from knowing that several friends and relatives—including Butterworth, Denis Browne, F. B. Ellis, and Adeline's younger brother Charles—had already made the ultimate sacrifice for their country. Their loss weighed on him (he told Holst that he dreaded "coming back to normal life with so many gaps"), and his near-daily encounters with death further emphasized the war's grim toll and senseless waste, strengthening his resolve to help end it.[7]

That opportunity came in early 1917 when his commanding officer recommended that he apply for a commission. His request was approved by April, and Vaughan Williams left for England on 16 June to enroll for training in the Artillery Officer's Cadet Unit. (Adeline may have asked her older brother Herbert, now Education Secretary for the Lloyd George administration, to pull some strings, supported by the fact that Private Vaughan Williams was ordered to report to the War Office in London rather than the RAMC training camp in Blackpool.) Steggles remembered his friend's tart farewell to his superiors, remarking that upon leaving, "I shall cease to be a man and become an officer."[8] Deemed too old to serve as a Royal Field Artillery subaltern, he was assigned instead to the Royal Garrison Artillery (RGA) for instruction on the use of six-inch howitzers, and reported for duty on 1 August 1917 at No. 2 RGA Officer Cadet School, Maresfield Park, Sussex.

Ironically, he began his officer training by violating the very rules that he would be expected to uphold. As when he joined the RAMC, Vaughan Williams was among the oldest cadets in the program. Faced with physical and intellectual demands that challenged soldiers half his age, he sought opportunities for solitude that would let him study without distraction. With the help of another cadet, John Tindall Robertson—who had taken over Steggles's assorted duties of care—he illicitly rented a room in a cottage outside the base, accessed via a camouflaged hole in the hedges surrounding the camp. This arrangement, along with careful time management, allowed them to evade patrols and secure the privacy needed to pass their exams. By late November, they were sent to Lydd, Kent, for a firing course to complete their training; while there, Vaughan Williams wrote a short appreciation of George Butterworth for his father, Sir Alexander Kaye Butterworth, to include in a memorial volume published the following year. On 23 December, both Vaughan Williams and Tindall Robertson received their formal commissions— Vaughan Williams as a second lieutenant—and three weeks' leave. They then reported to the Royal Artillery barracks in Bordon, Hampshire, before shipping out to France on 1 March 1918.

Now assigned to the 141st Heavy Battery, Vaughan Williams returned to Le Havre before moving up the line to Rouen to meet a major German attack (the Spring Offensive of 1918) on 21 March. Unfortunately, both he and Tindall Robertson, serving with the nearby 131st Heavy Battery, were not assigned to the howitzers on which they had been trained, but instead "to horse-drawn 60 pounder guns—completely different. So, knowing nothing of these guns, or how to use them, we were both put at wagon lines, in charge of the horses! Riding a horse was the only thing I ever knew [Vaughan Williams] to baulk at in his military career; but he scrounged himself a bicycle from somewhere and rode that instead."[9] Remarkably, Vaughan Williams safely transported all but one of the 200 horses through the ensuing retreat. His other responsibilities included supervising ammunition wagons headed to the front line and organizing teams and supplies for their journeys—crucial work carried out under extraordinarily perilous conditions at the western front. Yet his batman, A. J. Moore, remembered Vaughan Williams as "a most considerate officer. I do not ever remember hearing him speak contemptuously to a subordinate."[10] He was similarly respected by the men serving under him, even though he rarely fraternized with them outside of musical events and singing classes.[11]

Vaughan Williams stayed with the Heavy Battery through the armistice, but with increasing numbers of troops awaiting demobilization, the Army needed qualified people to organize opportunities for education, employment, and recreation. Vaughan Williams was therefore reassigned as Director of Music for the First Army of the British Expeditionary Forces (BEF) in France, headquartered in Valenciennes. According to his successor in the position, E. R. Winship, Vaughan Williams had plenty to do. "His work entailed visiting the divisions over a wide area, finding officers and other ranks from the various units who were interested in music and getting them to act as conductors to a choral society, orchestra or to take a class in music. At the time of his demobilization in February 1919 there were already nine choral societies, three classes, an orchestra and a band," including a choral society at the BEF headquarters under his direction, and he played piano and attempted to reassemble a disused organ in his spare time.[12] He was reviewed for promotion to first lieutenant, and although his commanding officer considered him "a most reliable and energetic officer," he was not recommended for advancement due to his age and because "he was most untidy in his ways and dress."[13]

Vaughan Williams's return home elicited a host of mixed feelings—relief at having survived foremost among them, along with the anticipation of returning to his wife and music. Yet he also had to face the dread of personal loss that he confessed to Holst back in 1916. Since then, Cecil Coles and Ernest Farrar had also fallen in the war, while another gap was created when his beloved mentor, Hubert Parry, succumbed to the flu pandemic of 1918. Another of Adeline's brothers, Edmund, died on Easter Sunday that year from peritonitis, just as Stella Duckworth had two decades earlier. Adeline's mother had also passed away (hit by a car outside her Chelsea home in August 1916), and so the burden of caring for Hervey had fallen to Adeline. In hopes of finding a better convalescent environment, she moved him to the Norfolk coastal town of Sheringham while Ralph was overseas, taking a series of rooms there in order to tend to her brother more easily. Thus upon returning to England, Vaughan Williams wound up splitting his time between Cheyne Walk, Dent's home in Cambridge (from February until at least June 1919), and no fewer than six different flats in Sheringham between August 1919 and May 1921, an unsettled situation that put some strain on the family finances.

Happily, this last point was ameliorated when Hugh Allen, Parry's replacement as Director of the Royal College of Music, invited Vaughan Williams to join the composition faculty (allegedly telling him to "come up to the RCM and be yourself one day a week").[14] It was a prestigious hire for the RCM, enhanced by the composer's receipt of an honorary doctorate in music from Oxford in June 1919, held in conjunction with events celebrating the Sheldonian Theatre's 250th anniversary. It may have been then that Allen made the offer to Vaughan Williams, who accepted and began teaching that September. His hiring was part of a larger series of curricular and staff reforms at the RCM, which also brought rising stars such as Holst, Colles, Howells, Adrian Boult, John Ireland, and Arthur Benjamin onto the faculty.

Vaughan Williams's professorship granted him powerful influence over the next generation of British composers. Even a partial list of his students—Stanley Bate, Ina Boyle, Howard Ferguson, Cecil Armstrong Gibbs, Ruth Gipps, Peggy Glanville-Hicks, Helen Glatz (née Hunter), Dorothy Gow, Ivor Gurney, Patrick Hadley, Imogen Holst, Gordon Jacob, Constant Lambert, Elizabeth Maconchy, Robin Milford, Michael Mullinar, Anna Russell, Cedric Thorpe Davie, and Grace Williams—constitutes a marquee lineup of postwar musical talent. Vaughan Williams's teaching methods were undogmatic, drawing upon the qualities he admired in Parry and Bruch. "What he taught was not a style of music," said Ruth Gipps, "but an attitude toward composition."[15] He eschewed textbooks in favor of models from historical literature (formulating exercises that obliged his students to apply those works' structural principles to their own compositions) and emphasized technique as the means to effectively express their artistic visions, never as an end in itself.[16] Most importantly, Vaughan Williams empowered his pupils to make their own creative decisions rather than relying on his pronouncements of their music's value.[17] "He directs you to be yourself," Michael Mullinar recalled. "[O]ne is soon conscious of nothing except how to find the best possible way of expressing what one has in mind."[18] Vaughan Williams's sympathetic approach resonated strongly with his numerous female students, whose aspirations he took far more seriously than did some of his contemporaries.[19] (For instance, he welcomed Anna Russell into his studio after Howells dismissed her efforts in lighter genres.) "None of the other professors looked at us as people," said Belinda Norman-Butler, "he did. He was always interested in us and in what we had to say about things."[20] In this capacity, he was endlessly patient, remembering how Bruch nurtured him when he most needed it. "I always try to remember the value of encouragement," he wrote. "Sometimes a callow youth appears who may be a fool or may be a genius, and I would rather be guilty of encouraging a fool than of discouraging a genius."[21] He mentored many of his students well beyond their time at the RCM by attending rehearsals of new works, promoting and facilitating performances of their music, and providing professional advice. Several of them (including Jacob, Lambert, and Mullinar) repaid him by assisting with the creation, arrangement, and performance of his own music. And finally, as he confessed to George McCleary, he enjoyed the work. "I like hearing the views and seeing the aims of the younger generation—it keeps me young!"[22]

When he was not teaching, he tended to stay in Sheringham—which, since it was a five-hour train journey from London, left him undisturbed to coax the embers of his inspiration back into flame. He began slowly, arranging multiple volumes of folk songs and carols for Stainer & Bell, and revising both the *Tallis Fantasia* and *A London Symphony*. He had already made some cuts to the latter for a performance in early 1918, and further revised the second, third, and fourth movements by August 1919. This version was first performed the following May, and catapulted the symphony to wide acclaim; *The Musical Times* deemed it "the result of deep thought and earnest aspiration, and . . . inspired by true love of beauty."[23] Several smaller works emerged soon after, the motet *O Clap Your Hands* and the *Three Preludes on Welsh Hymn-Tunes* foremost among them, along with the *Suite of Six Short Pieces for Pianoforte* and the *Suite de Ballet* for flute and piano. Two prewar compositions enjoyed belated premieres in 1920: the Four Hymns for tenor, viola, and orchestra— originally intended for the Three Choirs Festival of 1914—and *The Lark Ascending*, though not in its original form. Working with its dedicatee, Marie Hall, Vaughan Williams arranged a violin and piano version for a concert of the Avonmouth and Shirehampton Choral Society on 15 December 1920.

In addition to his work at the RCM, Vaughan Williams sought out other opportunities to reintegrate himself into British musical life. In November 1919, the newly revived Handel Society brought him on as conductor, and he accepted the music directorship of the Bach Choir two years later—a happy turn of events, for he had joined that en-semble in 1903 and had served on its Committee for several years.[24] Additionally, he recommended directing choirs for the LHMC in 1920 (on hiatus since the start of the war) and was re-elected as President of the Cambridge branch of the EFDS in November 1920. He became one of that organization's vice-presidents in 1921, about the same time as he began adjudicating for the Carnegie United Kingdom Trust's music publication scheme. He also continued writing regularly about music and musicians, including an extended appreciation of Holst (1920), tributes to Hubert Parry (1918) and Gervase Elwes (1921), and a meditative essay entitled "The Letter and the Spirit" (1920). After introducing its ostensible premise—that reading a score and listening to it are not equivalent actions, statements that he had been making since his Pokesdown lectures of 1902—Vaughan Williams made a striking assertion:

> Before going any further may we take it that the object of an art is to obtain a partial revelation of that which is beyond human senses and human faculties—of that, in fact, which is spiritual? And that the means we employ to induce this revelation are those very senses and faculties themselves? The human, visible, audible and intelligible media which artists (of all kinds) use, are symbols not of other visible and audible things but of what lies beyond sense and knowledge.[25]

He continues,

> Certain types of musical thinkers seem to have inherited the medieval fear of beauty—they talk about "mere beauty" and "mere sound" as if they were something to be feared and avoided. But in our imperfect existence what means have we of reaching out to that which is beyond the senses but through those very senses? [. . .] Surely, while music is the art of sound, it is the ear which must be taught its language.[26]

These are remarkable statements for a serious composer to make in 1920. One does not have to be a hard-line modernist to question postwar claims of beauty as a self-evident virtue, or spiritual enrichment as a marker of artistic value. But in taking this artistic position, Vaughan Williams was neither retreating from modernity, nor clinging to the past. He was in fact that rarest of things in postwar Britain: an idealist. Not because naiveté or privilege shielded him from reality, but because he was a person who, when confronted with the injustices, inequities, and shortcomings of the world, saw their opposition as a moral responsibility. Is the world ugly? Then it must be made beautiful. Do the people despair? Then they must remember hope. Does the spirit suffer? Then it must be made glad. While he never made such statements in so many words, the creative direction and thematic content of his postwar music strongly implies such concerns were at the forefront of his thinking. Such challenges could be taken up only by someone embodying unique combinations of inherited privilege and unselfish service, intellectual refinement and intuitive vision, social prestige and professional respect. To a degree matched by few other artists of his generation, Vaughan Williams had both the ability and desire to accept such a burden and the heart to bear it.

On 26 May 1921, Hervey Fisher died of complications from tuberculosis of the spine, the fourth of Adeline's siblings to die within a five-year period (her oldest sister, Florence, had died the previous March). The Vaughan Williamses returned to Cheyne Walk shortly thereafter, at which point Vaughan Williams informed pianist Vally Lasker about an important development. "The Past. Symph is practically finished now—c^d we possibly have a go at it (with a few friends to listen) one Sat: morning soon."[27] This is the earliest surviving reference to the *Pastoral Symphony*, the initial entry in a triptych of works—including the Mass in G Minor and the chamber opera *The Shepherds of the Delectable Mountains*—that consolidated and redefined the musical idiom known as pastoralism. Shortly thereafter, the orchestral version of *The Lark Ascending* had its London premiere on 14 June. Although it is rooted more firmly in a prewar conception of pastoralism, all four pieces mark a conspicuous shift toward a more introverted, subtle, and quietly intense style.

After a busy first half of 1922—which involved the first performances of the *Pastoral Symphony* in January and the motet *O Vos Omnes* in April, judging at the inaugural Stinchcombe Hill Musical Festival in Gloucestershire, directing three LHMC concerts, and a short trip to Holland—the Vaughan Williamses embarked for America at the end of May. They were guests of Carl and Ellen Stoeckel, founders of the Litchfield County Choral Union and Connecticut's Norfolk Festival, where Vaughan Williams conducted the American debut of the *Pastoral Symphony* on 7 June. It was praised by critic Oscar Thompson as "admirable in workmanship throughout, clarisonous [sic] in its varied scoring, and possessing a charm like that of the drifting skies and dreaming downs which it suggests."[28] But despite Thompson's inference, shared by many critics, Vaughan Williams had no such image in mind, though it was many years before its underlying inspiration—his own experiences on the war-torn fields of France—became public knowledge.

Ralph and Adeline took full advantage of their time in the United States, visiting Niagara Falls, New York City, Boston, the Berkshires, and rural Pennsylvania; they also reunited with Cecil Forsyth and their friends Bobby and Dorothy Longman. The Stoeckels treated them to all that American hospitality had to offer, and Vaughan Williams was captivated by gustatory experiences such as chicken salad and adding ice cream to coffee ("oh the American food—it's beyond powers of expression," he told Holst).[29] Upon returning to England in July, he made the final touches to *Hugh the Drover* before turning his attention to the RCM's inaugural production of *The Shepherds of the Delectable Mountains*. Queen Mary attended the performance, and Vaughan Williams was presented to her by Hugh Allen afterwards. Adeline's description of their exchange to her sister, Cordelia Curle, is unimprovable:

> Queen: Are you the composer? – I mean the composer of the 1ˢᵗ opera?
> R: Yes, Mam
> Queen: I thought the <u>dresses</u> were <u>very</u> nice—and the <u>scenery</u> quite charming.
> R: The students did it all themselves—

Then he received a gracious bow of dismissal & the next man was presented.[30]

On his fiftieth birthday he received a friendlier reception from Holst and a choir from Morley College, who serenaded the composer at Cheyne Walk with a part song written for the occasion by Holst's former student Jane Joseph. The Morleyites' heartfelt gesture reflected their esteem for Vaughan Williams's championing of their institution and his friendship with Holst, the dedicatee (along with his Whitsuntide Singers) of the newly completed Mass in G Minor, which was soon taken up by concert and liturgical choirs in England and abroad. Vaughan Williams must have been particularly gratified by the German premiere at Leipzig's Thomaskirche the following year. The director, Karl Straube, said that it "made a very deep impression on the whole audience, indeed has made your name popular in Leipzig, the musicians were fascinated and the 'connoisseurs' of music overpowered by the beauty of the composition; we all have to bring thanks to you, for giving us this refined masterpiece of musical art."[31] Like the

Pastoral Symphony and The Shepherds of the Delectable Mountains, the Mass in G Minor exuded a gently emphatic timelessness unlike almost anything else in contemporary British music, securing Vaughan Williams's place in the first rank of British composers and establishing him as a significant player on the international stage.

The Music of 1914–1922

ANY ASSESSMENT OF VAUGHAN WILLIAMS'S IMMEDIATE POSTWAR music must acknowledge several facts. First, the composer's wartime obligations largely precluded him from writing music between late 1914 and early 1919, so the works considered here represent those published or first performed between 1919 and 1922. Second, some of those compositions were completed in full or in part before the war, and so reflect stylistic tendencies aligned more closely with that era than with subsequent practices. Third, many works composed after the war's end share several traits: extensive counterpoint, evocations of older styles or genres, and associations with religious or spiritual topics. Finally, four works from this period—*The Lark Ascending,* the *Pastoral Symphony*, the Mass in G Minor, and *The Shepherds of the Delectable Mountains*—represent some of the most significant and influential contributions to English pastoral music in the twentieth century, and powerfully affected the tastes and aesthetics of British musicians and audiences for many years to come.

Ursula Vaughan Williams emphasized that Ralph's return from war "was not a simple and joyful release."[1] Beyond the gaps created by absent friends and the general challenges of readjusting to civilian life, "he faced a crisis that was both existential and spiritual: either forge a new mode of musical expression that would be creatively honest and culturally meaningful in the postwar world or begin a slow but inexorable descent into artistic irrelevance."[2] Obviously, the hoped-for revival of his abilities occurred, but it was a gradual process; there was no wellspring of music simply waiting to be tapped. Instead, Vaughan Williams approached his return to creative activity with his usual methodical diligence, beginning with the comparatively undemanding task of making a series of arrangements. Between 1919 and 1922, he set over forty folk tunes, popular airs, sea songs, carols, and hymns in multiple guises: for unaccompanied singer; solo voice and piano; choir with vocal soloist; and unison, male, or mixed choirs (a cappella or with accompaniment). Some represented entirely new undertakings, while others resumed projects that he had begun before the war. While most of the melodies he arranged were either his own or of anonymous origin, they also included musical and textual contributions from the likes of Shakespeare, Purcell, William Boyce, Robert Burns, and Charles Dibden, as well as non-English tunes such as the Scottish airs "Loch Lomond" and "Ca' the Yowes," and Stephen Foster's "Old Folks at Home," a popular number among the BEF choirs. The publishers for these songs were similarly diverse, ranging from prominent series like Stainer & Bell's Choral Library to the more obscure League of Arts for National and Civic Ceremony, which counted the four *Motherland Song Book* volumes and the *League of Nations Song Book* among its publications. Not all of these efforts were entirely successful,[3] but they provided a steady stream of material for Vaughan Williams to work with if and when inspiration waned.

Modest though the creative aspirations of these arrangements were, several of Vaughan Williams's earliest postwar compositions—Three Preludes on Welsh Hymn-Tunes (1920), the *Suite de Ballet* (1920), and the *Suite of Six Short Pieces for Pianoforte* (1921)—took similarly conservative and cautious approaches to their structure and layout. All three evoke Baroque- or Classical-era forms or genres, some featuring elaborate counterpoint and others referencing specific dance styles. His reason for writing such music may be inferred from a suggestion he later offered an American composition student. "You will not be wasting your time if, for a time you neglect free composition and make a <u>thorough</u> study of strict counterpoint, classical harmony, fugue and strict sonata form. You will then be fully equipped, your tools will be sharp and of tempered steel, ready for whatever use you wish to put them to."[4] By composing pieces based upon strict principles of form, rhythm, and/or voice leading, Vaughan Williams established well-defined boundaries within which he could hone any dulled edges he detected among his technical apparatus.

Coincidentally, such an approach mirrored many principles of neoclassicism, then gaining cachet thanks to figures such as Ravel and Stravinsky. It seems unlikely that an iconoclast like Vaughan Williams would have consciously aligned himself with this movement, but he was hardly the only postwar artist who turned to principles of order, balance, and clarity as both inspiration and balm for a soul battered by years of brutal conflict.

The Three Preludes are perhaps the most elaborate of the works just noted. Vaughan Williams had previously featured the tunes on which the preludes are based (William Owen's BRYN CALFARIA, J. D. Edwards's RHOSYMEDRE, and R. H. Prichard's HYFRYDOL) in *The English Hymnal* as nos. 319, 303, and 301, respectively. While not especially virtuosic, they hew closely to the improvisatory-sounding contrapuntal manner (if not always the sonorities) associated with the eighteenth-century chorale prelude, and demonstrate surprising levels of fluency for a composer not renowned for his organ technique—though they are dedicated to his more accomplished and long-suffering former teacher, Alan Gray. By comparison, the compact *Suite de Ballet* for flute and piano strikes a more contemporary note. Although two of its four movements ("Gavotte" and "Passepied") allude to specific Baroque dances, the suite lacks any obvious connection to ballet beyond its light and graceful manner. It was likely written for virtuoso flutist Louis Fleury in 1913—the two met in Stratford that year—but Vaughan Williams forgot he had done so until Fleury informed him about the first performance in March 1920.[5] All of the movements feature ternary form and practices found in many of the composer's other post-Parisian compositions, if with a more strongly pronounced neoclassical gloss. The A sections of the opening Improvisation, for example, layer pentatonic melodies in the flute over slow-moving dissonances in the piano, while the B section features a canon at the fifth between two diatonically ambiguous scales (each lacks a sixth scale degree, so are interpretable as either minor or Dorian). The jiglike Humoresque that follows pushes the sonic envelope even further, as the pentatonic set of the opening A section and the whole-tone collection of the following B section dissonantly unite in the concluding A′.

The deceptively simple *Suite of Six Short Pieces for Pianoforte* slightly intensifies the *Suite de Ballet*'s neoclassical aspect, even though its movement titles are more general and its harmonic and scalar profiles less outré.

Its textural clarity, graceful lines, and lightness of touch recall Ravel's *Le tombeau de Couperin*, as do the occasional quintal harmonies and frequent Picardy thirds. That Vaughan Williams should choose to follow his colleague's example of fastidious craftsmanship to revive his compositional muse makes sense, and while some movements (notably the Prelude and Slow Dance) could almost pass as Ravel pastiches, Vaughan Williams's own musical personality perceptibly emerges as the piece progresses, perhaps most so in the fifth movement (Rondo). The *Suite* also enjoyed an active afterlife. In 1923, Vaughan Williams collaborated with James Brown (editor for the Polychordia String Library) to arrange it for string orchestra, retitling it *The Charterhouse Suite*; it was this version that pianist Harriet Cohen adapted ten years later for piano and string orchestra.[6] Excerpts were also used for two ballets choreographed by Ninette de Valois at the Old Vic in 1929 and 1931 (*The Picnic* and *The Faun*), most likely at the recommendation of Vaughan Williams's former student Constant Lambert.[7]

Neoclassical elements also emerge in a song cycle from this era, if somewhat more tenuously and with a much earlier historical point of reference. *Merciless Beauty*, for high voice, two violins, and cello (though a piano may replace the string trio), was first performed in 1921 by the dedicatee, Steuart Wilson, and published the following year. It sports the subtitle "Three Rondels," alluding to a fourteen-line poetic form related to the medieval rondeau. The verses, attributed (perhaps speciously) to Chaucer, represent a thirteen-line variant of the form: the first three lines repeat as the last three, and lines one and two return as lines six and seven. Vaughan Williams makes the obvious choice to set the repeating text as a musical refrain in all three songs, following both standard medieval conventions and the approach often taken by Arnold Schoenberg in the twenty-one rondels of *Pierrot lunaire*, though there is no indication that Vaughan Williams looked to that cycle as a model. The first two poems—"Your Eyën Two" and "So Hath Your Beauty"—feature texts of courtly love, the austere if gently rhapsodic musical settings capturing the emotional quality of passion carefully held in check.[8] The final song ("Since I from Love") upends the somber atmosphere with its gleeful renunciation of love, expressed in music reminiscent of the Italian frottola or Parisian chanson, while the frequent meter changes evoke the naturalistic rhythmic inflections of English folk song. What particularly stands out is the songs' ease and fluency despite their limited musical material, and the degree to which the various influences meld into a cohesive and consistent style.

Vaughan Williams's evocation of past musical traditions carried over into sacred spheres as well, as represented by three short choral works published between 1920 and 1922. The earliest is the exuberant *O Clap Your Hands* for mixed chorus, organ, and small brass and percussion ensemble, with text taken from Psalm 47. Though brief, the fanfare-like melody and blocks of parallel triads that open and close the piece effectively contrast with the more restrained central section, in which chantlike declamation gives way to a short, rhythmically extended fugal treatment of the main theme. Its emotional effect could not be further from the mysterious desolation of the a capella motet *O Vos Omnes* (1922), first performed for Maundy Thursday services at Westminster Cathedral, where Richard Terry served as music director and organist. Terry ranked among the foremost scholars and conductors of liturgical music in England at the time, and Vaughan Williams admired his dedication to the revival and performance of English ecclesiastical works by Byrd, Tallis, Christopher Tye, Peter Philips, and many others. *O Vos Omnes* acknowledges that distinguished tradition, if not its specific idiom, with somber text from the Book of Lamentations pleading for mercy from a wrathful God. Few works in Vaughan Williams's catalogue elicit such bleakness—reinforced in the stark harmonies caused by withholding the men's voices for most of the piece—and it is tempting to link the motet's sentiments to the composer's experiences in the Great War, or to his pessimism about the world to which he returned. If that is the case, however, then it is an outlier in his postwar works that engage with themes of loss—such as *The Shepherds of the Delectable Mountains*, *Job*, and *Riders to the Sea*—which frame such sacrifices as humbling experiences necessary for redemption. *O Vos Omnes* lacks that resolution, closing instead with an urgent plea for repentance: "Jerusalem, convertere ad Dominum Deum tuum."

The most varied of these three liturgical works is *Lord, Thou Hast Been Our Refuge* (1921) for chorus, semi-chorus (or soloists) and orchestra or organ. The text is based on two versions of Psalm 90: one from the Book of Common Prayer, the other a metrical setting by Isaac Watts (with the incipit "O God, our help in ages past"). Vaughan

Williams's designation of this piece as a motet is technically incorrect—since the text is in English rather than Latin, it is an anthem—but the musical design resembles practices associated with French motets of the later fourteenth century by its use of seemingly incompatible musical sources. A solo melody for baritone opens the piece, declaimed in the manner of traditional psalmody, but is soon joined by a much slower (and strongly contrasting) choral statement of William Croft's metric hymn tune ST. ANNE, to which Watts's text was traditionally sung. As the two melodies progress, the latter stays firmly within the key of D major, but the solo melody fights its tonal pull, shifting between D major and minor while avoiding the tonic pitch at the ends of phrases. This conflict gives way at the end of the first verse to an extended passage of psalm-like choral homophony, interrupted by imitative phrases from the semi-chorus and quasi-responsorial lines from the solo baritone. The section closes with antiphonal exchanges between the chorus and semi-chorus, transitioning to an extended fugal passage from the orchestra that gradually intensifies, cutting out suddenly as the now-united choruses joyfully intone the opening psalmlike melody. The instruments, however, respond with the ST. ANNE theme in the manner of the opening section (redolent of how the tune YORK was treated in the Reigate production of *The Pilgrim's Progress*). The piece closes with an extended display of imitative polyphony shared between chorus and orchestra, a suitably elaborate illustration of the final exhortation "O prosper Thou our handywork." Coincidentally, Bach's "St. Anne" Fugue in E♭ (BWV 552) features a subject identical to the first phrase of Croft's melody. Vaughan Williams almost certainly knew this connection, making it especially appropriate that this work was published the same year that he accepted the Bach Choir directorship, when he would have been steeped in his predecessor's music.

Attractive and well-crafted as the pieces discussed to this point are, none occupies an influential position within the long arc of Vaughan Williams's career. But alongside these relatively modest efforts, a series of works emerged that systemized a stylistic approach to the expressive mode known as pastoralism. Their understated intensity and broad accessibility shaped the aesthetics of a generation of English composers—both positively and negatively—establishing a compelling alternative to more avant-garde or disruptive modernist practices while still engaging with and responding to contemporary British culture.

Pastoralism is difficult to define because it transcends boundaries of genre, mode, and style, allowing it to be reinterpreted and recast to reflect the proclivities of the artist or audience engaging with it.[9] From a topical perspective, pastoralism could invoke shepherds from Classical antiquity or the present day, Arcadian enclaves beyond the corrupting influences of the city, elegies for the dead, idealized rural landscapes, sites for spiritual introspection, and utopian fantasies, among other possibilities. From a musical perspective, pastoral compositions often display elements such as modally inflected scales, rhapsodic melodies with irregular phrase lengths, gently flowing rhythms, triadic yet tonally ambiguous harmonies, quiet dynamics, and light and transparent textures, all of which contribute to the generally understated and restrained expressive tone of such works. Such practices had existed for centuries by Vaughan Williams's day, and all of them are amply represented within early-twentieth-century British musical literature. However, prior to the Great War, music referred to as "pastoral" covered a wide stylistic and topical range, which has contributed to its often vague and ambiguous scholarly treatment. This scope narrowed significantly after the conflict, however, and it was Vaughan Williams, more than any other figure, who influenced that stylistic consolidation.

Pastoral elements sound in Vaughan Williams's music as far back as *In the Fen Country*, but his use of them increased after his return from Paris, audible in the String Quartet in G Minor, *On Wenlock Edge*, the *Five Mystical Songs*, the *Tallis Fantasia*, the *Phantasy Quintet*, and even *A London Symphony*. However, the most consistent integration of them may be heard beginning with two pieces completed by 1914, but revised and debuting after the war: Four Hymns for tenor, viola, and piano (or string orchestra), and *The Lark Ascending* for solo violin and orchestra.

The Four Hymns foreshadow Vaughan Williams's postwar approach to pastoralism in many ways. Cut from similar textual cloth as the *Five Mystical Songs*, the hymns' rhythmic and formal freedom runs counter to conventional expectations of such tunes as stolid and sober, uniting many gestures and practices heard elsewhere in Vaughan Williams's post-Parisian works. The spacious triadic harmonies that open "Lord!

Come Away!" create a similar effect as those of "From Far, from Eve and Morning" or the *Tallis Fantasia*, facilitating the tenor's free declamation. The hymn's focus on rhapsodic melody explains the through-composed form, although certain motivic gestures (like the rising figure on "Hosanna") return in modified guises to impose a sense of rhetorical shape. "Who Is This Fair One?" takes a different approach, as the strophic layout signaled in the first two verses gives way to increasing formal and rhythmic freedom, perhaps telegraphed by the opening melody's easy shifts between F minor and F Dorian. The text, by Isaac Watts, rides a fine line between sacred and earthly love, and Vaughan Williams's setting of it evokes the same kind of lush sensuousness characterizing *Flos Campi* and the *Magnificat*. The dark tones of the solo viola—Vaughan Williams's own instrument, which he often featured at points of intensely felt introspection—contributes greatly to this effect. It is also showcased in the extended solo that opens the beautifully languid "Come Love, Come Lord," though this tranquil movement ends with a quasi-bitonal clash between G Lydian and G minor. Its underlying triadic parallelism is replaced by the contrapuntal web spun throughout the "Evening Hymn," whose main melody includes both the "Searching for Lambs" motive and a figure that would later serve as the opening tune of the *Pastoral Symphony*. Although the Four Hymns do not rank among Vaughan Williams's more celebrated efforts, their significance as a gateway connecting his pre- and postwar idioms should not be underestimated, nor their engagement with pastoral conventions overlooked.

Arguably the first work to fully realize those conventions was *The Lark Ascending*. More than a century on from its first performance, it remains one of Vaughan Williams's most beloved compositions—indeed, one of the most popular pieces of British art music ever written. This very familiarity, however, makes it difficult to appreciate how unconventional and original it really is. Consider a very obvious question: what sort of work is it? Vaughan Williams dubbed it a "Romance for violin and orchestra," but its virtuosity and performing forces far exceed the conventions of nineteenth-century character pieces sporting that moniker. Yet its short, single-movement design precludes it from concerto status, and its lack of ostentatious display—despite its formidable technical demands—makes the description of "showpiece" somehow inappropriate, even with the presence of three cadenzas. It is sui generis, unlike almost anything else in the literature for violin and orchestra, and its uniqueness may explain the fascination it has exerted upon generations of listeners.

The score is preceded by an excerpt from George Meredith's eponymous poem of 1881:

> He rises and begins to round,
> He drops the silver chain of sound,
> Of many links without a break,
> In chirrup, whistle, slur and shake.
> . . . .
> For singing till his heaven fills,
> 'Tis love of earth that he instils,
> And ever winging up and up,
> Our valley is his golden cup
> And he the wine which overflows
> To lift us with him as he goes.
> . . . .
> Till lost on his aerial rings
> In light, and then the fancy sings.

Vaughan Williams's music captures Meredith's transcendent vision by eschewing naturalism—no literal birdsongs are quoted in this piece—in favor of an idealized lark whose "silver chain of sound" winds its way through the texture in rhapsodic coils. The ease and freedom the piece evokes goes well beyond the soloist's long-breathed (and occasionally unbarred) phrases, as Vaughan Williams's now-familiar employment of scalar ambiguity expands to such a degree that certain passages may be plausibly interpreted as belonging to three different heptatonic collections simultaneously.[10] Seventh and ninth chords emerge and vanish without resolution; pentatonic melodies float over modal harmonies; motives fragment and recombine with unprompted spontaneity. Yet that sonic freedom, paradoxically, can only be realized through intense control by the performers, particularly the soloist. The florid solo melody somehow resists tipping into the realms of Romantic excess, and despite the challenges posed by its rapid passagework and extensive double stops, it must sound easy and effortless throughout, an approach that may be compared to that of bel canto arias. It is a work that revels in the expansive and melancholic beauty of its own sound, without apology or embarrassment, soaring to picturesque heights that few in the postwar world still dared. Perhaps this is why *The Lark Ascending* has proven so resilient: in an increasingly noisy and exhausting world, it still provides a quiet space to dream.

The year 1922 was a propitious one for Vaughan Williams, for it witnessed the premieres of three great pastoral works: the *Pastoral Symphony*, *The Shepherds of the Delectable Mountains*, and the Mass in G Minor. Of these, the *Pastoral Symphony* has enjoyed perhaps the greatest rehabilitation of its reputation over the last century. During his lifetime, it was often treated as one of Vaughan Williams's least impressive symphonies: a gentle (if slightly dull) meditation on the English landscape that rejected the beckonings of postwar modernism. After his death, however, that perception changed drastically—perhaps most significantly with the revelation that it was not inspired by Cotswold villages or the Surrey hillsides, but by Vaughan Williams's own experiences with the RAMC in France, where he was charged with transporting the bodies of the dead and injured from the field.[11] Introducing this elegiac tradition to the work meant that "the symphony's invocation of the pastoral tradition is emptied and drained of many of its original codes and meanings," but also "deepened and enriched" by showing that tradition's potential for reinterpreting familiar gestures in new and compelling ways for contemporary audiences—a basic tenet of modernism.[12]

Similarly illuminating treatments have been applied to the *Pastoral Symphony's* underlying form and treatment of pitch resources, which continue Vaughan Williams's prewar tendencies toward musical designs that lend themselves to multivalent interpretations. The first movement, for example, may be fruitfully analyzed as either following the precepts of sonata-allegro form or adopting a rotational structure in the manner of Sibelius, but neither entirely captures its effect of organicism and inevitability.[13] This, despite passages that look disruptive in the score, such as the parallel triads centered around G Mixolydian that open the piece. They should clash uncomfortably against the G Dorian melody beginning in m. 4; yet this divergence barely registers. Instead, both figures seem like inchoate, fluid engagements with a shared central pitch leading up to the G pentatonic violin solo that follows in m. 9. The skill with which such contrasts are handled, facilitated in no small part by the masterfully understated orchestration, contribute to the work's pervasive tranquility and calm.

Vaughan Williams widens the harmonic conflict in the second movement, which opens by pitting F minor against the pentatonic collection C–D–E–G–A, interpretable as centering either on C or G. However, the main focus here is on the extended melodic continuity (or, to paraphrase Herbert Howells in his perceptive review of the piece, a tune that never ceases), resolving midway through the movement in a solo featuring the E♭ natural trumpet.[14] This striking passage was apparently inspired by a trumpeter the composer heard during his military training, though the exact details of when and where that happened are unclear. What seems all but certain, however, is that it was meant to evoke associations with the "Last Post," the trumpet call played at military funerals and remembrance ceremonies.[15] Its deeply moving gravitas contrasts with the restless, harmonically fluid orchestral material that precedes it, providing a brief moment of respite amid otherwise turbid and unstable surroundings.

The final two movements were salvaged in part from the sketches of an abandoned ballet. The music of the Scherzo was originally intended as a dance for elves and goblins, the folk-tinged result opening with a musical dialogue alternating between triple and duple meters, its galumphing progress interrupted by filigree passages for the winds and brisk marches from the brass.[16] One can only imagine what the antecedent was for the darkly intense finale, heralded and concluded by the bleak cries of a disembodied soprano voice. Here again, melodic continuity drives the movement's progress, but pitting two conflicting musical resources against each other: the rhythmically free soprano vocalise and a quasi-processional orchestral figure. The vocalise ultimately prevails, closing this delicate and restrained work with an expression of tragedy that is literally beyond words. The *Pastoral Symphony* is full of such dualities, perhaps a reflection of Vaughan Williams's attempt to capture the most prominent one of all: how to transform the wartime trauma that he experienced into an expression of terrible beauty that might help make a world full of loss—of friends and loved ones, of time, of hope—bearable once more.

Vaughan Williams addressed similar themes in *The Shepherds of the Delectable Mountains*, a one-act "pastoral episode" first performed at the RCM in June 1922. It is based upon a scene depicted near the end of the protagonist's journey in *The Pilgrim's Progress*, with various modifications—dropping the character of Hopeful, for instance, and adding material from the less familiar second part of Bunyan's allegory—and is the first of Vaughan Williams's settings to call the main character "Pilgrim" rather than "Christian." Vaughan Williams was clear about why he made the change: "I, on purpose, did not call the Pilgrim 'Christian' because I want the work to be universal and apply to any body [sic] who aims at the spiritual life whether he is Xtian, Jew, Buddhist, Shintoist or 5ᵗʰ [sic] day Adventist."[17] He was not entirely successful in his aim, as the Christian imagery and allusions are inescapable; nonetheless, the music imparts a meditative gentleness far removed from Bunyan's uncompromising evangelical faith, and the disquiet Pilgrim experiences at the end of his journey must have resonated with British listeners still struggling with the gaps created by the Great War, and the challenges their country faced in its wake.[18]

The manner in which the music underscores the drama is somewhat obvious, but no less effective because of that—artistic conventions arise because they work, and Vaughan Williams was happy to turn to them when appropriate. "Why should music be 'original?'" he asked. "The object of art is to stretch out to the ultimate realities though the medium of beauty. The duty of the composer is to find the *mot juste*. It does not matter if this word has been said a thousand times before as long as it is the right thing to say at that moment. If it is *not* the right thing to say, however unheard of it may be, it is of no artistic value."[19] Accordingly, the Shepherds' gently flowing conjunct melodies are supported by triadic harmonies suggesting both tonal and modal qualities; by contrast, dissonant chord successions frequently disrupt Pilgrim's chromatically inflected lines, highlighting his exhaustion from the journey and his fear at having to cross the River of Death. The paradise of the Celestial City awaiting him, however, is expressed by a pair of offstage female choirs, their unceasing stream of modally inflected imitative counterpoint unsullied by a single accidental, and set against joyous homophonic praises from the Shepherds. The whole is bookended by a solo viola, indicating—should further evidence be needed—the deeply personal associations the story held for the composer.

Vaughan Williams's final work of 1922 was the Mass in G Minor, though the key designation is something of a misnomer. Of the five movements, only the Kyrie I and II feature two flats in the key signature, and even there the actual center vacillates between G Dorian and

D Aeolian. "Mass around G Minor" describes it more accurately, for the various movements explore how G minor can be transformed or recast, and do so by uniting long-standing sacred music traditions with the innovations of postwar pastoralism. Richard Terry, who led the first liturgical rendition of the Mass in March 1923, remarked upon those qualities to the composer: "I'm quite sincere when I say that it is the work one has all along been waiting for. In your individual and modern idiom you have really captured the old liturgical spirit and atmosphere."[20] Some of those connections are obvious: the scoring for two choirs and vocal quartet parallels the *Tallis Fantasia*'s layout for double orchestra and string quartet, and the Sanctus begins with a contrapuntally layered transformation of the oscillating wind figure that opens the *Pastoral Symphony*. The textural contrasts, particularly in the Gloria and Credo, hearken back to Palestrinian techniques, and the occasional passages of text painting (the duple borrowings at "Genitum, non factum, consubstantialem Patri" in the Credo, for example) evoke the example of High Renaissance masters like Josquin. More subtle, however, is the way that Vaughan Williams draws upon choral practices spanning centuries—false relations, fauxbourdon, fugal and canonic imitation, cyclical motives, modal harmonies—and combines them with parallel root-position triads and fifths, pentatonicism, and surprising modulatory schemes.[21] The result sounds literally timeless, a fusion of techniques and idioms that pays tribute to the past without devolving into mere pastiche. It places Vaughan Williams firmly in the tradition of Tallis and Byrd, with whose music the Mass is so frequently compared, and like the other pastoral works of this era, it expresses Vaughan Williams's visionary spirit more eloquently than words ever could.

"New Heights and Depths and Mysteries"
(1923–1929)

Postwar Britain found itself irrevocably changed, and its musical life was no exception. With the death of Parry, Stanford's withdrawal from public life, and the gradual waning of Elgar's compositional activity (if not his reputation), a new generation of composers emerged in their stead, with Vaughan Williams at the helm. By 1923, he had made significant contributions to symphonic, choral, chamber, religious, solo vocal, and dramatic music; had established a reputation as a leading scholar of English folk song; was shaping young composers at the RCM; maintained an active conducting schedule; and showed no signs of slowing his compositional output. If anything, he was busier and more productive than ever before.

Having led his first concert with the Bach Choir, Vaughan Williams prepared to conduct one of the works he most admired early in 1923: Bach's *St. Matthew Passion*. More Bach soon followed with performances of the *St. John Passion* (using a smaller group drawn from the Bach Choir) and three cantatas for the Leith Hill Festival in April, along with the chance to direct the premiere of Holst's *Choral Hymns from the Rig Veda* on 7 April, a performance that gratified them both. "It's what I've been waiting for for 47½ years," wrote Holst. "The performance was so full of You—even apart from the places I cribbed from you years ago."[1] Another beneficiary of Vaughan Williams's professional generosity that spring was Dorothy Longman, the dedicatee of his Romance and Pastorale for violin and piano. "You couldn't have given me anything I should so like to have as your own music," Longman gushed. "You have sometimes doubted if I should care so much for your music, apart from our friendship—but you & your music are not apart they are one & that is why both mean what they do to me[.]"[2]

Unfortunately, these and other activities (including a holiday in northern Italy with Adeline) meant that Vaughan Williams was hard pressed to finish the ballet *Old King Cole*. "How I shall find time to score the old Ballet passes my comprehension," Vaughan Williams told Bernhard (later Boris) Ord, its conductor, less than two months before its May Week premiere in Cambridge at Nevile's Court, Trinity College.[3] The folk-inspired piece was performed for the Cambridge University Musical Society's (CUMS) Festival of British Music, and the score's late completion caused considerable stress. The dancers had only a piano score to work with in rehearsal, the rapid orchestrating and recopying resulted in error-filled parts, and the CUMS Orchestra's amateur players were alarmingly underrehearsed.[4] Nevertheless, the performance came off, and Vaughan Williams was satisfied with the result. "I thought the way you all invented the dances & interpreted the music was wonderful," he told producer John Burnaby. "Every gesture fitted the music exactly—which I have very seldom seen in a ballet."[5]

A dance-free selection of folk tunes debuted the following month when the Band of the Royal Military School of Music (RMSM) performed the *English Folk Songs Suite* on 4 July. Holst had enjoyed recent success with his Second Suite in F for military band, and as the Commandant of the RMSM, Col. J. A. C. Somerville, was a member of the Bach Choir, he likely raised the possibility of Vaughan Williams making a contribution to the genre.[6] Though the suite was scored for full wind ensemble, Gordon Jacob—one of Vaughan Williams's former RCM students, whose advice and assistance he regularly sought—made arrangements of it for both brass band and orchestra the following year.

The second half of 1923 was comparatively quiet, beginning with a short retreat to Danbury, Essex, where friend and former student Cecil Armstrong Gibbs rented the house next door to his own for Ralph and Adeline's use. At the time, Vaughan Williams was working on his oratorio *Sancta Civitas*, a striking departure from the pastoral works of the previous few years, though apparently undertaken alongside them.[7] Armstrong Gibbs remembered the composer coming over "to try over the sound of some hair-raisingly discordant passage" on his piano, since the rental house lacked one.[8] Vaughan Williams may also have been starting to think about future endeavors with the Bach Choir, including a concert featuring Holst's new *Ode to Death* and *Short Festival Te Deum* in December, and Bach's monumental Mass in B Minor the following May. One collateral result of the latter was his composition (with longtime choir member Gertrude Sichel) of twenty-five vocal exercises inspired by the Mass, published in 1924.

More religious music lay ahead that year, which opened with him inviting his old friend Martin Shaw to co-edit a new hymnbook called *Songs of Praise*. With *The English Hymnal* now firmly established among High Church congregations, Percy Dearmer asked Vaughan Williams if he would prepare a second collection for more popular use, particularly among children. Though disinclined to accept, Vaughan Williams did not trust anyone else to do the job correctly, so agreed to take on the task. However, his assent came with several conditions: he would work with a collaborator ("The said colleague to do all the work & that we shd share the credit and the royalties," he joked to Shaw), he would have the final say on any musical points, and there would be none of the compromises to popular taste that he felt had arisen with *The English Hymnal*.[9] With these stipulations established, he and Shaw got underway on the new volume, to which Vaughan Williams contributed five entirely new hymns and another twenty arrangements, mostly of English traditional tunes. A similarly popularizing motivation underlay his near-contemporaneous composition of a Magnificat and Nunc Dimittis, subtitled *The Village Service* (1925), which catered to the often-limited resources and skill sets of smaller parish choirs.

The first half of 1924 was marred by two deaths, the first of which was Stanford's on 29 March. Despite their complicated relationship, Vaughan Williams nevertheless wrote a short tribute for *Music & Letters*, and led the Bach Choir in a memorial concert that December. Stanford's death also vacated the Chair of Music at Cambridge, and Vaughan Williams's name circulated as a leading candidate; however, he felt that taking up an academic post "for which I am entirely unprepared, at the age of 51 w^d be rather an appalling prospect."[10] The Chair was awarded to Charles Wood, but passed to E. J. Dent, Vaughan Williams's preferred candidate, upon Wood's death in 1926.[11] Three months after Stanford's passing came Cecil

Sharp's. His health had declined since returning from a song-collecting expedition in the United States, but his last surviving letter to Vaughan Williams expressed his admiration for the *English Folk Songs Suite* and his hope to see *Hugh the Drover* in July. His death left the EFDS in some disarray, and it fell to Vaughan Williams and to Sharp's former assistant, Maud Karpeles, to sort out its administrative apparatus over the following months.

Summer 1924 featured several concerts showcasing Vaughan Williams's music, the most anticipated of which was the long-awaited debut of *Hugh the Drover*. Following five "private dress rehearsals" at the RCM, the public premiere on 14 July was produced by the British National Opera Company, directed by the young Malcolm Sargent. The critical response was generally positive, though opinions split as to whether an opera so "unmistakably English in character and atmosphere" was highly desirable or slightly embarrassing.[12] The opera's conspicuous use of folk songs drew recurring complaints from reviewers,[13] but the broader public response was enthusiastic, as epitomized by Bobby Longman: "Hugh is the thing, the whole thing, nothing but the thing, dear Ralph; it fills my heart up to the brim (has one's heart a brim?) Thank you ever so much for having written it."[14] Nevertheless, Vaughan Williams remained dissatisfied with the work overall, and repeatedly revised portions of both the music and libretto over the next three decades.

The Vaughan Williamses took their annual retreat in the wake of *Hugh*'s premiere to Oare, in Wiltshire. Dorothy Longman's sister, Mary Fletcher, invited them to use her home, and the comfortable setting and beautiful gardens helped Vaughan Williams begin writing a new work inspired by verses from the Song of Solomon. The lushly dissonant result—*Flos Campi*, a six-movement suite for viola, string orchestra, and wordless chorus—formed a striking contrast to a piece that he was finishing for violinist Jelly d'Aranyi: the quasi-neoclassical *Concerto Accademico*. Its second movement was salvaged from an abandoned concerto grosso, the other surviving movement of which became the *Toccata marziale* for military band.

It was around this time that the Vaughan Williamses grew increasingly concerned about Ivor Gurney. A pupil of both Stanford and Vaughan Williams, Gurney was a gifted poet and composer, making some of the century's most significant contributions to Anglophone art song. He was brilliant but eccentric, and the physical injuries and shellshock he suffered during the Great War exacerbated his tendency toward bipolar disorder. It became so pronounced by 1922 that his family had him committed to a series of institutions, the most long-term of which was the City of London Mental Hospital (also known as Stone House) in Dartford, Kent. The stigma surrounding mental illness—and the crude practices passing as treatment—meant that patients were often isolated by doctors and abandoned by friends and family. Because of Adeline's long experience caring for Hervey, however, and the memory of her brother Jack's psychological breakdown, asylums held no fears for her. Ralph too felt a duty of care for Gurney, both as a former student and a fellow veteran; the fact that Gurney turned up at 13 Cheyne Walk after escaping from Stone House early in 1923 speaks to their closeness.[15] The couple regularly visited Gurney at Dartford, bringing him books, music, and other gifts until his death in 1937, and often liaised with Marion Scott, Gurney's close friend, to ascertain his condition and to advocate for more humane treatment from the staff.

In tribute to his friend, Steuart Wilson mounted an all–Vaughan Williams concert on 27 March 1925, featuring several established numbers—*On Wenlock Edge*, *Merciless Beauty*, and the Four Hymns, dedicated to Wilson and specially arranged on this occasion for piano and string quartet—alongside four new song sets featuring texts by Shakespeare, Whitman, Irish poet Seumas O'Sullivan, and Fredegond Shove, Adeline's niece. Wilson repeated his performance of *Merciless Beauty* that September in Venice, the concluding portion of the two-part International Society for Contemporary Music (ISCM) Festival. The first half of the Festival had been held in Prague that May, with the *Pastoral Symphony* the lone piece of British music on the program. Vaughan Williams thought it came off poorly, as did Adeline, but she felt it got "a very good reception," an opinion shared by the critic for *The Musical Times*. He considered the *Pastoral* "not only the composer's finest achievement, but the finest work that has been produced in the English revival of music," and was surprised "to find how genuinely, and with what warmth, its delicate meditations were appreciated" by the foreign audience.[16]

That critic was Hubert Foss, the young and energetic director of Oxford University Press's newly founded Music Department. Until this point in his career, Vaughan Williams had signed with publishers on a work-by-work basis, and was growing frustrated dealing with bureau-cratic minutiae and inconsistent final products. When his friend and pa-tron Robert McEwan offered to privately publish *The Shepherds of the Delectable Mountains* in 1925, Vaughan Williams graciously refused, but the offer galvanized him to send it to OUP for consideration. Shrewdly realizing the prestige (and profit) that Vaughan Williams could lend his fledgling department, Foss accepted the work and came to an informal agreement with the composer that OUP would have rights of first con-sideration for any new compositions. This arrangement turned out spec-tacularly well for both parties, and Foss soon became one of Vaughan Williams's most trusted colleagues.

Both the *Concerto Accademico* and *Flos Campi* debuted in autumn 1925. While the latter was generally successful, Holst's tepid response to it—not to mention Vaughan Williams's own underwhelmed reaction to Holst's new *Choral Symphony* less than a month later—made Vaughan Williams concerned that an artistic gulf was opening between them. He attempted to rationalize his unsympathetic reaction to the *Choral Symphony*, but was very worried about it ("I couldn't bear to think that I was going to 'drift apart' from you musically speaking").[17] Holst was less troubled by the prospect of their changing tastes, telling his old friend that "occa-sionally drifting is necessary to keeping our stock fresh and sweet," and confessing that he found *Flos Campi* equally difficult to grasp. "But I'm not disappointed in *Flos*'s composer because he has not repeated himself. Therefore it is probably either an improvement or something that will lead to one."[18]

Having completed his work for *Songs of Praise*, Vaughan Williams was able to tackle several other projects in 1926. Beyond his responsibilities for the Bach Choir, the LHMC, and his regular engagement at the Three Choirs Festival, he was hard at work on a piano concerto, an operatic adaptation of *The Merry Wives of Windsor* (provisionally titled *The Fat Knight*), a chamber suite based on English folk songs, and a masque in-spired by *A Christmas Carol*. Coincidentally, it was around this time that Dearmer—yet again—asked Vaughan Williams and Shaw to edit another collection of religious melodies, and so work on *The Oxford Book of Carols* formed a backdrop to his other activities for the next two years.

Also in the background, but never far from his thoughts, was the growing unrest permeating British culture that culminated in the

General Strike of May 1926. Although he declared himself on the side of the miners and was disinclined to stand with members of his own class—though he suspected that he might in the end—Vaughan Williams was deeply troubled by the Strike's economic and social implications, so much so that he attempted to clarify his thoughts in an extended memorandum that he shared with Holst.[19]

> Isn't it our duty to support the govt as such even if in the end it has to resort to armed force? Is it wrong to be on the side of revolution if it came to that? I should not be against revolution by violence in the last resort (I don't think the status quo any thing to be proud of). But before I c^d do that & envisage the temporary anarchy which would follow I must be fairly certain that a better state of things is going to emerge. And have the side of revolution any scheme for the better government of the country to offer if they were victorious? I doubt it.
>
> [. . .]
>
> One cannot help benefiting by the gov^t action [of breaking the strike to prevent food shortages]—one is powerless to refuse the benefits—if one accepts the benefits must not one support the organization which provides them.[20]

Vaughan Williams's utilitarian perspective was not new; indeed, it had run like sap through the branches of his family tree for generations. His own political ideology, however, was informed by far more left-wing elements. He self-identified as a Radical while at Charterhouse; "read the Fabian tracts" upon arriving at Cambridge, where he converted to socialism "in opposition to the majority of undergraduates"; and claimed to have voted Radical or Labour in every election but one during his lifetime.[21] He later went so far as to tell Rutland Boughton, "It seems to me that all right minded people are communists, as far as the word means that everything should be done eventually for the common good."[22] That said, his conception of socialism aligned more with the philosophy of William Morris than Karl Marx, and shows that the idealism informing his aesthetics also colored his perception of real-world issues, if leavened by a countervailing pragmatism.

On 7 May, in the midst of the General Strike, *Sancta Civitas* had its inaugural performance at Oxford's Sheldonian Theatre. It takes the apocalyptic events surrounding the Second Coming of Christ as described in the Book of Revelation as its subject—interpolated with passages from the Sanctus of the Mass—yet it is preceded by a Greek epigraph from Plato's *Phaedo* in which Socrates, having described the soul's journey to the Elysian Fields, admits there is no empirical basis for such a belief. Vaughan Williams provided his own translation of the passage in a copy of the score he gave to Ivy Herbert:

> That these things are exactly as I have described, no sensible man will believe. But that this or something like it is true of our souls and their mansions, since we believe that the soul is immortal, appears to me worthy of belief and enough to justify some adventures of the ~~mind~~ imagination. For the venture is a noble one and it is right to sing of such things.[23]

Vaughan Williams claimed to prefer this piece, his only oratorio, to all his other choral compositions, though few critics initially agreed. *The Daily Telegraph* deemed it "ponderous, heavy-footed music," while Leigh Henry called it "a work of dull devotionalism." Even the usually sympathetic H. C. Colles found himself bewildered by the "disturbing new experience" the work evoked.[24] The London premiere by the Bach Choir in June was far more satisfactory. Harold Child confessed that he couldn't follow all of it, but "what I did understand just knocked me out." He complimented Vaughan Williams's treatment of the text: "over & over again you showed new heights & depths & mysteries & niceties in them. At the end I knew I'd heard one of the finest things in all music."[25] The most touching tribute, however, came from Elgar, who had long considered a similar topic as a sequel to his own oratorios *The Apostles* and *The Kingdom*. "I once thought of setting those words, but I shall never do that now, and I am glad I didn't because you have done it for me."[26]

More palatable for most listeners was the *Six Studies in English Folk Song*, first performed at the 1926 EFDS Festival. It was dedicated to cellist May Mukle, founder of the MM ("Mainly Musicians") Club, the only social club to which Vaughan Williams ever belonged. The work's success led to arrangements for clarinet, violin, and viola, and its accessibility and brevity have made it one of Vaughan Williams's most widely performed chamber pieces. Similarly accessible—if much odder—was the masque *On Christmas Night*, first performed in Chicago on Boxing Day 1926. Taking Dickens's *A Christmas Carol* as its starting point, the story underwent several unusual modifications: Scrooge is visited by only one spirit;

there are no visions of Scrooge's future, and the celebratory closing feast is replaced with a tableau of the Nativity before which Scrooge and Tiny Tim kneel in prayer. Vaughan Williams felt that it was still "*very* Dickensy and after all the whole thing is sentimental,"[27] but it nevertheless feels odd that he, of all composers, replaced Dickens's morally transformative conclusion with a scene of maudlin middle-class piety. A far more somber and dramatically powerful stage work also originated at this time: *Riders to the Sea*, a single-act *opera dialogue*. Perhaps Vaughan Williams's most dramatically satisfying opera (if also the grimmest), it took an unusually long time to compose; begun in 1925, it was not completed until 1932, and the first performance came another five years after that.

Significant changes to the Vaughan Williamses' personal lives were also afoot. R. O. Morris had been appointed head of music theory at the Curtis Institute in 1926, and thus he and Emmeline departed 13 Cheyne Walk. The house itself was beginning to present its own problems: it was threatened by major flooding after Christmas 1927 when part of the Chelsea Embankment collapsed, and Adeline's advancing arthritis meant the house's multiple floors posed a challenge. She had seriously injured herself by falling in 1922 (a regular occurrence even then), and another fall in October 1927 caused her to break her thigh "so badly that she was encased in plaster from head to toes" for several months.[28] Honorine Williamson, Morris's niece, was hired to assist with the household management, but Adeline's physical limitations were growing apparent.

Yet none of these events dampened Vaughan Williams's creative energies. While only one new work enjoyed a concert debut in 1927— an austerely moving cycle of Seven Housman Songs for voice and violin, expanded and retitled *Along the Field* in 1954[29]—*The Fat Knight* was well underway, and opportunities arose to write two other stage works. The first came from Cecil Sharp's sister Evelyn. Author, journalist, and suffragist, she approached Vaughan Williams with a libretto adapted from Richard Garnett's short story *The Poison Maid* (1888), itself based upon Nathaniel Hawthorne's *Rappaccini's Daughter* (1846). Only a month after receiving the first drafts of the story in July, Vaughan Williams had made "more or less complete sketches for six numbers" in the work that would become known as *The Poisoned Kiss*, and sent Sharp extended reflections on and revisions to the libretto over the next few months.[30] At almost exactly the same time Sharp contacted him, the composer was asked by his cousin Gwen Raverat if he would be interested in writing music for a ballet based on William Blake's *Illustrations from the Book of Job*. The scenario had originated with her brother-in-law, surgeon and Blake scholar Geoffrey Keynes. It took instant hold of Vaughan Williams, and he began poring over the illustrations, reading reference material that Raverat recommended, and drafting musical ideas for realizing Blake's visionary tableaux. Vaughan Williams and Shaw also finished their work on *The Oxford Book of Carols* that winter, and he produced a *Te Deum* for the installment of Cosmo Lang as the new Archbishop of Canterbury in December 1928.[31]

Reluctantly, Vaughan Williams resigned as director of the Bach Choir in February 1928. As Adeline wanted to find a more suitable house outside London, he felt it impractical to stay in the position. The blow was softened upon learning that Adrian Boult would be his replacement, to whom he provided a charmingly earnest list of suggestions for managing the group (e.g., "don't wait to start practice till everybody is ready—or you will never start at all").[32] The couple's decision to settle near Dorking made working with the LHMC more convenient, however, and Vaughan Williams's involvement increased significantly over the next several years. One of the earliest efforts came that summer, when he began sketching the first of four new pieces in honor of the LHMC's upcoming twenty-fifth anniversary while he was scouting locations for a new home.

Early in 1929, Vaughan Williams was thrust into rehearsals for the premiere of *Sir John in Love*—the replacement title for *The Fat Knight*—at the RCM. Dedicated to his old friend and colleague S. P. Waddington, "for all your help and encouragement in this and all my work," *Sir John* was the only stage work Vaughan Williams referred to simply as an opera, sans modifiers, and represents his most successful multi-act contribution to the genre.[33] He adapted the libretto himself ("which I am so proud of," he told Grace Williams), cutting some episodes from *Merry Wives* while incorporating materials from other Shakespearean plays and by contemporaneous poets.[34] Its lyrical beauty, brisk pacing, and engaging characters form a satisfying whole, even though the first performances at the RCM that March were shakier than the professional debut the following year at the Oxford Festival. It also inspired some spin-offs: the choral cantata *In Windsor Forest* (1931), and the Prologue, Episode, and

Interlude written for a production at the Bristol Opera School in 1933, though the Prologue was subsequently withdrawn.

By this time, Vaughan Williams had adopted a nickname that stuck with him for the rest of his life. He generally asked that "most of the young women of my acquaintance call me 'Uncle Ralph' when they wish to be respectful, 'V. W.' when otherwise inclined."[35] Younger male friends, such as Gerald Finzi and Robert de Ropp, also addressed him this way, although "Dr. Vaughan Williams" was a standard default for more formal situations or less intimate acquaintances. To de Ropp, Uncle Ralph was an avuncular cross between "the gentle, rotund, pipe-smoking Uncle Toby of *Tristram Shandy*" and a latter-day Papa Haydn, though this portrait reflected only one facet—albeit a prominent one—of Vaughan Williams's personality.[36] But he earned that reputation in part through his longtime and enthusiastic provision of assistance to friends and colleagues in need. Surviving letters from 1929 alone reveal him urging Grace Williams's father to let her continue studying composition at the RCM, assisting Diana Awdry in programming that year's Stinchcombe Festival, collaborating with Holst to help Rutland Boughton establish a Welsh opera festival, and taking it upon himself to complain to *The Times* on behalf of British composers frustrated by copyright laws and tired of their music's marginalization. More dispiriting events that year included the deaths of his old friends and fellow folk-song devotees Lucy Broadwood and Frank Kidson, for whom he wrote a pair of appreciations.[37] He particularly respected Broadwood's diligent work on behalf of English folk music, and had long valued her opinions on a range of subjects.

Following that year's demanding LHMC concerts—including Purcell's *King Arthur*, Parry's *Job*, and Haydn's *The Seasons*—the Three Choirs performance of *Sancta Civitas*, and the release of *Songs of Praise for Boys and Girls* (a follow-up to *Songs of Praise*, to which the composer contributed twenty-five arrangements but only one original tune), the Vaughan Williamses moved to Dorking on 6 October. The house they purchased had the Hindi name Chote Ghar ("Chote House"), which they immediately changed to White Gates. Its mock-Tudor exterior enclosed a large drawing room overlooked by a gallery, the whole bordered on three sides by a corridor leading off to additional rooms. The two great benefits were its size—there were six bedrooms, two bathrooms, and two additional half bathrooms, thus providing plenty of room for guests—and as all but the gallery and one bedroom were on one floor, it was far more accessible for Adeline.[38] The property covered nearly two acres and included a tennis court, a kitchen garden, a small orchard, and commanding views of the North Downs. Life at White Gates lacked the vibrancy of London, which Vaughan Williams loved and was sorry to leave (though he still traveled there regularly), but his new home provided a quiet and largely distraction-free setting for him to work. In another Haydnesque parallel, Vaughan Williams's remove from the city forced him to rely on his own resources and creativity, which—judging by the compositions of the next several years—not only remained vigorous, but also advanced toward unfamiliar and exciting new frontiers.

The Music of 1923–1929

T HE PREMIERE OF THE MASS IN G MINOR IN DECEMBER 1922 CLOSED
out Vaughan Williams's most intensely pastoralist period, a break
further demarcated by a lull in performances of new music during the
first half of 1923. The maximalist tendencies of works like the *Sea* and
London Symphonies were now largely purged from his style, while the
influences of French impressionism and English folk song were increasingly subsumed within a flexibly pandiatonic framework enriched by
modal and octatonic elements. Now fifty years old, Vaughan Williams
had fully attained the personal and highly distinctive musical idiom
that he had so diligently cultivated over the previous three decades,
and was well positioned to take advantage of it. Many of the pieces
he wrote in the 1920s plumbed new emotional depths and methods
of stylistic disruption, but within an unusually narrow ambit. Almost
every composition written during this time aligns with at least one of
the following four categories: religious music (in theme or application),
dramatic works, compositions showcasing solo string instruments, and
songs, whether newly composed or extant melodies featured in other
pieces.

The near-disastrous debut of *Old King Cole* did not provide an especially auspicious start to the era. Inspired by his continuing effort to find
alternatives to the classical balletic style he so disliked, Vaughan Williams
enlisted the EFDS's Cambridge branch to devise a scenario for which he
could write the music, the winner being Katherine Vulliamy's proposal

of *Old King Cole*. Drawing upon details from Edmund Spenser's *Faerie Queen*, the scenario expands the nursery rhyme into a full *scena*: King Cole of Colchester is visited by his daughter, the Empress Helena ("Queen Helena" in the score), who brings him a hookah pipe as a gift, though something goes wrong with it as he smokes. His cooks come to the rescue with a drinking bowl to slake his thirst; restored, he summons three fiddlers to compete for a prize from his daughter. He declares the Third Fiddler the winner, and the company marches off to dinner, but Helena gives her prize—a single rose—to the Second Fiddler, entirely absorbed in his world of music-making.

Although the score features original music (most notably, the opening series of variations inspired by the nursery rhyme's rhythmic scansion) the main focus is on arrangements of traditional folk and dance tunes, most prominently displayed in the fiddlers' solos. A "wild Fen-man" plays "Go and 'List for a Sailor," a dreamy romantic performs "A Bold Young Farmer"—preceded by a cadenza that bears more than a passing resemblance to *The Lark Ascending*—but the "folk clown" wins the competition with an energetic rendition of "The Jolly Thresherman," with references to other tunes throughout.[1] The dancing also derived from English folk traditions, particularly Morris dances, modified to fit the story; the Bowl Dance, for instance, adapts a Morris stick dance by replacing the wooden rods with cooks' ladles. Photographs from the Cambridge performance impart a good sense of the work's size and spectacle, but the tissue-thin scenario lacks dramatic weight. Vaughan Williams's next stage effort, the masque *On Christmas Night* (1926), repeats many of *Old King Cole*'s features and shortcomings. Growing out of a Christmas fantasia he wrote in 1921, this awkward adaptation of *A Christmas Carol* again makes extensive use of traditional English carols and dances throughout, including "Hunsdon House," "Haste to the Wedding," and "God Rest You Merry, Gentlemen," a technique also used in Holst's contemporaneous one-act opera *At the Boar's Head*. *On Christmas Night* also features several blackouts and tableaux that recall techniques from the Reigate production of *The Pilgrim's Progress*. Indeed, there is something Bunyanesque about Vaughan Williams's treatment of Scrooge, who is redeemed not by letting Dickens's secular "Spirit of Christmas" enter his heart, but by humbling himself before a vision of the Holy Family as "The First Nowell" plays in the background. This is, however, exactly as odd as it sounds, and despite multiple revisions to both music and plot, the work has failed to find an audience.[2]

Old King Cole and *On Christmas Night* exemplify Vaughan Williams's occasional tendency to compose works without much consideration for their long-term viability, or how they might align with standard repertory conventions. This shortsightedness may be explained in part by the growing financial security he enjoyed from his family allowance, his publishing royalties, his conducting and festival adjudication fees, and (by the 1920s) his teaching position at the RCM. These various income streams enabled him to be selective about accepting commissions, and write what he wanted without having to compromise his vision—sometimes resulting in quixotic or impractical creative decisions. For example, both *Old King Cole* and *On Christmas Night* generally eschew typical balletic practices, making them unlikely to be revived by professional dance companies. Analogous problems arise with his compositions for soloist and orchestra, which frequently combine relatively short durations with a lack of conspicuous virtuosity. This combination not only makes them difficult to program, but has also likely discouraged their wider adoption.

Ironically, even widely popular works were subject to critical condescension. *Hugh the Drover* exemplifies this phenomenon, as it inspired arguments about whether it represented a model to which English opera should aspire.[3] Vaughan Williams's characterization of the work as a "Romantic ballad opera" implied a comedy "on the lines of Smetana's 'Verkaufte Braut'" applied to English village life, set in a manner that was "not Wagnerian and not altogether Mozartian—but more the Mozartian with some of his squareness taken away—perhaps a certain amount of the Charpentier-Puccini conversational methods thrown in," while the story itself drew upon imagery from George Borrow's *I Zincali* and, unexpectedly, Richard Strauss's *Feuersnot*.[4] This characterization not only reflects Vaughan Williams's wide-ranging knowledge of the repertory, but also that he imagined *Hugh*'s design in terms of established practices. "I have no objection to the structure being more or less formal & conventional," he wrote to Child. "I think all opera has to be conventional (or perhaps I should say not realistic)," a revealing aside that clearly signaled both his intentions for *Hugh* and his broader conception of opera.[5] Yet it is not quite as conventional as one might expect. It is not technically a ballad opera, as it lacks spoken dialogue, but it also abjures recitative in favor of a flexible arioso delivery—so while there are discrete numbers scattered throughout, there is also a high degree of musical continuity.

Many reviews questioned whether the opera's conspicuous use of folk songs was appropriate or desirable, arguing that they were either stylistically incongruous, ill-fit the singers' voices, or came off as provincial. Such charges often reflect critical snobbishness more than the actual problem with their use: namely, that Vaughan Williams was less interested in their dramatic efficacy than their aesthetic appeal, evinced by his showcasing them in exclusively diegetic contexts and at dramatically static points. It is worth remembering that he began writing *Hugh* in 1910, the high point of his folk-song collecting activities, and was deeply invested in promoting the value of English folk culture to the widest possible audience. Yet he was also trying to create a distinctively national operatic style, and thought that a libretto "written to <u>real</u> English words—with a certain amount of <u>real</u> English music and also a <u>real</u> English subject might just hit the right nail on the head," particularly if the resulting work avoided playing to comic stereotypes of the rural yokel.[6] Unfortunately, this intense focus on the setting and the source materials came at the expense of the opera's emotional weight, resulting in a predictable storyline populated by stock character types rather than well-rounded personalities.

That being said, *Hugh the Drover* is exactly what Vaughan Williams intended it to be: a tuneful, charming, and lightly escapist work with a distinctively English gloss. It opens on a village fair in the Cotswolds during the Napoleonic Wars, where Mary bemoans her betrothal to the loutish butcher, John, at the instigation of her father, the town constable. Enter Hugh, a roving horse-wrangler who sweeps her off her feet, and challenges John to a prize fight with £50 and Mary's hand in marriage as the stake. Predictably, Hugh wins, but John accuses him of spying for the French; the villagers turn against him, and Hugh winds up imprisoned in the town stocks. The second act opens just before dawn the next morning—May Day—as Mary attempts to free Hugh, using the key she stole from her father. But she is caught in the act by the whole village, roused for the May revels: she is disowned by her father and spurned by John, and a squad of soldiers arrives to take Hugh away to prison. However, their sergeant recognizes the drover as an old friend who once saved his life, so Hugh is released and John conscripted in his place. Free once more, Mary and Hugh pledge their hearts to each other and to an itinerant life as the village bids them farewell.[7] Clearly, *Hugh the Drover* is not an opera concerned with issues of psychological complexity or dramatic innovation. It is a conventional, even clichéd work, but also a competent and entertaining first effort from an inexperienced compositional team, the lessons from which would inform many of Vaughan Williams's later dramatic efforts.

Hugh the Drover was the last of Vaughan Williams's prewar compositions to receive a performance during his lifetime, but another work waited nearly as long: Two Pieces for Violin and Pianoforte, published in 1923 and dedicated to Dorothy Longman. Comprising a Romance and Pastorale, they represent his earliest published foray into chamber music for solo instrument and piano, and were likely composed between 1912 and 1914. Though relatively slight, the two movements possess an understated intimacy and modal lyricism establishing them among his first compelling pastoral compositions. The introspective Romance for Viola and Piano likely dates from around the same time as the Two Pieces, though it is difficult to be certain, as it was discovered among Vaughan Williams's manuscripts following his death. It was first performed in 1962 by Bernard Shore, one of the most distinguished protégés of violist Lionel Tertis, for whom it may have originally been written.

One final piece with a possible prewar antecedent was the *English Folk Songs Suite* for military band (1923).[8] Although the suite originally featured four movements, Vaughan Williams cut the second ("Sea Songs") following the premiere but reissued it as a stand-alone piece in 1924.[9] The first movement may be derived from the now-lost *Fantasia on English Folk Song* from 1910, but more important is the connection with Holst's First Suite in E♭ and Second Suite in F for military band, completed before the war but revised before their premieres in 1920 and 1922. The two men would likely have spent field days discussing them, along with Holst's *A Somerset Rhapsody* (1910), a single-movement sequence of three folk-song settings for orchestra. In this sense, both composers' military band works align with their prewar compositional tendencies to showcase English traditional tunes in accessible instrumental settings for audiences unfamiliar with such melodies. The *English Folk Songs Suite* was particularly effective in this regard: each movement set three different folk songs distinguished by timbre, articulation, and/or key area, and Vaughan Williams was pleased to write something that he thought "would be an agreeable and salutary experience for [military] bandsmen."[10]

Vaughan Williams undertook another band piece in 1924 titled Concerto Grosso, but broke off after completing two movements. Ever resourceful, however, he recast the opening Allegro moderato as the *Toccata marziale* for military band. Unlike his previous effort, there are no folk songs in the *Toccata*. Rather, as the original and final titles imply, it is another neoclassical piece applying contemporary musical language within a Baroque-era genre. Rousing and energetic, it is more elegantly designed than the movements of the *English Folk Songs Suite*, focusing primarily on free and imitative contrapuntal textures in a through-composed setting, with many surprising modulations and dissonances (some of which may have resulted from copying errors that made their way into the published parts and score).[11]

The other movement from the abandoned Concerto Grosso found an unexpected new home in Vaughan Williams's Concerto in D Minor for Violin and String Orchestra (1925), where it served as the second movement.[12] It was originally titled *Concerto Accademico*, a strange choice for a composer who, despite his own associations with institutions of higher learning, remained suspicious of "that fear of self-expression which seems to be fostered by academic traditions."[13] But perhaps, like the cheeky tone he often employed in program notes, the title was an ironic acknowledgement of the concerto's many violations of precepts expected from a truly "academic" work. Its neoclassical orientation reinforces such a notion, even though that style's most typical signifiers (such as movement titles, formal organization, or rhythmic gestures) are absent or minimized. The outer movements' strongly defined rhythmic contours and fast tempi propel the piece in a manner rarely heard in Vaughan Williams's music; even calm passages are often paired with hemiolas or similarly disruptive metric effects. The central Adagio relaxes the otherwise frenetic pace, embracing a rhapsodic lyricism typical of Baroque concerti's slow movements, though that earlier period's evocation of vocality has been replaced by a melody far more idiomatic to the violin. The parallel triads, modal collections, and unusual dissonances further distance this piece from Baroque antecedents, but its urbanity, compactness, and textural transparency invite comparisons to the aesthetic and expressive qualities of the eighteenth-century concerto.

Vaughan Williams's neoclassical turn in the early 1920s may be connected to his directorships of the Handel Society and the Bach Choir. His rendition of the Mass in B Minor with the latter marked a high point of his tenure, and he brought to it a similarly idiosyncratic interpretation of Baroque musical conventions as he did to works like *Concerto Accademico* or the *Suite de Ballet*. He replaced the harpsichord with piano and organ, added figured bass in certain passages where none originally existed, and provided solos for the viola at certain points, such as the Agnus Dei. His decisions were based upon both a deep investment in the music and careful study of other interpretative models and opinions, most notably from Albert Schweitzer and Hugh Allen, who called the performance "exhilarating, & often astonishing."[14] Most importantly, Vaughan Williams's approach stemmed from his belief that Bach's music was as meaningful to the present as to the past, but required active, thoughtful artistic engagement from its performers to convey its expressive message. "We cannot perform Bach exactly as he was played in his time even if we wanted to," he wrote many years later, "and the question is, do we want to? I say emphatically, No! [. . .] The interpretation and with it the means of interpretation differ with each generation. If the music is ephemeral it will disappear with any change of fashion. If the music is really alive it will live on through all the alterations of musical thought."[15]

One may notice a parallel with Vaughan Williams's approach to collecting and editing English folk songs, another tradition whose constant reinterpretation he believed signified qualities of vitality and relevance rather than (as Cecil Sharp might assert) corruption or degradation. Vaughan Williams made several interpretive glosses to that tradition himself, and one of his most popular was the jewel-like *Six Studies in English Folk Song* (1926). His settings go beyond simple transcription, even though the songs are not developed far beyond their original designs, but their expressivity is intensified by accompaniments in which the piano is fully the soloist's equal. This is especially effective in the second movement (based on the tune "Spurn Point"), where the pianist's plaintive introductory figure turns out to be the climactic third phrase, as well as in the rollicking Allegro vivace that closes the piece, pitting the performers against each other as they quickly trade solo and accompanimental roles. The work's simple lyricism gives listeners some sense of the beauty Vaughan Williams must have perceived upon collecting such melodies, justification enough for their preservation.

This focus on beauty should not suggest that he was unconcerned with the expressive potential of a tune, particularly in liturgical music. He said as much in the introduction to *The English Hymnal*:

> No doubt it requires a certain effort to tune oneself to the moral atmosphere implied by a fine melody; and it is far easier to dwell in the miasma of the languishing and sentimental hymn tunes which so often disfigure our services. Such poverty of heart may not be uncommon, but at least it should not be encouraged by those who direct the services of the Church; it ought no longer to be true anywhere that the most exalted moments of a churchgoer's week are associated with music that would not be tolerated in any place of secular entertainment.[16]

Such considerations informed Vaughan Williams's conception of pieces like the *Magnificat and Nunc Dimittis* (1925) and the *Te Deum in G* (1928), but they also guided his approach on smaller scales, like selecting the hymns for *Songs of Praise*. According to Martin Shaw, Vaughan Williams insisted upon certain criteria for the collection: first, "that warm words should be married to an austere tune, and vice versa, in order to maintain the dignity necessary to public utterance as opposed to private, and to combine that with humanity. Secondly, the finest version of every tune, and not necessarily the earliest, should be the one printed. Thirdly, that fine melody, rather than the exploitation of a trained choir, should govern selection."[17] Vaughan Williams was pleased with the final product ("There's not a single tune in that I'm ashamed of," he told his cousin Frances Cornford), but found managing its subsequent revisions and spin-offs—including an enlarged version published in 1931, and *Songs of Praise for Boys and Girls* (1929)—increasingly tiresome.[18] "I won't do another hymn book," he told Joan Shaw (Martin's wife) around 1941. "I've done two other ones, not to mention (1) S[ongs of] P[raise] for blue eyed girls (2) S. P. for red braced boys (3) S. P. for one-eyed children between the ages of 7½ & 8¾ etc etc," so was ready to pass the baton.[19] Running parallel to *Songs of Praise* was *The Oxford Book of Carols* (1928), a compilation to which he brought the same breadth of geographic, temporal, literary, and stylistic diversity as he had *The English Hymnal*. He included four new carols of his own and arranged another twenty-three, and shared some lively (and, as usual, highly opinionated) exchanges with Lucy Broadwood after the volume's publication about its editorial and scholarly methodologies.[20]

Vaughan Williams's return to hymnody in the mid-1920s coincided with a renewed interest in art song, of which he completed five collections between 1925 and 1927. Though less familiar than his prewar efforts, many of these songs refine his established techniques and experiment with new ones. Particularly notable is their titular emphasis on the texts—Two Poems by Seumas O'Sullivan, Three Poems by Walt Whitman, Four Poems by Fredegond Shove, and Three Songs from Shakespeare, all of which debuted on the same concert in 1925—the centrality of which was reinforced by their overwhelmingly syllabic settings. The Shakespeare and O'Sullivan collections are relatively slight, though it is instructive to compare Vaughan Williams's new version of "Orpheus with His Lute" with his setting from 1902. Unsurprisingly, the easy lyricism and rich texture of the former marks a great advance over the latter's square rhythms and unimaginative accompaniment. Several entries in the Whitman and Shove sets, however, are more adventurous; he later identified "The New Ghost" from the latter as "one of my own songs that I like the best myself."[21] For example, the ground bass employed in the opening "Nocturne" from the Whitman poems comprises an asymmetrical octatonic set (D–E–F–F♯–G♯–A–B–C) that still contains the same number of major and minor seconds as the standard collection—another neoclassical union of traditional form and innovative musical language.[22] Similarly, "Motion and Stillness," the first of the Shove songs, shifts from F minor to what initially sounds like E major, but the addition of a conspicuous C♮ results in another asymmetrical octatonic collection. The quasi-whole-tone passage that follows initiates a set comprising the pitches of an F harmonic minor scale, but with C as the root. Yet all this disruption is mitigated by smooth, largely stepwise voice leading, and the slow harmonic changes create an illusion of stability where none should exist.

Vaughan Williams's most extended song contribution this decade was also the most unusual: *Along the Field* (1926). This now-canonical title was applied only in 1954, when the composer revised the Seven Housman Songs for publication, adding an eighth entry to this group of poems from *A Shropshire Lad* and *Last Poems* (1922). To make matters more confusing, Vaughan Williams originally wrote a total of nine songs—two of which were not sung at the first performances—and withdrew one of them ("The Soldier") upon revising the cycle.[23] Despite the nature of the source material, this collection forms an unexpectedly austere counterpart to *On Wenlock Edge*. With the accompaniment reduced to a single violin, the full textures and vibrant modal triads of the earlier work are replaced with disjunct melodies, dissonant harmonies, and highly independent part-writing. These tendencies reach their zenith in the essentially atonal "The Sigh That Heaves the Grasses," an unsettled elegy in which the dissonantly mismatched melody and accompaniment capture the poem's ambivalent and ambiguous response to loss—appropriately challenging music for such a complex emotional topic—a practice similarly pronounced in "The Half-Moon Westers Low" and "In the Morning." There are lighter and more accessible entries in the collection, such as "Fancy's Knell" and "Good-Bye," but the treatment of Housman's verses is far removed from the gentler pastoralism of the recent past.

Incongruous as the idiom of *Along the Field* is, it was far from unprecedented. A pair of works from 1925—the suite *Flos Campi* and the oratorio *Sancta Civitas*—represent two of Vaughan Williams's most challenging compositions of the decade, if not his entire career. *Flos Campi* earns this status for three major reasons: its unusual design, unorthodox performing forces, and complex harmonic idiom. Although Vaughan Williams called it a suite, its six movements are performed without a break, and are dominated by a solo viola and wordless chorus against a small orchestra. If anything, it is more akin to a concerto grosso or a tone poem, the latter classification justified by the unspoken epigraphs from The Song of Solomon heading each movement. The wordless chorus, although often commented upon, is not as groundbreaking as it might seem. Vaughan Williams used one as far back as *Willow-Wood*, and to similar effect at the end of *The Shepherds of the Delectable Mountains*; there is even precedent for its use in non-choral works like *Old King Cole*, while the soprano vocalise from the *Pastoral Symphony* represents a close expressive equivalent. The focus of that expression is slightly different in *Flos Campi*, though, centered as it is on the ache of longing for one's beloved.[24]

These erotic overtones notwithstanding, what really stands out is how the harmonic and timbral schemes convey the text's meaning without intoning a single word. Over about twenty minutes, *Flos Campi* progresses from a near-unclassifiable opening duet for oboe and viola—most plausibly interpretable as bitonal or bimodal, arguably with octatonic inflections—expressing the canticle's lovesickness, to passionate viola soliloquies in the second and fifth movements, and an unexpectedly martial turn in the fourth (appropriately expressed in parallel fourths from the orchestra). The pervasive diatonic counterpoint of the final movement (a realization of its simple motto "Set me as a seal upon thine heart") suggests a thematic and musical link with *The Shepherds of the Delectable Mountains*, where Pilgrim finds relief for his anguish and exhaustion upon arriving at the Celestial City, where he is greeted by the sounds of a celestial choir singing imitative lines untouched by chromaticism. Yet Vaughan Williams was quick to dissuade assumptions that *Flos Campi* "had an ecclesiastical basis" or was meant "to connote an atmosphere of 'buttercups and daisies.'"[25] What it ultimately communicates is difficult to say, but that may be the point. Love is a many-splendored thing, capable of encompassing beauty and pain, eros and agape, burning passion and quiet devotion. *Flos Campi* speaks with many of those voices in a manner as irrational and unpredictable and fascinating as love itself.

The religious associations of *Sancta Civitas* are more straightforward, even though Vaughan Williams's inclusion of the epigraph from Plato's *Phaedo* suggests that they should not be taken at face value. One alternative reading centers the apocalyptic experience of the Great War as an analogue for the end times described by John of Patmos, a parallel evoked by many British artists who served in the conflict and noted by subsequent commentators.[26] From a musical perspective, some of the most powerful moments appear during the battle between the armies of heaven and earth spanning rehearsal marks **9** to **22**, a stark contrast with the shimmering, slowly changing harmonies with which the work commences.[27] The Angel of the Lord and its forces are represented by a homorhythmic choir and fanfares of brass, their harmonies juxtaposing cross-relations and mediant shifts in unpredictable blocks that create an overwhelmingly triadic yet tonally unmoored texture. The earthbound forces are far less powerful, dispersed in points of imitation and deviating from the baritone soloist they ostensibly follow, and so they collapse in the face of heaven's united front.

A lament for the fall of Babylon follows, but like so much of Vaughan Williams's music evoking connections with war, hope ultimately emerges from despair. The vision of the new heaven and the new earth following the lament is mysterious yet utterly serene, heralded by a pentatonic violin solo and sustained in pandiatonic choral harmonies, a tantalizingly elusive vision of a better world. It is in these passages that *Sancta Civitas* embraces the oratorical tradition of privileging communal expression over that of the individual, a particularly English approach to the genre, and one that Vaughan Williams often returned to in his choral works. Few, however, conveyed that message in musical language so challenging and varied in so compact a guise. As Colles observed, "had Handel taken the Apocalyptic vision as his story . . . he would have produced an oratorio which it would take a complete evening to perform, whereas the modern composer with his more concentrated style passes all Heaven in review in half an hour."[28]

Colles's comment highlights Vaughan Williams's postwar tendency toward structural concision, which paid additional dividends when he returned to writing larger works at the end of the decade. This tendency is especially true of *Sir John in Love* (1929), a profound advance over *Hugh the Drover* in almost every way: characterization, pacing, dramatic efficacy, and musical cohesion. Although he began composing it in 1924, the inspiration most likely originated when he wrote the incidental music for *The Merry Wives of Windsor*, the play on which this opera is based, during his tenure with the Shakespeare Memorial Theatre Festival a decade earlier.[29] The story was a favorite of his, its combination of an unpretentious middle-class setting, well-defined characters, lightly subversive plot—in which clever women drive the action and confound the men—and conspicuous textual references to music playing to many of his interests. His adaptation streamlined Shakespeare's original story, but also fused additional dramatic and poetic material by Shakespeare and others into a seamless whole—no small challenge, given the large number of characters and subplots, ranging from scenes of romantic intrigue to comic interludes and emotionally revealing soliloquies.[30]

As in *Hugh*, Vaughan Williams again introduced various English folk and traditional melodies into the score, but better integrated them into the larger musical texture. Rather than framing the borrowed tunes as stand-alone events, he now uses them to literally underscore the plot or emphasize aspects of the characters' personalities, turning some of the melodies into reminiscence themes and largely de-emphasizing their origins.[31] (No small irony, then, that his *Fantasia on Greensleeves* (1934)— an arrangement juxtaposing that melody with the folk song "Lovely Joan"—remains one of his most popular orchestral works.) Vaughan Williams also insisted that the dances featured in the opera "must not be self consciously Hobbley-hoyish & 'Rustic'—neither must they be 'Dainty,'" a position consistent with his aim of humanizing the characters in *Hugh* and his dislike of classical ballet.[32] His efforts in this regard were far more successful here, as the characters are far more realistic than the thinly sketched figures of *Hugh the Drover*, and the solo and ensemble scenes more skillfully balanced.

Most importantly, the music reveals how much Vaughan Williams's artistic confidence and compositional skill had grown since 1910. While his now familiar triadic modal lyricism dominates the work, it is enhanced by more dissonant and tonally unstable language present in many of his compositions from the 1920s. This idiomatic approach enables him to capture the characters' wide emotional range—Ford's jealousy when he thinks his wife has been unfaithful, Evans's fear at his impending duel with Dr. Caius, Falstaff's confidence in his own schemes, the indignancy of the Windsor wives—with distinctive musical effects that still align with the opera's fundamental technical basis. If he treats such devices somewhat conservatively, *Sir John in Love* nevertheless represents Vaughan Williams's first large-scale application of a newly consolidated musical language and expanded creative range, a stylistically flexible and expressively diverse compositional idiom that would permeate his later works.

"An Awful Responsibility" (1930–1936)

THE MOVE TO DORKING INSPIRED MANY CHANGES IN VAUGHAN Williams's lifestyle. The fresh air and easy access to the outdoors led him to adopt or renew various hobbies: walking and cycling tours, tennis on the White Gates's grass court (Vaughan Williams and Morris apparently made a formidable doubles pair, "not that they moved very fast in any direction, but they made up for this immobility by their considerable combined cunning"),[1] horseback riding, gardening, and haymaking in the summertime; he even picked up his viola for the first time in many years. Friends, relatives, or guests regularly dropped by, some of whom became long-term residents. The first was Bob de Ropp, a first cousin once removed of Adeline's, who became estranged from his immediate family and moved in with the Vaughan Williamses around 1930. "I owe a great debt to the Vaughan Williamses," he later wrote, as they also paid for him to attend the Royal College of Science in London. "They put me back on my feet, gave me a game worth playing and a valid pattern on which to model my behavior."[2]

The fact that the Vaughan Williamses could so easily welcome a new household member (in addition to Honorine Williamson, who accompanied them on the move) reflects the fact that they were by now financially comfortable—so much so that in June 1931, Vaughan Williams turned down a $1000 commission ($17,000 in 2020) from Elizabeth Sprague Coolidge to compose a string quartet. Most of his money appears to come from the combination of his RCM salary (£112.14s.0d in 1928–1929, or almost $9300 in 2020),[3] publishing royalties, and occasional commissions. The allowance that had sustained him while young was less significant by this time, though his parents' investments (mostly in railroads) had done quite well. When Margaret Vaughan Williams died in 1937, her investment portfolio was worth £23,538—$2.06 million in 2020—but incredibly, Ralph turned down his share of the inheritance. No indications of a falling out with either his mother or brother exist, so presumably he decided that he didn't need the money and couldn't be bothered with it.[4]

Alongside his new activities and routines, public accolades continued to grow. In 1930, he was awarded the Cobbett Medal from the Worshipful Company of Musicians in recognition of services to chamber music, and the Royal Philharmonic Society's Gold Medal for outstanding musicianship. Coincidentally, Holst was awarded the same prize from the RPS only weeks later, which pleased Vaughan Williams more than his own receipt of it (he told Diana Awdry, tongue firmly in cheek, he considered such awards "only one of many polite hints that it is time to retire").[5]

Eight new works debuted in 1930, four of them at the LHMC. Each was written for and dedicated to one of the Festival's performing divisions: *Benedicite* (Towns), Three Choral Hymns (Div. I), *The Hundredth Psalm* (Div. II) and *Three Children's Songs for a Spring Festival* (Children's). The most significant musical event that year, however, was the premiere of *Job* at the Norfolk and Norwich Festival on 23 October. Since Diaghilev had rejected the scenario as unsuitable for the Ballets Russes, Vaughan Williams saw no prospect for its production. Instead, with considerable help from Holst to pare down the orchestration, he recast it as a concert piece for the Festival.[6] Geoffrey Keynes thought that the music was generally well received, but the loss of its dramatic aspect disappointed some reviewers. Even someone as sympathetic as Colles found it wanting: "A concert version of such a work can be little more satisfactory than is the orchestral accompaniment to a song-cycle without the singer," he wrote. "All that can be said is that the hearing of the music makes one want to have a realization of the ballet worthy alike of Blake and Vaughan Williams."[7]

Fortunately, such an opportunity came from the short-lived but influential Camargo Society. Founded in 1930, the London-based group filled the void left when the Ballets Russes collapsed after Diaghilev's death, attracting both money and talent: Constant Lambert served as ensemble director, Ninette de Valois and Lydia Lopokova as choreographers, and John Maynard Keynes—Lopokova's husband, and Geoffrey Keynes's brother—as treasurer. Although it lasted only until 1933, its productions of British ballets were commended for their quality and novelty, including *Job: A Masque for Dancing* in 1931, the production of which was eased thanks to Geoffrey Keynes's ability to front the initial expenses.[8] Keynes provided de Valois with copies of Blake's illustrations, which inspired her approach to the choreography; the sets and costumes were based on Gwen Raverat's designs; and Vaughan Williams enlisted Lambert to further thin the ensemble from eighty players to about thirty. Anton Dolin's powerfully athletic Satan was particularly lauded in early reviews, of which A. H. Fox-Strangways's was among the most enthusiastic: "Vaughan Williams's technique is now at its zenith; he can do what he wills to do; and through nearly all of this work he has not waited in vain for inspiration."[9]

In early 1931, Vaughan Williams's fifty-nine-year old sister, Meggie, died. Vaughan Williams wanted her role in the LHMC's founding to be properly memorialized, so he led Dorking's first full performance of Bach's *St. Matthew Passion* in her honor. It also inaugurated the new Dorking Halls, the long-awaited replacement for the spacious but otherwise inhospitable Drill Hall that had served as the Festival's home since 1922. The concert was held on 24 March—augmenting the usual LHMC activities the following month—and proved a deeply moving performance. Vaughan Williams later remembered that "when the seven hundred voices whispered 'be near me Lord' they made a magical sound which I shall never forget."[10] A second rendition followed in 1938, and the Passion's performance under his direction became an annual and much anticipated event in Dorking from 1942 through 1958.[11]

Vaughan Williams also witnessed the publication of two edited volumes in 1931 (an enlarged version of *Songs of Praise* and a set of country dances, collected mostly by Maud Karpeles, with whom he collaborated—with some resistance—on arrangements), and completed two major works: a long-delayed piano concerto and an early draft of the Symphony in F Minor. His brisk compositional pace continued into the new year. By late January 1932, he had completed a sketch for a *Magnificat* intended for that year's Three Choirs Festival; this followed a two-piano play-through of the Symphony in F Minor at St. Paul's Girls School on 6 January, attended by Holst and Finzi (with Vally Lasker and Helen Bidder performing). Holst was allegedly "puzzled by most of it and disliked the rest," and the two men spent several field days revising the work over the next two years.[12]

Their contact in 1932 was intermittent, however, as both spent extended periods in the United States. Holst left in January to take up the Horatio Lamb Lecturer position at Harvard, while Vaughan Williams arrived in New York on 13 October before going on to Bryn Mawr College in Philadelphia as that year's Mary Flexner Lecturer. His talks focused on the idea of national music, and represented the culmination of three decades' worth of thoughts on the subject. Two years later, they were published as *National Music*, the first collected volume of his prose. "Those lectures are only what I have been spouting for the last 20 years," he told Imogen Holst. "Now that they've appeared in print I shall never be able to spout them again."[13] *National Music* has been described as "a creative work rather than an academic study . . . not so much an account of what national music is, as an explanation of what Vaughan Williams would wish national music to be in an ideal world."[14] The lectures promote two largely incompatible ideas: first, that the elements of folk music should form the basis of any larger school of national music, and second, that national music reflected the amalgamation of composers' personal styles. In other words, Vaughan Williams believed that the construction of national music resulted both from musicians' intrinsic nature and their cultural nurturing, but had difficulty rectifying the contradictions that arose when privileged status was extended to folk song within such traditions. Problematic though it may be, it is also wide-ranging and engagingly written, providing considerable insight into Vaughan Williams's thoughts on the subject and the challenges to them that arose during his lifetime.

Vaughan Williams returned home by mid-December, and wrapped up the year by leading a Boxing Day performance in Cwmaman, Wales, where he directed a choir of unemployed miners in renditions of *Toward the Unknown Region* and the Four Hymns, Brahms's *Ein deutsches Requiem*, and the Sanctus from Bach's Mass in B Minor. The new year also started promisingly, as the Piano Concerto had its long-awaited debut on 1 February 1933. Harriet Cohen, the dedicatee, took the demanding solo part, supported by the BBC Symphony Orchestra under Boult. Despite mixed reviews, Vaughan Williams was extremely happy with Boult's rendering: "You have made impossible the composer's time-honoured excuse that the work would have sounded all right if it had been properly played—I could not have imagined a better first performance."[15] Subsequent revisions were delayed because of various events, most notably a doubly cracked fibula the composer sustained by slipping off a footpath in late June. Confined to bed, he decided to make the best of a bad situation by learning to play the clarinet. Though he was unsuccessful, the young woman he hired to teach him, Elizabeth Darbishire, soon became a regular visitor (along with her sister, Molly) to White Gates. The Vaughan Williamses formally purchased the house that year for around £3000 ($288,779 in 2020), and made plans for a thorough renovation, including the addition of an annex for Ralph's mother. Unfortunately, the undertaking was plagued with problems, forcing the Vaughan Williamses to spend extended stretches in London until late March 1934.

This was the first of several unfortunate events that year, most far more poignant. For example, Vaughan Williams decided to perform *The Dream of Gerontius* at that year's LHMC, and informed Elgar—whose health was in serious decline—of his intent. "I had been longing to do it for years, but had thought it too dangerous an experiment as I could not bear to do it badly," he wrote, adding that "it will be one of the great moments in my life when I stand with trembling baton to conduct it . . . and [the performers] shall think of you."[16] Three days after receiving this note, Elgar died, and so the concert became a memorial to English music's most distinguished representative. Elgar's daughter, Carice Blake, commended the choir's efforts and the beauty of their rendition: "It means so much to know you are teaching this generation to know & love his works and above all teaching them in such a splendid way."[17]

But an even greater loss was soon to come. Having suffered from a duodenal ulcer for several years, Holst underwent an operation to alleviate the increasingly intolerable pain. Tragically, his heart could not withstand the strain of surgery; he died on 25 May, aged only fifty-nine, a crushing blow to his old friend. "What are we to do without him," Vaughan Williams asked Imogen and Isobel Holst, "every thing seems to have turned back to him—what would Gustav think or advise or do."[18] He collaborated with the Holsts and Boult in preparing a memorial concert on 22 June, reluctantly agreeing to give an introductory talk, which "he [dreaded] very much and found it terribly difficult to write."[19] Soon after, he chaired a fundraising committee to create a dedicated music room and performance hall at Morley College named after Holst, securing pledges from contributors throughout Britain and the United States.

Vaughan Williams's reliance on Holst's criticism, encouragement, and judgment was not simply the indulgence of a long-standing habit, but part of his own creative process. He still doubted his own abilities and, despite his many successes and accolades, felt as though his creative aspirations had still gone unrealized. "In younger days when one thought one was going to do the real thing each time & each time discovered one hadn't done it, one said hopefully 'next time,'" he explained to Bobby Longman, "but when one touches on 65 one begins to wonder."[20] He was unsparing in assessments of his own music. "I wish I didn't dislike my own stuff so much when I hear it—it all sounds so incompetent,"[21] he wrote Maud Karpeles, while the reception of the Piano Concerto made him "sometimes feel inclined to tear up all my music & have nothing to do with public performance."[22] He knew he had these tendencies, as he told both Boult ("when one has lived in every note of a work one gets rather morbidly sensitive about it") and Grace Williams ("I never satisfy myself").[23] The loss of a staunch, perceptive, and sympathetic ally like Holst—one of the few truly intimate friends admitted to his own creative world—undoubtedly deepened his own self-critical tendencies.

His usual remedy for such feelings was to get on with the routine of work, and he had several projects lined up for the summer of 1934. He had been collaborating with E. M. Forster on a pageant play benefiting the Abinger Church Preservation Fund, and was preparing to direct both his *Magnificat* and Holst's *Te Deum* at that year's Three Choirs Festival. Unfortunately, following a long walk in Sussex after Holst's funeral, Vaughan Williams either cut his foot or acquired a blister that became infected, causing a septic abscess that left him bedridden for the second consecutive summer, forcing him to miss both events. Even being notified in July of his election to a life fellowship from the Worshipful Company of Musicians—only the second musician after Elgar to be so honored—provided little solace after such a dismal year.[24]

By September, Vaughan Williams was well enough to walk with a stick, and managed to direct a Proms performance on the 27th. The program included *A London Symphony*—recently revised for the third and final time—and two concert premieres: the *Fantasia on "Greensleeves,"* excerpted from *Sir John in Love* and arranged by Frank Greaves for strings, harp, and optional flutes; and *The Running Set*, a medley of English folk-dance tunes unveiled at the National Folk Dance Festival in January. Even though Adeline found it increasingly difficult to sit in a typical concert-hall seat, she accompanied Ralph to the performance. However, she still regularly attended rehearsals to provide feedback, and her husband continued to rely on her to review, copy, and correct his manuscripts.[25] The couple returned to London in November for the debut of the Suite for Viola and Small Orchestra, dedicated to and performed by Lionel Tertis with the London Philharmonic Orchestra, and to hear Lasker and Day play through the revised Symphony in F Minor. Boult and Arthur Bliss also attended the latter event, and Vaughan Williams thanked Bliss for his suggestions shortly after:

> You mustn't think that your advice has not been valuable because I have not exactly followed it—when I give advice to my pupils I tell them that they can do one of 3 things

> (a) accept it blindly—bad
> (b) reject it kindly—bad but not so bad
> (c) think out a 3rd course for themselves—sound.[26]

Few of Vaughan Williams's symphonies have had more wide-ranging reactions than his F Minor, unofficially known as the Fourth, which debuted on 10 April 1935. Attending the final rehearsals, Adeline told Curle she was pleased with the result. "The symph is emerging—& I now couldn't bear you <u>not</u> to hear it—last week I thought I c^dnt bear <u>anyone</u> to hear it! It was wonderful to get the 1st movement going this morning—It's powerful! I ought to have had more faith."[27] And indeed, reactions confirmed her conclusion. Maud Karpeles felt that it conveyed the troubled state of European politics in 1935, while Colles remarked that the "shockingly sophisticated" opening left the world of the *Pastoral Symphony* far behind, though he found considerable humor in the scherzo (which suggested the composer's "poisonous temper" to

Elizabeth Trevelyan), and admired its brilliant orchestration along with its unexpected levels of daring and gaiety.[28] Additionally, he noted its resemblance to the idiom of its dedicatee, Arnold Bax, who called it "the finest tribute of affection and comradeship that has ever been paid me and I shall value it all my life."[29] The public response was also generally enthusiastic. Edmund Rubbra said it conveyed an impression "of almost overwhelming power and beauty," Patrick Hadley "declared it has knocked Europe sideways," and Arthur Benjamin complimented "its sheer mastery, its vitality and its beauty."[30] Adeline, however, made special note of a letter "from a wireless listener unknown of <u>foul</u> abuse proud of having switched off after 3 minutes!"[31] Vaughan Williams's own self-effacing assessments of the piece are regularly quoted, but he reflected more thoughtfully upon the piece to Bobby Longman:

> I <u>do</u> think it beautiful—not, that I did not <u>mean</u> it to be beautiful because it reflects unbeautiful things—because we know that beauty can come from unbeautiful things (e.g. King Lear, Rembrandts School of Anatomy Wagners Niebelungs etc)
>
> As a matter of fact
>
> (1) I am not at all sure that I like it myself <u>now</u> all I know is that it is what I wanted to do <u>at the time</u>.
> (2) I wrote it not as a definite picture of anything external e.g. the state of Europe—but simply because it occurred to me like this—I can't explain why—I don't think that sitting down & thinking about great things ever produces a great work of art . . . a thing just comes—or it doesn't—usually doesn't.[32]

On 17 May, barely a month after the symphony's debut, Vaughan Williams was informed that King George V, as part of his Silver Jubilee birthday honors, wished to confer upon him the Order of Merit. Arguably the United Kingdom's most prestigious royal honor, the OM is limited to a membership of twenty-four and is the personal gift of the sovereign, given in recognition of meritorious service to the nation. Vaughan Williams had refused royal honors before, allegedly because he was uncomfortable with the obligations they implied. The same was true of Holst, whose political and spiritual beliefs—along with his aversion to public attention—made him indifferent to such recognition.

Vaughan Williams thought about his old friend when considering whether to accept, and of his own family's iconoclastic reputation.[33] "I hope you do not think I have betrayed my ancestry," he wrote to Lord Farrer, "but it seemed more modest to accept it without any fuss than to set my own judgement of myself against that of the authorities."[34] And so on 9 July, Vaughan Williams became the sixty-second recipient of the Order of Merit, joining his old friend George Trevelyan in its ranks.[35] "It's an awful responsibility to be chosen to 'represent' music," Vaughan Williams told Finzi, for he filled the vacancy created by Elgar's death, but he was deeply moved by the outpouring of good wishes from friends upon his investiture. One of the most charming came from Boris Ord, who told Vaughan Williams about a chorister who, while rehearsing *O Clap Your Hands*, asked "Oh, Sir, did the King give him an O. M. for writing music like this!" (In response, Vaughan Williams told him about "a small girl who asked her pfte mistress if I had had to pass an exam first!")[36]

Later that summer, he attended the International Folk Dance Festival, for which he had written a short *Flourish of Trumpets*; completed a choral suite on texts by John Skelton for the Norfolk and Norwich Festival ("It was due Aug 1st—and is only just ready now!" he fretted to Diana Awdry on 4 August); and accepted a commission from the Huddersfield Choral Society for its centenary celebrations in 1936.[37] Additionally, he began considering how he would disburse his own estate. In August, he approached Alexander Butterworth to propose that "a proportion of the fees and royalties on my compositions should go to the Butterworth trust. . . . with a special recommendation to the helping of young composers to get their works performed."[38] Memories of his own struggles undoubtedly spurred his advocacy for younger British musicians, and he often urged institutions such as the Macnaghten-Lemare Concerts and the BBC to program their music. He was annoyed by what he considered the Corporation's favorable treatment of foreign composers over British ones, yet he also encouraged certain pupils with firmly established musical voices—including Grace Williams, Stanley Bate, Peggy Glanville-Hicks, and Elizabeth Maconchy—to take advantage of continental training and pedagogy. Nevertheless, he felt strongly that solid musical technique could be acquired just as readily at home as abroad, and would provide the best basis for individual self-expression.[39]

Although not Master of the King's Music de jure, the post's current occupant (Walford Davies) asked Vaughan Williams for a work marking the death of George V in January 1936. In response, he composed the short choral song *Nothing Is Here for Tears*, featuring lines from Milton's *Samson Agonistes*, in less than a day; it was broadcast the following weekend as part of a BBC memorial concert. There was considerably more time available to prepare for the debut of *The Poisoned Kiss, or The Empress and the Necromancer* later that year. Billed as a "Romantic Extravaganza," it had an initial five-day run at Cambridge, beginning 12 May 1936, before moving to Sadler's Wells. Much of the surviving correspondence between Vaughan Williams and Evelyn Sharp shows how seriously Vaughan Williams took this light comic opera and how unsuitable Sharp was as a librettist, as the somewhat labored text was "flawed from the start by not committing either to a frothy romantic comedy or to a satirical fairy-tale."[40] Although the opera was financially unsuccessful, Vaughan Williams remained unbothered by that or the tepid critical response. "The fact remains," he told Sharp, "that people enjoyed our joint effort very much and some people came three times which would be impossible if they thought too badly either of words or music. [. . .] But I think we shall both agree that if it is ever done again we shall want to make omissions and alterations both in words & music," which he did two decades later.[41]

Following his regular engagement at the Three Choirs in Hereford that September—where he conducted the first performance of his Two Hymn-Tune Preludes along with the *Pastoral Symphony* and the Suite for Viola—Vaughan Williams headed to Norwich for the premiere of his Skelton choral suite, *Five Tudor Portraits*. He credited Elgar for its inspiration: at a Three Choirs Festival, the two had discussed Skelton "of whom I knew little then, except through the Anthologies. [Elgar] said 'You should make an oratorio out of Elinor Rumming.' He went on to point out how the metre of Skelton was often pure jazz," an observation that the rumbustious settings of "The Tunning of Elinor Rumming," "Epitaph on John Jayberd of Diss," and "Jolly Rutterkin" suggest Vaughan Williams took to heart.[42] The earthy verses caused some concern; one choral society was "jittery over Skelton—wants 'frowsy' & not blowsy—R taking a strong line—if you don't sing Skelton you don't sing Vaughan

Williams."[43] However, not everyone at Norwich appreciated Vaughan Williams's dedication to textual fidelity:

> The elderly Countess of Albermarle sat in the front row getting pinker and pinker in the face and, when the pink turned to purple, [soloist] Astra Desmond, thinking she was going to have a heart attack, was about to lean down from the platform and offer smelling salts. But before this aid could be given she rose to her feet, said "Disgusting" loudly and clearly, and marched out of the hall. When Ralph was told about it afterwards he said it certainly showed that the choirs' diction was good, and added reflectively, "A pity she didn't read the lines I didn't set."[44]

Less objectionable, if just as effective, were the texts for *Dona Nobis Pacem*, which debuted on 2 October 1936. Perhaps Vaughan Williams's most overtly political composition, he successfully avoided the trap that often snares such pieces: focusing too closely on specific details of contemporary events. Thus while the antiwar message was unmissable, the choice of texts—reflections on the American Civil War (by Whitman) and the Crimean War (from parliamentarian John Bright) paired with calls for peace from Scripture—bestowed a perspective that transcended the volatile circumstances of the day. The Huddersfield Choral Society's rendition was exceptionally fine, and Vaughan Williams led a broadcast performance the following month with the BBC Symphony Orchestra.

Unfortunately, aside from an outstanding rendition of the *Sea Symphony* by Boult in late October and an opportunity to meet Nadia Boulanger in November, the waning weeks of 1936 recalled the *annus horribilus* of 1934. The abdication of Edward VIII in December narrowly dodged the constitutional crisis that had been building for months, highlighting the government's apparent fecklessness with fascism ascendant on the continent. Closer to home, Adeline had broken her left arm in early October. While not serious, it underscored her escalating fragility and immobility, alleviated somewhat when she acquired a wheelchair in November. Most tragically, Hervey Vaughan Williams's wife, Constance, was hit by a bicyclist on 1 December outside the gates at Leith Hill Place and died the next day. Ironically, this blow revived his mother Margaret's increasingly precarious health, an act of sheer willpower in response to Hervey's distress, but she had been fighting an ongoing series of illnesses that had hung over White Gates like a cloud for months. These personal and environmental stresses, combined with Vaughan Williams's relentless work schedule, numerous professional obligations, and the still-raw pain of losing his closest friend had taken their toll. Now in his mid-sixties, Vaughan Williams was the éminence grise of English music, but was beginning to feel increasingly isolated, physically weary, and creatively exhausted.

The Music of 1930–1936

V AUGHAN WILLIAMS'S RAPID COMPOSITIONAL PACE DURING THE EARLY
1930s is striking, particularly given the number of large-scale pieces
he completed, but several factors contributed to it. Most importantly, he
had secured a technical idiom based in ambiguous scalar collections, unorthodox triadic relationships, rhythmic flexibility, and melodic lyricism
that could be adapted to an array of stylistic and expressive contexts.
Additionally, his close relationships with Hubert Foss at OUP and Adrian
Boult at the BBC facilitated the wide publication and performance of
his music, reinforcing his status as one of Britain's leading composers.[1]
This raised his public profile and likely emboldened him to take greater
creative risks, reflected in such works as the Piano Concerto, *Riders to the
Sea*, *Dona Nobis Pacem*, *Five Tudor Portraits*, *Job*, and the Fourth Symphony.
Yet these coexisted with far more demure compositions like *The Poisoned
Kiss*, the *Hymn Tune Prelude on "Song 13" by Orlando Gibbons*, a host of folk
arrangements and sacred pieces, and occasional works written for ama-
teur musicians and community celebrations.

The four pieces marking the LHMC's silver anniversary in 1930 combine those final two categories, and their varying levels of difficulty show
that Vaughan Williams took the artistic desires, abilities, and motivations
of amateurs as seriously as those of any professional. The most extended
of these works, the *Benedicite*, has an opening strongly reminiscent of
"Antiphon" from the *Five Mystical Songs*, a prelude to the choir's exuberant litany of blessings. This gives way to a more restrained second

section featuring the soprano soloist, notable for its lengthy melismas—a striking departure from Vaughan Williams's usual emphasis on naturalistic text declamation—backed by more restrained choral accompaniment. The final section alternates between imitative and homophonic textures, gradually building to a chorale-like finish as the soloist soars to a high B before the final cadence. Dedicated to the LHMC's Towns Division, it complements the Three Choral Hymns written for the Division I Choir, featuring texts by Miles Coverdale (1488–1569), Bishop of Exeter. If less extroverted than the *Benedicite*, they are no less expressive or technically demanding, and more formally concise. The same is true for the charming set of *Three Children's Songs* for the Children's Division, as well as the florid and freely imitative fantasia on *The Hundredth Psalm* dedicated to the Division II choir—a work Vaughan Williams would revisit many years later for a very different celebration.[2]

Vaughan Williams employed religious texts throughout his career, even in non-liturgical works, a predilection that served two aims. In many cases, he assumed that the texts would be familiar to many listeners, thus providing a point of reference for them to engage. But that apparent familiarity belied the artistic feint that often followed, where Vaughan Williams would reinterpret the verse or the story in unexpected ways. Few were more effective in this regard than the *Magnificat* (1932), born out of a desire "to lift the words out of the smug atmosphere which has settled down on it from being sung at evening service for so long."[3] Dedicated to contralto Astra Desmond—who, responding to Steuart Wilson's tut-tutting about young unmarried women singing Magnificats, told Vaughan Williams, "I'm a married woman with four children, why don't you write one for me"—it views the story of the Annunciation from Mary's perspective.[4] Holst's influence is more palpable here than in almost any of Vaughan Williams's other compositions, filtered through the harmonic idioms of *Flos Campi* and *Sancta Civitas*. It also looks ahead to the Symphony in F Minor, as the solo flute—used here to represent the Holy Spirit—anticipates a passage from the second movement. Here, however, its likely antecedents include Debussy's *L'après-midi d'un faun* or Ravel's *Shéhérazade*, overtly sensual works in which the flute straddles eroticism and otherworldliness, and that resonate even more powerfully from knowing that Vaughan Williams imagined the alto soloist expressing the voice of Mary yielding to her divine lover.[5] The *Magnificat* brings an underappreciated element of Vaughan Williams's religiously themed music into sharp relief: his focus on his subjects' humanity. Whether depicting the astonishment of Mary, the lovesickness of Solomon, or the soul-ache of Pilgrim, he responds seriously to their emotional states, and compels listeners to do the same. This attitude may also explain in part his longstanding attraction to Bach's Passions, in which the emphasis is less on Christ, the divine Son of God, as it is on Jesus, the human son of Mary—the story of a forsaken man who suffers because of other men's pride, venality, and cruelty, paying for their sins with his life.

But before Jesus's suffering, there was Job's. Vaughan Williams's so-called masque for dancing, an inspired interpretation of William Blake's extraordinary illustrations of loss and redemption, represents one of his greatest creative achievements. That it should occur within the realm of dance was surprising, given the unevenness of *Old King Cole* and *On Christmas Night*, but working with Raverat and Keynes likely helped correct (or stave off) potential problems of stagecraft that the composer could not always see when working alone. However, Vaughan Williams could be demanding when it came to the minutiae of stage productions, and this was particularly true for *Job*. While the production was ostensibly an artistic partnership, Keynes found himself increasingly marginalized (and annoyed) by Vaughan Williams's modifications to the scenario as work progressed.[6] One aspect of Keynes and Raverat's vision that was preserved, however, was the influence played by Joseph Wicksteed's assessment of Blake's illustrations, in which he argued that distinctions of good and evil correlated to the directions of right and left. The efficacy of *Job* on the stage arises in part from this congruence of the musical and dramatic visions, reinforced by Ninette de Valois's choreography.

The long-term critical estimation has positioned *Job* as uniting Vaughan Williams's pastoralist tendencies with more radical or conventionally modernist ones.[7] In this union, there is something of a parallel with the way in which Russian ballets, especially those of Stravinsky, assign divergent musical styles to contrasting character types, an approach complemented by Wicksteed's observations of Blake's imagery. Accordingly, the music for the heavenly host adopts the forms of early Baroque dances (the sarabande, pavane, and galliard), a neoclassical gloss gravitating toward modal and lyrical homophony, with largely diatonic melodies and undemonstrative accompaniments. The influence of Satan and his agents is far more disruptive, employing metric ambiguity, disjunct melodies, and dissonant harmonies often arising from polyphonic textures. Job is situated between these opposing forces, often receiving lyrical themes featuring modal or pentatonic pitch collections, but subject to fragmentation and counterpoint depending on the dramatic situation or musical context. The conclusion to the work is also revealing, in that it deviates from Blake's scenario returning Job to prosperity. Instead, Job remains "old and humbled, bereft of family and possessions," resigned to whatever fate God has in store. Once again, Vaughan Williams's protagonist is redeemed through personal sacrifice unaccompanied by material reward—only spiritual enlightenment, and a bitter enlightenment at that.[8]

If the road to *Job's* final realization was sometimes difficult, far less strained was the relationship Vaughan Williams cultivated with pianist Harriet Cohen, culminating in his dedication to her of the Piano Concerto in C Major (1933). The factors underlying their friendship are immediately apparent. Both were outgoing, charismatic, and flirtatious, and shared an admiration of Bach's music; Cohen's reputation stemmed in large part from her interpretations of his works. (Adeline, however, disliked Cohen intensely.)[9] The Concerto was not the only work connecting Vaughan Williams and Cohen: in 1930, he dedicated the *Hymn Tune Prelude on "Song 13" by Orlando Gibbons* to her, and later contributed his Choral and Choral Prelude on Bach's "Ach, bleib bei uns, Herr Jesu Christ" to the collection *A Bach Book for Harriet Cohen* (1932). The obscurity of these works is unfortunate, for they contain some of Vaughan Williams's most graceful and assured writing for the piano. Gibbons's melody acts as a cantus firmus; nestled within euphonious four-part counterpoint, it forms a stately complement to the transparent and gently flowing voices surrounding it.[10] The Choral and Choral Prelude freely arranges Bach's composition, which was itself transcribed from BWV 6, the cantata "Bleib bei uns, denn es will Abend werden." The opening melody of *that* work was based on the alto line from a 1594 chorale by German theorist and composer Seth Calvisius (1556–1615), so Vaughan Williams's treatment represented the third recasting of the tune. Like the *Hymn Tune Prelude*, the counterpoint is elegant and deliberate, reflecting the spirit of Bach's expression as much as Vaughan Williams's own technical skill. Finally, in 1933, he gave Cohen permission to arrange his own

Suite of Six Short Pieces (later, *The Charterhouse Suite*) for piano and string orchestra;[11] whether she also performed the six so-called teaching pieces from 1934 (later published as *A Little Piano Book*, 1984) is not known, but this attractive series of inventions and miniatures would have suited her talents well.[12]

Cohen was not the only soloist to reap the benefits of Vaughan Williams's friendship at this time. Henry Ley, the RCM's Professor of Organ, was the dedicatee of the Prelude and Fugue in C Minor, which debuted in 1930 and marked the end of an eventful transformation for the work. Originally written for organ, it was likely composed (or at the very least, sketched) in 1915, while Vaughan Williams was stationed at Saffron Walden. He presented it to Ley in 1921, who claimed that he "found it too difficult for an organ."[13] Evidently surprised by his colleague's verdict, Vaughan Williams undertook further revisions on it in 1923 and 1930, an auxiliary result of which was an arrangement of the piece for orchestra; it is this version that received the first public performance on 12 September. Allegedly inspired by Bach's Prelude and Fugue in C Minor, BWV 546, the homage is a very broad one. Notwithstanding the Prelude's motivic expansiveness and the complexity of the Fugue, the work's dissonant harmonies and disjunct contours align more closely with later pieces like *Job* or the Piano Concerto than with neoclassical compositions like the *Concerto Accademico*. The other notable solo work from the early 1930s is the Suite for Viola and Small Orchestra (1934), written for and dedicated to Lionel Tertis. Its eight movements divide into three groups: the Prelude, Carol, and "Christmas Dance" comprise a Christmas set, followed by two character pieces (Ballad and Moto Perpetuo) before concluding with a trio of dances—the Musette, "Polka mélancholique," and Galop. The expressive heart of the Suite beats within the beautiful Carol, but the movements cover an expansive range that requires both refined interpretive skills and athletic virtuosity from the soloist.

The same is true of the Piano Concerto, a work whose long-term neglect may be attributed to several factors, not least of which was Harriet Cohen herself. The concerto pushed Cohen's technique to its limits, her small handspan ("I cannot normally cover more than eight notes with each hand") unsuited to the piece's full chords and dense textures.[14] Yet she monopolized the concerto's performance in the years immediately following its premiere, and thus prevented it from being more widely heard.[15] Later generations of pianists have found its technical difficulty and lack of virtuosic flashiness an unappealing combination, and the fact that the work exists in multiple forms complicates questions of what constitutes the "definitive" version. Vaughan Williams made some of these modifications to suit his own tastes, such as cutting an allusion to Arnold Bax's Third Symphony from the end of the cadenza—Bax was, at the time, Cohen's lover—and may have made others to address Cohen's limitations.[16] The most substantive changes, however, came when it was adapted by Joseph Cooper for two soloists and orchestra in 1946 at Vaughan Williams's behest, yet this new arrangement did not supersede the single-piano version.[17]

Still, few performances of either have been forthcoming. The Piano Concerto has long been regarded as something of a problem child in Vaughan Williams's body of work. For the most part, it is not as tuneful as most of his repertory—exempting much of the second movement (Romanza), which contains some passages of near-Rachmaninovian lushness and expressive lyricism—nor it does it adhere to many of the standard structural expectations of the genre.[18] Moreover, its elaborate counterpoint, textural density, unusual sonorities, and sudden stylistic shifts can make it challenging to follow, and it invokes a forceful intensity rarely associated with Vaughan Williams's instrumental works—though not unprecedented.[19] Indeed, it extends his streak of writing works for soloist and ensemble that defy formal or generic conventions, balancing complicated juxtapositions of unconventional pitch collections against streams of diatonic parallel triads and complex chromatic counterpoint. It expanded the boundaries of his flexible harmonic palette to their furthest frontier, and continued his interwar fascination with neoclassicism, even though the stylistic connections to practices of earlier eras grew ever more tenuous. Like *In the Fen Country*, the Piano Concerto responds to the past while anticipating the future, the changes and transitions churning within it representing as yet unseen potential.

That potential was realized in the Symphony (No. 4) in F Minor, a work whose inspiration and meaning has been extensively debated since its debut in 1935. Frank Howes heard in it a "new note of sheer power— violence almost—[that] is characteristic of an age of electricity, speed and of Fascism," a response to ever-increasing technological and political instability.[20] More prosaically, Boult allegedly said that the composer began writing it "when he knew Adeline wasn't going to get better," while Ursula Vaughan Williams claimed that it was inspired by a review in *The Times* of a symphony performed at an ISCM Festival.[21] Such interpretations, however compelling, should be taken cautiously. That Vaughan Williams cared about the political situation in Europe, Adeline's health, and new developments in music may be taken as read, but those truths did not necessarily find a direct outlet in his compositions. As Hugh Ottaway perceptively noted, "if the Fourth was in fact triggered off by that description in *The Times*, then the underlying impulse, the pressure to create, must already have been very strong indeed."[22]

The most significant pressure shaping the development of Vaughan Williams's Fourth may have been the music of Beethoven.[23] Although the earliest sketches date from 1931, Vaughan Williams claimed that his first thoughts emerged in 1927, "at the time of the Beethoven Centenary," and that "musically I think it also grew from Beethoven . . . as I daresay you have noticed the opening chord is identical with the opening chord of the finale of Beethoven's 9th."[24] Vaughan Williams was ambivalent about Beethoven's music; he respected it, but in the way that one respects a dangerous animal or a loaded gun. He "hated Beethoven" when he entered the RCM, but a few years later regarded him as one of "the only composers worth considering"—along with Bach, Brahms, and Wagner—a position he later regarded as deeply snobbish.[25] He slew many sacred cows in an extended essay on Beethoven's Ninth Symphony, which he called "an unapproachable masterpiece" while asserting that it contained "plenty of banalities" that he found "hard to swallow."[26] Nevertheless, he later admitted that "the Beethoven idiom repels me, but I hope I have at last learnt to see the greatness that lies behind the idiom that I dislike."[27]

Vaughan Williams's Fourth Symphony represents a deeply personal response to the Beethovenian symphonic model, suggesting a new context for his famously self-deprecatory comment about it ("I don't know if I like it, but it's what I meant").[28] Particularly striking are its resemblances to Beethoven's Fifth Symphony, suggesting that Vaughan Williams's Fourth—so often characterized as one of his most radical compositions—in fact represents the climax of his engagement with neoclassicism. Much as Brahms's First Symphony responded to the symphonic challenge posed by Beethoven's Ninth, Vaughan Williams's Fourth questions the supremacy of that model on its own ground by engaging directly with Beethoven's Fifth. The first movements of both symphonies introduce two concise, pervasive motives, though where Beethoven fuses a rhythmic and melodic motive in a single figure, Vaughan Williams uses two melodic motives, which he identified in his program note for the work (Example 12.1a and b); in both works, these motives "unite the four movements and dominate the musical imagery."[29]

Vaughan Williams pointed out that the first motive was not the B–A–C–H figure (transposed, Motive 1 would be spelled B–A–H–B); however, the B–A–C–H motive *is* stated immediately before the first appearance of Motive 1 in mm. 6–7. Vaughan Williams's "crushed" version of B–A–C–H—its span reduced from three to only two half steps—would seem to neuter the original version's developmental and modulatory potential. Yet it forms the basis for most of the piece, constantly inspiring new treatments of the most unlikely and limited components. Similarly, the arpeggiated fourths opening the Scherzo recall the opening contour of the Scherzo in Beethoven's Fifth, a parallel extended further by its direct segue into the Finale. It is prepared and resolved identically in both pieces: motivic material drawn from the first movement gradually increases in volume and rhythmic dynamism before resolving in a massive chordal statement. In much the way Vaughan Williams distorted the B–A–C–H motive, he creates a similarly flattened-out take on the triad outlined at the beginning of Beethoven's finale to open his own final movement, turning it into "a series of 'oompahs' that get the music nowhere but simply stamp round and round."[30] Where the B–A–H–B distortion amplified the tension and concision of the model, the finale's transformation moves to the other extreme, skewering the original's pretentions to grandiosity by revealing the banality of the elements

Examples 12.1a and 12.1b Symphony (No. 4) in F Minor, principal motives

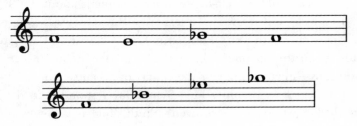

comprising it—a rhetorical gesture reinforced when the symphony's opening motive suddenly returns at the very close, negating all the effort that has gone before.[31]

Such economy of means and expressive bluntness permeates the work. The orchestration is unusually stark, pitting orchestral blocks against one another (almost certainly reflecting Holst's influence); the formal layouts are lean and uncluttered, reinforced by inventive tonal (or modal, or quasi-tonal) schemes; contrapuntal passages are tightly organized yet fully integrated within the fabric of the piece; and the metric scheme begets rhythmic contours of surprising subtlety and spontaneity. The result is "a twisted version of 'The Great German Masterpiece,'" in which Vaughan Williams engages contemporary German musical culture and his own anxiety of influence regarding the Beethovenian symphonic model, and overcomes them both.[32] William Walton's declaration that the F Minor was "the greatest symphony since Beethoven" may have been somewhat hyperbolic, but it validated Vaughan Williams's claim to that tradition, his mastery of it, and his exorcism of its power to bind him.[33]

Still, for all the commentary proclaiming that Vaughan Williams's Fourth Symphony meant that his past practices were now a closed book, the composer clearly did not think so. For instance, even though he had not collected any folk songs for nearly two decades, he still actively promoted and arranged them for various occasions and performers—usually on his own, but also with Maud Karpeles on *Twelve Traditional Country Dances* (1931) and *Folk Songs from Newfoundland* (1934), for which he wrote the piano accompaniments. He used the same voice-and-piano pairing for the Six English Folk Songs of 1935, but also arranged a clutch of part songs for publication in 1934, and Two English Folk Songs (1935) for voice and violin. Of slightly greater stature were a few folk-based compositions for orchestra. The best known is the *Fantasia on "Greensleeves*," but Vaughan Williams was most fond of *The Running Set* (1934). The name refers to an American dance of British origin rediscovered by Cecil Sharp; though the original tune was lost, it was danceable to any melody of an appropriate meter. Vaughan Williams's exuberant version opens by subjecting the tune "Barrack Hill" to an extended series of changing background variations, followed by renditions of "The Blackthorn Stick," "Irish Reel," and "Cock o' the North" before a final reprise of "Barrack Hill." He also wrote a brief *Flourish for Trumpets* based on the "Morris Call" for the International Folk Dance Festival of 1935, and interspersed a further mélange of folk tunes alongside various hymns and chants in *The Pageant of Abinger* (1934). This pageant fund-raiser depicted an imagined history of the eponymous Surrey village in six episodes, highlighting Abinger's stability amid transformative events like the Norman Invasion and the Civil Wars, but now threatened by uncontrolled urban sprawl. Though these sentiments were expressed in Forster's prose, Vaughan Williams shared them. (An amusing anecdote circulated that the Fourth Symphony, completed around the same time as the pageant music, "reflected Vaughan Williams's irritation over noisy arterial road construction near Dorking."[34])

The accessibility and tunefulness of *The Poisoned Kiss* aligns it with the folk-oriented works of this period, though its primary influence is not folk music, but English ballad opera. Vaughan Williams alluded to works in that tradition by John Gay (*Polly*, Gay's sequel to *The Beggar's Opera*) and Gilbert and Sullivan (including *The Mikado* and *The Yeoman of the Guard*) when he was corresponding with Evelyn Sharp about the libretto, which was clearly patterned after the model of mannered comedies by Oscar Wilde or W. S. Gilbert himself. The overarching storyline—a complicated tale of love and revenge centering on Tormentilla, a sorcerer's daughter raised on poisons intended to kill the first man she kisses—engages the usual tropes of mistaken identity and romantic intrigue that regularly tip into light-hearted absurdity.

However, there was a conspicuous gap between Vaughan Williams's broad vision for the piece and Sharp's ability to render suitable words, a problem he realized early on. "We've really got to make up our minds whether this is to be a musical comedy or real comic opera," he implored Sharp. "In musical comedy (or ballad opera) the music is purely incidental i.e. the music c^d be left out and the drama w^d remain intact. In comic opera at certain points (usually the finale) the drama is carried on through the music," and he pointed out examples of both practices merging in the libretto.[35] Sharp, unfortunately, lacked confidence in adapting the source material, and so Vaughan Williams took an active hand in cutting, reorganizing, rewriting, and editing her efforts, all the while cajoling her into crafting something he could work with. Unsurprisingly, the textual result was largely unsatisfactory. After multiple post-premiere revisions, Vaughan Williams finally purchased the copyright to the libretto after Sharp's death, and had the prose dialogue replaced with rhyming couplets.[36]

Not all of the problems with *The Poisoned Kiss* can be blamed on Sharp, however. For a romantic comedy, the music favors the romantic aspect far more than the comic. This is slightly puzzling, for Vaughan Williams himself was quite funny; examples of his ready wit and humor abound throughout his correspondence and writings. Yet when it came to composition, he bluntly stated, "I hate jokes in music," and generally lacked the Sullivanesque capacity or inclination to play the musical straight man.[37] That is, in passages where one would expect the score to recede and allow the words to shine, Vaughan Williams instead competes for the listener's attention, making it difficult for the libretto's clever wordplay to emerge. As a result, the most effective musical passages tend to be the most lyrical ones: the lullaby Tormentilla sings to her pet cobra in Act I, or her duets with the Empress ("Love breaks all rules") in Act III and with her would-be paramour, Amaryllis, in Act I ("Blue larkspur in a garden"). As flaws go, there are worse ones; however, the result is that *The Poisoned Kiss* falls short of what one would expect from an artist of Vaughan Williams's talent and wit. One suspects that the beauty of his lines would have been complemented by lighter, overtly comedic passages analogous to those in Mozart's *Die Zauberflöte*, a work in a similar vein that he admired very much.

Far more satisfying were two cantatas that debuted only a few months later: *Five Tudor Portraits* and *Dona Nobis Pacem*. Though their expressive aims were very different—the first, sonic studies evoking characters from a bygone era; the second, a succession of warnings and reflections of all-too-contemporary significance—both capture Vaughan Williams at the height of his compositional powers. Forging such wide stylistic ranges, vivid textual imagery, and subtle musical details necessitated a blazing creative fire, but the effort took its toll. By the end of the year, he was burnt out, uncertain if he would ever write another piece.

As with Vaughan Williams's religious works, *Five Tudor Portraits* highlights the humanity, both sublime and ridiculous, of John Skelton's characters. We have, representing the ridiculous, the "comely crinkled, wondrously wrinkled" brewer and taverner Elinor Rumming of Leatherhead; "the two-faced and fork-tongued" John Jayberd, parish clerk of Diss, Norfolk; and Jolly Rutterkin, a swaggering swell "as wise as a duck." The generic descriptions preceding these movements—Ballad, Burlesca, and Scherzo, respectively—indicate both their narrative content and dramatic tone. The larger-than-life Elinor Rumming is toasted in a sociable litany of anecdotes, rumors, memories, and tributes, an array reflected in the unpredictably sectional form (into which the wanderings of one Drunken Alice prove particularly diverting). John Jayberd receives a far less affectionate portrayal in the raucously grotesque requiem for men's chorus, which presages certain passages from Carl Orff's *Carmina Burana* (1937). Rather than commemorating his life, this satirical eulogy celebrates this quarrelsome and malicious clerk's death in a hodgepodge of Latin and English, careening between expostulations of splenetic fury and more leisurely recountings of his various sins. The closing Scherzo represents the opposite side of this coin: the dandified Rutterkin is clearly a wastrel of the first water, but the trumpet call and cries of "hoyda!" heralding his arrival convey his roguish charm, enhanced by the solo baritone's delightfully vacuous sartorial commentary.

For sublimity, however, we turn to Pretty Bess and Jane Scroop. Technically, it is not Bess we hear in this brief Intermezzo, but her heartbroken former lover. He is a simple man, and his plaint is straightforward and solemn, if not terribly imaginative. Appropriately, Vaughan Williams has assigned the baritone soloist a melody spanning only a ninth, with easy naturalistic declamation set against a reassuringly steady accompaniment—though the echoes from the chorus suggest greater depths beneath the seemingly artless facade. The emotional core of the work, however, lies in young Jane Scroop's lament on the death of her pet bird, Philip Sparrow, at the hand (or paw) of the churlish cat Gib. Unlike John Jayberd's funeral service, this is no parody. Even if Jane's earnest words did not make the case, the designation of this movement as a Romanza—which Vaughan Williams typically reserved for expressions of the most profound sincerity—tells us her grief was real and deeply felt. Her recounting of Philip's countenance and habits reminds us that the absence of everyday routines leave the biggest gaps when loved ones pass, while the chorus of birds weaves a breathtaking tapestry of sound in honor of their fallen comrade. Remarkably, this movement avoids any hint of mawkishness or sentimentality. For someone who allegedly was not very fond of children, Vaughan Williams understood them very well, and respected the honesty of their emotional responses enough to treat them with the seriousness that they deserved.

Dona Nobis Pacem strikes a very different tone, for the affairs it addressed were far less distant, and reflected Vaughan Williams's deep concerns about the political situation in Europe. Beginning in 1933, he made annual donations to the Society for the Protection of Science and Learning; his 1935 contribution went in support of an exhibition called "Artists against Fascism," and in 1936 he co-signed a letter, written to *The Times,* expressing support for Spain's Republican government. Given the backdrop of increasingly powerful fascist regimes in Germany and Italy—and the nascent threat posed by the British Union of Fascists at home—it is no surprise that Vaughan Williams's creative thoughts returned to the horrors of war.

Like his other pieces inspired by or connected to conflict, *Dona Nobis Pacem* ultimately expressed hope for a better future, but the path was neither straight nor easy. With the titular opening phrase employed as a refrain, the piece commences with three poems from Whitman's *Drum Taps* of 1865 ("Beat! Beat! Drums," "Reconciliation," and "Dirge for Two Veterans") that reflected his experience as a volunteer nurse during the American Civil War. Whitman evoked the chaos of total warfare in "Beat! Beat! Drums" more than half a century before blitzkrieg entered the lexicon, and so Vaughan Williams's music is appropriately apocalyptic, cramming fistfuls of words into irregular, unpredictable phrases against a tattoo of bugles and the thumping of terrible drums, a Dies Irae of man's own creation.

The terror cannot be sustained, however, and gives way to "Reconciliation," the shimmeringly transparent texture and sensitive text setting of which conveys some of the cantata's most ethereal music. The "Dirge for Two Veterans" that follows is the work's longest movement, and was in fact completed in 1911. Why Vaughan Williams set it aside at the time we do not know, but the links to his prewar idiom are audible in its rhythmic regularity and formal spaciousness. This contrasts with the starkly declaimed protest of Quaker and Radical parliamentarian John Bright against the Crimean War: "The Angel of Death has been abroad throughout the land; you may almost hear the beating of his wings. There is no one as of old . . . to sprinkle with blood the lintel and the two side-posts of our doors, that he may spare and pass on."[38]

This passage is succeeded by a wrenching choral reprise of "Dona nobis pacem," but as the text from the Book of Jeremiah that ensues makes clear: "We looked for peace, but no good came . . . The harvest is past, the summer is ended, and we are not saved."

And it is here, at the knife edge of despair, that Vaughan Williams offers a glimpse of salvation from the Book of Daniel: "O man greatly beloved, fear not, peace be unto thee, be strong, yea, be strong." Finally, the un-relenting grimness is tempered by expressions of hope: nation shall not lift up a sword against nation, mercy and truth are met, the nations are gathered together, and on Earth there is peace and goodwill. The music is initially joyous, releasing all the tension of the previous five movements, the energy gradually ebbing away into calm reflection. Yet hope seems more elusive than usual, for the final cadence is an uncertain resolution from a seventh chord on the submediant to the tonic. When the soloist sings her final E, "it does not bring a sense of completion or resolu-tion: peace may be present, and it may be possible, but it is a tentative, fragile thing."[39] The peace hoped for so fervently by those who heard this work was no less palpable to the composer, though for reasons that had as much to do with his own doubts and fears as with the shadow falling over Europe.

Photo 1 Arthur Vaughan Williams
(© Vaughan Williams Charitable Trust—
from the Collection of Ursula Vaughan
Williams)

Photo 2 Margaret Susan Vaughan Williams
with the family dog, Coffee (© Vaughan
Williams Charitable Trust—from the
Collection of Ursula Vaughan Williams)

Photo 3 Leith Hill Place (photograph by Robert Weedon)

Photo 4   Hervey Vaughan Williams, 1885
(© Vaughan Williams Charitable Trust—
from the Collection of Ursula Vaughan
Williams)

Photo 5   Meggie Vaughan Williams, 1885
(© Vaughan Williams Charitable Trust—
from the Collection of Ursula Vaughan
Williams)

Photo 6   RVW, 1885 (© Vaughan Williams Charitable Trust—from the Collection of Ursula
Vaughan Williams)

Photo 7   Charterhouse Public School, Godalming, 1888

Photo 8   RVW at Charterhouse, ca. 1889 (© Vaughan Williams Charitable Trust—from the Collection of Ursula Vaughan Williams)

Photo 9   Hubert Parry, 1893

Photo 10   Charles Wood (photograph by J. Palmer Clarke, courtesy of the Royal College of Music, London)

Photo 11   Charles Villiers Stanford, 1894

Photo 12   Maurice Ravel, 1910

Photo 13   Ralph ("Randolph") Wedgwood and RVW at Cambridge, 1890s (© Vaughan Williams Charitable Trust—from the Collection of Ursula Vaughan Williams)

Photo 14   "Rough music" at Hooton Roberts, 1901, L–R: Ivor Gatty, RVW, Adeline Vaughan Williams, Nicholas Gatty (© Vaughan Williams Charitable Trust—from the Collection of Ursula Vaughan Williams)

Photo 15   RVW, ca. 1903 (© Vaughan Williams Charitable Trust—from the Collection of Ursula Vaughan Williams)

Photo 16   Adeline Vaughan Williams, 1908 (© Vaughan Williams Charitable Trust—from the Collection of Ursula Vaughan Williams)

Photo 17   R. O. Morris, ca. 1920

Photo 18   Martin Shaw, 1928 (photograph courtesy of Isobel Montgomery Campbell)

Photo 19   Cecil Sharp, 1916

Photo 20   George Butterworth, ca. 1910

Photo 21 With the RAMC near Écoivres, 1916; RVW at far right, Harry Steggles second from right (© Vaughan Williams Charitable Trust—from the Collection of Ursula Vaughan Williams)

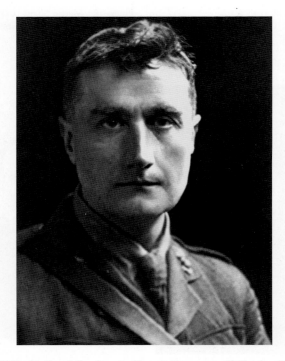

Photo 22 RVW in his Royal Garrison Artillery uniform, 1917 (© Vaughan Williams Charitable Trust—from the Collection of Ursula Vaughan Williams)

Photo 23   Gustav Holst and RVW hiking in the Malvern Hills, 1921 (photograph by W. G. Whittaker, © Vaughan Williams Charitable Trust—from the Collection of Ursula Vaughan Williams)

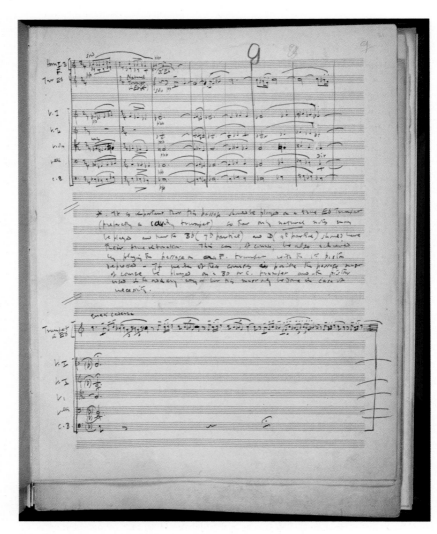

Photo 24   RVW's manuscript score for the *Pastoral Symphony*, second movement (©
Vaughan Williams Charitable Trust)

Photo 25   RVW, 1921 (photograph by E. O. Hoppé, © Vaughan Williams Charitable Trust—from the Collection of Ursula Vaughan Williams)

Photo 26   RVW in the garden at White Gates, 1930 (© Vaughan Williams Charitable Trust—from the Collection of Ursula Vaughan Williams)

Photo 27   Haymaking at White Gates, 1934, L–R: Bob de Ropp, Molly Darbishire, RVW, Elizabeth Darbishire (© Vaughan Williams Charitable Trust—from the Collection of Ursula Vaughan Williams)

Photo 28   Ursula Wood, 1936 (photograph by Somerset Murray, © Vaughan Williams
Charitable Trust—from the Collection of Ursula Vaughan Williams)

Photo 29   RVW with his cat, Foxy, 1948 (photograph by Dudley Styles, © Vaughan
Williams Charitable Trust—from the Collection of Ursula Vaughan Williams)

Photo 30   Adeline Vaughan Williams, 1948 (photograph by Rosamond Carr, © Vaughan Williams Charitable Trust—from the Collection of Ursula Vaughan Williams)

Photo 31   Gil Jenkins, 1945 (photograph by Walter Stoneman; © National Portrait Gallery, London)

Photo 32   Rehearsing with the Boyd Neel Orchestra, 1953

Photo 33   RVW and Ursula Vaughan Williams in Gloucester, 1954 (© Vaughan Williams Charitable Trust—from the Collection of Ursula Vaughan Williams)

Photo 34   In the drawing room at 10 Hanover Terrace, 1956

"One Has to Write as One Feels" (1937–1943)

I N EARLY 1937, VAUGHAN WILLIAMS OVERSAW THE PREMIERES OF AN
overture for an EDFS masque and two pieces (*Flourish for a Coronation*
and the *Festival Te Deum in F Major*) for the investiture of George VI,
while performances of the recently revised *In the Fen Country*, a revival
of *Hugh the Drover*, and the debut of *Riders to the Sea* all waited in the
wings. However, the strain of work and recent events was beginning to
show. Holst's death, deadline pressures, the unsettled political climate—all
contributed to Vaughan Williams feeling "absolutely dried up at present
and . . . feeling that I shall never again write a note of music."[1] Even
spending a few weeks in London with Adeline failed to help, for his
mother died on 20 November while they were there (only five months
after the death of Adeline's younger brother William). His spirits took
another hit when Ivor Gurney died on Boxing Day, and Ravel only two
days later.

Nevertheless, some sparks of inspiration still kindled. On 24 January
1938, he cautiously accepted an invitation from Henry Wood to write a
work for his forthcoming Jubilee Concert that October. Wood stipulated
only that it be "a choral work that can be used at any time, and for any
occasion," and gave Vaughan Williams free reign in choosing the text.[2]
The composer was less enthusiastic about receiving a ballet proposal
based on Edmund Spenser's *Epithalamion*, finding it "too realistic and
not idealized enough," excessively long, and overcomplicated.[3] Douglas
Kennedy had sent him the scenario at the behest of a young woman

who had previously offered an equally unsuitable balletic scheme for *The Ballad of Clerk Saunders*. After several months of three-way correspondence, Kennedy told Vaughan Williams to invite the woman to lunch—at her behest—so the two could talk it over in person. And so, on 31 March 1938, Vaughan Williams met Mrs. Joan Ursula Penton Wood, née Lock, known to her friends as Ursula.

Born in Malta to a military family connected with the Governor's office, Ursula Lock had an itinerant childhood, having been raised largely by her grandparents and later sent to boarding schools. She indulged streaks of self-reliance and romantic bohemianism during a brief stint as a student with the Old Vic in 1932—shortly before marrying Michael Wood, an army officer eleven years her senior—and in her writing of poetry. Although not especially musical herself, she remembered the powerful impact of hearing *Job* at Sadler's Wells, an experience that may explain why it was Vaughan Williams to whom she solicited her scenarios.

Despite their married statuses and forty-year age difference, Vaughan Williams and Wood were instantly attracted, much to their surprise. "He had, it seemed, expected a sensible matron in sensible shoes," while Wood had arrived in high heels; similarly, she had not "expected someone so large and so beautiful."[4] They had an expensive lunch at the Jardin des Gourmets, went to a movie, "ended up sitting by the Serpentine and talking about madrigal poems," and, before she saw him off at Victoria Station, shared a passionate kiss in a taxi.[5] She realized "I'd absolutely got it badly, very badly. I had fallen in love and that was very difficult. Thank goodness it happened."[6] The same was true for the composer. Within weeks, the two consummated an intense and deeply felt love affair. Vaughan Williams's letters to Wood over the next several months contain risqué comments, references to eagerly anticipated meetings in London, and reactions to her poetry. The depth of their intimacy—and the speed of its development—is indicated by a letter Vaughan Williams wrote in October 1938, after Wood attended a performance of the *Pastoral Symphony*:

> I'm glad you liked the symph. I did rather myself after many years. It is really <u>war time</u> music—a great deal of it incubated when I used to go up night after night in the ambulance waggon at Écoives [sic] & we went up a steep hill & there was a wonderful Corot-like landscape in the sunset—its [sic] not really Lambkins frisking at all as most people take for granted.[7]

The revelation of such a personal detail, so directly stated, about the inspiration behind one of his compositions is nearly unparalleled in Vaughan Williams's correspondence, and reveals his feelings for her more clearly than any number of epistolary double entendres about spending "evenings in woods."[8]

Around the same time that Vaughan Williams met Wood, Imogen Holst introduced him to Robert Müller-Hartmann. A German composer and refugee, he and his family had recently moved to Dorking, where they initially lived with mutual friends of the Vaughan Williamses, Jacob (Yanya) and Genia Hornstein.[9] Müller-Hartmann later served as one of Vaughan Williams's copyists—upon whom the composer increasingly relied by the 1930s, when such work became too onerous for Adeline—and became a trusted advisor and friend.

But all this was yet to come. In early 1938, Vaughan Williams was busy arranging the hymn tune MILES LANE ("All Hail the Power") for the Three Choirs Festival, preparing for another pageant collaboration with Forster (*England's Pleasant Land*) in July, and completing the *Serenade to Music*—for orchestra and a chorus of sixteen hand-picked vocalists— which he sent to Henry Wood in early June, shortly before an awkward award ceremony in Germany. The previous July, Prof. Hermann Fiedler of Queen's College, Oxford, informed Vaughan Williams that he had been nominated as Britain's inaugural recipient of the Shakespeare Prize from the Hanseatic University (today, the University of Hamburg). The award ostensibly recognized outstanding achievement in the arts, but the circumstances behind its dispensation were considerably murkier.[10] Vaughan Williams was no fool. His first impulse was to refuse, partly because such recognition of a British musician in Germany was "so unprecedented that I want to make sure that it is made only from a desire to recognise art and learning in this country." After informing Fiedler about his opposition to the Nazi government ("I belong to more than one English Society whose object is to combat all that the present German régime stands for"), he took some time to consider the offer before accepting in August.[11]

Vaughan Williams's rationalization notwithstanding, the Prize's presentation was of course a political gesture. It would not have been offered without the full knowledge of the Minister of Propaganda, Joseph Goebbels, though the British Foreign Office may not have been aware of this, and

Vaughan Williams clearly was not.[12] The award ceremony on 15 June 1938 came off without incident, although Vaughan Williams told Laurence Binyon that he had to make the Nazi salute on one occasion "where, after the health of the King of England there followed that of 'Unser Führer,'" likely at the dinner given in his honor that evening.[13] He was relieved to return home, but currency restrictions left him unable to claim the Prize's 10,000-mark honorarium (approximately £800 at the time, or just under $70,000 in 2020). Still, accepting the award weighed on his conscience. That November, he co-signed a letter to *The Times* with eighty-seven other public figures recording "our solemn protest, before the conscience of civilization, against the persecution of the Jews in Germany,"[14] and later invested considerable time and effort as Vice-Chair of the Dorking and District Committee for Refugees from Central Europe.

Having published the composer's settings of a Benedictus and Agnus Dei in 1938, OUP followed it in 1939 with a full set of Morning, Communion, and Evening Services. Vaughan Williams also wrote a short *Flourish for Wind Band* at Alan Bush's request to open a Festival of Music for the People on 1 April, and made enough progress with Wood on *Epithalamion* (now called *The Bridal Day*) to play through it at the end of the month. In fact, by June—with the world premiere of *Five Variants of "Dives and Lazarus"* in New York, a journey to Trinity College (Dublin) to receive an honorary Mus. Doc., and time spent writing his Suite for Pipes—it seemed that his "permanently sluggish imagination" was abating.[15] Particularly intriguing was a casual reference made in January 1939 about having "musical plans on hold which will occupy me for a long time."[16] What these entailed he did not say: possibly any of the projects previously mentioned, or the scenario for an opera based on the story of Belshazzar that he was considering. Most likely, however, it involved the earliest stages of sketching the Symphony (No. 5) in D Major, which he soon realized would convey a rather different tone than that of his previous contribution to the genre. He implied as much in a letter to an admirer of his Fourth Symphony: "Old age has brought a quieter method in what I am now writing (probably you would not like it so much!) After all one has to write as one feels—and if it is all right so much the better, if not so much the worse."[17]

Unfortunately, his priorities were irresistibly refocused by the outbreak of war in September 1939. In keeping with his past attitudes about the South African and 1914–1918 conflicts, he was ambivalent about the reasons for declaring war, but accepted its reality and was committed to its success. "It is wretched—but if we look on it merely as a bore we shan't push through with it—as we've got to do now unless we want to live perpetually in the state we are living now."[18] Though far too old to enlist, Vaughan Williams contributed to the war effort in other capacities. By October, he was working "with internees & evacuees & low-brow concerts for the troops,"[19] and helped Myra Hess organize her lunchtime concert series at the National Gallery. He also lent his name to an array of wartime arts organizations,[20] set up public lecture-concerts in Dorking under the title "Music in Wartime," and pursued such mundanities as digging a Victory Garden, supervising local fire-watchers, and collecting scrap metal door to door.[21]

As classes at the RCM were suspended because of the war, Vaughan Williams could dedicate himself to these and other activities, including composition. Before 1939 was out, he completed *A Hymn of Freedom*, notable for its publication in *The Daily Telegraph* just before OUP's official release.[22] He also began working on a piece playable for any instrumental ensemble, published in 1943 as *Household Music*, and arranged a series of mostly Elizabethan songs and dance tunes for a star-studded production of Shakespeare's *Twelfth Night* (which went unrealized until a performance in Kidderminster eight years later).[23] The continued disruption of RCM classes into 1940 led Vaughan Williams to retire after that year's Midsummer Term, but it also enabled him to accept more commissions than usual from the BBC and other national institutions between 1939 and 1945. Most of these works were of minor artistic importance, but fulfilled his desire to contribute to the war effort.

In August 1940, frustrated at the treatment of refugee musicians, he turned to his professional colleagues for help: "I feel that it is time that British musicians got together and looked for the release of their fellow musicians which are interned." He proposed expanding the scope of a governmental White Paper establishing categories of internees eligible for release. "Musicians do not appear to come under any category in the 'White Paper,'" Vaughan Williams observed, "but perhaps by a joint letter we could persuade the authorities to broaden their interpretation of 'work of national importance' . . . and to point out that to fructify the life of the country is of national importance and the fact that artistic and intelligent people who will spread the gospel of anti-Nazism are an asset to the country."[24] The proposal elicited the desired reforms, expanding coverage to "persons of eminent distinction who have made outstanding contributions to Art, Science, learning or Letters,"[25] and led the government to appoint Vaughan Williams as Chair of the Home Office Committee for the Release of Interned Alien Musicians. Over the next several years, he worked to improve conditions for all interned musicians—eminently distinguished and otherwise—securing the release of dozens. It is to his credit that he pursued this work while worried about the impact an influx of German and Austrian musicians might have on English musical life. He had expressed such concerns some years earlier to Jani Strasser, head of Glyndebourne's musical staff, and to Ferdinand Rauter in 1942, upon being invited to become a patron of the newly established Anglo-Austrian Music Society:

> We want your art and we want your help—Become Englishmen—try to assimilate our artistic ideals and then strengthen and fertilize them from your own incomparable art—But do not force a "Little Austria" on England—keeping itself apart from the "untouchables" and having its own musical life without any reference to the life going on around. This would not only be of no value to our country but would actually be a disservice—because people seeing this little body of musical aristocrats with their art perfected by generations of artistic endeavor would think that was the only art worth having and that they could reap without sowing by a mere mechanical imitation of Austrian music.[26]

Fortunately, Rauter understood that Vaughan Williams's comments represented a complicated mixture of admiration for the German musical tradition and concern about the vulnerability of Britain's; moreover, his refugee work helped counter the impression that these were the sentiments of a xenophobic Little Englander. Rauter reassured him that the organization encouraged "mutual understanding and esteem, so that we can work as friends and brothers, and in a happier future, reap what we have sown together,"[27] a sentiment Vaughan Williams heartily endorsed elsewhere. "I am as you know a convinced nationalist in all that concerns our individual & cultural life—But I believe this can only be achieved by living in unity with other nations in all those matters which are our common interest."[28]

All of these activities took place against a backdrop of personal loss. Several people close to Vaughan Williams died in 1940, including his old friends Maurice Amos and Donald Tovey, and Adeline's brother H. A. L. Fisher, but two deaths hit him particularly hard. The first was Dorothy Longman's in June, which led him to bleakly speculate, "Perhaps there will be no more happiness or peace for any of us now and we must be thankful for what has been."[29] He dedicated the beautifully stark motet *Valiant for Truth* to her memory, a setting from *The Pilgrim's Progress* commemorating the passage of that good man to his just reward. Her passing was followed only three months later by Honorine Williamson's. She had recently left White Gates for London, having married trumpeter Bernard Brown in February; tragically, she was killed in an air raid on 2 September. Her death devastated Adeline, to whom Honorine was almost a surrogate daughter, and Ralph as well. He initially visited her gravesite daily, then weekly, and was heartbroken to the point of tears when, after the passage of time and the addition of so many more cemetery plots, he could no longer find hers.

Vaughan Williams was naturally concerned for Wood's safety, since she was still in London at the beginning of 1940. They still met and wrote regularly, but he was increasingly guilty about his infidelity.[30] By October, Wood had relocated to Bude, Cornwall, where her husband was stationed at a radar unit. Vaughan Williams encouraged her to continue working at her poetry despite the circumstances. "My goodness what wonderful things to possess—to have beauty & to be able to <u>make</u> beauty. The Nazis can't destroy that."[31] He addressed similar issues in a short essay for *The Listener* ("The Composer in War Time") published in May, in which he considered not only the challenges the war presented for composers, but also the opportunities it provided for innovation. "Art is a compromise between what we want to achieve and what circumstances allow us to achieve. It is out of these very compromises that the supreme art often springs; the highest comes when you least expect it."[32]

Just before Christmas, *Six Choral Songs—To be Sung in Time of War* had its broadcast debut; shortly before, Boult approached Vaughan Williams with a commission from the BBC for a choral song (*England, My England*). It nearly didn't happen, however, because Vaughan Williams returned the commission over the Corporation's blacklisting of Alan Bush. The BBC objected to Bush's signing the People's Convention, a political manifesto linked to the Communist Party of Great Britain (to which Bush belonged), stating that any signatory "cannot be offered any further broadcasting engagements."[33] Despite disapproving of Bush's views, Vaughan Williams told the BBC Director General that he disagreed even more with their "victimization of private opinion."[34] He sent copies of his letter to Boult and *The Times*, which published it on 15 March; in response, the BBC hastily rescinded the ban, resulting in Bush's thanks and the renewal of the commission.

Vaughan Williams also made his initial foray into film music composition in 1940, writing the score for Ortus Films' *49th Parallel* (1941), which he described as "interesting & exasperating work . . . Writing in seconds to the stop watch is rather fun & composing & <u>scoring</u> extra bars during the rehearsal interval (5 minutes)."[35] The experience (and the money) led him to write five more film scores in as many years for commercial studios and government agencies, notably the Ministry of Information, and he wrote an extended essay on the subject in 1945.

Emmie Morris died of a heart ailment in May 1941; soon after, R. O. Morris came to live with the Vaughan Williamses at White Gates, where he stayed for several years—the latest in the ever-changing rota of relatives, friends, and refugees who found sanctuary there during the war. This included Ursula Wood, an increasingly regular visitor to Dorking. The intimate aspect of her relationship with Vaughan Williams remained secret, of course, including the fact that she had an abortion in May, and that Vaughan Williams may have been the father. Even more surprisingly, she gradually assumed a place in Adeline's affections previously held by Honorine Williamson, in part because Wood was willing to assist Ralph with various personal and professional responsibilities that Adeline no longer could.

One such obligation came from Mary Glasgow, Secretary-General of the Committee for the Encouragement of Music and the Arts (CEMA). Vaughan Williams joined the Committee following Walford Davies's death in March, and remained a member for several years after its reorganization as the Arts Council in 1946. The Leith Hill Musical Competition also underwent a transformation. In order to qualify for a Carnegie Grant, which was not available to musical competitions—only concerts—it was reorganized as the Leith Hill Festival Choir in 1940, dropping the competitive aspect until 1946. The year ended with Vaughan Williams completing a set of carol arrangements for British troops stationed in Iceland, and deciding that the nascent Fifth Symphony was ready for a play-through, "to see if I like it well enough to go on with it."[36] Finzi and Howells were invited to the rehearsal, and their positive assessment confirmed his own opinion about the piece, leading him to move ahead.

Despite his continued worries about a lack of inspiration, Vaughan Williams had completed drafts for no fewer than four pieces by April 1942. These included the Concerto in A Minor for Oboe and Strings, a revised version of the withdrawn Double Trio of 1939, *The Lake in the Mountains* for solo piano, and *The Airmen's Hymn* for unison chorus, all of which he submitted to OUP for safekeeping.[37] He also turned to his back catalogue, soliciting advice from Michael Mullinar on revising the piano part for *On Wenlock Edge*, revisiting his decade-old *Overture to Henry V* for brass band, and asking Müller-Hartmann to arrange the *Songs of Travel* for string orchestra. Even recent works came in for re-consideration: in May, he asked Harold Child to write words fitting the prelude from *49th Parallel* ("I believe it might make a good community song for some high falutin words about Canada or Freedom or Federal Union or something").[38] Child obliged, and OUP published the result ("The New Commonwealth") the following year.

In June 1942, Michael Wood—then in charge of antiaircraft defenses near Portsmouth—unexpectedly died of a heart attack. Since he was not stationed abroad, Ursula had not seriously considered the possibility of his death, let alone from natural causes, so the news came as an overwhelming shock; she injured her foot soon after and was left temporarily lame. Adeline, knowing that Wood's parents lived in Canada and were thus unable to help, invited her to recuperate at White Gates. Morris struck up an easy friendship with her, while Adeline's fondness for the young woman grew over the ensuing weeks. Wood's new living circumstances allowed her to observe Vaughan Williams's working habits firsthand. "To my infinite surprise [he] suggested I should bring my writing into the study while he worked, and cleared a patch on one of his tables for me. I sat in the window seat, he at his desk, dashing to the piano every now and then, or stopping to say something about anything in the world, from weather for gardening to a curious technical point about film music . . . or cross-questioning me about what I was doing."[39] After she returned to London, she followed his advice about making "a life in London your permanence & White Gates a series of episodes," and became one of the couple's most frequent guests.[40]

The unusual relationship between Ralph, Adeline, and Ursula highlights Vaughan Williams's complex and contradictory attitudes toward women (though such romantic triangles were not uncommon among the creative classes of this time, such as members of the Bloomsbury Group, or even the Hornsteins and Müller-Hartmanns). Growing up in a household run by women instilled an early respect in him for their authority, and he valued Adeline as an intellectual equal whose insightful criticism, talent, and assistance helped him build and sustain his career. Indeed, to a degree unusual for his time, he relied on women's advice and abilities throughout his life. Besides Adeline, some of the most prominent include Evangeline and Fanny Farrer, Lucy Broadwood, Ella Mary Leather, Maud Karpeles, Vally Lasker, Nora Day, Margery Cullen, and his sister, Meggie, all whom he treated, as he did his many female students, with the respect due to fellow professionals.

It is no secret that he was attracted by and attractive to intelligent and talented young women (to whom he referred as "nieces" or "nymphs"), whose beauty and attention he enjoyed and with whom he would flirt, often with delighted reciprocity.[41] Adeline was well aware of this behavior toward the nieces (to whom she was "Aunt Adeline" to his "Uncle Ralph"), and "recognized that their company gave him pleasure and thought it good for him, and she encouraged their visits."[42] However, he also took care to avoid overfamiliarity, teasing, or flirting when he knew it would make the recipient uncomfortable. His letters to Imogen Holst and Ina Boyle, for example, remain quite formal despite his long and cordial relationships with them.

Yet this behavior exists alongside his affair with Ursula Wood, who was not the only other woman to whom he had made romantic overtures while married. Bobby Longman, for instance, recalled his wife, Dorothy, once "showed me in the tower of Ludlow Castle a rough carving of 2 hearts intertwined which [she and Ralph] had done together some years before. How and why they were there I do not know." He continued,

> I remember D telling me that her mother had questioned her about going about so much with R—this was well before 1914—& had said "You are going it with R." I remember also a party someone gave after a concert—very

likely after the 1st performance of the London Symphony. R & D were by way of coming but did not appear & someone lightly said "oh, he's gone off with his pet." D told me once—probably in the mid 20's—that R had wanted to kiss her & that she had said "No R that would spoil it all." I think in some way they were in love with each other but D's remark puts the relationship into its proper place. I was not always wise & understanding about all this but—strange to say—it never affected my affection for R nor Adeline's for D. Adeline knew more about R than he knew himself! Later R took to going about with Fanny Farrer; this made D a little sad but their affection to each other remained to her death in 1940.[43]

Longman felt this account provided "a further insight into R's need for a woman's friendship, one who cd go about with him & be an intimate companion. Adeline alas after her illness cd not do this."[44]

There are some inconsistencies with Longman's statement, including identifying Adeline as invalid long before she was, and the ambiguity of "intimate companion," since it seems Dorothy rebuffed any sexual advances. But the broader implication—that a physical relationship was less important to Adeline than to Ralph—is highly plausible. According to Bob de Ropp, Adeline "was far more uptight about sex than Uncle Ralph. Unthinkable for her was another sexual scenario" because "such behavior was taboo. [Ralph] could never have got Aunt Adeline's consent to such a sensible arrangement. He was far too honest to deceive her—probably could not have done so, as she was amazingly intuitive, almost psychic, and would have known what was happening."[45] This comment echoes Longman's observation about Adeline's perceptiveness, while Jean Stewart described her as "a wise woman" with "great self-control."[46]

To that end, it is exceedingly likely that Adeline knew of her husband's affair with Wood; however, it also seems she was not only unconcerned by it, but used it to her advantage. By befriending Wood—and, by all accounts, Adeline's affection was entirely genuine—she was able to control their relationship's power dynamic. She was unthreatened by Wood's physical intimacy with her husband (indeed, she appreciated Wood's devotion to Ralph's needs, physical or otherwise, and thanked her regularly for assisting him on trips or at rehearsals) because she believed, correctly, that she retained an even deeper emotional intimacy with him. Wood confessed that this made her "*madly* jealous,"[47] because it relegated her to a position she never anticipated and could not counter. In Adeline, Wood met a woman as smart, strong, and confident as herself, qualities that she must have grudgingly respected—and that may explain Vaughan Williams's attraction to them both.[48]

In November 1942, Vaughan Williams celebrated his seventieth birthday, in honor of which the BBC broadcast a series of concerts. Frank Howes wrote a laudatory tribute in *The Listener*, while Elizabeth Maconchy, Cecil Armstrong Gibbs, Constant Lambert, and Gerald Finzi all honored him with compositional dedications. Vaughan Williams was embarrassed by the attention, but took the opportunity to repay the many compliments showered upon him. His response to conductor and keyboardist Arnold Goldsborough was typical:

> I was much moved by your generous letter. If I have helped to "lead" music & musicians at all then my 70 years have not been altogether wasted.
>
> You must not call yourself a "hack" musician—it is just what you are not. You have genius and power—but your genius does not run on routine lines—& for that reason you have never found a post worthy of your great powers.[49]

A slightly later message to Herbert Howells that praised his early Piano Quartet in A Minor (1916) touched on the reasons for the continued dissatisfaction with his own music.

> I daresay you are annoyed at having the "sins of your youth" praised—I feel the same when people single out the *Sea Symphony*—or rather I feel that perhaps all the rest of my life has been wasted—perhaps it is true of both of us & we have never got back the "first careless rapture" of our early works—but you have this advantage that you already knew your job in 1918.[50]

Yet he pressed on, writing film scores for *Coastal Command* and *The People's Land*, incidental music for a BBC radio play production of *The Pilgrim's Progress* (adapted by Edward Sackville-West), an arrangement of "The Blessing of the Swords" from Meyerbeer's *Les Huguenots*, and a pair of gifts: a short piano piece for Genia Hornstein—*A Winter Piece (for Genia)*—and two movements of a new string quartet delivered to a delighted Jean Stewart for her birthday. "I am still going about in a state bordering between tears and laughter," she wrote excitedly, "with an inane expression on my face which must be most trying for those who come into contact with me."[51]

The most important work of this period, however, was the newly completed Symphony in D Major, which he described as "all very quiet & not at all like the one before."[52] Boult summed up the general response in saying that he and his wife, Ann, "both feel that its serene loveliness is completely satisfying in these times & shows, as only music can, what we must work for when this madness is over."[53] This visionary quality places it squarely in the tradition of the *Pastoral Symphony*, another piece in which the tranquil expression belied the unsettled nature of its creation. But as the war raged on, Vaughan Williams's Fifth Symphony provided a glimpse of both the peace Britain fought for and the creative fire he felt had eluded him for so many years.

The Music of 1937–1943

F ROM A CREATIVE STANDPOINT, VAUGHAN WILLIAMS CLOSED OUT THE interwar period in much the same way that he initiated it: quietly, and with little apparent fuss. The large and varied works of the previous decade gave way to generally smaller and more intimate pieces, as though he were once again deliberately narrowing the focus of his imagination. Whether this was an attempt to consolidate his expressive vision or reflected his ongoing struggles with writer's block is unclear, but signs of this shift were apparent well before the privations of the Second World War made them all but inevitable.

One of the earliest examples of this change may be seen in the little-known but beautifully wrought Two Hymn-Tune Preludes for small orchestra, written in 1936 for the Three Choirs Festival, but included here because its modest scale and pastorally oriented expressive quality aligns better with subsequent works than with its more modernist contemporaries. Vaughan Williams's general disdain for Victorian hymn tunes notwithstanding, there were a few whose virtues he acknowledged, including EVENTIDE, by William H. Monk—the musical editor of *Hymns Ancient and Modern*—and J. B. Dykes's setting of DOMINUS REGIT ME. Considering that *The Poisoned Kiss*, *Five Tudor Portraits*, and *Dona Nobis Pacem* all debuted in 1936, the fact that he completed anything for the Three Choirs that year was remarkable enough; that the result should be two such exquisite and original treatments is astonishing. "Preludes" is the operative term, for these are free adaptations à la Bach: the scoring is delicate and transparent, with the melodic line always the central point of focus—whether in the oboe against a backdrop of slowly moving string suspensions in EVENTIDE, or woven amid the freely imitative texture of DOMINUS REGIT ME—conveying a sense of gentle inevitability as motives and melodies effortlessly spin out in both movements.

The past was also present in the *Flourish for a Coronation* and the *Festival Te Deum in F Major*, marking the coronation of George VI in 1937. Despite their titles, the *Festival Te Deum* was first performed at the coronation itself, while the *Flourish* had its premiere over a month earlier. Unfortunately, the *Festival Te Deum* does not rank among Vaughan Williams's best efforts. At once harmonically static and formally meandering, it offers little that is especially memorable, and those passages that are—like the melismas on "Lord" at the end of the first line—stand out for the wrong reasons. By contrast, the *Flourish* is an exciting work, full of pomp and grandeur. The title may imply a decorative fanfare for winds and percussion—a description befitting the slightly later *Flourish for Wind Band* (1939)[1]—but this choral-orchestral piece is more akin to a Georgian-era court ode. It is also one of the few works in which Vaughan Williams employs a large ensemble expressly to create a very loud noise indeed. The brass section alone calls for eight horns, six trumpets, three trombones, euphonium, and tuba; it also requires an alto saxophone, contrabassoon, bells, organ, and piano, though a more modestly scored alternative is available. But what is a coronation if not an excuse for flamboyance?[2] The opening of the *Flourish* provides this in spades: streams of notes in the winds and strings soar above a brass fanfare preceding the chorus's declaration of lines from First Kings: "Let the priest and the prophet anoint him king, and blow ye with the trumpet, and say, 'God save the King.'" This is succeeded by a *Largamente* for brass choir of conspicuously Handelian brilliance before alternating between choral arias and instrumental fanfares for the remainder of the first section. The second section adopts a contrastingly introspective tone: the tenors and basses open with a unison hymn tune beseeching the king to govern wisely and well, setting Chaucer's exhortation to King Richard II in his short poem *Lak of Stedfastnesse*, while the brief concluding passage reprises the opening fanfare, now set to text from the Agincourt Song.

The coronation works were the only newly completed ones debuting in 1937, not counting an English-language adaptation of Dvořák's *Te*

Deum (1892) for that year's Leith Hill Festival, or the Overture performed for an EFDS Masque but written in 1934.[3] However, one long-finished piece finally premiered late in the year: the single-act opera *Riders to the Sea*, a nearly verbatim adaptation of the eponymous drama by Irish playwright John Millington Synge.[4] Despite its modest dimensions, *Riders* represents one of Vaughan Williams's most thoroughly modernist works, both in terms of its musical language and bleakly fatalistic plot. Set on the Aran Islands off Ireland's west coast, the plot centers on Maurya, an old woman who has lost her husband and five of her six sons to the sea—one of them, Michael, only days earlier. Her last surviving boy, Bartley, insists on sailing to the horse fair at Connemara despite the threat of storms and Maurya's desperate pleas ("what is the price of a thousand horses against a son where there is one son only?"). Bartley leaves without the bread that his sisters Nora and Cathleen baked for his journey, so Maurya goes to intercept him; meanwhile, Nora and Cathleen determine that the clothes of a drowned man brought to them by the local priest are Michael's, and agonize how to tell their mother. She returns with the claim that she saw Michael riding behind Bartley on his way to the boat. Her daughters tell her otherwise—that Michael's body was washed ashore in Donegal—but Maurya recognizes the omen for what it is. Sure enough, a group of people arrive bearing a dripping burden: Bartley, drowned after being thrown onto the rocks by his pony. But Maurya's response is not despair, rather, blessed relief: "They are all gone now, and there isn't anything more the sea can do to me," she says. "It's a great rest I'll have now, and it's time surely."

As in *The Shepherds of the Delectable Mountains* and *Job*, Maurya's salvation hinges on the whim of either an incomprehensible God or pitiless Nature—here, possibly both—rather than her own actions. It is hard to read this recurring theme of redemption achieved through loss as anything other than a manifestation of survivor's guilt expressed by a veteran of the Great War, but it also suggests "that to acknowledge tragedy, however painful it may be, serves as a reminder that we have survived whatever trial has tested us."[5] Vaughan Williams often attempts to view tragedy through a lens of beauty, but *Riders to the Sea* tests that proposition's limits. The score's expressive efficiency arises largely from the degree to which octatonic sets dominate the musical language, although the opening of the work juxtaposes "areas of chromaticism and polytonality . . . with more stable, diatonic, modal passages," all linked by "common tones or elision of various scales."[6] As in *Job*, diatonicism frequently represents the enduring power of the human spirit, while octatonic scales and other unusual pitch collections embody nature's implacable force, but it can be difficult to tell where one ends and the other begins. *Riders to the Sea* is an appropriately dark composition for this time; though it clearly displays Vaughan Williams's mastery of technique, he remained doubtful about his own abilities and endurance—earlier in the year, he had flatly told Gerald Finzi that he was "no longer able to compose."[7] With his best friend dead, his wife increasingly fragile, and fascism rising in Europe, the future must have looked bleak indeed.

That changed after he met Ursula Wood in early 1938. To be clear, their affair did not effect an immediate cure for his writer's block, but from the very earliest days of their relationship, Vaughan Williams's letters to Wood mention books or poetry that he enjoyed, or react to those she sent or recommended, including her own poems. By the end of the year, their correspondence included extended discussions about text setting practices, suggesting that Vaughan Williams's imagination was stimulated not just by their physical relationship, but also from the discussions about literature—contemporary and classic, familiar and obscure—that he and Wood shared as their relationship deepened.

The *Serenade to Music* was the first tangible result of these exchanges. Vaughan Williams accepted the commission in late January, first met Ursula Wood in late March, and completed the *Serenade* by the beginning of June, just before leaving for Hamburg to accept the Shakespeare Prize. In this regard, his choice to set Lorenzo's soliloquy to Jessica from *The Merchant of Venice* was probably an unintentional coincidence; more revealing are its implications seen in the light of his affair with Wood, who allegedly assisted in its selection.[8] First, Lorenzo's words praising music were spoken to his beloved Jessica as they lay on the moonlit banks of Portia's house in Belmont. For Vaughan Williams, such a statement delivered under such conditions would indicate a deeply intimate confession, the kind reserved only for a very few who might understand. Second, it is worth remembering that Lorenzo and Jessica's love was taboo, representing as it did the union of a Christian and a Jew. This is not to suggest that Vaughan Williams was deliberately alluding to his own forbidden relationship by selecting this text—he was rarely so self-referential in his own music, and certainly not about such personal topics—but the coincidence is strikingly apposite.

From a musical perspective, the *Serenade* largely reverts to the lyrical, broadly diatonic idiom of *Sir John in Love*, Vaughan Williams's previous setting of Shakespeare. But there are no allusions to folk songs or traditional tunes, no Tudoresque mannerisms, no sense of anything archaic or obscure. Instead, we hear the inflections of the *Pastoral Symphony* and its attending works: the parallel triads, oscillating accompaniment, clear textures, and restrained instrumentation combine to form "the touches of sweet harmony" to which Lorenzo alludes. The voices, upon entering, elevate this paean to beauty into the realms of the ravishingly sublime; yet despite its overtly Romantic character, it eschews sentimentality or self-indulgence. Part of this restraint comes from Vaughan Williams's careful attention to the piece's form and design—particularly in the use of recurring motives, such as those for the solo violin, or the trumpet at the invocation of Diana. Broader rhetorical allusions are also present, reflecting the sorts of dramatic associations heard in *Job* and *Riders to the Sea*; for example, the darkly chromatic and dissonant section castigating "the man that hath no music in himself" descends to the lowest registers of the piece, threatening to unmoor its earlier tranquility. But Diana's trumpet sounds once more to announce the "right praise and true perfection" of music, restoring balance to the world and allowing the piece to end in a reassuring D major after a final exquisite ascent of the solo soprano.

Although Ursula Wood's influence on the *Serenade to Music* was largely indirect, she assumed the role of creative partner on *The Bridal Day*, a masque based on the scenario from Edmund Spencer's *Epithalamion* that led to her fateful first meeting with Vaughan Williams. It has a somewhat convoluted history: the composer began sketching it in late 1938, and had completed a draft by the following spring. A play-through went well enough that Douglas Kennedy scheduled a production at Cecil Sharp House for that autumn, but it was canceled by the outbreak of war. The work remained in limbo for several years until Hubert Foss pushed for its revival in 1952, which led to the BBC proposing a televised performance in 1953. The cast was quite fine—including Cecil Day Lewis as the narrator and Denis Dowling as the baritone soloist—and Vaughan Williams revised and slightly expanded the masque in preparation for the production, but was disappointed with the transmitted result. This led him to reconceive it as a choral cantata, which led to further revisions before its release as *Epithalamion* in 1957.[9]

The Bridal Day's classification as a masque reflects its varied theatrical practices: choral and solo singing, dramatic narration, mime, scenic tableaux, and dance. The supporting ensemble is unique in Vaughan Williams's catalogue: flute (doubling on piccolo), two violins, viola, cello, double bass, and piano, but is reduceable to piano and flute only.[10] The scenario celebrates the nuptials of a Bride and Bridegroom amid a Classically pastoral setting. As nymphs and Graces cavort with the couple's family and friends, the whole event takes place under the watchful eye of Juno, goddess of marriage, and the slightly blurrier gaze of Bacchus, who staggers his way through a Grotesque Dance in the fourth scene. The viola solo in this section—and the prominent role of the flute throughout—confirms the work's erotic basis, recalling comparable treatments for those instruments in *Flos Campi* and the *Magnificat*. But this masque is, on the whole, more joyous and extroverted than those predecessors, appropriately capturing its festive text (which Wood called "one of the few entirely happy love poems in the English language"), and the often pastoral-inflected music displays an ease and spontaneity befitting its subject.[11]

Similarly assured writing is present in the *Five Variants of "Dives and Lazarus,"* the result of a commission from the British Council for a work to represent England at the New York World's Fair of 1939. Strictly speaking, the work does not feature variants—that is to say, divergent examples of the same song collected in the field—so much as free variations emerging from Vaughan Williams's own imagination, not unlike the treatment applied in the Two Hymn-Tune Preludes or the Choral and Choral Prelude of 1932. Ironically, this approach means that the composer "modified [the melody] in transmitting it, just as a folk-singer does," literally creating his own so-called variants in the process.[12] The resemblance among them is clear, however, even when it involves changes to the meter (the first three variants are in $\frac{3}{4}$ time, which appears in no collected versions of the tune), the layering of voices in free and imitative counterpoint (as in the fourth variant), or the second variant's reduction of the B Aeolian melody to its barest outline.

The folk tune "Dives and Lazarus" was one of Vaughan Williams's favorites. He first encountered it in Lucy Broadwood and J. A. Fuller

Maitland's *English County Songs* (1893), and although he initially compared its impact to his discovery of Wagner's music ("I had that sense of recognition—'here's something which I have known all my life—only I didn't know it!'"), he also said that it gave "the same sense of the something [sic] peculiarly belonging to me as an Englishman" that he gleaned from the fifth of the *Enigma Variations*.[13] He later collected a version during a trip to Herefordshire in 1913, and featured a sternly martial setting of it in the *English Folk Songs Suite*.[14] The overall tone of the *Five Variants*, however, is far more mellow, not least due to the resonant orchestration for strings and harp, which evokes a textural spaciousness and timeless quality reminiscent of the *Tallis Fantasia*. Perhaps it was no accident that two melodies of such long-standing provenance—both dating from the sixteenth century—should inspire similar artistic responses.

These three compositions were the most significant to emerge in the first year of his relationship with Ursula Wood, but he completed several others as well. Not all were successful, such as the Double Trio for string sextet, withdrawn after its first performance in January 1939, and again after revising it for a second performance in 1942; it was eventually recast as the Partita for Double String Orchestra. Most of the others were more straightforward affairs, such an arrangement of the tune MILES LANE for the Three Choirs Festival of 1938—a hymn the composer admired enough to treat as the subject of a later essay[15]—or the full set of Services (Matins, Communion, and Evensong) in D Minor, dedicated to Craig Sellar Lang and the boys at Christ's Hospital boarding school in Horsham, Sussex. Written in mind of "college chapels and other churches [where] there is, besides the choir, a large body of voices" in the congregation, it allotted a unison part in a broadly accessible register and range to complement the choir's four-part harmonies.[16] Perhaps the most unusual work completed during this yearlong stretch was the Suite for Pipes (1939) for members of the Pipers Guild, one of the many musical organizations that counted Vaughan Williams as President. The titular instruments are not bagpipes, but an SATB quartet of bamboo flutes—handmade by guild members—resembling the tin whistle in design and sound, but in Vaughan Williams's hands, they also evoke the quality of a portative organ. The compact work opens with the rhapsodic and fanfarish Intrada, followed by three stylized dances (Minuet and Trio, Valse, and the sprightly closing Jig).[17]

Such pleasant diversions came to an unceremonious end once war had been declared in September. Although the war consumed Vaughan Williams's attention, it did not initially inspire much in the way of large-scale artistic responses. As early as spring 1940, he felt he had "for the present shot my bolt as regards war-time music," and continued complaining about writer's block.[18] Still, he produced a steady stream of minor and occasional works over the next few years that reflected the war's influence: several unison hymns (including "A Hymn of Freedom," "A Call to the Free Nations" and "The Airmen's Hymn"),[19] two stand-alone choral songs (*England, My England* and *The New Commonwealth*), and the collection *Six Choral Songs—To Be Sung in Time of War*, featuring texts by Percy Shelley. These are all rousing tunes aimed at general audiences, with patriotic or inspirational lyrics. One instrumental composition from this period should also be noted: the famously adaptable *Household Music: Three Preludes on Welsh Hymn Tunes* (1941). This example of *Gebrauchsmusik* reflects Vaughan Williams's exhortation that the war-time composer "serve the community directly through his craft if not through his art. [. . .] Would it not be a worthy object of the composer's skill to provide for . . . modest executants music worthy of their artistic imagination, but not beyond their technical skill?"[20] Accordingly, this suite may be performed on almost any combination of instruments, making it eminently suitable for the makeshift circumstances of wartime performance.[21]

From a creative standpoint, the most important works Vaughan Williams wrote during the war came in a new medium for him: film. In 1940, he offhandedly told his colleague Arthur Benjamin that he was interested in the possibility of writing cinematic music. Benjamin informed conductor and musical director Muir Mathieson, who contacted Vaughan Williams one Saturday to gauge his interest in scoring the film *49th Parallel*. The composer later recalled, "When I asked how long I could have to prepare it, the answer was, 'Till Wednesday,'" though this may be exaggerated.[22] There is no doubt, however, that he found the time restrictions hugely invigorating, because they concentrated his creative energies and forced him to work quickly and efficiently. He later recommended film scoring as "a splendid discipline . . . to all composition teachers whose pupils are apt to be dawdling in their ideas, or whose every bar is sacred and must not be cut or altered," and saw within the medium "potentialities for the combination of all the arts such as Wagner never dreamt of."[23]

Mathieson served as musical director on all of the films for which Vaughan Williams wrote scores between 1941 and 1944: two for the Ministry of Information (*Stricken Peninsula* and *49th Parallel*) and one each for the Crown Film Unit (*Coastal Command*), the British Council (*The People's Land*), and the Air Ministry in conjunction with the exiled Belgian government (*Flemish Farm*). Vaughan Williams's approach to writing film music differed from most composers, who typically synchronized their scores with the action shown on screen (a technique colloquially known as "Mickey Mousing"). Instead, he would provide "a score consisting of a continuous stream of music paralleling the action," which he then turned over to the musical director to fit to the final cut, but "remaining ever-ready to make whatever adjustments and alterations the director required."[24] Writing in this manner—much as one would work to the general scenario in a ballet—made it comparatively easy to later extract passages for concert suites or individual numbers. This was the case when the Prelude from *49th Parallel* was released in several different instrumental guises and, with a newly written textual trope from Harold Child, as the unison choral song *The New Commonwealth*. Such collaborations were mutually beneficial: film studios enjoyed the prestige of having Britain's most distinguished composer attached to their production, while Vaughan Williams was glad to contribute to the war effort.[25]

In addition to films, Vaughan Williams returned to a pair of dramatic antecedents during the war, beginning with incidental music for Shakespearean plays. In 1939, he arranged a series of traditional tunes alongside melodies by Orlando Gibbons, Thomas Morley, and Thomas Arne for a production of *Twelfth Night*, but the performance was delayed until 1947; he also scored a BBC production of *Richard II* in 1944 that was never broadcast.[26] The second revival, however, was far more significant: incidental music for a BBC radio transmission of *The Pilgrim's Progress* (1943), adapted by Edward Sackville-West and starring John Gielgud.[27] This is perhaps Vaughan Williams's best treatment of Bunyan's story, not least because he was freed from the limitations of the stage. Working in an entirely aural medium allowed the music to bear a greater amount of the dramatic weight, freed from the distractions of scenic elements—which, in practice, often fell far short of their imagined splendor. Particularly notable in this rendition is the extensive use of the *Tallis Fantasia* melody, which (along with the use of the hymn tune YORK in the prelude and epilogue) returns to practices he first employed in the Reigate scenes of 1906. New to this version, however, was a memorable melody replacing MONK'S GATE from the Reigate production. First sung by the character Help, it was later closely associated with the character of Christian—both here and in the subsequent Morality of 1951—and set to the text "who would true valour see" (Example 14.1). The dramatic significance of all three melodies was underscored by their successive reprise in the closing scene at the Delectable Mountains.

Supplementing this public return to Bunyan's tale was a more private engagement with it in the Symphony (No. 5) in D Major. It has a strong claim to being Vaughan Williams's most beloved symphonic work; certainly, it was warmly received at its debut on 24 June 1943 under Vaughan Williams's baton. Myriad influences intersect throughout its pages. He began writing it in 1938, soon after meeting Ursula Wood, who believed that she was at least partly responsible for inspiring its creation.[28] That same year, Vaughan Williams served as music director for the pageant *England's Pleasant Land*. Although he wrote music for only two scenes—an "Exit for the Ghosts of the Past" and a "Funeral March for the Old Order"—he incorporated elements from both into the symphony's first two movements.[29] As for Bunyan, the incidental music of 1942 was not

Example 14.1 "Who Would True Valour See," transcribed from the BBC Radio production of *The Pilgrim's Progress* (1943; Albion Records, ALBCD023/24, 2015)

the only *Pilgrim*-related score in progress. Having worked on a full operatic version of the story in fits and starts since about 1925, Vaughan Williams began suspecting that he would never finish it, so he scavenged portions of the score for use in the symphony. However, as he wound up completing the opera in 1949, there are several points of musical correlation between the two compositions.[30]

Thus inspired by obscurities and off-cuttings, Vaughan Williams returned to the world of symphonic composition—a world far different from that of its F-minor predecessor. That is not to suggest the Fifth marks an entirely new stylistic direction, for there are resemblances to both the *London* and *Pastoral* symphonies, particularly in terms of motivic design and harmonic language, respectively. Context too is key: just as the commemorative mode of the *Pastoral Symphony* evokes qualities of what Samuel Hynes calls an anti-monument—a rendering of war's sacrifices "without the value-bearing abstractions, without the glory, and without the large-scale grandeur"—the Fifth renders audible a vision of serenity and benediction, despite being composed under the circumstances of total war.[31] In both cases, Vaughan Williams imagines alternatives to a world that disappoints and frustrates, that erodes the soul, that suffers "woes which Hope thinks infinite." The composer had set that line from *Prometheus Unbound* in "A Song of Victory" only a few years earlier, but it is a later passage from that poem that encapsulates his own visionary spirit: "to hope till Hope creates / From its own wreck the thing it contemplates." To imagine beauty under such conditions, and to express that beauty so that others too might find hope within the wreckage— that is the mark of the true artist, and a challenge Vaughan Williams took up throughout his career.

Of course, as Hugh Ottaway perceptively notes, "the Fifth is not *all* serenity, any more than the Fourth is *all* violence" or the *Pastoral* is entirely tranquil.[32] The ostensible key of D Major, for example, is obscured from the outset (Example 14.2). Even Vaughan Williams was unsure of the tonality, initially designating it as G major—the opening key signature—an ambiguity reflecting two possible interpretations of the central pitch.[33] If it is D, then we are primed to hear the C pedal as a dissonance against the oscillating D–F♯ and A–E dyads that sound above it. If, however, we take G as the tonic, then the dissonance is explained by virtue of the initial sonority being a dominant ninth (D–F♯–A–C–E).

Example 14.2 Symphony (No. 5) in D Major, mvt. 1, mm. 1–8

Neither is quite correct. Instead, just as the Mass in G Minor techni-cally wasn't, this Symphony in D Major is "about" D major, in the sense of "approximately." The first eight measures feature a D Mixolydian col-lection, shifting to D Dorian when the clarinets lower the F♯ to F♮ in m. 9. But while the mode remains the same, its central pitch shifts—first ex-quisitely to F in m. 40, then five measures later to C—which means "the continuing pedal note becomes the fifth degree and finally the tonic," resolving the tension established from the outset.[34] But then, without warning, Vaughan Williams makes a pivot as breathtaking as the initial choral entrance in *A Sea Symphony* or the minor-to-major transforma-tion preceding the trumpet cadenza in the *Pastoral*: the C Dorian mo-dality is abandoned for the radiance of E major, a mediant modulation flanking and subtly positioning D as the fulcrum upon which the entire harmonic structure balances.

What is particularly remarkable about this design is its economy of means. The Fourth Symphony may have been an acrimonious homage to Beethoven, but it is the Fifth that, in the first movement's rigorous ex-ploration of a very limited amount of motivic material, is a more fitting tribute. But Vaughan Williams acknowledged a different composer in his dedication: Jean Sibelius, whose influence may be gleaned in the string writing of the Preludio's central section (one hesitates to call it a development), or in the deeply moving English horn solo at the beginning of the Romanza. This same passage sounds in *The Pilgrim's Progress* when Pilgrim arrives at the House Beautiful, one of the many concordances that commentators have seized upon to interpret this work, but this effort seems unnecessary. As we have seen many times, Vaughan Williams insisted upon splitting inspiration from interpretation. "It matters, of course, enormously to the composer what he was thinking about when he was writing a particular work," he said in 1919, "but to no one else in the world does it matter one jot."[35] He returned to this theme in a later tribute to Elgar. "The best composer is surely he who has the most beautiful melodies, the finest harmony, the most vital rhythm, and the surest sense of form," he wrote. "I lose patience with those people who try to put up Berlioz as a great composer . . . because he could give literary reasons for his beliefs, and do not see that a composer like Dvořák, a reed shaken by the wind, is far the greater man of the two because the wind was the divine afflatus."[36]

Divinely inspired or otherwise, Vaughan Williams's mastery of his craft is apparent throughout this symphony, whether in the finely wrought harmonic design of the Preludio, the Scherzo's Mendelssohnian sprightliness, the Romanza's intensely passionate lyricism, or the imaginatively flexible treatment of form in the closing Passacaglia, which brilliantly reprises the Preludio's opening material to launch a coda that ranks among the most delicately beautiful passages of music Vaughan Williams ever wrote. With the benefit of hindsight, we can forgive those who saw this work as a valedictory statement from the seventy-year-old composer, a fitting final contribution to the genre. For who could imagine not only that four more symphonies—and far more besides—were still to come, but also that his creative boundaries would continue expanding and his voice remain vital well into a future that few thought possible in 1943?

"I Live a Very Quiet Life Now" (1943–1951)

T HE CRITICAL AND POPULAR ACCLAIM RECEIVED BY THE FIFTH
Symphony, the stimulus of film and radio commissions, and the
emotional deepening of Vaughan Williams's relationship with Ursula
Wood lifted a weight from his creative shoulders, at least temporarily. He
completed several significant works in the latter half of 1943, including
the String Quartet in A Minor, the Oboe Concerto, and, rather opti-
mistically, a "Victory Anthem" that became known as *Thanksgiving for
Victory*.[1] It was unusual for Vaughan Williams to undertake a project so
closely tied to contemporary politics, much less by commission (in this
case, from the BBC), but that rarity should not imply he was himself
apolitical. He vociferously advocated for Federal Union, a movement
encouraging the creation of a "United States of Europe" encompassing
leading Atlantic democracies, later manifesting in bodies such as NATO
and the European Union. As Federal Union recognized the value of both
national sovereignty and international cooperation, it is no surprise that
it appealed to an idealist like Vaughan Williams. At the same time, he was
willing to engage with, and even defend, friends and colleagues with
opposing political views. His support of Michael Tippett, who refused
to comply with work directives required for conscientious objectors,
before a tribunal at Oxted Crown Court in 1943 is perhaps the best-
known example. Notable too are his exchanges with Alan Bush and
Rutland Boughton, both committed Communists, in which he argued
that music should not serve narrow political ideologies, and revealed his

incomprehension at how artists of integrity could believe otherwise. While his own privileged social status informed such a stance, it also reflected his broader position that music should be accessible to all, regardless of class, nationality, or political creed.

For the most part, however, wartime life for Vaughan Williams involved making whatever contributions he could on the home front. He maintained the Informal Hour concert series at the White Horse Assembly Rooms in Dorking, accepted the presidency of the Committee for the Promotion of New Music upon its foundation in 1943, and revived performances of Bach's *St. Matthew Passion* with the LHMC choirs in 1942. "I live a very quiet life now," he wrote to his old friend Fritz Hart. "Never leave home except occasionally for ½ a day to London on business," mainly because Adeline's increasingly precarious health made him reluctant to be away, even though plenty of people were available to help.[2] R. O. Morris was still in residence, and many of Adeline's friends and relatives passed through for extended periods, as did a series of married couples evacuated from London who assisted the regular household staff. More difficult was the residency of Ivy Herbert (a local pianist affiliated with the LHMC) and her friend Molly Potto, who stayed in the White Gates annex between 1943 and 1946. Their relationship with Morris and Adeline was often tense, not just because of the age difference and close proximity in shared quarters, but also because Herbert and Potto detested Ursula Wood, an attitude that led to multiple confrontations with Morris and Adeline.[3] Nevertheless, a mattress was provided for Ursula in the Vaughan Williamses' bedroom during her visits, and the flexible hours of her job—as a receptionist for Paul Nathan, a pediatrician and German refugee—let her assist Vaughan Williams during his regular visits to London. Adeline was grateful for the help, encouraged her visits to Dorking, and fussed over the younger woman's health and well-being ("I long to look after you a little," she wrote upon learning that Ursula had come down with the flu).[4]

One unexpected responsibility arose following Hervey Vaughan Williams's death on 30 May 1944. Ralph was one of three trustees for Hervey's will, which left to him Leith Hill Place and all of its household effects. He knew of Hervey's intent and had tried to convince him otherwise—knowing that proper management of the house, grounds, and tenants would encroach excessively on his work—but Hervey indicated that he could do whatever he liked with the property once it was his, so Ralph offered it to the National Trust. Though happy to accept, the Trust's agreement came with certain stipulations, as Vaughan Williams explained to Robert and Elizabeth Trevelyan, who currently lived next door at Tanhurst:

> They are anxious, I think, to have it but tell me that they must let the house and the immediate surroundings so as to give them an income to keep up the estate. So it is up to me, and you as neighbours to try and find a tenant who, at the same time, is desirable and rich . . . I think I should prefer a private tenant as they are likely to be more human in their relations with the cottagers and workmen—and I want to keep up the great tradition in that respect set up by my Grandfather [Josiah Wedgwood III], my mother and Hervey himself.[5]

Fortunately, the ideal tenants soon appeared. Ralph Wedgwood and his wife, Iris, had been searching for a country house for some time without success, so Vaughan Williams invited them to Leith Hill Place in August to see if it would suit their needs. The couple was delighted by the chance to live near Ralph and Adeline after decades apart, and so by November, Leith Hill Place was in the care of another generation of Wedgwoods. Soon after, Wedgwood reciprocated his cousin's generosity by presenting him with the manuscript score of *The Robin's Nest* (1878), Vaughan Williams's earliest surviving composition. It had somehow come into Wedgwood's possession, and the composer was amused by its return.[6]

Late 1944 was consumed by preparations for the concert premieres of the Oboe Concerto and the String Quartet in A Minor, and the recording of *Thanksgiving for Victory* with Boult and the BBC Symphony Orchestra.[7] Three other projects also occupied Vaughan Williams at this time. The first (and simplest) was the score for *Stricken Peninsula*, a Ministry of Information film showcasing Allied reconstruction efforts in Italy. Vaughan Williams was approached for the project by Muir Matheson, and waived his usual fee, considering the work a contribution to the war effort.[8] The second undertaking was considerably more complex: a new English-language edition of Bach's Mass in B Minor, a piece Vaughan Williams admired nearly as much as the *St. Matthew Passion*. He had conducted excerpts from it previously, and during his fire-watching shifts in the early 1940s decided to make his own edition and translation "adapted to the English liturgy," a pursuit that served as "a refuge for him" during the war.[9] Knowing it was unlikely to be widely used when he delivered it to OUP in autumn 1945, he offered to subsidize its publication, assuming a cost of around £400 (almost $23,500 in 2020). In fact, the actual cost was five times that; moreover, wartime restrictions on paper and manufacturing meant no British printer would touch it.[10] In the end, Vaughan Williams simply photocopied and distributed the manuscript parts to the Leith Hill choirs, who performed the Gloria, Sanctus, and Agnus Dei at the 1947 Festival.[11]

The third major project was the long-awaited completion of a libretto and score for a full-length opera on *The Pilgrim's Progress*. Vaughan Williams's renewed interest in the work stemmed from multiple sources: the BBC commission for the radio play of 1943, feedback from Wood on his treatment of the libretto, and his incorporation of passages from earlier drafts of it into the Fifth Symphony. Although he had finished a sketch by late 1945, it would still be some time before he was ready to submit the work to a play-through, but it now seemed as though its realization was a viable possibility.

Such optimism was warranted as the war finally drew to a close. Less than a week after Dorking's church bells rang out to celebrate V-E Day, the BBC broadcast *Thanksgiving for Victory*, though without the amount of promotion Vaughan Williams had expected. Still, life slowly began returning to normal, and Vaughan Williams could compose on a more or less full-time basis without war work demanding his attention. In its place, however, arose many administrative and professional obligations to the English Folk Dance and Song Society, CEMA, the LHMC, the Society for the Promotion of New Music, the Dorking Refugee Committee, the English Hymnal Committee, and numerous other boards, societies, festivals, and organizations clamoring for his attention and patronage.

But music remained as ever his primary focus, and the war's end tapped a wellspring of new talent and opportunities. Benjamin Britten's *Peter Grimes* hit London in June 1945 with only slightly less force than German bombs; Vaughan Williams attended the premiere, which led him to reread the poems of George Crabbe that inspired it. The Proms concerts also returned to the Royal Albert Hall, but without Henry Wood, who had died the previous August. Many of Vaughan Williams's works were programmed that season, including the concert debuts of *Thanksgiving for Victory* and *The Story of a Flemish Farm*, a suite that he thought featured "some of the best film music I have written."[12] Additionally, he was preparing for a revival of *Sir John in Love* at Sadler's Wells in early 1946, and turned his attention to works for piano: his Introduction and Fugue for Two Pianofortes, first performed on 23 March 1946, and *The Lake in the Mountains*, a short piece based on an episode from *49th Parallel*.[13]

He was also hard at work on a new symphony, this one in E minor. He completed drafts of the first two movements by February, though he confessed that he was "quite stuck" on the Scherzo.[14] Unlike his creative blocks of the previous decade, however, this one passed quickly, for he was able to inform Michael Mullinar by 21 May of the symphony's completion, and invited him to White Gates to play the work for a small group of listeners. In fact, Mullinar performed it three times over the course of a day in mid-July—broken up by dinner and poetry readings—and in recognition of his artistry and endurance, was named the symphony's dedicatee.[15]

A final pianistic contribution was yet to come in 1946: a two-soloist arrangement of the Piano Concerto. Vaughan Williams had been urged to make such an arrangement when the piece premiered, but never got around to it—perhaps because he wanted to see if the original version could succeed, and possibly because Harriet Cohen was fiercely protective of her claim to the work.[16] He turned to pianist Joseph Cooper (later the longtime host of the BBC panel show *Face the Music*) for assistance, and seems to have allowed him considerable latitude in making editorial decisions. Vaughan Williams also made some significant modifications himself, including the addition of a short cadenza and a complete reworking of the finale's close.[17]

Vaughan Williams's quick turnaround on the Concerto let him turn his attention to his first performance of Bach's *St. John Passion* in Dorking. He began recruiting a small choir of handpicked singers in October 1945, who became known as the Dorking Bach Choir; they rehearsed at White Gates through the winter before mounting a performance the following February. Concurrently, he completed a new score for Ealing Studios, *The Loves of Joanna Godden*. Its arrival in early December 1946 surprised Ealing's Director of Music, Ernest Irving, and for good reason. "Never in the history of Ealing, or for that matter of the world, has the score been finished before the film," he wrote. "It is the best music we have ever had here, and all the members of our little arcana were excited and delighted."[18]

Irving's charm, humor, and literary enthusiasm quickly endeared him to Vaughan Williams, and he was one of several new friends who entered the composer's life in the mid-1940s. These included Gil Jenkins, a high-ranking civil servant and amateur baritone. He was Gerald Finzi's supervisor at the Ministry of Transport, and it was through Finzi that Jenkins got to know both Wood and Vaughan Williams—intimately so, as he served as Vaughan Williams's best man in 1953 when the composer married Wood, with whom Jenkins also pursued extramarital liaisons. Another was Michael Kennedy, a young coder in the Royal Navy, who wrote to tell the composer how much he admired his Fifth Symphony. Vaughan Williams responded by saying that music formed "a means of communication and sympathy with people whom we may never meet in life (though I hope we may one day)."[19] Five years later, that long-deferred meeting with Kennedy—now music critic for *The Daily Telegraph*—took place in Manchester, kindling a warm friendship that led to Kennedy becoming one of the composer's authorized biographers.

Another important relationship arose with Roy Douglas, keyboardist and librarian for the London Symphony Orchestra (LSO), and a composer and arranger in his own right. Having served as Vaughan Williams's copyist for *Thanksgiving for Victory* and several films since 1942, Douglas received a surprising request in February 1947: "I have been foolish enough to write another symphony. Could you undertake to vet and then copy the score?"[20] Vaughan Williams's famously illegible handwriting carried over into his manuscript scores, occasionally so baffling that copyists needed to consult him in order to accurately render the parts. Douglas accepted the offer to assist with the Sixth Symphony, and worked closely with Vaughan Williams as copyist and musical consultant for the rest of the older composer's career.[21]

Work on the symphony consumed so much of Vaughan Williams's attention that he undertook only a few other short choral pieces in 1947. These included *The Souls of the Righteous*, a motet for the dedication of the Battle of Britain Chapel at Westminster Abbey; *The Voice out of the Whirlwind*, composed for the St. Cecilia's Day service of the Musicians Benevolent Fund; and a short tribute to Hubert Parry (*Prayer to the Father of Heaven*) for the Oxford Bach Choir. He had also committed to an audacious new film score for Ernest Irving, and by year's end was busily drafting numbers for *Scott of the Antarctic*. Initial recording sessions took place in February, with copious notes and suggestions exchanged in the interim (including an extended critique from Irving written entirely in iambic quadrameter).[22]

Such activity likely came as a relief to Vaughan Williams after all of the hullaballoo surrounding his seventy-fifth birthday. (Much less pomp had attended his and Adeline's fiftieth wedding anniversary three days earlier.) Still, with age came certain privileges: he advised the BBC on which of his pieces he would like to hear on a birthday concert—the Four Hymns, *Flos Campi*, and *Sancta Civitas*—enjoyed parties at Cecil Sharp House and the Dorking Halls (the latter replete with a magician, one of his favorite entertainments), received a new wireless set from the LHMC conductors, and attended a concert in his honor by the Croydon Philharmonic Society and the LSO, who performed the *Sea Symphony* and *Five Tudor Portraits*.

The year ended with a run-through of the Sixth Symphony by Boult and the BBC Orchestra at Maida Vale Studios on 16 December. Because of increasing deafness—likely caused by his proximity to heavy artillery in the Great War—Vaughan Williams had, as per his usual practice, invited a small group to provide feedback, particularly on issues of ensemble balance. Though many of the invitees had attended the piano play-through earlier in the summer, the orchestral rendition surprised and overwhelmed several of them—but not the composer. The very next day, Vaughan Williams sent Douglas an extended Scherzo revision based on what he had heard at the previous day's rehearsal, requesting one more round of changes before printing.[23]

For all that Vaughan Williams claimed to struggle with composition, his diligent and consistent work habits compensated for it. "You know that you cannot write a new piece of music like you can make a suit of clothes—just sit down and do it. The actual writing is often nothing; it is the mental preparation beforehand which counts."[24] He composed every day—often for extended periods, sometimes briefly—and usually had several projects going on at once. This habit also led him to revisit older works for possible improvement. One prominent example was the Partita for Double String Orchestra, a massive reworking of the Double Trio withdrawn in 1939 and revised in 1942. Now with an entirely new final movement (and considerable revision to the others), the BBC Third Programme broadcast its performance on 20 March 1948. Robert Müller-Hartmann was the work's dedicatee, an acknowledgement of his role in bringing both incarnations of the piece to fruition.

It was, however, the Symphony in E Minor that dominated that spring's musical landscape. Proof corrections, program notes, and rehearsals occupied Vaughan Williams's attention before the premiere on 21 April, a triumphant performance under Boult's direction that launched it to the forefront of the contemporary musical world. Despite its unusual qualities (such as the conspicuous use of the tenor saxophone, the lack of breaks between movements, and the closing Epilogue's haunting austerity), it logged a hundred performances around the world in just over two years. Vaughan Williams disliked critics' assignation of specific meanings to the work—Frank Howes's characterization of it as a "War Symphony" particularly got under his skin—feeling as he did that listeners should experience his compositions in whatever way most resonated with them. Still, even if he did not explicitly intend to depict the desolation of war in the symphony, he could not escape its broader influence as a shaping force, as remembered by composer Howard Ferguson: "The occasion was at one of those run-throughs [of the piece] at Maida Vale No. 1 . . . I said to him at the end of No. 6, 'That's a pretty grim piece'; to which he replied, '*I* call it The Big Three.' And that was the end of that."[25]

Having said that, Vaughan Williams strove to ensure that any performance of his music reflected his own aims as closely as possible, particularly when it came to dramatic works, for which he "would have liked to be producer, designer and repetiteur himself."[26] Examples abound of collaborative projects—*The English Hymnal, Hugh the Drover, Job, The Poisoned Kiss*—over the course of which he slowly, charmingly, firmly, and inexorably exerted more and more influence until his vision dominated the final product. Nowhere was this practice more evident than in his various settings of *The Pilgrim's Progress*, and it was to this that he returned in the wake of the Sixth Symphony's debut. In July, he asked Alan Frank to undertake "a little discreet publicising" about its existence, on the off chance that another composer might have been considering it.[27] Such a scenario was not as unlikely as it seemed. Only a few years earlier, just as Vaughan Williams had finished his initial sketch, Geoffrey Keynes asked if he would be interested in writing a masque based on Bunyan's story (the composer declined, somewhat sheepishly).[28] Considering the amount of time and effort he had invested in the opera, his anxiety at its potential usurpation is understandable. On 11 August, he sent the vocal score and libretto to Steuart Wilson (recently appointed the BBC's Director of Music) for consideration and held an informal play-through with Mullinar and a small group of guests in early December—singing all the parts himself—after which he sought dramaturgical advice from Clive Carey (a distinguished tenor and director, and Vaughan Williams's longtime friend) before beginning the orchestration.

As usual, many other obligations vied for his attention. Vaughan Williams learned that two biographies about him were underway in 1948, including one by Hubert Foss, at whose request he wrote the colorful and much-quoted "A Musical Autobiography" for inclusion in the volume. *Job* was revived at Sadler's Wells that spring (with new stage designs by John Piper, which Vaughan Williams disliked) and he led a concert rendition of it at the Three Choirs Festival in Worcester, along with the *Tallis Fantasia*. *Prayer for the Father of Heaven* and *Scott of the Antarctic* both debuted, the latter receiving a command performance a month before its public release. He was pleased with it, and permitted a recording of selections from the score on the condition "that it must not prevent my making later on a Symphony on the themes if ever I feel inclined to do so," an indication of where his imagination was already heading.[29] The year ended on a sad note, however, with the death of R. O. Morris on 15 December; Vaughan Williams pressed the BBC for a memorial concert in his honor.

Health issues were a growing concern at White Gates by 1949. Vaughan Williams's punishing work schedule and his concern for Adeline's condition took an increasing toll as he aged, physically and emotionally. Brutal colds were a common complaint, as was exhaustion after engagements like the LHMC. Additionally, his deafness was worsening (but mitigated by hearing aids), he had false teeth, and was overweight, though the latter was alleviated by the ministrations of a newly retained masseur. None of these maladies was particularly serious, but Adeline's condition had deteriorated over the previous few years. Although she was still taken out for occasional excursions and day trips as late as 1947, she was nearly immobile, confined to her wheelchair, and almost entirely reliant on other people for any physical task. Her mind, however, remained sharp.

Her increasingly deformed hands could not deter her from writing daily to Curle and/or Wood, presumably because they provided her only direct links to the outside world besides her husband. Fortunately, Wood and others assisted the couple on a regular basis, and White Gates had no shortage of visitors to enliven the atmosphere. One particularly distinguished guest was photographer Yousuf Karsh, who converted the main room into a makeshift studio for a day, capturing some of the most striking images of Vaughan Williams as a result. Earlier in the year, Vaughan Williams had also been convinced to sit for Jacob Epstein, who sculpted a bronze bust now held by the National Portrait Gallery.

A particularly touching concert occurred on 20 November, which entailed a private performance of two new works at White Gates: *An Oxford Elegy* and the *Fantasia (quasi variazione) on the "Old 104th" Psalm Tune*. Vaughan Williams arranged the concert for Adeline's benefit, though a few close friends also attended. Both compositions are for chorus and orchestra with soloists (an orator for the *Elegy*, and a pianist for the *Fantasia*), but Vaughan Williams employed reduced forces for this distinguished salon: the Schwiller String Quartet, eight members of the Tudor Singers, Michael Mullinar on piano, and Steuart Wilson as the reader. Other significant recent works included *Folk Songs of the Four Seasons*—a cantata commissioned by the National Federation of Women's Institutes (NFWI)—and the smaller Concerto Grosso for String Orchestra, both of which premiered in 1950. He also decided at the height of summer that "it is about time I started thinking about the 'Sinfonia Antarctica,'" which meant retrieving his *Scott* music from Irving to begin sketching the new composition.[30]

These works all marked a turn toward projects associated with people or institutions of personal significance to Vaughan Williams. In addition to helping spearhead a fundraiser to reconstruct the war-damaged Cecil Sharp House, he collaborated with Ernest Irving on a new film score (*Bitter Springs*) and with Ursula Wood on *The Sons of Light*, a cantata for which she wrote the text. Vaughan Williams also completed three choral songs on Shakespearean texts for Cecil Armstrong Gibbs and wrote a short section of "solemn music" to conclude the *Masque of Charterhouse*, recently revived by the school's new Director of Music, John Wilson. These pieces came at the expense of several requests for new works— Vaughan Williams turned down at least four prospective commissions during the first half of 1950—and of time spent on the project in which he was most invested: *The Pilgrim's Progress*. Nevertheless, a performance of that work at Covent Garden was confirmed by May, and the ensuing months were consumed by interviews with prospective producers and conductors, score revisions and copying, and the endless details involved with mounting a production of this scale. The amount of work he faced would have challenged a man half his age, but he thrived on it. Conducting engagements, festival performances, concert premieres, administrative activity, and the usual raft of correspondence filled any gaps not taken up by revision and rehearsal of the opera (or "Morality," as he called it), and the thought of seeing his efforts finally realized undoubtedly fueled his pace.

Yet the final result proved bitterly disappointing. In the weeks leading up to the debut of *The Pilgrim's Progress* on 26 April, Douglas and Wood were uneasy about the quality of the production. Douglas called the final result a "shabby miscreation" and later indicated that while "musically the standard of performance was reasonably good . . . the scenery and costumes, the staging, lighting, and production generally—all these fell short of the composer's conception."[31] The emphasis on static tableaux, the lack of a female lead, and the story's uncompromising religiosity would have presented an uphill battle for success anywhere, much less Covent Garden, but Vaughan Williams flatly rejected suggestions that it was more suited to a cathedral setting. He was unmoved by the cool critical response ("They won't like it . . . and I don't care, it's what I meant, and there it is"), but immediately began thinking of ways to improve it for its next performance, however unlikely that might have seemed.[32]

But worse was soon to come. Adeline's health declined precipitously in April, with doctors visiting almost daily. She was suffering regular fevers and had lost the use of her hands, and was so weak that she was barely able to listen to the radio broadcasts of *The Pilgrim's Progress*. She rallied slightly in early May, reassuring her husband enough for him to venture briefly to London. Tragically, however, while he was attending a rehearsal of *Toward the Unknown Region* on 10 May, Adeline died at home. Vaughan Williams's grief likely mingled with relief that her suffering had finally ended, but her loss cut deeply. Adeline Fisher had believed in him when few others did, kindled his artistry, facilitated his career, and resolutely supported him for over half a century as one of his few musical and emotional intimates. "I go on with my work as usual which is what she wants I feel sure," he told Elizabeth Trevelyan.[33] But his stiff upper lip belied his anguish, glimpsed briefly when he confessed that Adeline's death meant that "now I am all alone."[34]

The Music of 1943–1951

ALTHOUGH REGULARLY NOTED, IT BEARS REPEATING THAT VAUGHAN
Williams enjoyed a level of late career productivity matched by few
other composers. Five of his nine symphonies premiered after his seventieth birthday, as did two concerti, an opera, and numerous choral works,
cantatas, chamber pieces, and film scores. His creative scope and language
continued expanding as well. Like the compositions he completed in the
aftermath of the Great War, many of the works first performed between
1943 and 1951 favor smaller-scale genres or designs and more intimate
forms of expression, with careful attention to detail and surprising—if
still accessible—modifications, transformations, or ambiguations of otherwise familiar materials and processes. However, with the exceptions of
the Fifth and Sixth Symphonies—and, with several caveats, *The Pilgrim's
Progress*—the compositions of this period have generally failed to gain
hold in either the standard performing repertory or within assessments
of Vaughan Williams's musical legacy, for several possible reasons. First, by
the war's end, Vaughan Williams had enjoyed a position of artistic prominence for well over three decades. As new pieces appeared, it may have
been difficult for them to compete for attention against those from his
growing back catalogue. Additionally, many of these new pieces, their
professionalism and artistry notwithstanding, were simply impractical
from either financial or performing standpoints; their failure to gain
early traction has thus led to their marginalization. Finally, a new generation of English composers and critics began to emerge, many of whom

took issue with the music and the aesthetic values that Vaughan Williams had long promoted, such as his continued advocacy for the relevance of folk song and a robust culture of "national music" for England. Vaughan Williams could weather such criticism fairly easily, however, and was increasingly more motivated by his own creative impulses, the need to manage Adeline's declining health, and a desire to collaborate with artists whom he admired than by critical opinion.

The Concerto for Oboe and Strings (1944) represents one of the first examples of this phenomenon. Despite its small scale, the concerto has proven curiously resistant to analysis, in part because its motives are so densely and thoroughly interwoven that it can make determining the actual sections quite difficult, even in the first movement's ostensible rondo form (which comes off more like a neoclassical gloss on ritornello form as a result).[1] And yet, the modal language emphasized throughout also grants the work an appropriately pastoral quality. The finale was based on a scherzo discarded from the Fifth Symphony, but the rippling cadenzas of that movement and the initial *Rondo pastorale* invite comparisons with *The Lark Ascending*.[2] Like it, the virtuosity of the Oboe Concerto aligns less with Romantic showstopping grandiosity than with the nimbleness, ease, and precision expected in a concerto grosso, a parallel further reinforced by the understated ensemble and the second movement's unusual pairing of minuet with musette. Nevertheless, as suggested by its dedication to Léon Goossens, the soloist faces no shortage of technical or expressive challenges.

Comparable subtlety and complexity also appear in the String Quartet in A Minor (1944), subtitled "For Jean on Her Birthday." This alludes to its dedicatee, Jean Stewart: violist for the Menges Quartet, Ursula Wood's close friend, and one of the composer's favorite "nieces." Appropriately, the viola takes the lead in all four movements, from the unorthodox pentatonic set (D–E–F–G–A♭) initiating the Prelude and returning throughout in a ritornello-like manner, to the gently lyrical melody framing the Epilogue's radiantly (and almost exclusively diatonic) contrapuntal web. Less thoughtful is the key designation, which is even more tenuous than usual. In fact, the first movement is the only one ending in A minor, and the remaining three eschew that key altogether. This inclination toward tonal ambiguity may be a holdover from the Fifth Symphony, suggested further by the resemblance of its movement titles (Preludio, Scherzo, Romanza, Passacaglia) with those of the Quartet (Prelude, Romance, Scherzo, Epilogue). Other compositions are also effectively evoked. The Romance's double-stopped *senza vibrato* lines recall the texture of the *Tallis Fantasia* (even though the tone correlates more with Beethoven's late quartets), alongside hints of the key conflicts and tritone emphasis later displayed in the Sixth Symphony.[3] More tenuous is Vaughan Williams's claim that the Scherzo's opening theme came from *49th Parallel*; more likely, it was inspired by material from that film rather than based off of a specific passage within it.[4]

The same description applies to the impressionistic piano piece *The Lake in the Mountains* (1947). Dedicated to Phyllis Sellick following her premiere performance of the Concerto for Two Pianos (with her husband, Cyril Smith), its tranquil, rhythmically fluid contours elicit an effect of mysterious beauty—one could easily mistake it for an obscure work by Debussy—that far outstrips its cinematic source material, foreshadowing similar techniques of thematic transformation that would coax *Sinfonia Antartica* into existence. One final keyboard composition, the Introduction and Fugue for Two Pianofortes, was dedicated to Sellick and Smith and debuted on 23 March 1946, almost exactly eight months before the Concerto for Two Pianos. Rarely performed, it is a difficult work in many respects: technically and physically demanding, texturally dense, structurally complex, thematically intricate, and formally spacious. The fugue is by far the dominant partner, but its two primary themes grow out of the introduction's opening passage, unexpectedly alluded to in the midst of the fugue's expansive treatment of its own thematic material. Double fugue, canon, and free counterpoint are all present, interspersed with episodes displaying a Bach-like flair for continuous development. Like Vaughan Williams's other neoclassical compositions, it will never be mistaken for the genuine article, but the influence that Bach's music exerted upon it unmissable.

More firmly anchored in the present was *Thanksgiving for Victory* (1945) for narrator, soprano solo, chorus, children's choir, and orchestra. Acting on behalf of the BBC, Boult approached Vaughan Williams in August 1943 to see if he would be willing "to write a Victory Anthem, to be used at the end of the war."[5] After consulting with James Welch (the BBC's Director of Religious Broadcasting) about the lyrics, Vaughan Williams submitted a sketch of the work on 15 December, and promptly forgot about it. Unfortunately, so did the BBC:

> About June 1944 I had an agitated telephone call from Adrian Boult. "How about that Victory Anthem? It may be wanted any minute, please get to work on it." I replied "You've already had it for nearly six months." So a hue and cry was made, and it was, I believe, found forgotten in a drawer. So then after wasting six idle months, I had to revise, partly rewrite, and wholly orchestrate the work all in a hurry, which was the one thing I did not want to do for a great occasion. However it got finished fairly soon. I went to Bedford and we had a very successful recording.[6]

Thanksgiving for Victory is a celebratory counterweight to *Dona Nobis Pacem*, a national expression of gratitude and relief after six years of privation and loss. A compact sectional work, it assembles diverse texts on the subjects of victory and salvation taken from Scripture, Shakespeare's *Henry V*, and the rousing poem "Land of Our Birth" from Kipling's *Puck of Pook's Hill*.[7] Unusually among noncommercial composers, Vaughan Williams designed the work with the technical advantages of broadcasting in mind, particularly the ability to fade the ensemble beneath the speaker—an element that presents certain challenges in live performance.[8] Still, its aims were deliberately populist, adopting relatively straightforward (if often distantly related) successions of major keys in keeping with the joyous occasion. It is also a strangely guileless work. However skeptically we may eye Kipling's tub-thumpingly patriotic verses, or know today that phrases like "violence shall be no more heard in thy land" will prove disappointingly hollow, the spirit is very much Vaughan Williams's, kindling hope amid the darkness with the words of the prophet Isaiah: "the Lord hath anointed me to proclaim liberty to the captives . . . to comfort all that mourn; to give them beauty for ashes, the oil of joy for mourning, the garment of praise for the spirit of heaviness."

Vaughan Williams's engagement with religiously themed music continued with three motets completed between 1947 and 1948. *The Souls of the Righteous*, written for the dedication of Westminster Abbey's Battle of Britain Chapel on 10 July 1947, is the most straightforward of the three, a restrained yet moving setting of commemorative text from the Wisdom of Solomon, contrasting slow choral lines against solos from soprano and baritone. *The Voice out of the Whirlwind* took as its musical starting point the "Galliard of the Sons of the Morning" from *Job*, expanding it and assigning text from the verses where God reminds Job exactly who was in charge. The work was first performed by choir and organ for the St. Cecilia's Day service at the Church of St. Sepulchre, Holborn in 1947; Vaughan Williams orchestrated it for a Leith Hill Musical Festival (LHMF) performance in 1951.[9] The most striking of the three, however, is *Prayer to the Father of Heaven*, commissioned for the Oxford Festival of Music by British Composers in May 1948, the centenary of Parry's birth. Accordingly, Vaughan Williams dedicated the composition "to the memory of my master Hubert Parry not as an attempt palely to reflect his incomparable art, but in the hope that he would have found in this motet (to use his own words) 'something characteristic,'" a phrase Parry often applied when assessing his pupils' efforts.[10] Overall, the bold dissonance treatment and close textures recall choral works by Anglo-Canadian composer Healey Willan (1880–1968)—the unusual sound perhaps a cheeky allusion to the many sins Vaughan Williams committed against "correct" voice leading while under Parry's tutelage—but the effect of such strange harmonies, particularly coupled with John Skelton's prophetic text, is vibrant and compelling.

The small number of pieces debuting between 1945 and 1947 may misleadingly suggest that Vaughan Williams was not especially busy during that period. In fact, besides arranging a suite based upon the incidental music from *Flemish Farm* (first performed at a Proms concert in July 1945),[11] he completed the film score for *The Loves of Joanna Godden* by the end of 1946, oversaw the debut of the Concerto for Two Pianos, and finished revising his Double Trio in its new guise as the Partita for Double String Orchestra (1948). Now expanded to chamber orchestral proportions, the Partita added double basses—but not second violins—renamed the opening Fantasia as "Prelude," and replaced the closing Rondino with a new movement titled "Fantasia."[12] Even with this restructuring, the work still seems unsatisfactory, though it is difficult to say why—perhaps some combination of the dense textures, complicated rhythmic counterpoint, and uncharacteristic lack of melodic emphasis. In fact, the Partita gives the impression of Vaughan Williams deliberately working outside his comfort zone, focusing on aspects of rhythmic and metric intricacy that, if penned by Paul Hindemith, Michael Tippett, or Constant Lambert, likely would pass without comment. The most successful and

Example 16.1a   Symphony (No. 6) in E Minor, mvt. 2, mm. 1–5 ("Two Hot Sausages" motive)

Example 16.1b   Symphony (No. 6) in E Minor, mvt. 4, mm. 1–3 ("Miserable Starkey" motive)

least mannered example is the third movement, "Intermezzo (Homage to Henry Hall)," the subtitle of which pays tribute to the popular leader of the BBC Dance Orchestra, and displays a swaggeringly chic quality not especially common in Vaughan Williams's music.[13]

Much of his energy, however, was focused on his Symphony (No. 6) in E Minor, begun in 1944 and finished three years later. Like the previous two symphonies, the Sixth contains numerous and often subtle musical references. Most commonly noted are two rhythmic figures—one opening the second movement, the other at the beginning of the finale—originally written for (or inspired by music from) *Flemish Farm*, but never used. The players of the London Symphony Orchestra allegedly labeled these motives "Two Hot Sausages" and "Miserable Starkey," based on their rhythmic accentuation (Example 16.1a and b).[14]

Vaughan Williams did, however, extract several passages from *Coastal Command* for use here, some quite closely from the source material.[15] Additionally, Malcolm Sargent claimed that the Scherzo's tenor saxophone solo paid tribute to the members of the West Indian Dance Orchestra and their leader, Ken "Snakehips" Johnson, killed when the West End club where they were engaged, the Café de Paris, was bombed by the Germans in March 1941.[16] Despite some critical disdain regarding the saxophone's presence, Vaughan Williams staunchly defended its use. When asked if a bass clarinet could replace it as a cost-saving measure, he replied that the saxophone "is essential to the work. I am tired of boiling down my work so that it can be played by two banjos and a harmonium . . . If [orchestras] cannot run to a Saxophone I fear they cannot do the Symphony. You might as well play it without double basses."[17]

Vaughan Williams revealed a more personal detail to Michael Kennedy several years later. "With regard to the last movement of my No. 6. I do NOT BELIEVE in meanings and mottos as you know, but I think we can get in words nearest to the substance of my last movement in 'we are such stuff as dreams are made on, and our little life is rounded by a sleep.'"[18] The significance of his slight misquotation of Shakespeare becomes clearer if placed in context. It concludes a short monologue by Prospero the magician in *The Tempest*: having conjured spirits to stage a masque for his daughter, Miranda, and her recently betrothed fiancé, Ferdinand, he abruptly ends the performance to face his unfinished business with the monstrous Caliban. Alert to the couple's surprise at his actions, he quickly assuages their concerns:

> Our revels now are ended. These our actors,
> As I foretold you, were all spirits and
> Are melted into air, into thin air:
> And, like the baseless fabric of this vision,
> The cloud-capp'd towers, the gorgeous palaces,
> The solemn temples, the great globe itself,
> Yea, all which it inherit, shall dissolve
> And, like this insubstantial pageant faded,
> Leave not a rack behind. We are such stuff
> As dreams are made on, and our little life
> Is rounded with a sleep.[19]

Prospero reminds his audience that his magic is illusory, ethereal, the stuff of dreams and visions—just as our own tiny lives, legacies, and achievements are rendered insignificant against the backdrop of eternity.

This seems a compelling way to account "for the extreme contrast in the Sixth Symphony between the turbulence of the first three movements and the protracted *pianissimo* Epilogue": as a struggle to defy the inevitability of entropy and decay, knowing that you will fail.[20] In this respect, the first movement mounts the strongest offensive against symphonic conventions and boundaries. It forgoes sonata–allegro form in favor of a quasi-rotational approach applied to its three primary theme groups, the divisions between which overlap and blur. The ostensible key signature of E minor seems more a general suggestion rather than a specific designation, but with a level of interplay between diatonic, modal, octatonic, and hexatonic collections that is exceptional even by Vaughan Williams's now-familiar embrace of harmonic ambiguity.[21] Similarly, the meters are constantly undermined by syncopations, borrowed rhythms, hemiolas, and off-beat accents; only the final *Tranquillo* statement of the third theme at **15** is unaffected by such disruptions. The second movement (Moderato), by contrast, eschews rhythmic variety in favor of the gradual, unrelenting intensification of the "two hot sausages" figure— perhaps Vaughan Williams's rejoinder to Constant Lambert's jibe, alluded to in the symphony's program note, that "the whole trouble with a folk song is that once you have played it through there is nothing much you can do except play it over again and play it rather louder."[22] Though not borrowed from a folk source, such a process here results in near-unbearable dramatic tension.

This discomfort is further emphasized by the subtle juxtaposition of B♭ and E as the second movement's central referential pitches. This relationship takes on even greater prominence in the Scherzo, which opens with all twelve chromatic pitches presented in a rising sequence of paired tritones (Example 16.2). This eventually becomes, for want of a better term, the "principal subject" of a movement that Vaughan Williams unhelpfully described as "fugal in texture but not in structure."[23] Like the first movement, the Scherzo undergoes strange transmutations, negotiating "an unstable dialogue between a counterpoint that persistently congeals into melody and accompaniment, and a thematic homophony that persistently dissolves into counterpoint," the paradoxical absurdity of which is complemented by a Shostakovian secondary melody.[24] It is also here that the saxophone's infamous solo appears, but its legato suaveness degenerates into a ploddingly brutal and mechanistic reprise from the full orchestra, a hint that the piece's myriad transformations—formal, textural, rhythmic, harmonic—have finally reached their limits. In literary terms, we have achieved narrative collapse, the breakdown of a coherent path forward. The Sixth Symphony's Epilogue, a desolate quasi-fugue, is the musical analogue to this: its ponderously static subject showcases the most important structural and motivic intervals of the previous movements—the tritone, minor third, and minor second—and the two

Example 16.2 Symphony (No. 6) in E Minor, mvt. 3, mm. 1–7 (indicating tritone pairings)

sixteenth–eighth-note rhythmic pattern that dominated the Moderato. But all the passion and vitality of those gestures have melted into thin air, their dynamism replaced by dissolution and disillusion. Their power spent, they "drift about contrapuntally" (in the composer's words) until their inherent pointlessness is confirmed by the E-minor triad closing the piece—a destiny foretold from the start.[25] One senses that Holst would have admired such a sentiment expressed in such uncompromisingly austere terms, as he did himself in *Egdon Heath* and *The Planets,* particularly "Neptune, the Mystic." But if we cast Vaughan Williams as Prospero in this scenario, then the spell conjured in the Sixth Symphony by the Wizard of White Gates was a dark one indeed for many listeners. Deryck Cooke described the experience of hearing the Epilogue as "nothing short of cataclysmic . . . an ultimate nihilism . . . every drop of blood seemed frozen in one's veins," though it did not prevent the work from quickly attaining international acclaim.[26]

With the Sixth Symphony completed, Vaughan Williams turned his attention to a cluster of amateur-oriented compositions: *Folk Songs of the Four Seasons* (1950), the Concerto Grosso for String Orchestra (1950), and a cantata called *The Sons of Light* (1951). All three were "large-scale community music-making events" that premiered at the Royal Albert Hall, the largest of which was the 3000-voice chorus at the inaugural Singing Festival for the National Federation of Women's Institutes (NFWI) that performed *Folk Songs of the Four Seasons*. Vaughan Williams almost certainly wrote the work at the behest of his old friend Fanny Farrer, now the General Secretary of the NFWI, and received carte blanche in selecting the text and design.[27] The choral-orchestral result was a series of folk songs and carols—plus the medieval rota "Sumer Is Icumen In"—outlining the calendar year. It was tailored for the three divisions of the choir: the largest sang in unison, and the second and third in parts, the third performing unaccompanied. The five-movement Concerto Grosso adopted a similar three-part stratification, applied here to the 400-strong string orchestra of the Rural Music Schools Association. It evokes predecessors like Britten's *Simple Symphony* or Holst's *Holberg* and *St. Paul Suites*: short, well-written pieces engaging to hear and gratifying to play for amateurs and professionals alike. The divisions are for a concertino group, a tutti ensemble ("who can play in the 3rd position, and simple double stops"), and an ad lib body of "less experienced players," including those "who prefer to use only open strings."[28] The almost Handelian result combines an array of relatively simple parts into a richly textured whole, making this one of Vaughan Williams's last and most fluent neoclassical compositions. Somewhat less effective was *The Sons of Light*, a three-movement cantata written for the massed choirs of the Schools' Music Association of Great Britain. It once again fulfilled a request from an old friend—violist Bernard Shore, now chief music inspector of schools—and some 1150 choristers (plus orchestra) took part in the premiere. The texts, written by Ursula Wood, were inspired by stories of creation myths; of these, the most imaginatively set was the second movement's "The Song of the Zodiac," featuring distinctive episodes assigned to each of the twelve astrological signs.

These broadly accessible pieces were balanced by two more unusual ones, both completed in 1949: *An Oxford Elegy* and the *Fantasia (quasi variazione) on the "Old 104th" Psalm Tune* for piano, chorus, and orchestra.

The melody featured in the latter was written by Thomas Ravenscroft for his *Whole Booke of Psalms* (1621), with text from an earlier metrical version attributed to Thomas Sternhold and John Hopkins ("My soul, praise the Lord, speak good of his name").[29] The *Fantasia* resists easy classification. Beethoven's Fantasia, op. 80 represents one of its few antecedents, but Vaughan Williams makes greater use of the choir; additionally, his scoring is considerably thicker and the texture often busier than Beethoven's.[30] The title also raises questions. Was Vaughan Williams treating variation form so loosely that it evoked the more freewheeling fantasia, or did this particular fantasia adopt an approach to thematic transformation that broadly aligned with variation form? Such taxonomic issues little concerned the composer, who was always more interested in a piece's expressive effect than its adherence to convention. That said, it also means that the *Fantasia on the "Old 104ᵗʰ"* is somewhat difficult to grasp. Despite its brevity—only lasting about fifteen minutes—it feels slightly overstuffed as it strains to encompass the variety of techniques, timbres, and textures on display over the course of a prelude, seven variations, and coda. Virtuosic cadenzas, free and fugal counterpoint, and expansive chorales for soloist and ensemble pass in review, all loosely organized around a central mode of D Aeolian, and in frequently striking harmonizations. Unfortunately, its difficulty, expansive performing forces, and expense mitigate against its being more widely taken up.

The combination of orator, chorus, and orchestra featured in *An Oxford Elegy* is similarly uncommon, but had a recent analogue in *Thanksgiving for Victory*. Although longer than its predecessor, the *Elegy* is smaller in scale, employing a chamber ensemble and only two texts, both by Matthew Arnold: excerpts from *The Scholar Gypsy* and *Thyrsis*. Vaughan Williams had long admired Arnold's verse, but his early settings of *Dover Beach* and *The Future* were either lost or incomplete, and he never realized his long-desired goal of writing an opera based on *The Scholar Gypsy*. His approach here, however, is particularly effective, keeping the central focus on the text by assigning most of it to the speaker. Selections from the two poems, ingeniously and sensitively interwoven against languorous and unhurried music, gently invoke the melancholic aspect of English pastoralism, a tranquil and nostalgic vision befitting the city of dreaming spires.

Through all of this postwar activity ran the thread of dramatic music. Vaughan Williams completed scores for three Ealing Studios films between 1946 and 1950: *The Loves of Joanna Godden* (completed 1946, released 1947), *Scott of the Antarctic* (1948), and *Bitter Springs* (1950). That last was a collaboration with Ernest Irving, who arranged and scored "thematic material supplied by Vaughan Williams" for about half of the numbers, but wrote the remainder himself.[31] It was *Scott of the Antarctic*, however, that exerted the strongest grip on Vaughan Williams's imagination; he wound up writing more than twice as much music as was eventually used in the film, though he would reuse both canonic and castoff passages in *Sinfonia Antartica* a few years later.[32] The music for *Joanna Godden* came easily as well—he was especially proud of rising to the challenge to musically depict foot-and-mouth disease—but later found himself unable to remember anything he had written for it, although the studio extracted ten episodes from the soundtrack for gramophone release in 1948.[33] Vaughan Williams experienced another uncharacteristic memory lapse with the short propaganda film *Dim Little Island* (1949), made under the auspices of the Central Office of Information. Most of the soundtrack features excerpts from *Five Variants of "Dives and Lazarus,"* but it also includes brief arrangements of the folk songs "Pretty Betsy" and "The Pride of Kildare" and voice-over narration from the composer himself, although he later denied having worked on the film at all.[34]

He also wrote a small amount of incidental music for two non-cinematic dramas. The first was a revival of *The Masque of Charterhouse*, a pageant from 1911 tracing the founding and history of his old school. For this revised performance of 1950, Vaughan Williams arranged the hymn tune AUCTOR OMNIUM BONORUM—composed by Johann Lohner but adapted by J. S. Bach, with Latin text by former Charterhouse headmaster William Haig Brown—and new "Solemn Music" for the closing scene, which featured an orchestral setting of the school hymn, the *Carmen Carthusianum*.[35] He also composed three short musical episodes for a radio adaptation of Thomas Hardy's *The Mayor of Casterbridge* (1951) produced by the BBC West of England Service, much of which he later recast as *Prelude on an Old Carol Tune* (1952). The tune in question was "On Christmas Night the Joy-Bells Ring," which dominates the fabric of the first two movements ("Casterbridge" and "Intermezzo"), while the third, rather fragmentary section ("Weyhill Fair") conveys Michael Henchard's panic at the realization that he sold his wife while in a drunken stupor the night before, thus putting the events of the story into motion.[36]

All of these dramatic works, however, were dwarfed by the culminating effort of this period. *The Pilgrim's Progress* debuted at Covent Garden on 26 April 1951, indirectly linking it with the Festival of Britain that opened the following week.[37] Nearly half a century in the making, it incorporated music and dramatic elements from the Reigate production of 1906, *The Shepherds of the Delectable Mountains* (1922), the BBC radio production from 1943, and the Fifth Symphony. It was the success of these last two that apparently spurred the composer to complete the opera, although he had drafted substantial portions of Acts I and II between 1925 and 1936. Unfortunately, the result was a beautiful disappointment, let down by subpar production values at the premiere and, more importantly, Vaughan Williams's dramatic sensibilities.

While Vaughan Williams had an extremely specific dramaturgical vision for *The Pilgrim's Progress*, it had few operatic antecedents. Rutland Boughton's "choral drama" *Bethlehem* (1915), adapted from the Coventry Nativity Play, was one; indeed, Vaughan Williams's designation of *The Pilgrim's Progress* as a "Morality" rather than an opera acknowledges its literary roots, for Bunyan's allegory follows the tradition of medieval morality plays like *Everyman* that edified as well as entertained. "You must remember that the Opera is to be acted almost like a ritual and not in the ordinary dramatic sense,"[38] Vaughan Williams explained to E. J. Dent, the closest parallels he could think of being Act I of *Parsifal* and the initiation scene from *Die Zauberflöte*. He also told Steuart Wilson that it was "not 'dramatic'—but then it is not meant to be. Whether this is a good excuse I do not know. It is more of a ceremony really than a drama."[39] Yet he insisted to both Boughton and Foss that "it is essentially a stage piece and not for a cathedral," even though some critics believed that the meditative and overtly religious atmosphere suggested otherwise.[40] It is, in some ways, a dramatic equivalent of the Sixth Symphony, in that it explores notions of transformation and eternity. The whole story, Bunyan reminds us, is "in the similitude of a dream," calling up comparisons to the baseless fabric of Prospero's visions, and posing difficulties for effective staging.

The root of the problem lies with the near-static first act, the tempo marking of which rarely exceeds Moderato, a practice that continues into the slightly livelier opening scene of Act II ("The Arming of the Pilgrim"). Following the Prologue delivered by Bunyan, Pilgrim meets the Evangelist, who sends him on his way toward the Wicket Gate; the ineffectual warnings of Pilgrim's Neighbours constitute the only minor obstacle, which is summarily dealt with. Following a tumultuous instrumental interlude, the next scene opens with an exhausted Pilgrim arriving at the House Beautiful—but what tribulations he has faced in the interim, we do not know. Introducing an intervening conflict or challenge (the Slough of Despond, for example) could have enlivened both the dramatic pacing and musical variety. Instead, the lack of action results in a curiously passive protagonist for whom the King's Highway seems little more threatening than a four-lane thoroughfare with regular service stations.

Dyneley Hussey's sympathetic assessment correctly observes that Vaughan Williams's sense of drama is unconventional—not unlike his interpretations of Bach's music—but argues that the unfamiliar treatment only seems "static because it is less concerned with physical movements than with inward conflicts."[41] While this critique is accurate, the challenge lies in conveying that to audiences (though it appears that the Cambridge revival of 1954 was more successful in this regard than the premiere production at Covent Garden). Nevertheless, by the time Pilgrim confronts Apollyon in Act II, scene 2, three quarters of an hour has passed with little more than expository scenes, reflective meditations, and static tableaux to show for it. This lack of action may be why Vaughan Williams's assignation of a monotone to Apollyon sometimes comes in for criticism—it represents yet another example of unchanging sameness—even though it is absolutely the correct decision, dramatically and musically: Apollyon's soul is evil, and therefore without music. The remaining scenes strike a better balance between action and reflection, and the repose of the Delectable Mountains, a near-seamless integration of music from the one-act opera of 1922, should be an appropriate reward after Pilgrim's journey, but it does not feel that way. Even though the second half of the work more effectively conveys the physical and spiritual dangers Pilgrim faces, the broader sense of his struggle to overcome his initial lack of faith—both in God and in himself—is largely lost.

Vaughan Williams's decision to retain the general order of scenes from the Reigate production must be judged a misstep. Perhaps thinking that it would save him further effort, he instead locked himself into a musico-dramatic template that he had long since surpassed.[42] This is a great shame, because much of the music in The Pilgrim's Progress is wonderful.

The use of the noble hymn tune YORK at the beginning and end is radiantly sublime, and several episodes—Lord Lechery's song at Vanity Fair (added after the premiere), the duet for the By-Ends, and the Woodcutter Boy's song preceding it—unerringly hit their targets. Even when the dramatic efficacy ebbs, the score rarely does, a characteristic observed by Pilgrim himself when arriving at the House Beautiful: "Music in the house; music in the heart; music in heaven for joy that I am here," a statement perfectly reflecting Vaughan Williams's own spiritual credo.

"Worthy of the Cause Which He Serves"
(1951–1958)

ADELINE'S DEATH PRECIPITATED A HOST OF CHANGES AT WHITE GATES. Her immobility and Vaughan Williams's general indifference to his surroundings meant that the house had become shabby: peeling paint, ragged linen, and general disorder ruled, so Vaughan Williams, Wood, and Curle set to work clearing out and cleaning up, sometimes with un-expectedly emotional results.[1] Vaughan Williams and Wood's relationship also shifted. For years, she had publicly played the role of the composer's secretary and assistant, the truth known or guessed only by a few, but that began to change. She and Vaughan Williams holidayed together in Hythe (Kent) and Cambridge that July, and he presented her "an allow-ance or a present or what you will of £200 a year," which allowed her to move to a two-bedroom flat in Fitzrovia.[2] She chose it ostensibly so that Vaughan Williams "could have a room as a *pied à terre*" after evening events in London, a less taxing alternative to the late-night commutes he had undertaken while Adeline was alive.[3] Wood also gently encouraged him to enjoy the benefits of his advancing age and distinguished repu-tation, both socially and professionally. His acceptance of an honorary doctorate from the University of Bristol in December, the first music degree ever awarded by that institution, combined both, as he was able to reunite with his old friend Arnold Barter (longtime conductor of the Bristol Philharmonic) during his visit.

As ever for Vaughan Williams, though, work came first. He sent a variety of revisions to *The Pilgrim's Progress* to Roy Douglas early in summer 1951, the result of several lengthy exchanges with E. J. Dent, of which the addition of Lord Lechery's Song is the best known. Yet several other production shortcomings still persisted, particularly the costume for Apollyon that resembled "a cross between an Assyrian figure and the Michelin [Man]."[4] He also undertook minor revisions to all of his symphonies but the *London* upon learning that John Barbirolli was planning to conduct his full symphonic cycle for the Hallé Orchestra's 1951–1952 season. Vaughan Williams led *A Sea Symphony* himself with that ensemble in March 1952, at which point he revealed to Barbirolli the existence of *Sinfonia Antartica*. Though it was too late to add to that season's roster, Barbirolli delightedly accepted the offer to lead its debut the following January.

While these symphonic and operatic works dominated 1951 and 1952, several smaller works also emerged. *An Oxford Elegy* finally had its public premiere on 19 June 1952, and Vaughan Williams arranged the *Prelude on an Old Carol Tune* from his music for the BBC's radio production of *The Mayor of Casterbridge*. He also mooted the idea of writing an essay collection to Alan Frank at OUP, possibly stimulated by some reminiscences that the BBC requested from him in honor of Stanford's centenary. The most surprising project, however, was a Romance in D♭ for Harmonica, written after Vaughan Williams attended a concert by Larry Adler, one of that instrument's most distinguished performers. Adler found it a considerable challenge, but at the first London performance at a Proms Concert in September 1952, it elicited an immediate encore from the Albert Hall audience, a rarity for a new work.[5]

Similarly unusual circumstances surrounded the revival of *The Bridal Day*. Though the work was completed in 1939, its premiere was canceled by the war. However, the BBC offered to televise a first performance in conjunction with Queen Elizabeth's coronation in 1953, so Vaughan Williams and Wood toured a studio in March 1952 to see how it might work. The composer remained doubtful. "How a whole masque is to get into a frame about 12 inches square passes my comprehension," he confessed to Foss,[6] but nevertheless decided to move forward with revisions. He and Wood also took the opportunity to holiday in France for about two weeks that May—his first trip abroad since 1938, and presaging several more.

On 11 October 1952, the eve of Vaughan Williams's eightieth birthday, the leader writers of *The Times* paid tribute to his long and storied career:

Happy is the man who lives long enough to look back on the accomplishment of the work he set out, or was fated, to do and to see its fruits being harvested. Happier still is he who in age finds his creative powers undiminished, whose radical mind is still unblunted and whose prophetic vision is still penetrating enough to bring new revelations of truth.[7]

The sentiments expressed by the editors were echoed by friends, colleagues, and admirers from around the world, including Queen Elizabeth, who sent a congratulatory telegram from Balmoral that joined the many other cards, letters, and gifts sent to White Gates. The Incorporated Society of Musicians held a dinner in Vaughan Williams's honor, where Herbert Howells led a fulsome and eloquent toast to "the man most fitted to receive the admiration, gratitude, and proud affection . . . of countless thousands the world over who have come under the spell of his genius."[8] Less embarrassing for Vaughan Williams, who hated being the center of attention on such occasions, were the numerous celebratory concerts to which he was invited and, in some cases, for which he chose the program. These included the London Philharmonic's birthday concert, led by Boult on 12 October and featuring *A Song of Thanksgiving*, the Symphony in D Major, *Flos Campi*, and *The Sons of Light*; and another mounted in Dorking the day before, consisting of *An Oxford Elegy*, *Five Mystical Songs*, the *Benedicite*, and his arrangement of *Old Hundredth*.

Once the celebrations had died down and the thank-you notes were all written, Vaughan Williams returned to composition. He had been commissioned to write a piece for Queen Elizabeth's coronation, was recasting passages from *The Sons of Light* for a short choral song cycle, and oversaw Roy Douglas's arrangement of a suite extracted from *Folk Songs of the Four Seasons*. Looming largest was *Sinfonia Antartica*, a late-November rehearsal of which inspired several alterations that Vaughan Williams and Douglas carried out over the following month. Around this time, rumors arose that Douglas was orchestrating (or claiming to orchestrate) Vaughan Williams's new works, a misconception that may have resulted from the composer's running joke of introducing Douglas, his copyist, as "the man who writes my music for me."[9] He was horrified to learn that his remark had been misconstrued, more concerned about its effect on Douglas's reputation than his own, and quashed the allegations as soon as he learned of their existence. Fortunately, this was the only significant shadow cast over the premiere of *Sinfonia Antartica* on 14 January 1953. Rehearsals with Barbirolli and the Hallé went smoothly, and the performance was warmly received by the Manchester audience, though its five movements and filmic origins inspired a considerable amount of discussion about whether it counted as an "actual" symphony. Ernest Irving, the dedicatee, wittily parried such critiques, responding to one complaint about the work's bleakness by "point[ing] out that Scott was not out on a beano and that the Antarctic plateau was no Hampstead Heath."[10]

Vaughan Williams left such critical debates to others, for his attention had turned to more personal concerns. Just before he and Wood traveled to Manchester for *Antartica*'s debut concert, and after attending a performance of *Tristan und Isolde*, he asked her to marry him. She accepted, and the two were wed in a quiet ceremony at St. Pancras Parish Church on 7 February—an unsurprising event to many of their friends, and one that many later credited for reviving the composer in the twilight of his career. The couple soon began looking for a new home in London, which necessitated the sale of White Gates and, somewhat more reluctantly for Vaughan Williams, resigning as conductor for the LHMF, although he stayed on as its President and continued directing annual performances of the *St. Matthew Passion* in Dorking. The newlyweds eventually took a lease on a beautiful John Nash–designed terrace house across from Regent's Park at 10 Hanover Terrace, where they moved in September. Gil Jenkins had a room kept for him in the new house as well, a somewhat unusual arrangement explained by the fact that Jenkins and Ursula had been carrying on an affair since the mid-1940s, with Vaughan Williams's knowledge and tacit sanction, which apparently continued after the composer's marriage to Wood.[11]

The months prior to the move were full of activities. Following the Passion performances and the LHMF, the Vaughan Williamses honeymooned in Italy in April and May. They returned home only weeks before the coronation on 2 June, for which Vaughan Williams had written a short anthem (*O Taste and See*) and made a congregational arrangement of *The Old Hundredth*, adapted from the 1929 setting he had made for the LHMC. This work occurred against the backdrop of rehearsals for *Riders to the Sea* and *Hugh the Drover* at Sadler's Wells, along with other coronation concerts, including one sponsored by the Arts Council (at which Vaughan Williams's part song "Silence and Music," part of the collaborative cycle *A Garland for the Queen*, had its first performance), the BBC's televised premiere of *The Bridal Day*, and the royal commission of Benjamin Britten's *Gloriana* at Covent Garden. Although Vaughan Williams privately admitted that he didn't care much for the opera, the unsympathetic public response roused him to defend it in *The Times*:

> I do not propose, after a single hearing, to appraise either the words or the music of *Gloriana*. The important thing to my mind, at the moment, is that, so far as I know, for the first time in history the Sovereign has commanded an opera by a composer from these islands for a great occasion. Those who cavil at the public expense involved should realize what such a gesture means to the prestige of our own music.[12]

Old friends and former students streamed through White Gates in the months before the Vaughan Williamses departed, but such pleasantries were disrupted by the death of the composer's trusted colleague Hubert Foss in late May, a loss that was deeply felt. At the same time, Vaughan Williams was reviewing proofs of his forthcoming essay collection (sporting the cumbersome title *Some Thoughts on Beethoven's Choral Symphony with Writings on Other Musical Subjects*), was collaborating once more with Martin Shaw to co-edit a collection of carols for OUP, and was pushing himself to finish a new work, "only emerging [from his study] to sleep & have meals."[13] The piece in question was *Hodie*, a choral-orchestral setting of the Nativity story, which he had begun the previous winter and completed in August. A play-through in early September inspired a few changes, including the addition of an aria at the request of Eric Greene, the prospective tenor soloist. Soon after, Vaughan Williams began revising *Along the Field* for a recording that, unfortunately, was never released, but the new version received a performance in May 1955.

Vaughan Williams spent most of late 1953 settling in at Hanover Terrace, which soon became a popular spot for friends and musicians to gather. Ursula established a series of "Singeries," monthly gatherings of friends who enjoyed singing part songs and social drinking, with

Vaughan Williams conducting the sometimes excessively convivial group. Distinguished professional guests also dropped in for rehearsals or musicales, including the tubist of the London Symphony Orchestra, Philip Catelinet, for whom the composer wrote a concerto in 1954 to mark the orchestra's fiftieth-anniversary concert, and Frederick Grinke, who gave a private performance of Vaughan Williams's new Violin Sonata in early September.

Much of 1954, however, was taken up by travel. The bitter winter was made more tolerable by a triumphant performance of *The Pilgrim's Progress* at Cambridge in late February. Although the early rehearsals boded ill, the end result was a far more effective realization of Vaughan Williams's vision than Covent Garden's, and he was enormously grateful to producer Dennis Arundell and conductor Boris Ord for their inspired efforts. Once the Passion performances and the LHMF had wrapped up in late April, the Vaughan Williamses took a two-week holiday in northern Italy (visiting Pisa, Florence, Siena, and Rome) before a more extended trip to the United States that autumn. Vaughan Williams's old friend Keith Falkner, now Professor of Voice at Cornell University, had invited the composer to Ithaca as a visiting professor for the term, a sojourn that he expanded into a nationwide lecture tour. This required clearing his calendar, which had the side benefits of allowing him to prepare for the September premiere of *Hodie* at Worcester for the Three Choirs Festival—which he directed, along with *Flos Campi* and the *Pastoral Symphony*—and work on his latest large-scale project: a new symphony.

Although ostensibly in residence at Cornell for the fall term, Vaughan Williams only spent about five weeks there between late September and early December, though they were filled with activities. He delivered a series of lectures under the rubric "What Is the Background of Music?" (repeated partially or in full during his tour), published the following year as *The Making of Music*. He also worked with composition students, conducted the Buffalo Philharmonic on campus on 9 November, and was honored by a concert from the Cornell Orchestra and Choirs. Though the performances all went well, and the musicians were inspired to work with Vaughan Williams (and he with them), the flares of temper that often accompanied his conducting were in evidence. One outburst was captured on film by a trumpeter who missed his cue in rehearsal, while

another was barely sublimated during the actual concert performance of
A London Symphony when it turned out that Vaughan Williams's prepared
score was accidentally replaced with a new, unmarked one. Ironically,
"he was so angry that he gave one of the best performances of his life."[14]
Only in rehearsals or performances would this otherwise unassuming
man reveal such levels of rage. Nearly all musicians who worked with
him understood that these furious blasts, though always quick to subside,
stemmed not from egotistic vanity at being disobeyed, but from frustration at their collective failure—himself included—to meet his enormously high standards. A compliment he paid to Martin Shaw's artistry
applied just as much to himself: only "the very best . . . is alone worthy
of the cause which he serves," a reflection of his lifelong respect for and
devotion to his art.[15]

The Vaughan Williamses left Ithaca in early October for a month-
long lecture tour and holiday that took them across the continent. The
composer spoke at and attended concerts in his honor at the University
of Toronto, the University of Michigan, and Indiana University, and
stopped at Niagara Falls and Chicago before setting off on a three-day
train journey to California. After a short residency at UCLA, the couple
took a week-long break in Santa Barbara, where Vaughan Williams
completed a set of Gaelic song arrangements and attended a *Riders to
the Sea* double bill at UCSB: Synge's play followed by his own opera. He
was so impressed by the results that he hosted the student opera cast at
his hotel for tea.

Following a stop at the Grand Canyon, Vaughan Williams returned
to Cornell by early November, remaining there (aside from a concert in Buffalo) until the end of the month. He and Ursula then went
on to New York, where, as guests of Rudolf Bing, they attended two
performances at the Metropolitan Opera and visited old friends James
and Rebecca Friskin (née Clarke) and Peggy Glanville-Hicks. Their final
stop was New Haven, where Vaughan Williams received Yale University's
Howland Memorial Prize. Holst had been awarded the same prize exactly thirty years earlier, and Vaughan Williams invoked the memory of
his old friend several times in his acceptance speech, a valedictory effort drawing from his entire corpus of writings and lectures of the previous half-century.[16] The voyage back to England on the *Queen Mary*
provided an appropriately luxurious end to the tour, and the Vaughan

Williamses were back at Hanover Terrace in time to host their now-annual Christmas carol Singery.

In an appropriate display of holiday spirit, Vaughan Williams generously donated some of his American earnings to the LHMF and (anonymously) to the journal *Music & Letters*, which was in danger of folding, and used an unexpected windfall from the Performing Arts Society to support a young composer, John South.[17] In the following months, he made further donations to offset the legal costs for a slander case brought against the ISCM, and ensured that Harold Child's widow would receive his share of royalties for *The New Commonwealth*. Although these represented only the latest entries in his long charitable history, he began thinking about codifying his approach to it more formally. By now quite wealthy, Vaughan Williams admitted he was "not interested in money, except as a means of not having to think about it," so he turned to colleagues for counsel on how best to secure his philanthropic legacy.[18] By summer 1955, Vaughan Williams had received a series of initial guidelines from his accountant, Albert ("Bert") Sturgess, on channeling his performing rights fees into an endowment benefiting musicians and musical organizations. In 1956, this was officially organized as the RVW Trust; since then, it has contributed millions of pounds toward recordings, educational programs, festivals, concerts, performing ensembles, and individual musicians across the United Kingdom.[19] This philanthropy may also explain why he co-signed a series of letters to *The Times* over the next few years with regard to copyright legislation that would affect royalty rates and mechanical reproduction rights (and thus the amount of money available to the Trust).

Several smaller works debuted in the first half of 1955, including the Prelude on Three Welsh Hymn Tunes for brass band, the choral song cycle drawn from *The Sons of Light* (titled *Sun, Moon, Stars, and Man*), *Song for a Spring Festival* (written for the LHMF), and *Diabelleries*, a set of variations by diverse composers written for Anne Macnaghten's New Music Group concert series.[20] He also completed the song "Hands, Eyes and Heart" for Keith Falkner, a mixed choral arrangement of Patrick Hadley's *Fen and Flood*—of which he was the dedicatee—and unexpectedly decided to revise his almost thirty-year-old masque *On Christmas Night*. But it was the new Symphony in D Minor—the first whose title contained an identifying ordinal, the Eighth—that demanded most of his attention. He held his usual play-through for friends in mid-April, and gave it to John Barbirolli to review shortly afterward, with the caveat that it would not be ready for that summer's Cheltenham Festival. Only by August had he wrestled it into a satisfactory form, sending it to OUP for safekeeping until Roy Douglas could undertake copying and editing duties in October.

When he wasn't composing, Vaughan Williams was either attending concerts, traveling, or both. The Vaughan Williamses visited Cornwall for the May Day observances at Padstow, and then went on to Cambridge for May Week, followed by Ipswich to celebrate Martin Shaw's eightieth birthday, Cheltenham for the Festival, and the New Forest at the express invitation of Sven and Juanita Berlin, self-described gypsies who invited the composer to hear them sing. International destinations also made it onto their itinerary, including a nearly month-long journey through Greece, capped off with visits to Venice, Solesmes, and St. Malo. A final trip to Ireland came in October, where Vaughan Williams delivered the inaugural address for the University of Cork's Arnold Bax Memorial Lecture.

The first half of 1956 largely mirrored that of the previous year. Taking precedence was the Eighth Symphony—which Vaughan Williams revised further upon returning from Cork, and again following a play-through in February—around which orbited several satellites completed at about the same time, including *A Choral Flourish*, music for the film *The England of Elizabeth*, the motet *A Vision of Aeroplanes*, and a pair of organ preludes on Welsh folk songs. Unsurprisingly, the Symphony exerted the greatest pull on the public's imagination following its premiere in May under Barbirolli, the dedicatee. Letters and reviews praised the genial and timbrally colorful work, with one notable exception. Nine-year-old Tom Whitestone had attended the London premiere, and wrote to Barbirolli saying he should perform Haydn rather than Vaughan Williams. Barbirolli passed the letter on to the composer, who took it quite well:

Dear Tom

Sir John Barbirolli has sent me your letter to him—I am glad you like Haydn; he is a very great man & wrote beautiful tunes.

I must one day try to write a tune which you will like.

Yrs affectionately,

R. Vaughan Williams[21]

A bout with phlebitis required several weeks of bed-rest in June and July, but Vaughan Williams kept himself occupied by finishing *Epithalamion* (a cantata extracted from *The Bridal Day*) and acquiring the copyright of the libretto to *The Poisoned Kiss* so that he and Ursula could revise it. They completed the initial textual alterations by the end of August, and Ursula transformed the dialogue from prose to rhymed couplets by year's end (though the musical alterations were not finished until early 1957). He was able to attend the Three Choirs Festival in Gloucester that September and reunite with a host of friends and colleagues, including Rutland Boughton and the Finzis, who drove the Vaughan Williamses out to the site in rural Gloucester (Chosen Hill) that inspired Finzi's new choral work *In Terra Pax*. Sadly, this was the last meeting between the two men. A visit to the sexton's cottage on Chosen exposed Finzi to chicken pox; unbeknownst to the Vaughan Williamses, his immune system was already compromised by Hodgkin's lymphoma, and he died three weeks later.[22] The tragedy was compounded by the deaths of George Trevelyan's wife, Janet, and of Ralph Wedgwood during the first week of September. Vaughan Williams wrote letters to *The Times* to supplement the printed obituaries for Wedgwood and Finzi, whose passings cast a pall over the Vaughan Williamses' trip to Majorca that autumn.

Vaughan Williams's own health remained surprisingly robust for a man in his mid-eighties. Energetic and lively, he rarely suffered from anything more serious than occasional colds and bouts of exhaustion from overwork, but Ursula worried about the strain his unceasing activity placed upon him. More seriously, upon returning from an early summer holiday in Austria, he was diagnosed with acute anemia and, shortly after, a cancerous prostate. Surgery followed in mid-August, and his convalescence was speedy and uneventful. He spent several weeks resting at home and with Joy Finzi and her sons in Ashmansworth, but Ursula kept the details out of the press. Fortunately, he had fully recovered by late September, and thus was able to attend the premiere of *Epithalamion* at the Royal Festival Hall, and enjoy the many celebrations accompanying his eighty-fifth birthday. Concerts, parties, and tributes lasted through October, which also witnessed the debuts of the Variations for Brass Band (a test piece for the National Brass Band Championship) and the

Flourish for Glorious John, a gift to Barbirolli in observance of the Hallé's centenary season.

At the end of October, Vaughan Williams revealed the existence of the Symphony No. 9 in E Minor to Barbirolli, the earliest ideas for which had likely gestated alongside those of the Eighth, and he organized a play-through on 2 November. It inspired the usual numerous revisions, which he made while once again laid up with phlebitis. Once the edits and the illness had run their course, Vaughan Williams turned his attention to music for *The Vision of William Blake*, a film produced for the bicentennial of Blake's birth. After seeing the rough cut of the film on 10 December, he completed his *Ten Blake Songs* for voice and oboe before the end of the year.

The demands of conducting the annual Dorking performances of the *St. John* and *St. Matthew Passion* had become increasingly heavy, so Vaughan Williams decided that the 1958 concerts would be his last. The performances that year were outstanding; indeed, he called the second of the two *St. Matthew* concerts "the best we have done."[23] It is all the more fortunate that this performance was professionally recorded—a unique historical document, revealing both the idiosyncrasies and the expressive depth of Vaughan Williams's approach to the work, along with the level of performative skill he could extract from a largely amateur chorus and ensemble.[24] Rehearsals for the Ninth Symphony soon followed, including one that Vaughan Williams funded out of his own pocket. For whatever reason, he was more apprehensive about this symphony than usual, and continued making minor cuts and alterations right up to its debut on 2 April. While perhaps more elusive than some of his others, it nevertheless garnered positive responses from press and public alike, but with occasional undertones of skepticism mixed among them.

In addition to the Passions and the symphony, Vaughan Williams also spent time in March composing three vocalises for Margaret Ritchie, and had progressed far enough on the first act of a new opera called *Thomas the Rhymer*—for which Ursula was writing the libretto—to schedule a play-through of the first scene with Roy Douglas on 8 April. But exhaustion was setting in, so it was with considerable relief that the couple left for an extended holiday in Italy, with stretches in Naples bookending a longer stay on the island of Ischia as guests of William and Susanna

Walton. The surroundings powerfully stimulated Vaughan Williams's imagination, for he wrote music for the opera nearly as fast as Ursula could produce the text, and their joint productivity continued after returning home in May. Just as work on the initial sketches wrapped up in July, Vaughan Williams was approached by Simona Pakenham—a young woman who had recently befriended the couple, and author of a book on the composer's music—about arranging some carols and composing incidental music for a Nativity play she had recently written called *The First Nowell*. He was happy to oblige, splitting his attention between the two dramatic works over the next several weeks. With few other significant projects in the pipeline, Vaughan Williams was able to take on some non-compositional responsibilities (including fundraising for a folk music library at Cecil Sharp House and fighting cuts to the BBC's Third Programme) and further travel, including to Nottingham for an honorary degree, and to Cambridge and Lincolnshire for concerts and time with friends. He also underwent a second surgery on his prostate in late July, which caused him to miss a performance of *Flos Campi* in King's Lynn and a dress rehearsal of *Sir John in Love*.[25] As before, his recovery was swift—he attended a Proms performance of his Ninth Symphony in early August, and soon after went touring around Dorset and Wiltshire with Ursula and Joy Finzi—but tragically brief.

At 3:40 in the morning on 26 August, the day he was scheduled to attend the inaugural recording sessions for the Ninth Symphony, Ralph Vaughan Williams died suddenly and quietly at home of a coronary thrombosis. He was cremated at Golders Green three days later, with only a small group of intimates in attendance at the memorial that followed, and his ashes were moved to Westminster Abbey in preparation for his funeral service on 19 September.[26] An enormous congregation of relatives, colleagues, musicians, well-wishers, and diplomats came to pay their respects, the event preceded by Boult leading the London Philharmonic Orchestra in the *Five Variants of "Dives and Lazarus,"* Bach's Double Violin Concerto, and excerpts from *Job*.[27] Music also permeated the service, including Vaughan Williams's own Coronation arrangement of *The Old Hundredth*, heard as the procession returned from the gravesite and vividly remembered by Rutland Boughton: "The sun that burst through the south windows of Westminster Abbey at the very moment of his funeral fanfares seemed perfectly to seal the triumphant memorial of that generous soul."[28] Vaughan Williams's modest memorial tile lies in the North Choir aisle, between those of Elgar and Stanford, a testament to the impact that he and his music had not only on British culture, but also the lives of countless friends and admirers. "Great artist," Boughton confirmed. "Better still, and rarer, a Great man."

The Music of 1951–1958

B Y THE MID-TWENTIETH CENTURY, VAUGHAN WILLIAMS'S PLACE IN
British music began undergoing a complicated process of renegoti-
ation. Four monographs dedicated to his music were published between
1950 and 1957, some of which pushed a stridently nationalistic view of
him that trod uncomfortably close to hagiography. At the same time, the
voices dissenting from such a view grew louder and more numerous.
As younger composers like Benjamin Britten and Michael Tippett rose
to international prominence, certain critics accused Vaughan Williams of
embodying an outdated approach to English music that embraced pro-
vinciality, amateurishness, and conservatism, both political and aesthetic—
charges that his indifference to serialism (among other high modernist
practices) seemed only to reinforce.[1] Both portrayals misrepresented and
grossly oversimplified Vaughan Williams's philosophy and his contributions
to British musical life, but they were also all but inevitable. No other figure
had contributed to the nation's musical life for so long and in so many
areas—composition, education, scholarship, administration, historical
preservation, artistic advocacy, philanthropy, performance—which meant
that reckoning with his influence was necessary for those negotiating the
paths that British music was taking in the postwar world.

Yet even as late as 1951, the composer himself still had several
contributions left to make. While the final three symphonies and the

cantata *Hodie* are the best known, Vaughan Williams also continued turning out smaller-scale and occasional pieces, such as the exquisite Three Shakespeare Songs (1951) for mixed choir. It was written in 1949 and dedicated to Cecil Armstrong Gibbs, who had asked Vaughan Williams if he could compose a test piece for the British Federation of Music Festivals. Vaughan Williams turned him down, but some weeks later Gibbs received an envelope containing the three pieces and a note: "Here is a good-will offering for Xmas. I expect you have already chosen something else. If not these are at your service."[2] The texts of the first two songs ("Full Fathom Five" and "The Cloud-Capp'd Towers") come from *The Tempest*; the latter quotes the lines from Prospero's speech that undergirded the Sixth Symphony, and ends with an evocation of its predecessor's closing major-minor contrast. The Mendelssohnian lightness of the final song ("Over Hill, Over Dale") reflects its origins in *A Midsummer Night's Dream*; like the others, it uses minimal motivic resources to maximal effect, creating strange and otherworldly sounds from the simplest of materials. The same applies, though in a slightly different context, to the Romance in D♭ for Harmonica (1952). It reflects Vaughan Williams's interest in unusual timbres and instruments, a tendency he was increasingly apt to indulge as he aged; as late as 1956, he was researching the range and abilities of the piano accordion, for purposes unknown.[3] All this is to say that the Romance, while thoroughly professional in its comportment and design, cannot quite escape the label "novelty piece," though it is striking just how seriously Vaughan Williams took the challenge of writing it. The long, rhapsodic solo lines invoke familiar practices from *The Lark Ascending*—another work classified as a "Romance"—with considerable chromatic fluidity and chordal parallelism on display from both soloist and orchestra.

These two compositions were the only significant ones to debut between summer 1951 and January 1953, when *Sinfonia Antartica* received its first performance.[4] Custom dictates that any discussion of this work begin by explaining the title's odd spelling (it was originally *Sinfonia Antarctica*, but when the combination of Latin and Greek words was pointed out, Vaughan Williams opted for *Antartica* to maintain lexical consistency), and noting its basis in music written for Ealing Studios' *Scott of the Antarctic* (1948).[5] While this origin called the work's symphonic status into question for several commentators, *Sinfonia Antartica* follows many of the same practices as Vaughan Williams's three previous symphonies: transformative cyclical themes, large-scale structural links, and consecutive hexatonic juxtapositions, used most conspicuously to expand the Prelude's first theme group.[6] More likely, certain critics found the notion of aesthetic overlap between mass entertainment and high art tacky, presumptuous, and damaging to the values embodied in the latter.[7] Such insecurities have largely dissipated with the passage of time, enabling us to more easily perceive *Sinfonia Antartica* as the starkly moving artistic statement that it is.

Several writers have identified the passages from *Scott of the Antarctic* employed in *Sinfonia Antartica*, but Vaughan Williams did not make those links explicit for listeners.[8] Rather, each of the five movements is preceded by an unspoken epigraph, shifting the focus from specific elements of the film to its broader themes and values (the virtue of endurance, the persistence of love, awe at nature's grandeur).[9] This shift likely reflected the composer's own evolving conception of Scott's *Terra Nova* expedition and the mythology surrounding it. The story of Captain Robert Falcon Scott's doomed journey to the South Pole in 1910–1911, commonly framed as a story of British determination in the face of overwhelming odds, had long captured Britons' imaginations.[10] In preparation for writing the film score, Vaughan Williams read Apsley Cherry-Garrard's *The Worst Journey in the World* (1922), a memoir by one of the expedition's only survivors. Ursula Vaughan Williams stated that "Ralph became more and more upset as he read about the inefficiencies of the organization; he despised heroism that risked lives unnecessarily, and such things as allowing five to travel on rations for four filled him with fury."[11] While the film portrayed Scott's expedition as exemplifying tragic but heroic fortitude, Vaughan Williams clearly felt that the deaths of the polar team members were both an unnecessary and appalling sacrifice.

Ultimately, his musical response led to the creation of an anti–*Pastoral Symphony*. Like that piece, *Sinfonia Antartica* initially seems to depict a particular landscape, but it in fact plumbs the darker corners of the human spirit. In the *Pastoral Symphony*, Vaughan Williams confronted the horror of war as a veteran who saw its cost firsthand, and accepted the obligation to create something better in its wake. *Sinfonia Antartica*, by contrast, implies the opposite: not only did the *Terra Nova* explorers fail to reach the pole before Roald Amundsen's Norwegian team, but also Scott himself seemingly abjured responsibility for the tragedy that followed ("The causes of the disaster are not due to faulty organization, but to misfortune in all risks which had to be undertaken") and was lionized despite his failure.[12] This lack of accountability for those in charge was familiar during the Great War as well, making the return of the wordless soprano from the *Pastoral Symphony*—now backed by a small women's chorus and the inhuman whir of a wind machine—seem like an especially poignant and bitterly cold tribute to the dead.

A more literal form of anti-pastoralism arises from the evocative depiction of the Antarctic wastes. Pastoral geography typically evokes hospitable, inviting spaces, and the pastoral music most frequently associated with such sites is similarly gentle and accessible. The inspirational role of the beautiful but war-torn French countryside on the *Pastoral Symphony* has already been noted, while Ursula Vaughan Williams noted that *Sinfonia Antartica* challenged her husband "to find musical equivalents for the physical sensations of ice, of wind blowing over the great, uninhabited desolation, of stubborn and impassable ridges of black and ice-covered rock, and to suggest man's endeavour to overcome the rigours of this bleak land and to match mortal spirit against elements."[13] All this is exemplified in the third movement ("Landscape"), which draws upon passages from the *Scott* score associated with the scaling of Beardmore Glacier, the main access point to the Antarctic plateau. The movement deliberately conveys a sense of place that is not beautiful and tranquil, but uncanny and terrifying. Framed by unsettled *Klangfarbenmelodie* generated from the flutes, horns, harp, and assorted percussion, the first theme group's ponderous stasis—a sonic metaphor for the tedious sameness confronting the explorers scaling the glacier's face—is conveyed by relentless ostinati, slow-moving harmonies, and cyclical motives. This eventually gives way to an unsettling unison statement from the full orchestra, then a tentative chorale-like figure from the horns and lower winds before the unison statement returns. A second rotation of the whole process begins at rehearsal mark **6**, but the chorale is given over this time to the organ, whose shocking timbral contrast hits with shattering intensity.[14] Unlike the Corot-like landscape that Vaughan Williams saw from the hill near Écoivres, the vision from the glacier's summit is one of desolation— quite literally, the end of the world. It is perhaps the single most disquieting moment in the composer's entire catalogue, inverting the organ's redemptive and divinely benevolent associations to depict the bleak and pitiless majesty of a frozen hellscape, an infinity of ice promising only death. It is difficult to imagine a less convivial subject for the composer, but Vaughan Williams had just entered his ninth decade of life; with Adeline's death and the apparent failure of *The Pilgrim's Progress* still palpable, it is perhaps unsurprising that such inhospitable and coldly distant visions might resonate with him. There are, of course, lighter moments in the symphony—the Scherzo and Intermezzo break the tension of the odd-numbered movements—but overall, it extends the existential crisis expressed in the Sixth Symphony, with no obvious resolution in sight.

For Britain, however, a new day appeared to be dawning as the young Princess Elizabeth ascended to the throne. In October 1952, Vaughan Williams met with William McKie, organist at Westminster Abbey, to discuss the prospect of contributing music for the Coronation the following summer. He rejected writing another *Te Deum*—but did so anyway in 1954, to little effect—gave permission for use of the English translations of the Credo and Sanctus from his Mass in G Minor, and proposed composing a short anthem. The result was *O Taste and See*, a setting of Psalm 34:8, performed as the Queen took Communion. Its simple beauty outlived the occasion; only three years later, Vaughan Williams received a letter from the Budo Festival Choir of Kampala, Uganda, winners of the 1955 Namirembe Music Festival, for which *O Taste and See* was the test piece. Additionally, Vaughan Williams offered to do "a mess-up of 'Old Hundredth,'" a rather breezy description for one of the venerable hymn tune's finest extended treatments.[15] The opening fanfare (mustering "all available trumpets") and closing verse came from his setting for the LHMC Division II Choir (1930); the Doxology is particularly notable for its multiple deceptive cadences. In between, he featured the harmonization from *Songs of Praise* in the second verse, a soaring trumpet descant in the third, and a fauxbourdon by John Dowland in the fourth. Notably, the first and last verses called for congregational participation, a Coronation ceremony first.[16] One final piece, *Silence and Music*, fulfilled an Arts Council commission for a successor to Thomas Morley's *The Triumphs of Oriana* (1601) in honor of the new Elizabethan age. Ten composers, including Bliss, Howells, Finzi, and Tippett, were invited to contribute part songs to the compendium (entitled *A Garland for the Queen*), with Vaughan Williams's the fourth in the series. Featuring text by Ursula Vaughan Williams, *Silence and Music* was dedicated "to the memory of Charles Villiers Stanford, and his Blue Bird," an homage to the grave and restrained beauty of that work by his former teacher.

Far more ebullient was the Concerto in F Minor for Bass Tuba (1954), perhaps the composer's most engaging contribution to the genre; as Vaughan Williams put it, "The music is fairly simple and obvious and can probably be listened to without much previous explanation."[17] One suspects that, as a violist, he sympathized with tubists' relegation to the lower ranks of instrumental prestige. His response—a tuneful and tightly structured composition that is by turns lyrical and virtuosic— works because it takes the instrument seriously, exploring sonorities and techniques that reveal its technical abilities and expressive depths. Several passages anticipate ideas explored elsewhere; for instance, the opening of the Romanza bears a strong resemblance to XI: Lullaby from *Hodie*, and the extensive use of hemiola received similarly thorough application in the Eighth Symphony. The Concerto also adheres to Vaughan Williams's well-established practices of tonal ambiguity, not least by employing F Phrygian as the primary collection in the first movement, while the last opens by outlining a collection centered on F (F–G–A–B–C–D♭–E♭) combining aspects of Lydian and Aeolian scales. As usual, the Romanza represents the heart of the composition, the tuba's rhapsodic potential fully exploited to unexpectedly moving effect. Unlike the Romance for Harmonica, this is no occasional or novelty piece, but a compelling demonstration of Vaughan Williams's continued ability to extract beauty even from the most unexpected sources.

Such skills, however, were not always as warmly received following the Second World War as after the First, as the Christmas cantata *Hodie* (1954) demonstrated. Its formal layout—fifteen movements plus a two-part epilogue—parallels Bach's *St. Matthew Passion*, which has fifteen scenes and two exordia. The commonalities continue from a textual standpoint, as both compositions alternate between scriptural passages and meditative poems. In the case of *Hodie*, the former derives mostly from the Gospel according to Luke—the recitational delivery of which serves to unify the work—while the latter includes contributions by John Milton, Thomas Hardy, George Herbert, William Drummond, and Ursula Vaughan Williams. This accessible and largely joyous piece conveys the Nativity's mystery and magic with an almost childlike sense of wonder (perhaps most vividly in the pomp of XIV: The March of the Three Kings), but it inspired some remarkably vitriolic criticism, including complaints that "Vaughan Williams has said nothing new," notwithstanding that "an 'avant garde' and difficult Christmas cantata is surely the last thing that even a critic wants to hear."[18] Yet Vaughan Williams might have agreed with those critics. "I've not had a new musical idea since I was 30," he once told Christopher Finzi, who found such a statement "completely incomprehensible at the time. I can understand it now. He was mining his own ideas, digging them out. He was exploring inside not outside."[19]

In fact, from a stylistic perspective, *Hodie* is surprisingly wide-ranging, juxtaposing simple four-part chorales and recitatives for treble choir and continuo with complex chromatic, pentatonic, and modal collections underpinned by unorthodox harmonies. Broadly speaking, this split divides narrative texts (i.e., taken from Scripture) or descriptions of earthly and material subjects from texts on metaphysical or spiritual topics, not unlike the approaches taken in *The Shepherds of the Delectable Mountains*, *Riders to the Sea*, and *Job*. What is new, however, is how he unites these opposing tendencies from the outset before breaking them apart in subsequent movements. Despite the initial key signature of E♭ major, the opening fanfare—later sung to the text *Hodie Christus natus est*—comprises a six-note scale centered around B♭ (B♭–C♭–D♭–E♭–G–A) that cannot be derived from any standard collection; its closest equivalents are B♭ melodic minor with a lowered second, or B♭ Phrygian with a raised seventh, each lacking the fifth scale degree. However, as this collection simultaneously embodies aspects of both key (representing the earthly and ephemeral) and mode (representing the divine and eternal), it is a canny musical symbol of the union of God and man in Christ. A few subsequent movements occupy comparably liminal spaces between humanity and divinity, including IX: Pastoral ("The Shepherds Sing"), in which a shepherd keeps catching glimpses of a world beyond his own, implied by the persistent chromatic passages within the otherwise diatonic setting. Even more poignant is Movement VII, a setting of Thomas Hardy's poem "The Oxen," which alludes to the myth that animals could talk on Christmas Eve:

> So fair a fancy few would weave
> In these years! yet, I feel
> If someone said on Christmas Eve,

"Come; see the oxen kneel,
In the lonely barton by yonder coomb
Our childhood used to know,"
I should go with him in the gloom,
Hoping it might be so.

This is the only text written from a contemporary perspective, with all of modernity's attendant doubts in train. But the narrator's skepticism is tempered by hope in a mystical promise that he cannot quite dismiss, signaled by the persistent chromaticism and parallel triads heard within the predominantly E Aeolian setting. These appear alongside movements of simple and intimate beauty, such as the gently meditative XI: Lullaby, or the entirely diatonic V: Choral ("The Blessed Son of God"), which banish such misgivings to focus instead upon the promise of Christmas. Vaughan Williams undertook another Christmas work in 1958, the Nativity play *The First Nowell*, based on Simona Pakenham's adaptation of medieval pageants that showcased arrangements of various hymns and carols. Vaughan Williams had finished only about two-thirds of the score when he died, but left enough sketches and drafts to allow Roy Douglas to complete the remainder in time for a first performance in December 1958.[20]

The pace and scope of Vaughan Williams's writing in the 1950s is remarkable by any measure, and was not limited to large-scale pieces. A clutch of part songs appeared between 1954 and 1955, three of which were arrangements of Gaelic songs (though he evidently wrote a fourth, its identity and whereabouts currently unknown).[21] The other two compositions were original: the austerely moving *Heart's Music* (1954), featuring text by Thomas Campion (1567–1620), and *Song for a Spring Festival* (1955), a setting of a short poem by Ursula Vaughan Williams performed exclusively to open the Leith Hill Musical Festival.[22] Another work was inspired by choral music, but written for brass band. The Prelude on Three Welsh Hymn Tunes (1955) is related to the Three Preludes for organ of 1920, and features two of the same melodies: BRYN CALFARIA—now simply CALFARIA—and HYFRYDOL. RHOSYMEDRE was replaced with Thomas John Williams's EBENEZER (no. 108 in *The English Hymnal*), which opens the work and returns between the renditions of CALFARIA and HYFRYDOL. Vaughan Williams wrote it for the International

Staff Band of the Salvation Army—having been impressed upon hearing them perform in Dorking—and his graceful, rhythmically fluid treatment of these dignified hymn tunes demonstrates his facility for continuous polyphony.

Vaughan Williams's final chamber work was also one of his most substantial. The Sonata in A Minor for Violin (1954), written for and dedicated to violinist Frederick Grinke, is a difficult piece in several respects, not least the technical demands placed on both soloists, and its twenty-five-minute duration places it among the composer's longest non-symphonic instrumental works. The opening Fantasia's rhythmic fluidity, pervasive hemiola, and general harmonic scheme owes a debt to the violin sonatas of Debussy and Ravel and to Bach's sonatas and partitas for solo violin, given the extended passages of multiple stops. By contrast, the angular and motoric Scherzo displays a rhythmic drive and acerbic edginess recalling Prokofiev or Bartók. Even more surprising was Vaughan Williams's use of the variation theme from the finale of his own Quintet in C Minor (1905), withdrawn almost four decades earlier, as the subject for the Sonata's own closing set of variations. The haunting opening statement gives way to a series of increasingly inventive and elaborate treatments, evoking neoclassical, impressionistic, folk-inspired, and pastoral idioms. The final variation places the theme in counterpoint with the opening Fantasia's melody, followed by a brief, *Lark Ascending*–style cadenza and an affirming A-major coda.

The increasingly extroverted character of the post-*Antartica* compositions arguably peaked with its successor in the genre, the Symphony No. 8 in D Minor (1956). Much as *Sinfonia Antartica* represents the polar opposite of the *Pastoral Symphony*, so the Eighth is the affirming equivalent of the Fourth's ambivalent stance toward Beethoven. Appropriately, it shares the key signature (though used here in the relative minor), tunefulness, and succinct dimensions of Beethoven's Eighth Symphony, and has been similarly characterized as relatively light and unassuming. Certainly it was composed at a far more congenial time in the composer's life than was *Sinfonia Antartica*: he had remarried, had begun to travel more widely, had celebrated his eightieth birthday and the Coronation festivities, and finally had witnessed a production of *The Pilgrim's Progress* that vindicated his creative efforts. Given such developments, his creation of such a timbrally colorful and expressively buoyant work is unsurprising. Its distinctive sonic palette is perhaps its most widely discussed feature. Although the full orchestra is used in the opening Fantasia, only winds and brass are employed in the Scherzo, while the Cavatina features bowed string instruments exclusively. The closing Toccata was originally titled "Toccata colle campanelle," alluding to the extensive use of "all the 'phones and 'spiels known to the composer," including glockenspiel, tubular bells, vibraphone, celesta, and tuned gongs (added at the last moment, and at no small expense, after Vaughan Williams heard them in a performance of *Turandot*).[23] Felix Aprahamian memorably dubbed the result a "Gloucestershire gamelan," but most commentators found it excessively noisy and/or snidely criticized the vibraphone's presence.[24]

This focus on instrumental color means that the symphony's tight structural organization is often overlooked. The first movement, for instance, sports the unusual title "Fantasia (Variazioni senza tema)," perhaps alluding to the fact that the second and fifth variations were the first to be written; hence the composer's wry description of the movement as "seven variations in search of a theme."[25] The process of simplification that led to the so-called first variation—which, for all practical purposes, acts as the theme—reveals a primary motive of two consecutive perfect fourths (Example 18.1).

Successive variations employ diminished, augmented, and inverted versions of that interval before returning to the initial pair of perfect fourths in the final variation, creating an effect of departure and return

Example 18.1   Symphony No. 8 in D Minor, mvt. 1, mm. 1–4

Example 18.2   Symphony No. 8 in D Minor, mvt. 4, mm. 9–14 ("A theme")

Example 18.3   Symphony No. 8 in D Minor, mvt. 4, mm. 29–34 ("B theme")

analogous to sonata–allegro form.[26] Subsequent movements also employ fourths in conspicuous motivic and structural contexts, particularly the finale, which takes the form of a modified rondo. Following an opening flourish that shifts between D major and D minor—a figure the composer described as a "sinister exordium"—the A theme is a pentatonic melody that features three interlocking fourths, while the B theme emphasizes that interval by outlining it with almost every change in direction (Examples 18.2 and 18.3).

All this should not suggest that the Eighth lacks any external associations, but those that exist are comparatively subtle. Some are self-referential: the Toccata's theme evokes the "Galliard for the Sons of the Morning" from *Job*, while the orchestration and harmonizations of the first movement's variations elicit strong connections with nearly all of Vaughan Williams's previous symphonies.[27] Other allusions are more obscure. For instance, Italian composer Gian Francesco Malipiero (1882–1973) composed a work for piano and orchestra titled *Variazioni senza tema* (1923), which Vaughan Williams heard at the 1925 ISCM Festival. It too features seven variations based on a four-note motive comprising interlocking perfect fourths; however, the opening motive in Vaughan Williams's first movement was more likely borrowed from Holst's hymn tune Valiant Hearts (1925). Additionally, the main melody and the closing passage of the Cavatina were inspired by the chorale "O Sacred Head" from Bach's *St. Matthew Passion*, and the broad parallels with Beethoven's Eighth Symphony have already been noted.[28] A further connection with those composers also stands out:

> To my mind, two composers and two only . . . have been able to write music which is at the same time serious, profound, and cheerful—Bach in the "Cum Sancto" of the B minor Mass and Beethoven in the finale of the Choral Symphony. Incidentally both these movements are in D major.[29]

This observation suggests that Vaughan Williams's emphasis on D major in the Toccata—a largely cheerful movement regularly interrupted by a "sinister exordium"—was no coincidence. If the first movement of the Eighth reviewed the accomplishments of his own career, then the finale acknowledges the debt he owed to the two composers whose music he respected and with whose influence he struggled above all others.

The Eighth Symphony was not Vaughan Williams's only late composition to revisit his earlier works. Following the BBC's disappointing production of *The Bridal Day*, and perhaps realizing that a relatively brief piece with a large cast faced long odds for future performances, Vaughan Williams transformed the masque into a cantata for baritone, mixed chorus, and small orchestra. The result (*Epithalamion*, 1957) restored Edmund Spenser's original poetic title, slightly expanded some of the masque's musical numbers, and added text to others originally written for dancers alone. Another example appeared in *The England of Elizabeth* (1957), a short film chronicling the first Elizabethan age. The music is continuous for the twenty-five-minute- long documentary; while most of the material was original, Vaughan Williams quoted both Thomas Tallis's anthem *If Ye Love Me* and the theme from his own orchestral impression *The Solent*, the latter recurring in various guises throughout the film (some of which did not make the final cut).[30]

Vaughan Williams completed several smaller projects while he was working on the Eighth and Ninth Symphonies. The Two Organ Preludes Founded on Welsh Folk Songs (1956) are relatively unremarkable miniatures: an almost exclusively diatonic Romanza on "The White Rock," and a free-flowing, more chromatically inflected Toccata on "St. David's Day." Far more virtuosic organ writing is displayed in *A Vision of Aeroplanes* (1956), one of Vaughan Williams's strangest and most difficult choral works. The anthem's disorienting swirl of sound recalls the battle between the forces of heaven and earth in *Sancta Civitas*, effectively conveying the bizarre visions described in Ezekiel 1. It is a world away from the euphonious and flowing treatment of Psalm 33 in *A Choral Flourish* (1956), whose unusual title was echoed in the *Flourish for Glorious John* (1957) celebrating the centenary season of the Hallé Orchestra and its director, John Barbirolli.[31]

Among the last pieces Vaughan Williams completed was the Variations for Brass Band, written as the First Section test piece for the 1957 National Brass Band Championship of Great Britain.[32] The challenges of variation form had recently occupied him in the *Fantasia (quasi variazione) on the "Old 104th" Psalm Tune*, the Violin Sonata, the Eighth Symphony, and the chamber compilation *Diabelleries* (1955), for which he wrote a single variation on Alfred Scott-Gatty's tune "Oh! Where's My Little Basket Gone?" His final contribution to the genre—and an impressive capstone to his band literature—is the most straightforward, if challenging for amateur ensembles. The eleven brief variations cover a wide stylistic and expressive range, from dignified chorales to a breezy waltz. The *Andante maestoso* theme again invokes the *Solent* melody, with other passages recalling sections from *Hodie*—notably XII: Hymn—and the Eighth Symphony, while anticipating passages from Vaughan Williams's final major work: Symphony No. 9 in E Minor.

The seeds of the Ninth Symphony may have been sown as early as 1955, when the composer alluded to "having a flirtation with [the tuba's] young cousin the flügel horn," but he did not begin sketching the symphony in earnest until 1956, much of it at the Finzis' house in Ashmansworth.[33] He completed drafts of the first three movements by August of that year, and the finale by October, but the revision process was alarmingly protracted, with final copies of the orchestral parts completed only two days before the first performance.[34] Moreover, the work was underrehearsed, the program note reveals Vaughan Williams at his most flippant, and it seems as though Malcolm Sargent had taken certain interpretive liberties that were less than effective, leading to a distinctly cool reception in some corners of the press.[35] As usual, Vaughan Williams was unbothered by his detractors. "I don't think they can quite forgive me for still being able to do it at my age," he told a friend, a remark that suggests he knew the quality of his work and was aware of the partisan response it faced.[36]

Today, that quality stands more clearly revealed through the wealth of sketches and rough copies of the score. Vaughan Williams typically destroyed these, but as his surviving symphonic manuscripts were on display at the Royal Festival Hall in conjunction with the premiere—the RPS was the symphony's dedicatee—he decided to preserve those of the Ninth "as I thought it might be useful to show the scaffolding."[37] As a result, more information on the development and revision of the Ninth Symphony exists than for almost any of his others, and their study reveals a complex web of programmatic allusions spun throughout. Some of these—such as the overlapping evocations of Thomas Hardy's *Tess of the D'Urbervilles*, Salisbury Cathedral, Stonehenge, and the Ghostly Drummer of Salisbury Plain—are now generally familiar, but others—such as music by Bach, Elgar, and Paul Dukas; Hardy's *The Mayor of Casterbridge*; the Great War; and, almost inevitably, *The Pilgrim's Progress*—remain relatively obscure, if no less compelling.[38] In keeping with the habits of a lifetime, Vaughan Williams withheld such details. "It is quite true that [the second] movement started off with a programme, but it got lost on the journey— so now, oh, no, we never mention it—and the music must be left to speak for itself."[39] However, his long-standing and near-pathological distrust of overt programs seems misplaced here. Vaughan Williams believed that a program's literary cachet could be used to justify an inferior composition and lead to undeserved success, yet the Ninth Symphony presents a case in which awareness of the programmatic elements illuminates the details of an already finely crafted work, nowhere more so than in the second movement.[40]

That fastidious attention to craftsmanship results in a subtle and often understated composition—"complex, but not complicated," as Ravel would say.[41] Like the previous two symphonies, the large ensemble includes unusual or rarely employed instruments—including three saxophones, contrabassoon, and a massive battery of percussion alongside the aforementioned flugelhorn—but these are employed with deliberation and care, largely avoiding the thick textures occasionally heard in *Sinfonia Antartica* and the Eighth. The thematic resources are enormously wide ranging (Vaughan Williams identified twenty-four distinct themes in his program note) and evoke associations with a host of earlier works, from *Sinfonia Antartica* to the Sixth Symphony and *The Solent*, manifesting in the second movement's flugelhorn solo. The harmonic and formal scheme is no less varied, allowing for such unusual feints as letting the B♮ of the (mostly) E Phrygian first subject in the opening Moderato maestoso to infiltrate the G-minor second subject, reversing the usual sonata-form expectation that the second key area displace the first, and from which "a major-minor conflict, a Phrygian relationship, and a tritonal one" are derived and explored.[42] The first of these resolves at the very end with E major seemingly victorious as the opening theme returns one last time, usurping the ostensible home key for an unexpectedly optimistic conclusion—later used to similarly moving effect by Shostakovich to conclude his own final symphony. It forms an appropriate denouement to Vaughan Williams's symphonic pantheon, which attained a level of artistic consistency, stylistic variety, expressive power, and enduring appeal within the genre nearly unmatched in the twentieth century.

And so this survey ends as it began: with a miscellany of songs. The most extended are the *Ten Blake Songs* (1958), though only eight were used in the film for which they were commissioned. It seems likely the revision of *Along the Field* only two years earlier inspired the pairing of voice with oboe rather than piano. The stark and often tonally unstable result resembles the earlier treatment of Housman's poems, whether in the astringent counterpoint of "A Poison Tree," the oboe's skirling accompaniment in "The Piper," the expressive anguish of "Cruelty Has a Human Heart," or the sweetly cloying phrases of "The Lamb," a poem Vaughan Williams hated, and was annoyed to have effectively set.[43] The *Three Vocalises* (1958), the final piece he completed before his death, feature similarly unusual duets between clarinet and soprano.[44] Because their ranges overlap, there are interesting exchanges—especially in the Prelude—that adumbrate the use of *tintinnabuli* in the music of Arvo Pärt, the overall effect one of wistful longing.

The final collection, the so-called *Four Last Songs*, comprises pieces written between 1954 and 1958: "Menelaus" (originally "Menelaus on the Beach at Pharos," 1954), "Hands, Eyes, and Heart" (1955), "Tired" (1956), and "Procris" (1958). Though regularly claimed to be early entries for two separate song cycles—one based on themes from Classical mythology, the other a series of love songs, all setting texts by Ursula

Vaughan Williams—there is evidence to suggest otherwise.[45] More than six decades on from his first songs composed for Parry at the RCM, we see the final fruits from a composer whose sensitivity to literature and the expressive potential of the human voice kept him engaged with the genre throughout his career. As James Day eloquently describes them, "here there is tenderness without nostalgia, austerity of expression but not of feeling," a still youthful passion tempered by the lucidity of experience and knowledge.[46] All of this is beautifully conveyed in the gentle intimacy of "Tired," in which only a single accidental disturbs the otherwise exclusively diatonic language, but belies a tension between the opening melody—in D♭ Ionian—and the B♭ Aeolian implications of its accompaniment. The central section unites voice and piano in F Aeolian before returning to the opening material, the two parts reconciling in D♭ at the very close. It is an appropriate piece on which to end, for in it we hear the spontaneity and easy rhythmic flow of folk song, a Ravelian clarity of texture, pastoralism's parallel fifths and triadic modality, and the deeply felt sincerity of expression that Vaughan Williams strove to impart in every work he wrote throughout his long and distinguished career.

Calendar

Year	Age	Life	Contemporary musicians and events
1872		Ralph Vaughan Williams born, 12 Oct. at Down Ampney, Gloucestershire, son of Rev. Arthur Vaughan Williams (1834–1875) and Margaret Susan Vaughan Williams (née Wedgwood) (1842–1937).	Scriabin born, 6 Jan.; Bantock 4 years old; Bizet 34; Brahms 39; Bruckner 48; Debussy 10; Delius 10; Dvořák 31; Elgar 15; Liszt 61; Mahler 27; Parry 25; Satie 6, Stanford 20; R. Strauss 8; Verdi 59; Wagner 59. First Italian performance of Verdi's *Aida* (Milan), 7 Feb.[a] Foundation stone of Bayreuth Festspielhaus laid, 22 May.
1873	1		Reger born, 19 Mar.; Rachmaninoff born, 1 Apr. Tchaikovsky's Second Symphony, (Moscow), 7 Feb.; Liszt's *Christus* (Weimar), 29 May.
1874	2		Schoenberg born, 13 Sept.; Holst born, 21 Sept.; Ives born, 20 Oct. *Boris Godunov* (St. Petersburg), 8 Feb.; Verdi's *Requiem* (Milan), 22 May.
1875	3	Arthur Vaughan Williams (40) dies, 9 Feb. Ralph's mother, brother, and sister move to Leith Hill Place, Surrey.	Sterndale Bennett (58) dies, 1 Feb.; Ravel born, 7 Mar.; Bizet (36) dies, 3 June; S. Coleridge-Taylor born, 15 Aug. Bizet's *Carmen* (Paris), 3 Mar.; Tchaikovsky's First Piano Concerto (Boston), 25 Oct.

Year	Age	Life	Contemporary musicians and events
1876	4		S. S. Wesley (65) dies, 19 Apr.; Falla born, 23 Nov. Grieg's *Peer Gynt* (Oslo), 28 Feb.; first *Ring* cycle at Bayreuth, 13–17 Aug.; Brahms's First Symphony (Karlsruhe), 6 Nov.
1877	5		Dohnányi born, 27 July; Quilter born, 1 Nov. Tchaikovsky's *Swan Lake* (Moscow), 4 Mar.
1878	6	First surviving composition, *The Robin's Nest*. Begins music lessons with his aunt Sophy Wedgwood.	Boughton born, 23 Jan.; Holbrooke born, 6 July. Gilbert and Sullivan's *HMS Pinafore* (London), 25 May.
1879	7	Begins to learn the violin.	Frank Bridge born, 26 Feb.; Ireland born, 6 July; Respighi born, 9 July; Cyril Scott born, 27 Sept. Brahms's Violin Concerto (Leipzig), 1 Jan.
1880	8	Passes correspondence course in music theory.	Bloch born, 24 July; Offenbach (61) dies, 4 Oct.; Willan born, 12 Oct. Parry's *Prometheus Unbound* (Gloucester), 11 Sept.
1881	9		Bartók born, 25 Mar.; Musorgsky (42) dies, 28 Mar.; Miaskovsky born, 20 Apr.; Enescu born, 19 Aug. Gilbert and Sullivan's *Patience* (London), 23 Apr.
1882	10	First visit abroad, to France.	Malipiero born, 18 Mar.; Stravinsky born, 17 June; Grainger born, 8 July; Kodály born, 16 Dec. Wagner's *Parsifal* (Bayreuth), 26 July.
1883	11	Goes to Field House School at Rottingdean.	Wagner (69) dies, 13 Feb.; Casella born, 25 July; Berners born, 18 Sept.; Bax born, 6 Nov.; Webern born, 3 Dec. Brahms's Third Symphony (Vienna), 2 Dec. Royal College of Music opens, 7 May.

Year	Age	Life	Contemporary musicians and events
1884	12	During his school days, takes violin lessons from William Quirke and piano lessons from Charles T. West. Regularly attends concerts in Brighton.	Smetana (60) dies, 12 May. Bruckner's Seventh Symphony (Leipzig), 30 Dec.
1885	13		Berg born, 7 Feb.; E. Farrar born, 7 July; Butterworth born, 12 July; Wellesz born, 21 Oct. Gilbert and Sullivan's *The Mikado* (London), 14 Mar.
1886	14		Ponchielli (51) dies, 16 Jan.; R. O. Morris born, 3 May; Liszt (74) dies, 10 May; R. Clarke born, 27 Aug. Saint-Saëns's Third Symphony (London), 19 May.
1887	15	Enters Charterhouse School, playing the violin and later viola in the orchestra.	Borodin (53) dies, 27 Feb.; Villa-Lobos born, 5 Mar.; Price born, 9 Apr.; N. Boulanger born, 16 Sept.; Macfarren (74) dies, 31 Oct. Stanford's Third ("Irish") Symphony (London), 27 June.
1888	16	Organizes joint concert of compositions by himself and his friend H. Vivian Hamilton.	Coles born, 7 Oct. Verdi's *Otello* (Milan), 5 Feb.; Parry's *Blest Pair of Sirens* (London), 17 May.
1889	17		Boyle born, 8 Mar.; Boult born, 8 Apr. Mahler's First Symphony (Budapest), 20 Nov.
1890	18	Visits Munich and hears *Die Walküre*. Enters the Royal College of Music, where he studies harmony with F. E. Gladstone, composition with Parry, and organ with Parratt.	M. Hess born, 25 Feb.; Ibert born, 15 Aug.; Gurney born, 28 Aug.; Franck (67) dies, 8 Nov.; Martinů born, 8 Dec.

Year	Age	Life	Contemporary musicians and events
1891	19	Begins private composition study with Parry.	Delibes (54) dies, 16 Jan.; Prokofiev born, 23 Apr.; C. Porter born, 9 June; Bliss born, 2 Aug. Sullivan's *Ivanhoe* runs for 160 nights at the new Royal English Opera House (London).
1892	20	Enters Trinity College, Cambridge, where he reads History and works for his MusB under Charles Wood. Studies organ under Alan Gray. Meets Hugh Allen (organ scholar of Christ's College). Attends *Tristan und Isolde* in London, conducted by Mahler (32).	Honegger born, 10 Mar.; Tailleferre born, 19 Apr.; Lalo (69) dies, 22 Apr.; Sorabji born, 14 Aug.; Milhaud born, 4 Sept.; Howells born, 17 Oct. Sibelius's *Kullervo* (Helsinki), 28 Apr.; Tchaikovsky's *The Nutcracker* (St. Petersburg), 18 Dec.
1893	21	Early composition performed at the Cambridge University Music Club.	E. Goossens born, 26 May; L. Boulanger born, 21 Aug.; A. Benjamin born, 18 Sept.; Gounod (75) dies, 18 Oct.; Tchaikovsky (53) dies, 6 Nov. Verdi's *Falstaff* (Milan), 9 Feb. Bournemouth Municipal Orchestra founded.
1894	22	Takes MusB degree at Cambridge. Composes *Vexilla Regis* as degree exercise.	Piston born, 20 Jan.; Chabrier (53) dies, 13 Sept.; Warlock born, 30 Oct.; Moeran born, 31 Dec. Dvořák's Ninth Symphony "From the New World" (New York), 16 Dec.; Debussy's *Prélude à l'après-midi d'un faun* (Paris), 23 Dec.
1895	23	Takes History BA at Cambridge. Resumes studies at the Royal College of Music, studying composition with Stanford. Hired as organist at St. Barnabas Church, S. Lambeth.	Jessye born, 20 Jan.; W. G. Still born, 11 May; Orff born, 10 July; Hindemith born, 16 Nov. Queen's Hall Promenade Concerts founded, conducted by Henry J. Wood.

Year	Age	Life	Contemporary musicians and events
1896	24	Visits Bayreuth.	A. Thomas (84) dies, 12 Feb.; C. Schumann (76) dies, 20 May; Bruckner (72) dies, 11 Oct.; Thomson born, 25 Nov.; Sessions born, 28 Dec. Dvořák's Cello Concerto (London), 19 Mar.; Beach's *"Gaelic"* *Symphony* (Boston), 30 Oct. Stanford's *Shamus O'Brien* runs for over 100 performances in London.
1897	25	Marries Adeline Fisher, 9 Oct. Studies with Max Bruch in Berlin.	Cowell born, 11 Mar.; Brahms (63) dies, 3 Apr.; Korngold born, 29 May. Dukas's *The Sorcerer's Apprentice* (Paris), 18 May.
1898	26	Settles in London at 16 Lord North Street, Westminster, later moving to 5 Cowley St. Completes String Quartet in C Minor, Quintet in D Major, and Serenade in A Minor. Passes FRCO exam.	R. Harris born, 12 Feb.; Gershwin born, 25 Sept. S. Coleridge-Taylor's *Hiawatha's Wedding Feast* (London), 11 Nov. Folk-Song Society founded.
1899	27	Signs lease for 10 Barton Street. Receives ARCM in Theory and Composition; takes doctoral exam and viva at Cambridge. Completes *The Garden of Proserpine* and *A Cambridge Mass*.	Poulenc born, 7 Jan.; Auric born, 15 Feb.; Hadley born, 5 Mar.; R. Thompson born, 21 Apr.; Ellington born, 29 Apr.; J. Strauss II (73) dies, 3 June; Chausson (44) dies, 10 June; Chávez born, 13 June; Krása born, 30 Nov.; Barbirolli born, 2 Dec.; Revueltas born, 31 Dec. Elgar's *Enigma Variations* (London), 19 June.
1900	28	Meets Cecil Sharp. Completes *Bucolic Suite*. Attends disastrous first performance of Elgar's *Dream of Gerontius* in Birmingham, 3 Oct.	Weill born, 2 Mar.; Antheil born, 9 July; Copland born, 14 Nov.; Sullivan (58) dies, 22 Nov.; Bush born, 22 Dec. Puccini's *Tosca* (Rome), 14 Jan.

Year	Age	Life	Contemporary musicians and events
1901	29	Takes MusD at Cambridge. Completes *Heroic Elegy and Triumphal Epilogue*. Serenade in A Minor (Bournemouth), 4 Apr.	Verdi (87) dies, 27 Jan.; Stainer (60) dies, 31 Mar.; Rubbra born, 23 May; Partch born, 24 June; R. Crawford (later Seeger) born, 3 July; Finzi born, 14 July; Rodrigo born, 22 Nov. Accession of Edward VII, 22 Jan.
1902	30	First published composition, "Linden Lea." *Bucolic Suite* (Bournemouth), 10 Mar. Completes *Fantasia for Piano and Orchestra* and numerous songs. Begins giving regular University Extension Lectures and writing articles for *The Vocalist*.	Duruflé born, 11 Jan.; Walton born, 29 Mar. Debussy's *Pelléas et Mélisande* (Paris), 30 Apr.
1903	31	Begins collecting folk songs. Writes "Conducting" and "Fugue" entries for Grove's *Dictionary*. Composes *Willow-Wood, Silent Noon, Burley Heath, The Solent*, and many vocal works. Begins writing *A Sea Symphony*.	Wolf (42) dies, 22 Feb.; A. Coleridge-Taylor born, 8 Mar.; L. Berkeley born, 12 May; Khachaturian born, 6 June. Elgar's *The Apostles* (Birmingham), 14 Oct.
1904	32	Begins work as music editor of *The English Hymnal*. Composes *In the Fen Country* and *Songs of Travel*. *The House of Life* (London), 2 Dec. Goes on a wide range of folk-song collecting expeditions.	Dallapiccola born, 3 Feb.; Dvořák (61) dies, 1 May. Mahler's Fifth Symphony (Cologne), 18 Oct. London Symphony Orchestra founded.
1905	33	Edits Purcell's *Welcome Songs* (Part I) for the Purcell Society. Continues collecting folk songs, including a particularly fruitful expedition to Norfolk in Jan. *Pan's Anniversary* (Stratford-upon-Avon), 24 Apr. First Leith Hill Festival, 10 May. Moves to 13 Cheyne Walk, Chelsea, 1 Nov.	Tippett born, 2 Jan.; Blitzstein born, 2 Mar.; Rawsthorne born, 2 May; Lambert born, 23 Aug. Strauss's *Salome* (Dresden), 9 Dec.

Year	Age	Life	Contemporary musicians and events
1906	34	*The English Hymnal* published. Composes *Norfolk Rhapsodies*. Incidental music for *The Pilgrim's Progress* (Reigate), 1 Dec.	Grace Williams born, 19 Feb.; Arensky (44) dies, 25 Feb.; Lutyens born, 9 July; Shostakovich born, 25 Sept. Smyth's *The Wreckers* (Leipzig), 11 Nov.
1907	35	*Toward the Unknown Region* (Leeds), 10 Oct. Goes to Paris to study with Ravel.	Maconchy born, 19 Mar.; Imogen Holst born, 12 Apr.; Grieg (64) dies, 4 Sept.; Roy Douglas born, 12 Dec.
1908	36	Returns from Paris. Leads extension lecture series at Morley College. Revises *Willow-Wood*.	MacDowell (47) dies, 23 Jan.; Rimsky-Korsakov (64) dies, 21 June; Messiaen born, 10 Dec. Elgar's First Symphony (Manchester), 3 Dec.
1909	37	String Quartet in G Minor (London), 8 Nov.; *On Wenlock Edge* (London), 15 Nov.; incidental music for *The Wasps* (Cambridge), 26 Nov.	Albéniz (48) dies, 18 May. R. Strauss's *Elektra* (Dresden), 25 Jan.
1910	38	*Fantasia on a Theme by Thomas Tallis* (Gloucester), 6 Sept.; *A Sea Symphony* (Leeds), 12 Oct. Edits second volume of Purcell's *Welcome Songs*. Agrees to direct the Palestrina Society. Begins work on *Hugh the Drover*.	Barber born, 9 Mar.; Mary Lou Williams born, 10 May; Balakirev (71) dies, 29 May. Stravinsky's *Firebird* (Paris), 25 June. Accession of George V, 6 May.
1911	39	*Pageant of London* opens (London), 8 June; *Five Mystical Songs* (Worcester), 14 Sept.	Ursula Lock (later Wood, later Vaughan Williams) born, 15 Mar.; Mahler (50) dies, 18 May; Menotti born, 7 July. R. Strauss's *Der Rosenkavalier* (Dresden), 26 Jan.
1912	40	*Fantasia on Christmas Carols* (Hereford), 12 Sept.	Massenet (70) dies, 13 Aug.; S. Coleridge-Taylor (37) dies, 1 Sept.; Cage born, 5 Sept.; Glanville-Hicks born, 29 Dec. Ravel's *Daphnis et Chloé* (Paris), 8 June; Schoenberg's *Pierrot lunaire* (Berlin), 16 Oct.

Year	Age	Life	Contemporary musicians and events
1913	41	Composes extensive amounts of incidental music for Shakespeare Memorial Theatre Festival.	Dello Joio born, 24 Jan.; Bonds born, 3 Mar.; Britten born, 22 Nov. Stravinsky's *Rite of Spring* (Paris), 29 May.
1914	42	*Phantasy Quintet* (London), 23 Mar.; *A London Symphony* (London), 27 Mar. Enlists as a private in the RAMC.	Boughton's *The Immortal Hour* (Glastonbury), 26 Aug. Great War begins, 4 Aug.
1915	43	Posted to Dorking with 2/4ᵗʰ London Field Ambulance. Unit moves to Watford in April, and in May to Saffron Walden.	Goldmark (84) dies, 2 Jan.; Scriabin (43) dies, 27 Apr.; Persichetti born, 6 June; Taneyev (58) dies, 19 June.
1916	44	Posted to Sutton Veny, Wiltshire, and then to Écoivres, France, 22 June. Transferred to Salonika, Greece, arriving 30 Nov., moving on to Katerini, 15 Dec.	Granados (48) dies, 24 Mar.; Ginastera born, 11 Apr.; Babbitt born, 10 May; MacCunn (48) dies, 2 Aug.; Butterworth (31) killed in action, 5 Aug. Elgar's *For the Fallen* (London), 3 May.
1917	45	Receives commission in the Royal Garrison Artillery; departs Greece for England, 16 June, reporting for duty at the RGA Officer cadet school, Maresfield Park, 1 Aug.	Joplin (49) dies, 1 Apr.; Harrison born, 14 May. Satie's *Parade* (Paris), 18 May. Russian Revolution begins, 8 Mar.
1918	46	Serves in France with RGA; appointed Director of Music, First Army, BEF, Valenciennes.	L. Boulanger (24) dies, 15 Mar.; Debussy (55) dies, 25 Mar.; Coles (29) killed in action, 26 Apr.; Boito (76) dies, 10 June; Bernstein born, 25 Aug.; Farrar (33) killed in action, 18 Sept.; Parry (70) dies, 7 Oct. Holst's *The Planets* (London), 29 Sept. Armistice declared, 11 Nov.

Year	Age	Life	Contemporary musicians and events
1919	47	Demobilized in Feb. Appointed professor of composition at the RCM. Awarded honorary DMus at Oxford. Appointed conductor of the Handel Society.	Leoncavallo (61) dies, 9 Aug. Elgar's Cello Concerto (London), 27 Oct.
1920	48	Revised version of *A London Symphony* (London), 4 May; *Four Hymns* (Cardiff), 26 May.	Earl Kim born, 6 Jan.; Fricker born, 5 Sept.; Bruch (82) dies, 2 Oct. Holst's *Hymn of Jesus* (London), 25 Mar.
1921	49	Appointed conductor of the Bach Choir. *The Lark Ascending* (London), 14 June.	Gipps born, 20 Feb.; Piazzolla born, 11 Mar.; Husa born, 7 Aug.; Humperdinck (67) dies, 27 Sept.; M. Arnold born, 21 Oct.; Saint-Saëns (86) dies, 16 Dec.
1922	50	*Pastoral Symphony* (London), 26 Jan.; *The Shepherds of the Delectable Mountains* (London), 11 July. Visits USA to conduct *Pastoral Symphony* at Norfolk (CT) Festival. Mass in G Minor (Birmingham), 6 Dec.	Xenakis born, 1 May; G. Walker born, 27 June. Bliss's *A Colour Symphony* (Gloucester), 7 Sept. British Broadcasting Company founded, 18 Oct.
1923	51	*Old King Cole* (Cambridge), 5 June; *English Folk Song Suite* (Twickenham), 4 July.	Ligeti born, 28 May; Rorem born, 23 Oct. Stravinsky's *Les Noces* (Paris), 13 May; Walton's *Façade* (London), 12 June.
1924	52	*Hugh the Drover* staged at the RCM, 4 July, and by the British National Opera Company under Malcolm Sargent (London), 14 July.	Nono born, 29 Jan.; Stanford (71) dies, 29 Mar.; Busoni (58) dies, 27 July; Fauré (79) dies, 4 Nov.; Puccini (65) dies, 29 Nov. Gershwin's *Rhapsody in Blue* (New York), 12 Feb.; Schoenberg's *Erwartung* (Prague), 6 June; Janáček's *The Cunning Little Vixen* (Brno), 6 Nov.

Year	Age	Life	Contemporary musicians and events
1925	53	Four song cycles debut (London), 27 Mar.; *Flos Campi* (London), 10 Oct.; Violin Concerto (London), 6 Nov. *Songs of Praise* published, with RVW and Martin Shaw as music co-editors. Meets Hubert Foss; enters informal publishing agreement with OUP.	Boulez born, 25 Mar.; Satie (59) dies, 1 July; Berio born, 24 Oct. Berg's *Wozzeck* (Berlin), 14 Dec.
1926	54	*Sancta Civitas* (Oxford), 7 May; *Six Studies in English Folk Song* (London), 4 June; *On Christmas Night* (Chicago), 26 Dec.	Henze born, 1 July; Charles Wood (60) dies, 12 July. Puccini's *Turandot* (Milan), 25 Apr.; Bartók's *The Miraculous Mandarin* (Cologne), 27 Nov. UK General Strike, 4–12 May.
1927	55	Seven Housman Songs (later revised as *Along the Field*), concert debut (Bradford), 20 Mar.	Stravinsky's *Oedipus Rex* (Paris), 30 May; Janáček's *Glagolitic Mass* (Brno), 11 Sept. BBC incorporated, 1 Jan.
1928	56	Resigns conductorship of Bach Choir. Co-editor, with Martin Shaw, of music for *The Oxford Book of Carols*.	Musgrave born, 27 May; Janáček (74) dies, 12 Aug; Stockhausen born, 22 Aug. Weill's *Die Dreigroschenoper* (Berlin), 31 Aug.
1929	57	*Sir John in Love* (London), 21 Mar. Moves to White Gates, Dorking, 6 Oct. Composes four works for performance at the Silver Jubilee of the Leith Hill Festival in 1930.	Previn born, 6 Apr. Walton's Viola Concerto (London), 3 Oct. US and UK stock markets crash, ushering in Great Depression.
1930	58	Concert performance of *Job* (Norwich), 23 Oct. Receives RPS Gold Medal.	Takemitsu born, 8 Oct.; Warlock (36) dies, 17 Dec. Stravinsky's *Symphony of Psalms* (Brussels), 13 Dec. BBC Symphony Orchestra makes its public debut under Adrian Boult, 22 Oct.

Year	Age	Life	Contemporary musicians and events
1931	59	Leads first Dorking performance of Bach's *St. Matthew Passion*, 24 Mar. *Job* staged in London, 5 July.	Nielsen (66) dies, 2 Oct.; M. Williamson born, 3 Oct.; Gubaidulina born, 24 Oct.; d'Indy (80) dies, 2 Dec. Walton's *Belshazzar's Feast* (Leeds), 8 Oct.; Still's *Afro-American Symphony* (Rochester, NY), 28 Oct.
1932	60	*Magnificat* (Worcester), 8 Sept. Named Mary Flexner Lecturer at Bryn Mawr College (PA), lectures from which are published as *National Music*. Elected President of the English Folk Dance and Song Society.	John Williams born, 8 Feb.; Sousa (77) dies, 6 Mar.; Hugh Wood born, 27 June; A. Goehr born, 10 Aug.
1933	61	Piano Concerto (London), 1 Feb. Revised edition of *The English Hymnal* published.	Duparc (85) dies, 13 Feb.; Penderecki born, 23 Nov.; Górecki born, 6 Dec. Price's Symphony No. 1 (Chicago), 15 June. Hitler comes to power in Germany.
1934	62	*The Running Set* (London), 6 Jan.; *Pageant of Abinger* (Abinger, Surrey), 14 July; *Fantasia on "Greensleeves"* (London), 27 Sept.; Suite for Viola (London), 12 Nov.	Elgar (76) dies, 23 Feb.; Holst (59) dies, 21 Mar.; Delius (72) dies, 10 June; Birtwistle born, 15 July; P. M. Davies born, 8 Sept.; Schnittke born, 24 Nov. Shostakovich's *Lady Macbeth of the Mtsensk District* (Leningrad), 22 Jan.
1935	63	Symphony (No. 4) in F Minor (London), 10 Apr. Receives OM, 9 July.	Dukas (69) dies, 18 May; Terry Riley born, 24 June; Pärt born, 11 Sept.; Maw born, 5 Nov.; Berg (50) dies, 24 Dec. Gershwin's *Porgy and Bess* (New York), 10 Oct.; Walton's First Symphony (London), 6 Nov.

Year	Age	Life	Contemporary musicians and events
1936	64	*The Poisoned Kiss* (Cambridge), 12 May; *Five Tudor Portraits* (Norwich), 25 Sept.; *Dona Nobis Pacem* (Huddersfield), 2 Oct.	Glazunov (70) dies, 21 Mar.; Richard Rodney Bennett born, 29 Mar.; Respighi (56) dies, 18 Apr.; S. Reich born, 3 Oct.; E. German (74) dies, 11 Nov. Britten's *Our Hunting Fathers* (Norwich), 25 Sept. Accession of Edward VIII, 20 Jan. Accession of George VI, 11 Dec.
1937	65	*Flourish for a Coronation* (London), 1 Apr.; *Festival Te Deum* performed at George VI's Coronation Service, 12 May; *Riders to the Sea* (London), 30 Nov.	Glass born, 31 Jan.; Keiko Abe born, 18 Apr.; Derbyshire born, 5 May; Gershwin (38) dies, 11 July; Gurney (47) dies, 26 Dec.; Ravel (62) dies, 28 Dec. Shostakovich's Symphony No. 5 (Leningrad), 21 Nov.
1938	66	Meets Ursula Wood, 31 Mar. *England's Pleasant Land* (Westcott, Surrey), 9 July; *Serenade to Music* (London), 5 Oct. Begins work on *The Bridal Day.*	Bolcom born, 26 May; Tower born, 6 Sept. Hindemith's *Mathis der Maler* (Zürich), 28 May; Copland's *Billy the Kid* (Chicago), 6 Oct.
1939	67	*Five Variants of "Dives and Lazarus"* (New York), 10 June.	Zwilich born, 30 Apr.; L. Andriessen born, 6 June; W. Carlos born, 14 Nov. Bartók's Second Violin Concerto (Amsterdam), 23 Mar. WWII begins, 1 Sept.
1940	68	First film score: *49th Parallel. Six Choral Songs—To Be Sung in Time of War* broadcast 20 Dec. Retires from the RCM.	Revueltas (40) dies, 5 Oct. Finzi's *Dies Natalis* (London) 26 Jan.; Britten's *Les Illuminations* (London), 30 Jan.; Tippett's Concerto for Double String Orchestra (London), 21 Apr.; Bartók's Divertimento (Basel), 11 June.

Year	Age	Life	Contemporary musicians and events
1941	69	*Household Music* (London), 4 Oct. Completes incidental music arrangements for *Twelfth Night*. Serves as chair for Home Office Committee for the Release of Interned Alien Musicians. Joins CEMA.	Frank Bridge (61) dies, 10 Jan.; H. W. Davies (71) dies, 11 Mar.; Hailstork born, 17 Apr. Rachmaninoff's *Symphonic Dances* (Philadelphia), 3 Jan.; Messiaen's *Quatuor pour la fin du temps* (Görlitz), 15 Jan.; Barber's Violin Concerto (Philadelphia), 7 Feb.
1942	70	Composes score for the film *Coastal Command*.	Zemlinsky (69) dies, 16 Mar.; M. Monk born, 20 Nov. Shostakovich's Symphony No. 7 (Kuibishev), 5 Mar.; Copland's *Rodeo* (New York), 16 Oct.
1943	71	Symphony (No. 5) in D Major (London), 25 June; incidental music for *The Pilgrim's Progress* broadcast by the BBC on 5 Sept. Music for the films *The People's Land* and *The Story of a Flemish Farm* composed.	Schwantner born, 22 Mar.; Rachmaninoff (69) dies, 28 Mar.; Holloway born, 19 Oct. Ellington's *Black, Brown and Beige* (New York), 23 Jan.
1944	72	Oboe Concerto (Liverpool), 30 Sept.; String Quartet in A Minor ("For Jean on Her Birthday") (London), 12 Oct.	Tavener born, 28 Jan.; Smyth (86) dies, 11 May; Krása (44) murdered at Auschwitz, 17 Oct.; Beach (77) dies, 27 Dec. Tippett's *A Child of Our Time* (London), 19 Mar.; Bartók's *Concerto for Orchestra* (Boston), 1 Dec.
1945	73	*Thanksgiving for Victory* broadcast, 13 May. Music for the film *Stricken Peninsula* completed.	Mascagni (81) dies, 2 Aug.; Webern (61) dies, 15 Sept.; Bartók (64) dies, 26 Sept.; Rutter born, 24 Oct. Britten's *Peter Grimes* (London), 7 June. WWII ends, 2 Sept.

Year	Age	Life	Contemporary musicians and events
1946	74	Introduction and Fugue for Two Pianos (London), 23 Mar. With Joseph Cooper, arranges and revises Concerto for Two Pianos from his Piano Concerto (London), 22 Nov. Music for the film *The Loves of Joanna Godden* composed.	Bantock (78) dies, 16 Oct.; Falla (69) dies, 14 Nov. Stravinsky's Symphony in Three Movements (New York), 24 Jan.; Britten's *The Young Person's Guide to the Orchestra* (Liverpool), 15 Oct.
1947	75	*The Souls of the Righteous* (London), 10 July; *The Voice out of the Whirlwind* (London), 22 Nov.	J. Adams born, 15 Feb.; Casella (63) dies, 5 Mar. Korngold's Violin Concerto (St. Louis), 15 Feb.
1948	76	Broadcast of Partita for Double String Orchestra (revised from Double String Trio (London), 21 Jan. 1939), 20 Mar.; Symphony (No. 6) in E Minor (London), 21 Apr.; *Prayer to the Father of Heaven* (Oxford), 12 May. Music to the film *Scott of the Antarctic* completed.	Wolf-Ferrari (72) dies, 21 Jan.; R. O. Morris (62) dies, 14 Dec. First Aldeburgh Festival opens, 6 June.
1949	77	*An Oxford Elegy* and *Fantasia (quasi variazione) on the "Old 104th" Psalm Tune* privately performed (Dorking), 20 Nov. Music and narration by RVW used in the film *Dim Little Island*.	S. Paulus born, 24 Aug.; R. Strauss (85) dies, 8 Sept. Messiaen's *Turangalîla-Symphonie* (Boston), 2 Dec.
1950	78	*Folk Songs of the Four Seasons* (London), 15 June; public debut of *Fantasia on the "Old 104th"* (Gloucester), 6 Sept.; Concerto Grosso (London), 18 Nov.	Weill (50) dies, 3 Apr.; Miaskovsky (69) dies, 9 Aug.; Moeran (55) dies, 1 Dec.; L. Larsen born, 24 Dec. R. Strauss, *Four Last Songs* (London), 22 May.
1951	79	*The Pilgrim's Progress* (London), 26 Apr.; *The Sons of Light* (London), 6 May. Adeline Vaughan Williams (80) dies, 10 May.	A. Davis born, 20 Feb.; Schoenberg (76) dies, 13 July; Lambert (45) dies, 21 Aug. Stravinsky's *The Rake's Progress* (Venice), 11 Sept.; Britten's *Billy Budd* (London), 1 Dec.

Year	Age	Life	Contemporary musicians and events
1952	80	Romance for Harmonica (New York), 3 May; public debut of *An Oxford Elegy* (Oxford), 19 June.	Knussen born, 12 June; Saariaho born, 14 Oct. Accession of Elizabeth II, 6 Feb.
1953	81	*Sinfonia Antartica* (Manchester), 14 Jan. Marries Ursula Wood, 7 Feb. Arrangement of *The Old Hundredth Psalm Tune* performed at coronation of Queen Elizabeth II, 2 June; *The Bridal Day* broadcast by BBC television, 5 June. Moves to 10 Hanover Terrace, London.	Prokofiev (61) dies, 4 Mar.; Price (66) dies, 3 June; Quilter (75) dies, 21 Sept.; Bax (69) dies, 3 Oct.; Crawford Seeger (52) dies, 18 Nov. Elvis Presley makes his first Sun Records recordings, 18 July.
1954	82	Tuba Concerto (London), 13 June; *Hodie* (Worcester), 8 Sept.; Violin Sonata broadcast, 12 Oct. Visiting professor at Cornell University, lectures from which are later published as *The Making of Music*.	Daugherty born, 28 Apr.; Weir born, 11 May; Ives (79) dies, 19 May. Britten's *The Turn of the Screw* (Venice), 14 Sept.; Walton's *Troilus and Cressida* (London), 3 Dec.
1955	83	*Prelude on Three Welsh Hymn Tunes*, broadcast 12 Mar. Music composed for the film *The England of Elizabeth* (released 1957).	Enescu (73) dies, 4 May; Honegger (63) dies, 28 Nov.; B. Sheng born, 6 Dec. Tippett's *The Midsummer Marriage* (London), 27 Jan.
1956	84	Symphony No. 8 in D Minor (Manchester), 2 May; *A Vision of Aeroplanes* (London), 4 June. RVW Trust established.	Charpentier (95) dies, 18 Feb.; Finzi (55) dies, 27 Sept. Stockhausen's *Gesang der Jünglinge* (Cologne), 30 May.
1957	85	*Epithalamion* (London), 30 Sept.; Variations for Brass Band (London), 26 Oct.	Sibelius (91) dies, 20 Sept.; Korngold (60) dies, 29 Nov. Poulenc's *Dialogues des Carmelites* (Milan), 26 Jan.
1958	[85]	Symphony No. 9 in E Minor (London), 2 Apr.; *Ten Blake Songs* (London), 8 Oct.; *The First Nowell* (London), 19 Dec. RVW dies in London, 26 Aug.	Holbrooke (80) dies, 5 Aug. Tippett's Second Symphony (London), 5 Feb.; Britten's *Noye's Fludde* (Aldeburgh), 18 June; Stravinsky's *Threni* (Venice), 23 Sept.

[a] Unless otherwise indicated, composition dates refer to first performance.

List of Works

While comprehensive, this list is not exhaustive, particularly regarding the availability of various arrangements and editions of RVW's original works. Readers are referred to Michael Kennedy's *Catalogue of the Works of Ralph Vaughan Williams* (*CVW*), second edition—on which this list is based—for a more detailed reckoning. Given limitations of space, publication details are provided for those compositions either published for the first time or receiving significant new editions (not just reprints) since *CVW* was released, with the exception of Section **IX**. A variety of minor corrections have also been applied to clarify some of the entries in *CVW*. Unless otherwise noted, works representing the composer's earliest juvenilia (i.e., written prior to 1888) have been relegated to Section **X.B**.

I. Stage Works

A. Operas

1. *The Shepherds of the Delectable Mountains.* One act. Libretto by RVW from John Bunyan. Later incorporated into *The Pilgrim's Progress.* First performance: London, Royal College of Music, 11 July 1922.
2. *Hugh the Drover, or Love in the Stocks.* Two acts. Libretto by Harold Child. Dedication: "To Sir Hugh Allen from Author and Composer." First performance: London, Royal College of Music, 4 July 1924. A further scene was added in 1933 at the beginning of Act II, but marked "optional" in the more extensive revisions to this work completed in 1956. The aforementioned scene is present in the vocal score published in 1959, but not in subsequent editions. See also *A Cotswold Romance* (**IV.B.31**).
3. *Sir John in Love.* Four acts. Libretto adapted by RVW from Shakespeare's *The Merry Wives of Windsor* and other sources. Dedication: To S. P. Waddington. First performance: London, Royal College of Music, 21 March 1929. A Prologue, Episode, and Interlude were also composed for performance at Bristol Opera School, 30 October 1933. The Prologue has been withdrawn. The Episode and Interlude are included in editions of the full opera's score published after 1971. Publication: Critical edition, ed. David Lloyd-Jones, OUP, 2021. See also *In Windsor Forest* (**IV.B.14**).
4. *The Poisoned Kiss, or The Empress and the Necromancer.* Three acts. Libretto by Evelyn

Sharp, later amended and edited by RVW and Ursula Vaughan Williams. First performance: Arts Theatre, Cambridge, 12 May 1936.

5. *Riders to the Sea.* One act. Minimal adaptation of J. M. Synge's play by RVW. First public performance: London, Royal College of Music, 1 December 1937.

6. *The Pilgrim's Progress.* A Morality. Prologue, four acts, and epilogue. Libretto adapted from John Bunyan by RVW, with interpolations from the Bible and verses by Ursula Wood. First performance: Royal Opera House, London, 26 April 1951. See also *Seven Songs from* The Pilgrim's Progress (**V.42**).

B. Masques, Ballets, Pageants, and Other Musico-Theatrical Works

1. *Pan's Anniversary.* A masque in twelve parts, to a scenario by Ben Jonson. Original music composed and arranged by RVW; dances from Elizabethan virginal music and English folk tunes arranged for orchestra by Gustav Holst. First performance: Stratford-upon-Avon, 24 April 1905.

2. *The Pageant of London.* Held in conjunction with the 1911 Festival of Empire. Frank Lascelles, pageant master; W. H. Bell, musical director. RVW was responsible for Part 2, scene 5: "The London of Merrie England: May Day Revels in the Days of Henry VIII" (compiled by Alice Gomme, Allan Gomme, and Cecil Sharp). Comprises twelve short movements, featuring arrangements of English folk tunes and dances and the Reading Rota ("Sumer Is Icumen In"). Orchestrated by Cecil Forsyth. First public performance: Crystal Palace, Sydenham, 8 June 1911.

3. *Old King Cole.* A ballet for orchestra and chorus ad lib. Scenario by Katherine Vulliamy. First performance: Nevile's Court, Trinity College, Cambridge, 5 June 1923.

4. *On Christmas Night.* Masque, adapted from Dickens's *A Christmas Carol* by RVW and Adolf Bolm. Dedication: "To Douglas Kennedy, with thanks for his splendid 'Watchman.'" First performance: Eighth Street Theatre, Chicago, 26 December 1926. Substantially revised in 1935 and 1955.

5. *Job, A Masque for Dancing.* Scenario by Geoffrey Keynes, Gwendolyn Raverat, and RVW, inspired by William Blake's *Illustrations of the Book of Job.* Dedication: To Adrian Boult. First performance (concert version): Norwich, 23 October 1930. First staged performance: Cambridge Theatre, London, 5 July 1931. Publication: Critical edition, ed. Julian Rushton, OUP, 2018.

6. *The Pageant of Abinger.* Scenario by E. M. Forster. Written for mixed chorus and military band, comprising arrangements of traditional tunes, hymns, and chants. First performance: Old Rectory Garden, Abinger, Surrey, 14 July 1934. See also "O How Amiable" (**IV.D.6**).

7. *England's Pleasant Land.* Pageant, scenario by E. M. Forster. Written for mixed chorus and military band. Score by various composers, including RVW, who contributed the music for Act II, scene 1 ("Exit of the Ghosts of the Past" and "The Funeral March for the Old Order"). First performance: Milton Court, Westcott, Surrey, 9 July 1938.

8. *The Bridal Day.* A Masque by Ursula Wood, founded on Edmund Spenser's *Epithalamion.* For baritone soloist, speaker, dancers, mimers, mixed chorus, and small instrumental ensemble. First public performance: 5 June 1953, BBC Television. See also *Epithalamion* (**IV.B.38**).

9. Music for *The Masque of Charterhouse*. Includes "Solemn Music" for the final scene, and RVW's arrangement of the hymn tune Auctor Omnium Bonorum. First performance: Founder's Court, Charterhouse School, Godalming, Surrey, 12 July 1950.
10. *The First Nowell*. Nativity play for soloists, mixed chorus, and small orchestra. Libretto by Simona Pakenham, adapted from medieval pageants. Twenty movements based on or featuring arrangements of traditional tunes by RVW, eight of which were edited and completed by Roy Douglas following the composer's death. First performance: London, Theatre Royal, Drury Lane, 19 December 1958.

II. Incidental Music for Plays, Films, and Radio

A. Music for Stage Dramas

1. Scenes Adapted from Bunyan's *The Pilgrim's Progress* (John Bunyan, adaptation by Evelyn Ouless). A prelude, music for twelve episodes, and an epilogue were composed. Eight numbers survive: Prelude; The Arming of Christian; Christian and Apollyon; The Fight between Christian and Apollyon; Vanity Fair; The Death of Faithful; Final Scene; Epilogue. First performance: Reigate Priory, Surrey, 1 December 1906. Publication: Full score, Promethean Editions, 2008; piano rehearsal edition, 2014.
2. *The Wasps* (Aristophanes, trans. H. J. Edwards). Incidental music commissioned by the Greek Play Committee, Cambridge. Eighteen numbers in three acts. Overture; Act I: Introduction, Melodrama and Chorus, The Wasps' Serenade, Chorus (Allegro molto), Chorus (Allegro moderato), Melodrama and Chorus (Allegro), Melodrama and Chorus (Moderato). Act II: Entr'acte and Introduction, Melodrama and Chorus, March-past of the Witnesses, Parabasis. Act III: Entr'acte, Introduction (followed by repeat of Entr'acte from **E**), Melodrama, Chorus, Melodrama, Chorus and Dance. First performance: Cambridge, 26 November 1909. Publication: Vocal score, performing edition for narrator, voices, and orchestra, English trans. by David Pountney, Faber Music, 2010. See also *Aristophanic Suite in Five Movements* (**III.C.10**).
3. Incidental music to Greek plays. First performance of choruses: 31 May 1912, Royal Court Theatre, London.
    (a) *The Bacchae* (Euripides, trans. Gilbert Murray). For solo contralto, SSA women's chorus, and orchestra. One surviving chorus: Thou Immaculate on High. Publication: Study score, Promethean Editions, 2019.
    (b) *Iphigenia in Tauris* (Euripides, trans. Gilbert Murray). Prelude and four choruses. 1. Dark of the Sea; 2. Bird of the Sea Rocks; 3. Oh, Fair the Fruits of Leto Blow; 4. Go Forth in Bliss. Publication: Study score, Promethean Editions, 2019.
    (c) *Electra* (Euripides, trans. Gilbert Murray). Two choruses: 1. Onward O Laboring Tread; 2. O for the Ships of Troy. Publication: Study score, Promethean Editions, 2019.
4. Incidental music to *The Death of Tintagiles* (Maurice Maeterlinck). First performance: June 1913.
5. Incidental music to *The Blue Bird* (Maeterlinck). Composed 1913. First public performance: Dorchester Abbey, Dorchester-on-Thames, 24 May 2019.

6. Incidental music for various plays, all performed at the Shakespeare Memorial Theatre, Stratford-upon-Avon, for that institution's 1913 Festival.
   (a) *King Richard II* (William Shakespeare). Thirty-two numbers, mostly fanfares and entrance music. Three more extended movements were newly composed: March for Richard's entrance, Agnus Dei for soprano and organ, and Prelude to Act V. Seven of the remaining movements are arrangements of traditional tunes, both secular and sacred. First performance: 21 April 1913.
   (b) *The Merry Wives of Windsor* (Shakespeare). One page only survives, marked "molto moderato." First performance: 22 April 1913.
   (c) *King Henry IV, Part 2* (Shakespeare). The music was almost entirely arranged from Tudor and traditional sources. Six items survive, all arrangements: an Alman from the *Fitzwilliam Virginal Book*, "Half Hannikin," "Princess Royal," "Lady in the Dark," Dowland's *Pavana Lachrimae* (for strings), and the carol "Angelus ad Virginem." First performance: 23 April 1913.
   (d) *King Henry V* (Shakespeare). Two items survive, one of them the Agincourt Song, the other the song "J'aimons les filles" (Act III, scene 7). First performance: 24 April 1913.
   (e) *King Richard III* (Shakespeare). Four items survive, one based on the Hampshire "Dargason"; one adapted from the music to *King Richard II* (**II.A.6.a**); a march for Richard's entrance in Act III, scene 4; and a fanfare for Richard's defeat at Bosworth. First performance: 26 April 1913.
   (f) *Much Ado about Nothing* (Shakespeare). Two items survive, one an allegro in D major in two parts (nos. 1–2), the other a short passage for viola (no. 6). First performance: 28 April 1913.
   (g) *The Devil's Disciple* (George Bernard Shaw). Comprising arrangements of "The British Grenadiers," the March from Handel's *Judas Maccabaeus*, and a verse of "Yankee Doodle." First performance: 29 April 1913.
7. Incidental music for *Twelfth Night* (Shakespeare). Twenty-six numbers, comprising arrangements of music by Orlando Gibbons, Thomas Morley, Thomas Arne, and various sixteenth- and seventeenth-century traditional songs and dances. Instrumentation includes strings, pipe, and tabor. First performance: The Playhouse, Kidderminster, 1947.

B. Film Music

1. *49th Parallel*. First screening: Odeon Cinema, Leicester Square, 8 October 1941. See also *The New Commonwealth* (**IV.B.28**) and *The Lake in the Mountains* (**VII.A.10**).
2. *Coastal Command*. First screening: Plaza Cinema, Piccadilly Circus, 16 October 1942. A suite of seven movements was arranged by Muir Mathieson, six of which were first broadcast from Manchester on 17 September 1942.
3. *The People's Land*. First screening (private): Ministry of Information, 17 March 1943.
4. *Flemish Farm*. First screening: Leicester Square Theatre, London, 12 August 1943. See also *The Story of A Flemish Farm* (**III.C.21**).
5. *Stricken Peninsula*. Trade-shown in October 1945.
6. *The Loves of Joanna Godden*. First screening: New Gallery Cinema, 16 June 1947.

7. *Scott of the Antarctic.* Twenty-eight items were composed, six of which were not used in the film. First screening: Royal Film Performance, Empire Theatre, Leicester Square, London, 29 November 1948. First public screening: Odeon Theatre, Leicester Square, London, 3 December 1948. Publication: Full score, ed. Martin Yates, OUP, 2018. See also *Sinfonia Antartica* (**III.A.7**).

8. *Dim Little Island.* Includes excerpts from *Five Variants of "Dives and Lazarus"* (**III.C.20**). First screening: Edinburgh Film Festival, 1949.

9. *Bitter Springs.* Music arranged and scored by Ernest Irving from thematic material supplied by RVW. First screening: Gaumont Cinema, Haymarket, London, 10 July 1950.

10. *The England of Elizabeth.* First screening: Leicester Square Theatre, March 1957. Two suites were adapted from the film by Muir Mathieson: *Three Portraits from "The England of Elizabeth"* and *Two Shakespeare Sketches from "The England of Elizabeth."*

11. *The Vision of William Blake.* Included excerpts from *Job* (**I.B.5**). First public screening: Academy Cinema, London, 10 October 1958, though the Blake Society received an earlier private screening. See also *Ten Blake Songs* (**V.46**).

C. Music for Radio

1. Incidental music for *The Pilgrim's Progress.* Radio play based on Bunyan's allegory, adapted by Edward Sackville-West. First broadcast 5 September 1943.

2. Incidental music for *Richard II.* Radio play based on Shakespeare. Composed 1944; never transmitted. Publication: Full score, Promethean Editions, 2014.

3. Incidental music for *The Mayor of Casterbridge.* Radio play based on the novel by Thomas Hardy. Includes the following items: I. Casterbridge; II. Intermezzo; III. Weyhill Fair. Ten episodes, the first transmitted on 7 January 1951. Publication: Full score, Promethean Editions, 2011. See also *Prelude on an Old Carol Tune* (**III.C.23**).

III. Music for Large Instrumental Ensembles

A. Symphonies

1. *A Sea Symphony* (Walt Whitman). For soprano, baritone, mixed chorus, and orchestra. Four movements: I. A Song for All Seas, All Ships; II. On the Beach at Night, Alone; III. Scherzo (The Waves); IV. The Explorers. Dedication: To R. L. W. [Ralph Wedgwood]. First performance: Leeds, 12 October 1910.

2. *A London Symphony.* For orchestra. Four movements: I. Lento—allegro risoluto; II. Lento; III. Scherzo (Nocturne); IV. Andante con moto. Dedication: To the memory of George Butterworth. First performance: Queen's Hall, London, 27 March 1914.[1] First performance, revised version: Queen's Hall, London, 18 March 1918. First performance, second revision: Queen's Hall, London, 4 May 1920. First performance, third revision: Queen's Hall, London, 22 February 1934.

3. *Pastoral Symphony.* For full orchestra, with soprano (or tenor) voice. Four movements: I. Molto moderato; II. Lento moderato; III. Moderato pesante; IV. Lento. No dedication. First performance: Queen's Hall, London, 26 January 1922. Publication: Critical edition, ed. David Matthews, Faber Music, 2016.

4. Symphony in F Minor. For full orchestra. Four movements: I. Allegro; II. Andante moderato; III. Scherzo; IV. Finale con epilogo fugato. Dedication: To Arnold Bax. First performance: Queen's Hall, London, 10 April 1935. Publication: Critical edition, ed. David Matthews, OUP, 2018.
5. Symphony in D Major. For full orchestra. Four movements: I. Preludio; II. Scherzo; III. Romanza; IV. Passacaglia. Dedication: To Jean Sibelius, without permission. First performance: Royal Albert Hall, London, 24 June 1943. Publication: Critical edition, ed. Peter Horton, OUP, 2008.
6. Symphony in E Minor. For full orchestra. Four movements: I. Allegro; II. Moderato; III. Scherzo; IV. Epilogue. Dedication: To Michael Mullinar. First performance: Royal Albert Hall, London, 21 April 1948. Publication: Critical edition, ed. David Lloyd-Jones, OUP, 2011.
7. *Sinfonia Antartica*. For full orchestra, soprano soloist, and women's chorus. Five movements: I. Prelude; II. Scherzo; III. Landscape; IV. Intermezzo; V. Epilogue. Dedication: To Ernest Irving. First performance: Free Trade Hall, Manchester, 14 January 1953. Publication: Critical edition, ed. David Matthews, OUP, 2012.
8. Symphony No. 8 in D Minor. For full orchestra. Four movements: I. Fantasia (Variazioni senza tema); II. Scherzo alla marcia (per stromenti a fiato); III. Cavatina (per stromenti ad arco); IV. Toccata. Dedication: To John Barbirolli. First performance: Free Trade Hall, Manchester, 2 May 1956. Publication: Critical edition, ed. David Lloyd-Jones, OUP, 2016.
9. Symphony No. 9 in E Minor. For full orchestra. Four movements: I. Moderato maestoso—tranquillo; II. Andante sostenuto; III. Scherzo (Allegro pesante); IV. Andante tranquillo. Dedication: To the Royal Philharmonic Society. First performance, Royal Festival Hall, London, 2 April 1958. Publication: Critical edition, ed. Alain Frogley, OUP, 2017.

B. Orchestral Works Featuring Instrumental Soloist(s)

1. *Fantasia for Pianoforte and Orchestra*. Composed 1896–1902; revised twice in 1904. In one movement (six sections). First performance: Dorchester Abbey, Dorchester-on-Thames, 1 June 2012. Publication: Full score, ed. Graham Parlett, OUP, 2012.
2. *The Lark Ascending*. Romance for violin and orchestra. Composed 1914, revised 1920. Dedication: To Marie Hall. First performance (violin and piano arrangement): Shirehampton Public Hall, 15 December 1920. First performance of orchestral version: Queen's Hall, London, 14 June 1921.
3. *Flos Campi*. Suite for solo viola, small wordless mixed chorus (SATB), and small orchestra. Six movements, each headed by an extended quotation from The Song of Solomon. Dedication: To Lionel Tertis. First performance: Queen's Hall, London, 10 October 1925. Publication: Critical edition, ed. Julian Rushton, OUP, 2014.
4. Concerto in D Minor (*Concerto Accademico*). For violin and string orchestra. Three movements: I. Allegro pesante; II. Adagio—tranquillo; III. Presto. Movement II originally written as the second movement of the abandoned Concerto Grosso (see **III.D.3**). Dedication: To Jelly d'Arányi. First performance: Aeolian Hall, London, 6 November 1925.

5. *Fantasia on Sussex Folk Tunes.* For violoncello and orchestra. Dedication: To Pablo Casals. First performance: Queen's Hall, London, 13 March 1930. Withdrawn by the composer. Publication: Full score, OUP, 2015. Arrangement for piano and cello by Julian Lloyd Webber and John Lenehan, OUP, 1984. Transcription for viola by Martin Outram, OUP, 2018.

6a. Concerto in C Major for Pianoforte and Orchestra. Dedication: To Harriet Cohen. First performance: Queen's Hall, London, 1 February 1933.

6b. Concerto for Two Pianofortes and Orchestra. Adapted from **III.B.6a** by Joseph Cooper in collaboration with RVW. First performance: Royal Albert Hall, London, 22 November 1946.

7. Suite for Viola and Small Orchestra. Eight movements in three groups. Group 1: Prelude, Carol, Christmas Dance; Group II: Ballad, Moto perpetuo; Group III: Musette, Polka mélancolique, Galop. Dedication: To Lionel Tertis. First performance: Queen's Hall, London, 12 November 1934.

8. Concerto in A Minor for Oboe and Strings. Three movements: I. Rondo pastorale; II. Minuet and Musette; III. Finale (Scherzo). Dedication: To Léon Goossens. First performance: Philharmonic Hall, Liverpool, 30 September 1944.

9. *Fantasia (quasi variazione) on the "Old 104th" Psalm Tune.* For piano solo, mixed chorus (SATB), and orchestra. Text attributed to Thomas Sternhold and John Hopkins. First performance (private): White Gates, Dorking, 20 November 1949. First performance (public): Gloucester Cathedral, 6 September 1950.

10. Romance in D♭ for Harmonica. For harmonica, string orchestra, and piano. Dedication: To Larry Adler. First performance: Town Hall, New York, 3 May 1952.

11. Concerto in F Minor for Bass Tuba and Orchestra. Three movements: I. Allegro moderato; II. Romanza; III. Finale: Rondo alla tedesca. Dedication: to the London Symphony Orchestra. First performance: Royal Festival Hall, London, 13 June 1954. Publication: Critical edition, ed. David Matthews, OUP, 2012.

C. *Other Orchestral Works*

1. Serenade in A Minor. For small orchestra. Five movements: I. Prelude; II. Scherzo; III. Intermezzo and Trio; IV. Romance; V. Finale. First performance: Winter Gardens, Bournemouth, 4 April 1901. Publication: Full score, ed. Julian Rushton, OUP, 2012.

2. *Bucolic Suite.* For orchestra. Four movements: I. Allegro; II. Andante; III. Intermezzo; IV. Finale. First performance: Winter Gardens, Bournemouth, 10 March 1902. Publication: Full score, ed. Julian Rushton, OUP, 2012.

3. *Heroic Elegy and Triumphal Epilogue.* For orchestra. First performance: Royal College of Music, London, 5 March 1901. Publication: Full score, Faber Music, 2008.

4. *In the New Forest.* Four impressions for orchestra.
   a. *Burley Heath.* Left unfinished; score completed by James Francis Brown. First public performance: Dorchester Abbey, Dorchester-on-Thames, 23 May 2014. Publication: Full score, ed. James Francis Brown, OUP, 2013.
   b. *The Solent.* First performance: 19 June 1903, venue unknown. Material from this piece was reused in *A Sea Symphony* (**III.A.1**), the incidental music to *The England of Elizabeth* (**II.B.10**), Variations for Brass Band (**III.D.13**), and the Ninth Symphony (**III.A.9**). Publication: Full score, ed. James Francis Brown, OUP, 2013.

    c. *Harnham Down*. First performance: Queen's Hall, London, 12 November 1907. Publication: Full score, ed. James Francis Brown, OUP, 2013.

    d. *Boldre Wood*. First performance: Queen's Hall, London, 12 November 1907. Unpublished, MS lost.

5. *Symphonic Rhapsody*. For orchestra. First performance: Winter Gardens, Bournemouth, 7 March 1904. MS destroyed.

6. *In the Fen Country*. Symphonic Impression for Orchestra. Completed 1904, revised 1905 (twice) and 1907, orchestration revised 1935. First performance: Queen's Hall, London, 22 February 1909. Dedication: To R. L. W. [Ralph Wedgwood].

7. *Norfolk Rhapsody No. 1 in E Minor*. First performance: Queen's Hall, London, 23 August 1906. Revised prior to a subsequent performance at the Winter Gardens, Bournemouth, 21 May 1914.

8. *Norfolk Rhapsody No. 2 in D Minor*. First performance: Park Hall, Cardiff, 27 September 1907. Publication: Full score, edited and completed by Stephen Hogger, OUP, 2014.

9. *Norfolk Rhapsody No. 3 in G Minor and Major*. First performance: Park Hall, Cardiff, 27 September 1907. MS lost.

10. *The Wasps: Aristophanic Suite in Five Movements*. I. Overture; II. Entr'acte; III. March-past of the Kitchen Utensils; IV. Entr'acte; V. Ballet and Final Tableau. First performance: Queen's Hall, London, 23 July 1912. See also **II.A.2**.

11. *Fantasia on English Folk Song: Studies for an English Ballad Opera*. In three sections; possibly reworked as *English Folk Songs Suite* (**III.D.1**). First performance: Queen's Hall, London, 1 September 1910. MS lost.

12. *Fantasia on a Theme by Thomas Tallis*. For double string orchestra and string quartet. First performance: Gloucester Cathedral, 6 September 1910. Revised 1913 and 1919. Publication: Full score, new edition, Faber Music, 2010.

13. Prelude and Fugue in C Minor. For orchestra. First (orchestral) performance: Hereford Cathedral, 12 September 1930. See also **VII.B.2**.

14. *The Charterhouse Suite*. See **VII.A.5**.

15. *The Running Set*. Founded on traditional dance tunes, for medium orchestra. First performance: Royal Albert Hall, London, 6 January 1934.

16. *Fantasia on "Greensleeves."* Adapted from *Sir John in Love* (**I.A.3**) and arranged by Ralph Greaves for strings and harp with optional flute(s). First performance: Queen's Hall, London, 27 September 1934.

17. Two Hymn-Tune Preludes. For small orchestra. I. Eventide (W. H. Monk); II. Dominus Regit Me (J. B. Dykes). First performance: Hereford Cathedral, 8 September 1936.

18. *An EFDS Medley*. Overture for orchestra, founded on English folk tunes. Composed 1934. First performance: Royal Albert Hall, London, 9 January 1937. See also **III.D.10**.

19. Partita for Double String Orchestra. Revised version of the withdrawn Double Trio (1939; see **VI.11**). Four movements: 1. Prelude; II. Scherzo ostinato; III. Intermezzo (Homage to Henry Hall); IV. Fantasia. Dedication: to R. Müller-Hartmann. First performance in this form: BBC Third Programme broadcast, 20 March 1948.

20. *Five Variants of "Dives and Lazarus."* For strings and harp. First performance: Carnegie Hall, New York, 10 June 1939. Also arranged for concert band by Stephen Gregson, OUP, 2004.

21. *The Story of a Flemish Farm.* Suite for orchestra. Seven movements: I. The Flag Flutters in the Wind; II. Night by the Sea. Farewell to the Flag; III. Dawn in the Barn. The Parting of the Lovers; IV. In a Belgian Café; V. The Major Goes to Face His Fate; VI. The Dead Man's Kit; VII. The Wanderings of the Flag. First performance: Royal Albert Hall, London, 31 July 1945. See also **II.B.4**.

22. Concerto Grosso. For string orchestra, in three groups: concertino, tutti, and ad lib. Five movements: I. Intrada; II. Burlesca ostinata; III. Sarabande; IV. Scherzo; V. March and Reprise. First performance: Royal Albert Hall, London, 18 November 1950.

23. Prelude on an Old Carol Tune. Founded on incidental music written for Hardy's *The Mayor of Casterbridge.* The carol tune is "On Christmas Night the Joy-Bells Ring." First performance: BBC broadcast, 18 November 1952. See also *The Mayor of Casterbridge* (**II.C.3**).

24. *Flourish for Glorious John.* For full orchestra. Written in honor of the Hallé Orchestra's centennial season, and its conductor, John Barbirolli. First performance: Free Trade Hall, Manchester, 16 October 1957. Unpublished in original form; arranged for wind ensemble by John Boyd (Ludwig Music, 1998).

D. Works for Military, Wind, or Brass Band

1. *English Folk Songs Suite.* For military band; transcribed in 1924 by Gordon Jacob for full orchestra and for brass band. Three movements: I. March: "Seventeen Come Sunday"; II. Intermezzo: "My Bonny Boy"; III. March: "Folk Songs from Somerset." First performance: Kneller Hall, Twickenham, 4 July 1923.

2. Sea Songs. Quick march for military and brass bands. Based on "The Princess Royal," "Admiral Benbow," and "Portsmouth." Originally the second movement of the *English Folk Songs Suite* (**III.D.1**). Probable first performance as a stand-alone work: British Empire Exhibition, Wembley, between 24 and 31 May 1924.

3. Concerto Grosso. For military band. Two movements: I. Allegro moderato; II. Molto adagio. Unperformed and unpublished. See also *Toccata marziale* (**III.D.4**) and *Concerto in D Minor* (**III.B.4**).

4. *Toccata marziale.* For military band. Originally written as the first movement of the abandoned Concerto Grosso (**III.D.3**). First performance: British Empire Exhibition, Wembley, between 24 and 31 May 1924.

5. *Henry the Fifth.* Overture for brass band. Composed 1933. First performance: Maurice Gusman Concert Hall, Miami, Florida, 3 October 1979.

6. *The Golden Vanity.* March for military band. Composed 1933.

7. Flourish of Trumpets for a Folk Dance Festival. For brass band. Based on the Morris Call, collected by Cecil Sharp. First performance: London, International Folk Dance Festival, Royal Albert Hall, 17 July 1935.

8. *England's Pleasant Land.* See **I.B.7**.

9. Flourish for Wind Band. Written at the request of Alan Bush to open a pageant associated with the Festival of Music for the People. First performance: Royal Albert Hall, London, 1 April 1939.

10. *A Folk Dance Medley.* Adaptation of **III.C.18** for military band, arranged by RVW and Gerrard Williams. First performance: BBC broadcast, 27 March 1940.

11. March Suite Founded on English Folk-Tunes.[2] For military band. First performance: BBC broadcast, 27 March 1940.

12. Flourish for Three Trumpets. First performance: Stafford, Borough Hall, 19 March 1951.
13. Prelude on Three Welsh Hymn Tunes. For brass band. Based on the tunes EBENEZER, CALFARIA, and HYFRYDOL. First performance: BBC broadcast (on *Listen to the Band*), 12 March 1955.
14. Variations for Brass Band. First performance: National Brass Band Championship of Great Britain, Royal Albert Hall, London, 26 October 1957. Also arranged for orchestra by Gordon Jacob (with revision by Frank Wright). First performance: Birmingham Town Hall, 8 January 1960.

IV. Choral Works

A. Student Compositions

1. *Music, When Soft Voices Die* (Percy Shelley). Part song for male voices. First performance: Cambridge University Musical Club, 18 November 1893.
2. *Vexilla Regis*. Hymn for soprano solo, mixed five-part chorus (SSATB), strings, and organ. Composed 1894; MusB degree exercise. Four movements: I. Vexilla Regis; II. Impleta Sunt; III. O Crux; IV. Fons Salutis. First performance: St. Mark's Cathedral, Minneapolis, 30 May 2009.
3. *Peace, Come Away* (Alfred, Lord Tennyson). For four voices and small orchestra. Dated 27 September 1895.
4. Three Elizabethan Songs. Likely composed between 1892 and 1895. For chorus (SATB). 1. Sweet Day (George Herbert); 2. The Willow Song (William Shakespeare); 3. O Mistress Mine (Shakespeare). First performance (probable): Shirehampton Public Hall, 5 November 1913.
5. *Sonnet 71 ("A Poor Thing but Mine Own")* (Shakespeare). For six voices (SSATBB). Likely composed between October 1895 and March 1896. Publication: No. 1 of *Two Partsongs*, Faber Music, 2007.
6. *Echo's Lament of Narcissus* (Ben Jonson). Madrigal for double chorus. Likely composed between October 1895 and March 1896. Publication: No. 2 of *Two Partsongs*, Faber Music, 2007.
7. *Vine, Vine and Eglantine* (Tennyson). Vocal valse for SATB and piano. Dated 16 March 1896.
8. *To Sleep* (Tennyson). For choir (SATB) and orchestra. Undated, likely composed ca. 1895–1896.
9. *Come Away, Death* (Shakespeare). Likely composed between 1896 and 1902. SSATB.
10. *A Cambridge Mass*.³ For soloists (SATB), mixed double chorus, and orchestra. Completed 1899 as MusD degree exercise. Five movements: I. Credo; II. Offertorium; III. Sanctus; IV. Hosanna; V. Benedictus. First performance: Fairfield Halls, Croydon, 3 March 2011. Publication: Vocal score, ed. Alan Tongue, Stainer & Bell, 2011; full score, 2012.

B. Works for Chorus and Orchestra

1. *The Garden of Proserpine* (Algernon Swinburne). For soprano solo, chorus (SATB), and orchestra. Completed 1899. First performance: Dorchester Abbey, Dorchester-on-Thames, 31 May 2011. Publication: Vocal score, Stainer & Bell, 2011.

2. *Willow-Wood* (D. G. Rossetti). Cantata for baritone or mezzo-soprano solo and orchestra. Four movements, performed without breaks: I. Adagio quasi andante; II. Andante con moto; III. Adagio quasi andante; IV. Allegro quasi andante. First performance (solo with piano accompaniment): St. James's Hall, London, 12 March 1903. Revised 1908, adding women's chorus ad lib. First performance of revised version: Philharmonic Hall, Liverpool, 25 September 1909. Publication: Vocal score, Stainer & Bell, 2005.

3. *Sound Sleep* (Christina Rossetti). For female voices (SSA) and pianoforte. Dedication: Mrs. [Margaret] Massingberd. First performance: Spilsby, Lincolnshire, 27 April 1903.

4. *Toward the Unknown Region* (Whitman). Song for chorus (SATB) and orchestra. Dedication: To F. H. M. [Florence Maitland]. First performance, Leeds Town Hall, 10 October 1907.

5. Three Nocturnes (Whitman). For baritone solo, semi-chorus, and orchestra. I. Smile O Voluptuous Cool-Breath'd Earth; II. Whispers of Heavenly Death; III. Out of the Rolling Ocean. Nos. I and III are dated 18 August 1908; No. II is dated 11 January 1908. First performance of No. II: Gloucester Cathedral, 18 August 2001. First performance of full set: Maida Vale Recording Studios, 12–13 October 2015. Publication: Full score, Faber Music, 2017; movements I and III orchestrated by Anthony Payne, based on RVW's short score. Stand-alone version of II published as *Nocturne: Whispers of Heavenly Death*, full score, Faber Music, 2013.

6. *A Sea Symphony*. See **III.A.1**.

7. *Five Mystical Songs* (George Herbert). For baritone soloist, mixed chorus (SATB) ad lib, and orchestra. 1. Easter; 2. I Got Me Flowers; 3. Love Bade Me Welcome; 4. The Call; 5. Antiphon. First performance; Worcester Cathedral, 14 September 1911.

8. *Fantasia on Christmas Carols* (trad.). For baritone soloist, mixed chorus (SATB), and orchestra. First performance: Hereford Cathedral, 12 September 1912.

9. *Lord, Thou Hast Been Our Refuge* (Psalm 90). Motet for chorus (SATB), semi-chorus (SATB), and orchestra (or organ). First documented performance: St. Paul's Cathedral, London, 26 June 1921.

10. Fanfare: "So He Passed Over . . ." For double chorus of women's voices (SA), trumpets, cello, double bass, and bells. Completed 1921.

11. *Flos Campi*. See **III.B.3**.

12. *Sancta Civitas* (*The Holy City*). Oratorio for tenor and baritone soloists, mixed chorus (SATB), semi-chorus, distant chorus, and orchestra. Text from the KJV of the Bible and the Sanctus of the Mass.[4] First performance: Sheldonian Theatre, Oxford, 7 May 1926. Publication: Vocal score, ed. Havergal Brian, Faber Music, 2008; full score, 2014.

13. *Te Deum in G* (Book of Common Prayer). For Decani and Cantoris (SATB men's and boys' voices) with organ or orchestra. Orchestration by Arnold Foster. First performance: Canterbury Cathedral, 4 December 1928.

14. *In Windsor Forest* (Shakespeare et al.). Cantata for mixed chorus (SATB) and orchestra. Music and text adapted from the opera *Sir John in Love* (**I.A.3**). Five movements: I. The Conspiracy; II. Drinking Song; III. Falstaff and the Fairies; IV. Wedding Chorus; V. Epilogue. First performance: Queen's Hall, London, 14 April 1931.

15. *The Hundredth Psalm*. For mixed chorus (SATB) and orchestra. Words from Psalm 100 and Doxology from Daye's Psalter, 1561. Dedication: To LHMC [Leith Hill Musical Competition] Division II. First performance: Drill Hall, Dorking, 29 April 1930.

16. Three Choral Hymns. For baritone (or tenor) solo, mixed chorus (SATB), and orchestra. Texts by Miles Coverdale, those for nos. II and III after Martin Luther. Three movements: I. Easter Hymn; II. Christmas Hymn; III. Whitsunday Hymn. Dedication: To LHMC Division I. First performance: Drill Hall, Dorking, 30 April 1930.

17. Three Children's Songs for a Spring Festival (Francis Farrar). Unison voices with string accompaniment. Three movements: 1. Spring; 2. The Singers; 3. An Invitation. Dedication: To LHMC Children's Division. First performance: Drill Hall, Dorking, 1 May 1930.

18. *Benedicite*. For soprano, mixed chorus (SATB), and orchestra. Text from The Song of the Three Holy Children (the Apocrypha) and "Hark, My Soul, How Everything" (John Austin). Dedication: to LHMC Towns Division. First performance: Drill Hall, Dorking, 2 May 1930.

19. Magnificat. For contralto solo, women's choir (SA), solo flute, and orchestra. Words adapted from the Bible. Dedication: To Astra Desmond. First performance: Worcester Cathedral, 8 September 1932.

20. *Five Tudor Portraits* (John Skelton). For contralto (or mezzo-soprano), baritone, mixed chorus (SATB), and orchestra. Five movements: I. The Tunning of Elinor Rumming (Ballad); II. Pretty Bess (Intermezzo); III. Epitaph on John Jayberd of Diss (Burlesca); IV. Jane Scroop (Her Lament for Philip Sparrow) (Romanza); V. Jolly Rutterkin (Scherzo). First performance: St. Andrew's Hall, Norwich, 25 September 1936.

21. *Nothing Is Here for Tears* (John Milton). Choral song (unison or SATB) with accompaniment for pianoforte, organ, or orchestra. Composed upon the death of King George V. First performance: London, BBC broadcast concert, 26 January 1936.

22. *Dona Nobis Pacem*. Cantata for soprano and baritone soloists, mixed chorus (SATB), and orchestra. Texts from the KJV, Whitman, and John Bright, and the Christian liturgy. Five sections: I. Agnus Dei (Liturgy); II. Beat! Beat! Drums! (Whitman); III. Reconciliation (Whitman); IV. Dirge for Two Veterans (Whitman);[5] V. The Angel of Death—We looked for peace—O man, greatly beloved—The glory of this latter house—Nation shall not lift up a sword against nation (John Bright and KJV). First performance: Huddersfield Town Hall, 2 October 1936.

23. Flourish for a Coronation. For mixed chorus (SATB) and orchestra. Three movements: I. Let the Priest and the Prophet Anoint Him King . . . (The Bible); II. O Prince, Desire to Be Honorable . . . (Geoffrey Chaucer); III. Now Gracious God He Save Our King . . . (The Agincourt Song). First performance: Queen's Hall, London, 1 April 1937.

24. Festival Te Deum in F Major (Book of Common Prayer). For mixed chorus (SATB) and organ or orchestra. First performance: Westminster Abbey (coronation service for George VI), 12 May 1937.

25. *Serenade to Music* (Shakespeare). For sixteen solo voices (4S, 4C, 4T, 4B) and orchestra.[6] Dedication: "Composed for and dedicated to Sir Henry Wood on the occasion of his jubilee, in grateful recognition of his services to music." First performance: Queen's Hall, London, 5 October 1938.

26. *Six Choral Songs—To Be Sung in Time of War* (P. Shelley). For unison voices with piano or orchestra. I. A Song of Courage; II. A Song of Liberty; III. A Song of Healing; IV. A Song of Victory; V. A Song of Pity, Peace, and Love; VI. A Song of the New Age. First performance: BBC broadcast concert, 20 December 1940.

27. *England, My England* (W. E. Henley). Choral song for baritone soloist, double choir, unison voices, and orchestra. Additional version for unison voices and piano or orchestra, with optional descant on final verse. First performance: BBC broadcast concert, 16 November 1941.

28. *The New Commonwealth* (Harold Child). For unison voices with piano or orchestra. Music adapted from the Prelude to *49th Parallel* (see **II.B.1**). First known performance (in arrangement for TTBB unaccompanied choir): St. Mary's Church, Dorchester, 9 December 1943.

29. *Thanksgiving for Victory* (renamed *A Song of Thanksgiving*, 1952). For soprano solo, speaker, mixed chorus (SATB), and orchestra. Texts from the Bible (including the Apocrypha), Shakespeare, and Rudyard Kipling. First performance: recorded in London, 5 November 1944, for BBC broadcast, 13 May 1945.

30. *The Voice out of the Whirlwind.* Motet for mixed chorus (SATB) and orchestra or organ. Adapted from "Galliard of the Sons of the Morning" (*Job: A Masque for Dancing*, scene viii; see **I.B.5**). First performance: Church of St. Sepulchre, Holborn Viaduct, London, 22 November 1947.

31. *A Cotswold Romance.* Cantata for tenor and soprano soloists, mixed chorus (SATB), and orchestra. Adapted from the opera *Hugh the Drover* (see **I.A.2**) by Maurice Jacobson. Ten movements: I. The Men of Cotsall; II. Sweet Little Linnet; III. Song of the Road; IV. Love at First Sight; V. The Best Man in England; VI. Alone and Friendless; VII. The Fight and Its Sequel; VIII. Hugh in the Stocks (Gaily I Go to Die); IX. Mary Escapes;[7] X. Freedom at Last. First performance: Central Hall, Tooting Broadway, London, 10 May 1951.

32. Folk Songs of the Four Seasons (trad.). Cantata for women's voices (SSAA) and orchestra. Five movements: I. Prologue; II. Spring; III. Summer; IV. Autumn; V. Winter. First performance: Royal Albert Hall, London, 15 June 1950.[8] Publication: Critical edition and vocal score, ed. Graham Parlett, OUP, 2022.

33. *An Oxford Elegy* (Matthew Arnold). For speaker, small mixed chorus (SATB), and small orchestra. First performance (private): White Gates, Dorking, 20 November 1949. First performance (public): The Queen's College, Oxford, 19 June 1952.

34. *Fantasia (quasi variazione) on the "Old 104th" Psalm Tune.* See **III.B.9**.

35a. *The Sons of Light* (Ursula Wood). Cantata for mixed chorus (SATB) and orchestra. Three movements: I. Darkness and Light; II. The Song of the Zodiac; III. The Messengers of Speech. Dedication: To Bernard Shore. First performance: Royal Albert Hall, London, 6 May 1951.

35b. *Sun, Moon, Stars, and Man* (Ursula Wood). Four songs for unison voices with strings and/or piano, adapted from sections of *The Sons of Light*. I. Horses of the Sun; II. The Rising of the Moon; III. The Procession of the Stars; IV. The Song of the Sons of Light. First performance: Birmingham Town Hall, 11 March 1955.

36. *The Old Hundredth Psalm Tune ("All People That on Earth Do Dwell")* (William Kethe). Arranged for mixed choir (SATB), congregation, orchestra, and organ. First performance: Westminster Abbey (coronation service for Elizabeth II), 2 June 1953.

37. *This Day (Hodie)*. Christmas cantata for soprano, tenor, and baritone soloists with mixed chorus (SATB), boys' voices, organ (optional), and full orchestra. Sixteen movements: I. Prologue (text from Vespers for Christmas Day); II. Narration (Gospels of Matthew and Luke, KJV); III. Song (Milton); IV. Narration (Gospel of Luke); V. Choral (Coverdale, after Luther); VI. Narration (Gospel of Luke and the Prayer Book); VII. The Oxen (Thomas Hardy); VIII. Narration (Gospel of Luke); IX. Pastoral (Herbert); X. Narration (Gospel of Luke); XI. Lullaby (William Ballet); XII. Hymn (William Drummond); XIII. Narration (Gospel of Matthew); XIV. The March of the Three Kings (Ursula Vaughan Williams); XV. Choral (Anon. and Ursula Vaughan Williams); XVI. Epilogue (Gospel of John and Milton's Nativity Hymn). Dedication: To Herbert Howells. First performance: Worcester Cathedral, 8 September 1954.

38. *Epithalamion* (Spenser). Cantata founded on the masque *The Bridal Day* (see **I.B.8**), for baritone, mixed chorus, and small orchestra. Words chosen by Ursula Vaughan Williams from Spenser's *Epithalamion*. Eleven movements: I. Prologue; II. Wake Now; III. The Calling of the Bride; IV. The Minstrels; V. Procession of the Bride; VI. The Temple Gates; VII. The Bellringers; VIII. The Lover's Song; IX. The Minstrel's Song; X. Song of the Winged Loves; XI. Prayer to Juno. First performance: Royal Festival Hall, London, 30 September 1957.

C. Choral Works and Part Songs (Unaccompanied)

Note: Apart from the Five English Folk Songs (see **IV.C.7**), this list does not include choral arrangements of folk songs, which may be found in Sections **VIII.A** and **IX**. For choral arrangements of hymn tunes, see **VIII.B** and **IX**.

1. "Rise Early Sun" (René Gatty). SATB. First performance: Hooton Roberts, Yorkshire, September 1899. Unpublished, but performed with missing tenor part reconstructed by Roy Douglas at Hooton Roberts, 1972.

2. "Ring Out Your Bells" (Philip Sidney). SSATB. Dedication: To Lionel Benson, Esq. & the members of the Magpie Madrigal Society. First performance: unknown, likely a private performance by the Magpie Madrigal Society, ca. 1902.

3. "Rest" (Christina Rossetti). SSATB. Dedication: To Lionel Benson, Esq. & the members of the Magpie Madrigal Society. First performance: St. James's Hall, London, 14 May 1902.

4. "Fain Would I Change That Note" (Anon.). Canzonet for four voices (SATB). Composed 1907. First known performance: Music Hall, Aberdeen University, 15 December 1908.

5. "Love Is a Sickness" (Samuel Daniel). Ballet for four voices (SATB). Likely composed 1913.

6. *O Praise the Lord of Heaven* (Psalm 148). Anthem for two full choirs and semi-chorus. First performance: London, St. Paul's Cathedral, 13 November 1913.

7. Five English Folk Songs. Freely arranged for mixed chorus (SATB).[9] Five movements: 1. The Dark-Eyed Sailor; 2. The Springtime of the Year; 3. Just as the Tide Was Flowing; 4. The Lover's Ghost; 5. Wassail Song. First performance not known. First London performance: Guy's Hospital Musical Society, 1 May 1914.

8. *O Vos Omnes ("Is It Nothing to You?")*. Text from the Maundy Thursday Office of Tenebrae. Motet for mixed voices (SSAATTBB) with alto solo. Dedication: To Dr. R. R. Terry. First performance: Westminster Cathedral, 13 April 1922.

9. Mass in G Minor. For soloists (SATB) and double chorus, with organ part ad lib. Five movements: I. Kyrie; II. Gloria; III. Credo; IV. Sanctus—Osanna I—Benedictus—Osanna II; V. Agnus Dei. Dedication: To Gustav Holst and his Whitsuntide Singers. First performance: Birmingham Town Hall, 6 December 1922. A Communion Service in English was subsequently adapted by Maurice Jacobsen and revised by RVW.

10. *Valiant for Truth* (John Bunyan). Motet for mixed chorus (SATB), with optional organ or pianoforte. First performance: London, St. Michael's Church, Cornhill, 29 June 1942.

11. Chant for Psalm 67 (*Deus Misereatur*). First performance: St. Martin's Church, Dorking, 14 October 1945.

12. *The Souls of the Righteous* (The Wisdom of Solomon). Motet for treble (or soprano), tenor, and baritone soloists and mixed chorus (Treble ATB or SATB). First performance: Westminster Abbey, for the dedication of the Battle of Britain Chapel, 10 July 1947.

13. *Hymn for St. Margaret* (St. Margaret) (Ursula Wood). Unison voices. Composed January or February 1948. No. 748 in *Hymnal for Scotland*.

14. *Prayer to the Father of Heaven* (John Skelton). Motet for mixed chorus (SATB). Dedication: "To the memory of my master Hubert Parry not as an attempt palely to reflect his incomparable art, but in the hope that he would have found in this motet (to use his own words) 'something characteristic.'" First performance: Sheldonian Theatre, Oxford, 12 May 1948.

15. Three Shakespeare Songs. For mixed chorus (SATB). 1. Full Fathom Five; 2. The Cloud-Capp'd Towers; 3. Over Hill, over Dale. Dedication: To C. Armstrong Gibbs. First performance: Royal Festival Hall, London, 23 June 1951.

16. *O Taste and See* (Psalm 34). Motet for mixed choir (S [or treble] ATB), with organ introduction. First performance: Westminster Abbey (coronation service for Elizabeth II), 2 June 1953.

17. *Silence and Music* (Ursula Vaughan Williams). For mixed chorus (SATB). No. 4 of *A Garland for the Queen*. Dedication: To the Memory of Charles Villiers Stanford, and his Blue Bird. First performance: Royal Festival Hall, London, 1 June 1953.

18. *Heart's Music* (Thomas Campion). Song for mixed chorus (SATB). Dedication: Written for Wilfrid Dykes Bower and the St. Thomas's Hospital Musical Society. First performance: Church of St. Sepulchre, Holborn Viaduct, London, 25 November 1954.

19. *Song for a Spring Festival* (Ursula Vaughan Williams). For mixed chorus. Written for and given to the Leith Hill Musical Festival in April 1955, to be performed nowhere else. First performance: Leith Hill Musical Festival, Dorking Halls, 15 April 1955.

20. *A Choral Flourish* (Psalm 32). For mixed chorus (SAT and high BarB) with introduction for organ or two trumpets. In Latin, with English version as alternative; English text from Psalm 33, KJV. Dedication: To Alan Kirby. First performance: Royal Festival Hall, London, 3 November 1956.

D. Works for Choir or Unison Voices and Piano or Organ Accompaniment

For folk songs, extant hymns, and traditional tunes arranged in this manner, see Sections **VIII** and **IX**.

1. *Darest Thou Now, O Soul* (Whitman). Unison song for voice and piano or strings. Likely composed in 1905, but not published until 1925.

2. *O Clap Your Hands* (Psalm 47). Motet for mixed chorus (SATB) and organ. First known performance: St. John's College Chapel, Cambridge, 21 November 1920.

3. *Let Us Now Praise Famous Men* (Ecclesiasticus). Unison song, with accompaniment for pianoforte, organ, or small orchestra. Orchestration by Arnold Foster. First documented performance: St. Andrew's Congregational Church, West Ealing, 11 November 1923.

4. Magnificat and Nunc Dimittis (*The Village Service*). Mixed chorus (SATB) and organ. Composed 1925.

5. *The Pilgrim Pavement* (Margaret Ridgeley Partridge). Hymn for soprano solo, mixed chorus (SATB), and organ. First performance: Cathedral of St. John the Divine, New York City, 10 February 1935.

6. *O How Amiable* (Psalms 84 and 90). Anthem for mixed chorus (SATB) and organ. Originally composed for *The Pageant of Abinger* (see **I.B.6**). Dedication: to F. F. [Frances Farrer]. First performance: the Old Rectory Garden, Abinger, Surrey, 14 July 1934.

7. LITTLE CLOISTER (Percy Dearmer). Hymn tune for unison voices and organ. Counterpart to no. 262 in *Songs of Praise*. Composed 1935.

8. Services in D Minor. For unison voices, mixed choir (SATB) and organ.[10] Morning Service: I. Te Deum; II. Benedictus; III. Jubilate. Communion Service: I. Kyrie; II. Responses; IIIa. Before the Gospel; IIIb. After the Gospel; IV. Creed; V. Sursum Corda; VI. Sanctus; VII. Benedictus Qui Venit; VIII. Agnus Dei; IX. Gloria. Evening service: I. Magnificat; II. Nunc Dimittis. Dedication: Written for and dedicated to Dr. C. S. Lang and his singers at Christ's Hospital. Composed 1939.

9. "A Hymn of Freedom" (Canon G. W. Briggs). For unison voices with pianoforte or organ. First performance: Queen's Hall, London, 31 December 1939. See also **IV.D.11**.

10. "A Call to the Free Nations" (Canon G. W. Briggs). Hymn for choral or unison singing. Composed 1941. See also **IV.D.11**.

11. *Five Wartime Hymns* (Canon G. W. Briggs). For unison voices with piano or organ, by RVW, Martin Shaw, and Ivor Atkins. **IV.D.9** and **IV.D.10** were the first two items in this collection. Published 1942.

12. "The Airmen's Hymn" (Victor Bulwer-Lytton). Unison song with piano or organ. Composed 1942.

13. Te Deum and Benedictus. Unison voices or mixed voices (with occasional optional harmony) with accompaniment of organ, harmonium, or piano. Composed 1954.

14. *A Vision of Aeroplanes* (Ezekiel). Motet for mixed chorus (SATB) and organ. Dedication: To Harold Darke and his St. Michael's Singers. First performance: St. Michael's Church, Cornhill, 4 June 1956.

V. Songs (for Solo Singer and Piano Unless Otherwise Noted)

Note: Two significant modern compilations of RVW's songs exist: *Ralph Vaughan Williams Song Album* (2 vols., Boosey & Hawkes, 1985) and *Vaughan Williams Collected Songs* (3 vols., OUP, 1993). Songs belonging to these collections will be so designated at the end of their respective entries by publisher (BH or OUP) followed by the volume number in which the song appears.

Folk song and traditional tune arrangements for voice(s) and piano are in Section **VIII**.

1. "Summum Bonum" (Robert Browning). Likely composed 1891.
2. "Crossing the Bar" (Alfred, Lord Tennyson). For mezzo-soprano or baritone. Composed 1892.
3. "Wishes" (by "T," from the *Cambridge Observer*, August 1893). Composed 1893.
4. "The Virgin's Cradle Song" (Samuel Taylor Coleridge). First performance: Cambridge University Musical Club, 3 November 1894. Very likely the same as "A Cradle Song," published in *The Vocalist* (April 1905). (BH 2)
5. "To Daffodils" (Robert Herrick). Two distinct settings exist, one dated 3 July 1895.
6. "Dirge for Fidele" (Shakespeare). For two mezzo-sopranos and piano. Likely composed ca. 1895.
7. *Three Settings from Rumpelstiltskin* (Florence Bell). 1. Lollipop's Song; 2. Spinning Song; 3. Rumpelstiltskin's Song. Likely composed between 1896 and 1897.
8. Two Vocal Valses (Tennyson). 1. Spring. Dated 17 February 1896. 2. Winter. Dated 16 March 1896.
9. "Rondel" (Algernon Swinburne). For contralto or baritone. Likely composed between October 1895 and March 1896. First performance (probable): Bechstein Hall, London, 28 May 1906.
10. "How Can the Tree but Wither?" (Thomas, Lord Vaux). Likely composed 1896. First known performance: 5 June 1907. (OUP2)
11. "Claribel" (Tennyson). Likely composed between 1896 and 1902. First performance (probable): Bechstein Hall, London, 2 December 1904. (BH1)
12. "Linden Lea" (sometimes "In Linden Lea," William Barnes). Subtitled "A Dorset Folk Song." Composed 1901. RVW's first published work (in *The Vocalist* 1, no. 1, April 1902). Dedication: To Mrs. Edmund Fisher. First performance: Hooton Roberts Musical Union, Yorkshire, 4 september 1902. (BH1)
13. "Blackmwore by the Stour" (William Barnes). Subtitled "A Dorset Folk Song." Composed 1901. First performance: Hooton Roberts Musical Union, 4 September 1902. (BH1)
14. "Whither Must I Wander?" (Robert Louis Stevenson). First performance: St. James's Hall, London, 27 November 1902. Later incorporated into *Songs of Travel* (see **V.24**).
15. "Boy Johnny" (Christina Rossetti). Dedication: To J. Campbell McInnes, Esq. First performance: Oxford, Commemoration Week, June 1902. (BH1)
16. "If I Were a Queen" (C. Rossetti). First performance: Exeter, 16 April 1903. (BH2)
17. "Tears, Idle Tears" (Tennyson). Dedication: To J. Francis Harford, Esq. First performance: St. James's Hall, London, 5 February 1903. (BH2)
18. "Silent Noon" (D. G. Rossetti). First performance: London, St. James's Hall, 10 March 1903. Later incorporated into *The House of Life* (see **V.23**).
19. "Orpheus with His Lute" (Shakespeare). Composed 1902. Dedication: To Miss Lucy Broadwood. First performance: Bechstein Hall, London, 2 December 1904. See also **V.37**.
20. "When I Am Dead, My Dearest" (C. Rossetti). Composed 1903. First performance: Aeolian Hall, London, 28 November 1905.
21. "The Winter's Willow" (Barnes). First performance unknown. Published in *The Vocalist* 2, no. 20 (November 1903). (BH1)
22. Two Vocal Duets (Walt Whitman). For soprano, baritone, piano, and string quartet, with violin obbligato. 1. The Last Invocation; 2. The Love-Song of the Birds. The

first completed 23 July 1904. First performance: Reading Town Hall, 24 October 1904. Publication: Full score and parts, ed. Marcus DeLoach, Stainer & Bell, 2017.

23. *The House of Life* (D. G. Rossetti). A cycle of six sonnets: 1. Love-Sight; 2. Silent Noon; 3. Love's Minstrels; 4. Heart's Haven; 5. Death in Love; 6. Love's Last Gift. First performance: Bechstein Hall, London, 2 December 1904.

24. *Songs of Travel* (Stevenson). A cycle of nine songs: 1. The Vagabond; 2. Let Beauty Awake; 3. The Roadside Fire; 4. Youth and Love; 5. In Dreams; 6. The Infinite Shining Heavens; 7. Whither Must I Wander?; 8. Bright is the Ring of Words; 9. I Have Trod the Upward and the Downward Slope.[11] First performance: Songs 1–8, Bechstein Hall, London, 2 December 1904. First complete performance: BBC Home Service broadcast, 21 May 1960. Orchestral arrangement of songs 1, 3, and 8 by RVW, 1905; orchestral arrangement of remaining songs by Roy Douglas, 1961–1962. (No. 1 in BH1; nos. 3 and 8 in BH2)

25. "Ye Little Birds" (Thomas Heywood). First performance: Aeolian Hall, London, 3 February 1905. MS destroyed.

26. "The Splendour Falls" (Tennyson). Published in *The Vocalist,* 4, no. 38 (May 1905). First performance (probable): Northern Polytechnic Institute, Islington, 14 October 1905. (BH1)

27. "Dreamland" (C. Rossetti). First performance: Aeolian Hall, London, 31 October 1905. (BH1)

28. "The Rock of Rubies" (Robert Herrick). First known performance: Aeolian Hall, London, 18 May 1906. MS lost.

29. "Buonaparty" (Thomas Hardy). First documented performance: Aeolian Hall, London, 26 October 1908. (BH2)

30. "The Sky above the Roof" (Paul Verlaine, trans. Mabel Dearmer). Composed 1908. First documented performance: Public Hall, Worcester, 13 April 1912. (BH1)

31. "Is My Team Ploughing?" (A. E. Housman). Likely composed 1908; this version for voice and piano. First performance: Aeolian Hall, London, 25 January 1909. Later incorporated into *On Wenlock Edge* (see **V.32**).

32. *On Wenlock Edge* (Housman). For tenor voice, piano, and string quartet. Six songs: 1. On Wenlock Edge; 2. From Far, from Eve and Morning; 3. Is My Team Ploughing?; 4. Oh, When I Was in Love with You; 5. Bredon Hill; 6. Clun. First performance: Aeolian Hall, London, 15 November 1909. Also arranged by RVW for tenor and orchestra. First performance (orchestral version): Queen's Hall, London, 24 January 1924.

33. Four Hymns. For tenor voice, with accompaniment of piano or string orchestra, and viola obbligato. I. Lord! Come Away (Bishop Jeremy Taylor); II. Who Is This Fair One? (Isaac Watts); III. Come Love, Come Lord (Richard Crashaw); IV. Evening Hymn (trans. from the Greek by Robert Bridges). Dedication: To J. S. W. [Steuart Wilson]. First performance (orchestral version): Cardiff, 26 May 1920.

34. *Merciless Beauty* (attrib. Chaucer). Three rondels for high voice, two violins, and cello. 1. Your Eyën Two; 2. So Hath Your Beauty; 3. Since I from Love. First performance: Aeolian Hall, London, 4 October 1921.

35. "It Was a Lover and His Lass" (Shakespeare). Part song for two voices and piano. First documented performance: Music Hall, Aberdeen, 21 April 1923.

36. Two Poems by Seumas O'Sullivan (James Starkey). 1. The Twilight People; 2. A Piper. First performance: Aeolian Hall, London, 27 March 1925. (No. 1 in OUP2)

37. Three Songs from Shakespeare. 1. Take, O Take Those Lips Away; 2. When Icicles Hang by the Wall; 3. Orpheus with His Lute. (No. 3 differs from **V.19**.) First performance: Aeolian Hall, London, 27 March 1925. (OUP1)
38. Four Poems by Fredegond Shove. 1. Motion and Stillness [dated 1922]; 2. Four Nights; 3. The New Ghost; 4. The Water Mill. First performance: Aeolian Hall, London, 27 March 1925. (OUP2)
39. Three Poems by Walt Whitman. 1. Nocturne; 2. A Clear Midnight; 3. Joy, Shipmate. Joy! First performance: Aeolian Hall, London, 27 March 1925. (OUP1)
40. *Along the Field* (A. E. Housman). Eight songs for voice and violin. 1. We'll to the Woods No More; 2. Along the Field; 3. The Half-Moon Westers Low; 4. In the Morning; 5. The Sigh That Heaves the Grasses; 6. Good-Bye; 7. Fancy's Knell; 8. With Rue My Heart Is Laden. A ninth song ("The Soldier") was withdrawn.[12] Originally billed as Seven Housman Songs; the later title was applied upon the cycle's revision in 1954.[13] First performance (broadcast): BBC, 8 August 1926. First public concert performance as Seven Housman Songs: Motley Street Cinema, Bradford, 20 March 1927, by Joan Elwes (soprano) and Dettmar Dressel (violin).[14] First public performance as *Along the Field*: Wigmore Hall, London, 26 May 1955.
41. "The Willow Whistle" (M. E. Fuller). For voice and pipe. Undated, but probably contemporary with the *Suite for Pipes* (1939; see **VI.12**). First performance: Holy Trinity Church, Hinckley, Leicestershire, 16 October 1982.
42. Seven Songs from *The Pilgrim's Progress* (Bunyan, Ursula Vaughan Williams, and Scripture). For voice and piano. Nos. 1–3 and 5 for baritone, no. 4 for soprano solo or duet, nos. 6–7 for soprano. Modified from their original forms in the Morality *The Pilgrim's Progress* (see **I.A.6**). 1. Watchful's Song (Nocturne). Dedication: To Bryan Drake. 2. The Song of the Pilgrim. Dedication: To Douglas Robinson and the members of the chorus at Covent Garden. 3. The Pilgrim's Psalm. Dedication: To Arnold Matters. 4. The Song of the Leaves of Life and the Water of Life. Dedication: To Elizabeth Abercrombie and Monica Sinclair. 5. The Song of Vanity Fair. Dedication: To whoever shall first sing it [Thorsteinn Hannesson]. 6. The Woodcutter's Song. Dedication: To Iris Kells. 7. The Bird's Song. Dedication: To Adèle Leigh. (All OUP3)
43. "In the Spring" (Barnes). Composed 1952. Dedication: To the members of the Barnes Society. First performance unknown. (OUP2)
44. "Menelaus on the Beach at Pharos" (Ursula Vaughan Williams). Dedication: To Keith Falkner. First performance: Cornell University, Ithaca, NY, 14 November 1954. See also **V.48**.
45. "Hands, Eyes and Heart" (Ursula Vaughan Williams). Completed by 7 March 1955. First performance: Christchurch, New Zealand, recital broadcast by New Zealand Broadcasting Corporation, 21 December 1956. See also **V.48**.
46. *Ten Blake Songs.* For voice and oboe. Composed Christmastide 1957. 1. Infant Joy; 2. A Poison Tree; 3. The Piper; 4. London (oboe tacet); 5. The Lamb; 6. The Shepherd (oboe tacet); 7. Ah! Sunflower; 8. Cruelty Has a Human Heart; 9. The Divine Image (oboe tacet); 10. Eternity. Eight of these songs were used for the film *The Vision of William Blake* (**II.B.11**). Dedication: To Wilfred Brown and Janet Craxton. First concert performance: BBC broadcast, 8 October 1958.
47. Three Vocalises. For soprano voice and B♭ clarinet. I. Prelude; II. Scherzo; III. Quasi menuetto. Dedication: To Margaret Ritchie. First performance: Free Trade Hall, Manchester, 8 October 1958.

48. *Four Last Songs* (Ursula Vaughan Williams). 1. Procris; 2. Tired; 3. Hands, Eyes and Heart; 4. Menelaus. First performance of cycle: BBC Home Service, 3 August 1960. (OUP1)

VI. Chamber Music

1. Pianoforte Trio in G. For violin, cello, and piano. Performed at Charterhouse School Hall, Godalming, Surrey, 5 August 1888.
2. String Quartet in C Minor. Composed winter 1897–1898. Four movements: I. Allegro; II. Andantino; III. Intermezzo; IV. Variazione con finale fugato. First performance: Oxford and Cambridge Musical Club, 30 June 1904. Publication: Full score and parts, Faber Music, 2002.
3. Quintet in D Major. For clarinet, horn, violin, cello, and piano. Composed 1898. Four movements: I. Allegro moderato; II. Intermezzo; III. Andantino; IV. Finale. First performance: Queen's Hall (small hall), London, 5 June 1901. Publication: Full score and parts, ed. Bernard Benoliel, Faber Music, 2002.
4. Quintet in C Minor. For violin, viola, violoncello, double bass, and piano. Three movements: I. Allegro con fuoco; II. Andante; III. Fantasia (quasi variazioni). Completed 27 October 1903, revised 1904 and 1905. First performance: Aeolian Hall, London, 14 December 1905. Withdrawn after 8 June 1918. Publication: Full score and parts, ed. Bernard Benoliel, Faber Music, 2002. See also **VI.16**.
5a. *Ballade and Scherzo.* For two violins, two violas, and cello. Completed 22 May 1904. First known performance of Scherzo: British Library Conference Center, London, 20 February 2001. Publication: Full score and parts for *Scherzo* only (published with **VI.5b**), Faber Music, 2002.
5b. *Nocturne (By the Bivouac's Fitful Flame) and Scherzo (founded on an English Folksong).* For two violins, two violas, and cello. Revised and retitled version of **VI.5a**, completed 1 October 1906. Scherzo is entirely different from that of **VI.5a**. First known performance: British Library Conference Center, London, 20 February 2001. Publication: Full score and parts (published with *Scherzo* of **VI.5a**), Faber Music, 2002.
6. String Quartet in G Minor. Four movements: I. Allegro moderato; II. Minuet and Trio; III. Romance; IV. Finale. First performance: Novello's Rooms, London, 8 November 1909. Revised 1921. First performance of revised version: London, 6 March 1922.
7. *Phantasy Quintet.* For two violins, two violas, and cello. Completed 1912. Four continuous movements: I. Prelude; II. Scherzo; III. Alla sarabanda; IV. Burlesca. Dedication: To W. W. Cobbett, Esq. First performance: Aeolian Hall, London, 23 March 1914.
8. *Suite de Ballet.* For flute and pianoforte. Likely composed 1913. Four movements: I. Improvisation; II. Humoresque; III. Gavotte; IV. Passepied. First performance: 62 Cadogan Place, London, 20 March 1920.
9. Two Pieces for Violin and Pianoforte. Likely composed between 1912 and 1914; published 1923. I. Romance; II. Pastorale. Dedication: To D. M. L. [Dorothy Longman]. First known performance: BBC Newcastle broadcast, 5 November 1924.
10. *Six Studies in English Folk Song.* For cello and piano. I. Adagio; II. Andante sostenuto; III. Larghetto; IV. Lento; V. Andante tranquillo; VI. Allegro vivace. Dedication: To

May Mukle. First performance: Scala Theatre, London, 4 June 1926. Alternative versions for violin, viola, or clarinet, and for cello and orchestra.

11. Double Trio. For two violins, two violas, and two cellos. Four movements: I. Fantasia; II. Scherzo ostinato; III. Intermezzo (Homage to Henry Hall); IV. Rondino. First performance: Wigmore Hall, London, 21 January 1939. Revised version, first performance: National Gallery, London, 12 October 1942. Withdrawn in this form, but further revised (with new finale) as Partita for Double String Orchestra (see **III.C.19**).

12. Suite for Pipes. Composed 1939. Four movements: I. Intrada; II. Minuet and Trio; III. Valse; IV. Finale: Jig. Dedication: The Pipers' Guild Quartet. First performance: Chichester, August 1939.

13. *Household Music: Three Preludes on Welsh Hymn Tunes.* For string quartet or alternative instruments, and horn ad lib. Composed 1940. I. CRUG-Y-BAR (Fantasia); II. ST. DENIO (Scherzo); ABERYSTWYTH (eight variations). First documented performance (orchestral version): Bournemouth, 25 November 1940. First documented performance (original version): Wigmore Hall, London, 4 October 1941.

14. *Fantasia on "Linden Lea."* For oboe, clarinet, and bassoon. Composed 1942–1943 for John Parr of Sheffield. First performance unknown.

15. String Quartet in A Minor (For Jean on Her Birthday). Composed 1942–1944. Four movements: I. Prelude; II. Romance; III. Scherzo; IV. Epilogue—Greetings From Joan to Jean. First performance: National Gallery, London, 12 October 1944.

16. Sonata in A Minor. For violin and piano. Three movements: I. Fantasia; II. Scherzo; III. Tema con variazione. Dedication: To Frederick Grinke. The finale is based on the final movement of the withdrawn Quintet in C Minor (see **VI.4**). First performance: BBC broadcast, 12 October 1954.

17. Romance for Viola and Pianoforte. Date of composition unknown; likely between 1912 and 1914. First performance: The Arts Council, 4 St. James's Square, London, 19 January 1962.

VII. Keyboard Works

A. Piano

1. *The Robin's Nest.* Composed 1878. RVW's first known composition. First public performance: BBC North of England Home Service broadcast, 16 November 1964.

2. Short Piece for Pianoforte. Dated 16 July 1897. Dedication: Adeline from Ralph.

3. *Andante sostenuto.* Dated 17 July 1904. Dedication: "For your [Adeline Vaughan Williams's] birthday."

4. *Pezzo ostinato.* Dated 27 January 1905.

5. Suite of Six Short Pieces for Pianoforte. I. Prelude; II. Slow Dance; III. Quick Dance; IV. Slow Air; V. Rondo; VI. Pezzo ostinato. First performance unknown. Arranged for string orchestra as *The Charterhouse Suite* by James Brown in collaboration with RVW (1923), itself adapted for piano and string orchestra by Harriet Cohen (1933).

6. *Hymn Tune Prelude on "Song 13" by Orlando Gibbons.* Composed 1928. Dedication: To Harriet Cohen. First performance: Wigmore Hall, London, 14 January 1930.

7. Six Teaching Pieces for Pianoforte. Book I—Two Two-Part Inventions: l. Andante con moto; 2. Allegro moderato. Book II—1. Valse Lente; 2. Nocturne. Book III—1. Canon; 2. Two-Part Invention. Composed and published in 1934; rereleased as *A Little Piano Book*, OUP, 1984.

8. *A Winter Piece (for Genia* [Hornstein]). With love from Uncle Ralph. First performance: New Year's Day, 1943.

9. Introduction and Fugue for Two Pianofortes. Dedication: For Phyllis [Sellick] and Cyril [Smith]. First performance: Wigmore Hall, London, 23 March 1946.

10. *The Lake in the Mountains.* Based on music from *49th Parallel* (see **II.B.1**). Dedication: To Phyllis Sellick. Published 1947.

B. Organ

1. Three Preludes Founded on Welsh Hymn-Tunes. Composed 1920. I. BRYN CALFARIA; II. RHOSYMEDRE; III. HYFRYDOL. Dedication: To Alan Gray. First performance unknown.

2. Prelude and Fugue in C Minor. Likely begun 1915. Initial version for organ completed in 1921, revised 1923 and 1930, including arrangement for orchestra. Dedication: To Henry Ley. First performance (orchestral arrangement): Hereford Cathedral, 12 September 1930. First documented performance (organ): University of Birmingham, 3 May 1931. See also **III.C.13**.

3. Passacaglia on B. G. C. Composed for the Bride [Barbara Gordon Clark, née Lawrence]. First performance: 9 September 1933.

4. *A Wedding Tune for Ann* [Wilson, née Pain], *27 October 1943.* First performance: St. James Church, Shere, Surrey, 27 October 1943.

5. *A Wedding Canon (2 in 1 Infinite).* Dedication: "For Nancy [Elias, née Harvey], 30 May 1947, with love from Uncle Ralph."

6. Two Organ Preludes Founded on Welsh Folk Songs. I. Romanza ("The White Rock"); II. Toccata ("St. David's Day"). Composed 1956.

VIII. Arrangements

A. Folk Songs and Folk Dances

For substantial published collections of folksong arrangements by RVW, see **IX.A** and **B**.

1. "Entlaubet ist der Walde" (German *Volkslied*, English text by Walter Ford). Voice and piano. Dedication: To Walter Ford. First performance: St. James's Hall, London, 27 November 1902.

2. "Wanderlied" (German *Volkslied*, English text by Walter Ford). Voice and piano. Arranged 1902. Dedication: To Walter Ford. First performance: St. James's Hall, London, 10 November 1905.

3. "Adieu" (German *Volkslied*, trans. A. Foxton Ferguson). Soprano and baritone duet with piano. First performance: Exeter, 16 April 1903.

4. "Cousin Michael" (German *Volkslied*, trans. A. Foxton Ferguson). Soprano and baritone duet with piano. First performance: Exeter, 16 April 1903.

5. "Think of Me" (German *Volkslied*, trans. A. Foxton Ferguson). Soprano and baritone duet with piano. First performance: Steinway Hall, London, 22 March 1904.

6. Two French Folk Songs. Voice and piano. 1. Chanson de quête. 2. La ballade de Jésus Christ. Likely arranged in 1904.

7. "The Jolly Ploughboy" (Sussex folk song). TTBB, 1908; for unison chorus with piano, 1912.

8. "The Winter Is Gone" (English folk song). TTBB, 1912.

9. "Ward the Pirate" (English folk song). Mixed chorus (SATB) and orchestra, 1912.

10. "Tarry Trowsers" (English folk song). Mixed chorus (SATB) and orchestra, 1912.

11. "The Carter" (English folk song). Mixed chorus (SATB) and orchestra, 1912.

12. *The Minehead Hobby-Horse* (English folk dance). Orchestra, 1912.

13. *Phil the Fluter's Dancing* (English folk dance). Flute and strings, 1912.

14. Five English Folk Songs—see **IV.C.7**.

15. "The Turtle Dove" (English folk song). TBB, with pianoforte ad lib and solo part for tenors and baritones, 1919. Also arranged for mixed voices (SSATB), 1924; and for unison voices with piano or orchestra, 1934.

16. "A Farmer's Son So Sweet" (English folk song). Male choir (TBarB) with piano ad lib, or mixed choir (SSATBarB), 1921. Dedication: To the English Singers.

17. "Ca' the Yowes" (Scottish folk song, text by Robert Burns). Tenor solo and mixed chorus (SATB), 1922. Transcribed by Herbert Pierce for TTBB chorus, 1925.

18. "High Germany" (English folk song). Male choir, tenor and bass solos, and piano ad lib, 1923.

19. "The Lawyer" (English folk song). Mixed voices (SSATBB). First performance: London, 13 June 1927.

20. "An Acre of Land" (English folk song). TTBB choir with piano ad lib, 1934; unaccompanied mixed choir (SATB), 1934; and for unison voices with piano (from *Folk Songs of the Four Seasons*, **IV.B.32**), 1950.

21. "John Dory" (English folk song). Unaccompanied mixed choir (SATB), 1934.

22. "The Ploughman" (English folk song). TTBB voices with piano ad lib, 1934.

23. Two English Folk Songs. For voice and violin. 1. Searching for Lambs; 2. The Lawyer. Dedication: To Margaret Longman. Published 1935.

24. Six English Folk Songs. For voice and piano. 1. Robin Hood and the Pedlar; 2. The Ploughman; 3. One Man, Two Men; 4. The Brewer; 5. Rolling in the Dew; 6. King William. Published 1935; also for TTBB with optional accompaniment, 1934.

25. "Le paradis" (French folk song) Voice and harp (or piano). First performance: Institut Français du Royaume-Uni, 17 November 1952.

26. *Three Gaelic Songs* (English-language version by Ursula Vaughan Williams). 1. Dawn on the Hills (S'tràth chuir a'ghrian); 2. Come Let Us Gather Cockles (An téid thu bhuain mhaoraich); 3. Wake and Rise (Mhnàthan a'ghlinne so!). Unaccompanied mixed choir (SATB), arranged October 1954.

B. *Hymn Tunes, Carols, Chorales, and Other Sacred Music*

1. "Que Dieu se montre seulement." (Huguenot battle hymn, attr. Mattias Greiter). Voice and piano. First performance: Leighton House, London, 30 January 1905.

2. *The English Hymnal*. See **IX.A.2a**.

3. Evening Hymn (Henry Purcell). Voice and string orchestra. First performance: Manchester Town Hall, 22 February 1912.

4. "And All in the Morning (On Christmas Day)" (Derbyshire carol). Mixed chorus (SATB) and orchestra, 1912.
5. Choral and Choral Prelude. Based upon *Ach bleib' bei uns, Herr Jesu Christ* ("Now Cheer Our Hearts This Eventide," BWV 649) by J. S. Bach (after Seth Calvisius). Freely arranged for piano by RVW. Published in the anthology *A Bach Book for Harriet Cohen*, 1932.
6. *My Soul Praise the Lord* (William Kethe, slightly adapted). For mixed choir (SATB), unison singing (with descant), and organ (or strings and organ), 1935.
7. *Te Deum* (by Antonin Dvořák, English adaptation by RVW). For soprano and bass, mixed chorus (SATB), and orchestra. First performance: Royal Albert Hall, London, 9 January 1937.
8. Benedictus and Agnus Dei, in *Liturgical Settings of the Holy Communion* (ed. J. H. Arnold). Congregational portions of the service are set to traditional melodies, 1938.
9. *All Hail the Power* (text by Edward Perronet). Set to William Shrubsole's tune MILES LANE, for unison (congregation) and mixed chorus (SATB) with organ or orchestra. Dedication: To Ivor Atkins. First performance: Worcester Cathedral, 4 September 1938.
10. Two Carols (trad., freely translated by Ursula Wood). For mixed choir (SATB). 1. Come Love We God; 2. There Is a Flower (Es ist ein' Ros'), 1945.
11. *God Bless the Master of This House* (from the "Sussex Mummers' Carol"). Unaccompanied mixed chorus (SATB), 1956.
12. *Schmücke dich, O liebe Seele*. Based upon the chorale fantasia by J. S. Bach (BWV 180). For violoncello and strings. First performance: Friends' House, Euston Road, London, 28 December 1956.

C. Traditional and Popular Tunes

1. "The Willow Song" (trad.). Voice and piano. Dated 19 February 1897.
2. "Réveillez-vous, Piccars" (French, fifteenth century, English adaptation by Paul England). Voice and piano. First performance: Church Room, South Street, Eastbourne, 19 October 1903.
3. "Jean Renaud" (French, fifteenth century, English adaptation by Paul England). Voice and piano. First performance: St. James's Hall, London, 11 February 1904.
4. "L'amour de moy" (French, fifteenth century, English adaptation by Paul England). Voice and piano. First performance: London, St. James's Hall, 11 February 1904.
5. "Quand le rossignol" (Châtelain de Coucy, late twelfth century/early thirteenth century). Voice and piano. First performance: Leighton House, London, 18 November 1904.
6. "Down among the Dead Men" (Old English air). TTBB arrangement made in 1906 for the Reigate production of *The Pilgrim's Progress* (see **II.A.1**).
7. "The Spanish Ladies" (trad.). Voice and pianoforte, 1912; also unison and mixed voices, 1912.
8. "Alister McAlpine's Lament" (Scottish air, words by Robert Allan). Unaccompanied mixed voices (SATB), 1912.
9. "Mannin Veen" (Manx traditional melody). For mixed chorus (SATB), 1913.
10. "Our Love Goes Out to English Skies" (Henry Purcell, lyrics by Harold Child).

Adapted from Queen Zempoalla's March in Purcell's *Indian Queen* (1695). Unison or mixed choir (SATB), 1920; with string accompaniment, 1924.

11. "The Lass That Loves a Sailor" (Charles Dibdin). Unison or mixed choir (SATB), soprano solo, and piano, 1921.

12. "The Mermaid" (traditional English). SATB choir with soprano solo, or unison choir with piano, 1921.

13. "Heart of Oak" (William Boyce). Unison choir and piano, or male voices (TTBB), or SATB choir with soprano solo and piano, 1921.

14. "The Farmer's Boy" (old English air). Male voices (TTBB), 1921.

15. "Loch Lomond" (Scottish air). Male voices (TTBB) with baritone solo, 1921; mixed choir (SSATB), 1931.

16. "Old Folks at Home" (Stephen Foster). Male voices (TTBB) with baritone solo, 1921.

17. *Mr. Isaac's Maggot* (traditional English country dance tune). Clarinet, pianoforte, triangle, and strings. First performance: Village Hall, Abinger, Surrey, January 1925.

18. *"The Giant" Fugue* (J. S. Bach). Transcription for string orchestra, by RVW and Arnold Foster, of BVW 680 ("Wir glauben all' an einen Gott"), 1925.

19. "Epithalamium" (adaptation by RVW of an old English air, text by John G. Brainard). Arranged for two violins, viola, cello, and double bass by Henry P. Schmitt. For Carl Stoeckel. Dated 30 October 1925.

20. *Fantasia on "Greensleeves."* See **III.C.16.**

21. "I'll Never Love Thee More" (from John Playford's *The English Dancing Master*, words by James Graham, First Marquis of Montrose). Unaccompanied mixed voices (SATB), 1934.

22. "The World It Went Well with Me Then" (old English air). TTBB unaccompanied, 1934.

23. "Tobacco's but an Indian Weed" (old English air). TTBB unaccompanied, 1934.

24. *Diabelleries.* Variations by RVW, Howard Ferguson, Alan Bush, Alan Rawsthorne, Elizabeth Lutyens, Elizabeth Maconchy, Gerald Finzi, Grace Williams, and Gordon Jacob on the tune "Oh! Where's My Little Basket Gone?" (attrib. Alfred Scott-Gatty). For flute, oboe, clarinet, bassoon, horn, trumpet, string quartet, and double bass. First performance: Arts Council, 4 St. James's Square, London, 16 May 1955.

D. *Miscellaneous Arrangements*

1. "The Blessing of the Swords." English-language adaptation of the scene from Jacob Meyerbeer's *Les Huguenots*. Mixed chorus (SATB) and orchestra, 1942.

2. *Fen and Flood* (libretto by Charles Cudworth). Cantata for male chorus (TTBarB) and orchestra by Patrick Hadley; arranged for soprano and baritone soloists and mixed chorus (SATB) by RVW. First performance (for soloists with two pianos and miscellaneous instruments): Gonville and Caius College, Cambridge, 12 June 1955. First performance, SATB and orchestra: St. Nicholas's Chapel, King's Lynn, 27 July 1956.

IX. Edited Collections

Note: This section does not account for all arrangements of folk songs, hymns, and other melodies made after the initial publication of the volume(s) listed. For such details, please consult the appropriate entry in *CVW*.

A. Collections Edited by Vaughan Williams

1. *Works of Henry Purcell*, vol. XV ("Welcome Songs, Part I"). Edited for the Purcell Society. Five songs: 1. Welcome, Viceregent of the Mighty King (Z. 340); 2. Swifter, Isis, Swifter Flow (Z. 336); 3. What Shall Be Done in Behalf of the Man? (Z. 341); 4. The Summer's Absence Unconcerned We Bear (Z. 337); 5. Fly, Bold Rebellion (Z. 324). Publication: Novello, 1905.

2a. *The English Hymnal,* with tunes. Percy Dearmer, Thomas Lacey, Athelstan Riley, et al., eds.; RVW, musical editor. Publication: OUP, 1906.

   a. Original tunes contributed by RVW: 152 (DOWN AMPNEY); 524 (RANDOLPH); 624 (SALVE FESTA DIES); 641 (SINE NOMINE).

   b. Tunes derived from folksongs, arranged by RVW, and under his copyright: 15 (FOREST GREEN); 23 (DENT DALE); 186 and 611 (RODMELL); 239 and 385 (SUSSEX); 295 (DANBY); 299, 572, and 594 (GOSTERWOOD); 402 (MONK'S GATE); 525 (FARNHAM); 562 (KING'S LYNN); 595 (EAST HORNDON); 597 (HERONGATE); 607 (INGRAVE).

   c. Tunes arranged by RVW, not under his copyright: 7 (HELMSLEY); 16 (NEWBURY); 20 (THIS ENDRIS NYGHT); 29 (A VIRGIN UNSPOTTED); 42 (WAS LEBET, WAS SCHWEBET); 89 (ANIMA CHRISTI); 90 (DE PROFUNDIS); 145 (IN BABILONE); 212 (ST. PATRICK); 213 (AVE MARIS STELLA); 221 (KING'S LANGLEY); 249 (DEO GRACIAS); 268 (AR HYD Y NOS); 275 (LODSWORTH); 294 (DEVONSHIRE); 308 (ADORO TE, No. 2); 317 (Modes vii and viii); 326 (PANGE LINGUA); 344 and 609 (HORSHAM); 355 (HAMBRIDGE); 379 (RUSPER); 388 (ST. ISSEY); 389 (SHEPTON-BEAUCHAMP); 390 and 599 (SHIPSTON); 417 (STELLA); 437 (MORIAH); 448 (FITZWILLIAM); 485 (SANDYS); 488 (CAPEL); 490 (ST. COLUMBA); 498 (MENDIP); 514 (LLANSANNAN); 574 (KINGSFOLD); 579 (FORTUNATUS); 591 (FARNABY/LEW TRENCHARD); 601 (EARDISLEY); 606 (ST. HUGH); 638 (ST. AUSTIN/SOUTHILL); 654 (FARNABY); 656 (BRIDGEWATER/LANGPORT).

   d. Tunes arranged by RVW, but not attributed to him until the revised edition (1933): 18 and 38 (ST. VENANTIUS); 65 (JESU CORONA); 123 (SOLEMNIS HAEC FESTIVITAS); 125 (REX GLORIOSE); 129 and 480 (ORIENTIS PARTIBUS); 159 (ADESTO SANCTA TRINITAS); 165 (CHRISTE SANCTORUM); 181 (DEUS TUORUM MILITUM); 208 (DIVA SERVATRIX); 242 (COELITES PLAUDANT); 653 (PROMPTO GENTES ANIMO).

2b. Revised edition (OUP, 1933). RVW added three new tunes to this edition: 273 (MAGDA); 368 (KING'S WESTON); and 541 (WHITE GATES). He also adapted three others—91 (VALOR); 157 (WICKLOW); and 638, part 3 (STALHAM)—and harmonized those for 18 (ROUEN) and 58–60 (O INVIDENDA MARTYRUM).

3. *Works of Henry Purcell*, vol. XVIII ("Welcome Songs, Part II"). Edited for the Purcell Society. Four songs: 1. From Those Serene and Rapturous Joys (Z. 326); 2 Why, Why Are All the Muses Mute? (Z. 343); 3. Ye Tuneful Muses (Z. 344); 4. Sound the Trumpet (Z. 323). Publication: Novello, 1910.

4. *Selection of Collected Folk Songs.* Vol. I. Arranged for voice and pianoforte by Cecil Sharp and RVW. Eight songs previously arranged by RVW were included: 8. Down by the Riverside; 9. Farmyard Song; 12. I Will Give My Love an Apple; 15. My Boy Billy; 22. The Carter; 25. The Female Highwayman; 26. The Fox; 31. The Painful Plough. Publication: Novello, n.d., but likely 1917.

5. *The Motherland Song Book.* Four volumes, Stainer & Bell, 1919.
   a. Volume III: Sea Songs. For unison and mixed voices, selected and edited by RVW. The following tunes were arranged by him: 1. The Arethusa; 5. Full Fathom Five; 6. Jack the Sailor (TTBB); 8. We Be Three Poor Mariners (TTB).
   b. Volume IV: Sea Songs. For unison and mixed voices, selected and edited by RVW. The following tunes were arranged by him: 1. The Golden Vanity; 3. Just as the Tide Was Flowing; 9. The Spanish Ladies.

6. *Eight Traditional English Carols.* Arranged for voice and piano, and for unaccompanied mixed choir (SATB). 1. And All in the Morning (On Christmas Day); 2. On Christmas Night; 3. The Twelve Apostles; 4. Down in Yon Forest; 5. May-Day Carol; 6. The Truth Sent from Above; 7. The Birth of the Saviour; 8. The Wassail Song (unison only). Publication: Stainer & Bell, 1919.

7. *Twelve Traditional Carols from Herefordshire.* Collected, edited, and arranged for voice and piano, or for unaccompanied mixed choir (SATB), by Ella Mary Leather and RVW. 1. The Holy Well; 2. The Holy Well (second version); 3. Christmas Now Is Drawing Near at Hand; 4. Joseph and Mary (to the tune There Is a Fountain); 5. The Angel Gabriel; 6. God Rest You Merry, Gentlemen; 7. New Year's Carol; 8. On Christmas Day (All in the Morning); 9. Dives and Lazarus; 10. The Miraculous Harvest (or The Carnal and the Crane); 11. The Saviour's Love; 12. The Seven Virgins (or Under the Leaves). Publication: Stainer & Bell, 1920.

8. *Twenty-five Vocal Exercises Founded on Bach's* Mass in B Minor. Edited and arranged by Gertrude Sichel and RVW. Publication: Stainer & Bell, 1924.

9a. *Songs of Praise.* Text editor, Percy Dearmer; music editors, Martin Shaw and RVW. Publication: OUP, 1925.
   i. Original tunes composed and/or contributed by RVW: 37 (Magda); 41(i) (Oakley); 110 (Sine Nomine); 123(i) (Cumnor); 185 (Guildford); 217 (Down Ampney); 406 (Randolph); 443 (King's Weston); 445(i) (Salve Festa Dies).[15] Publication: London, OUP, 1925.
   ii. Tunes arranged by RVW and under his copyright, not present in *The English Hymnal*: 12 (Danby; different arrangement than that in *The English Hymnal*); 51 (Macht Hoch die Thür); 163(ii) (Valor); 182 (Ach! Wan Doch Jesu, Liebster Mein); 200(ii) (Eventide, descant); 226 (Regina); 246 (Crüger, descant for verse 3); 249 (Freuen wir Uns); 293 (Wächterlied); 296 (Il Buon Pastor); 327 (Engadine); 330 (Londonderry); 352(ii) (Essex); 353 (Milites); 372 (St. Gabriel); 408 (Mariners); 415 (O Mentes Perfidas); 438 (Hardwick); 440 (Bamberg); 442 (Resonet in Laudibus).

9b. *Songs of Praise for Boys and Girls.* Editors as for *Songs of Praise.* Publication: London, Oxford University Press, 1929.
   i. Original tunes composed and/or contributed by RVW: 95 (Marathon), adapted from the Processional Chorus (no. 12) in *The Wasps* (**II.A.2**).

ii. Tunes arranged by RVW and under his copyright: 1 (HARDWICK); 5 (HORSHAM); 8 (SHIPSTON); 9 (TAVISTOCK); 13 (BANBURY); 23 (RODMELL); 27 (COME, FAITHFUL PEOPLE); 29(i) (BRIDGWATER); 29(ii) (LANGPORT); 33 (SOLOTHURN); 56 (MONK'S GATE); 57 (PLEADING SAVIOUR); 58 (STOWEY); 60 (EAST HORNDON); 64 (HERONGATE); 65 (QUEM PASTORES LAUDAVERE); 69 (EARDISLEY); 72 (HAMBRIDGE); 76 (ST. HUGH); 80 (GOSTERWOOD); 83 (EPSOM); 93 (RESONET IN LAUDIBUS); 94 and 105 (MAGDALENA); 109(i) (ST. AUSTIN); 109(ii) (FARNHAM).

9c. *Songs of Praise*, enlarged edition. Editors as for *Songs of Praise*. Publication: OUP, 1931. All of RVW's arrangements from the first edition were retained except for REGINA, LONDONDERRY, and EAST HORNDON.

    i. Original tunes composed and/or contributed by RVW: 126 (MANTEGNA); 302 (MARATHON); 319(ii) (ABINGER); 432 (FAMOUS MEN); 489 (WHITE GATES).

    ii. Tunes arranged by RVW and under his copyright: 59 (ST. OLAF'S SEQUENCE); 65 (HELMSLEY); 164 (COBBOLD); 205 (DORKING); 232 (OSLO); 353 (CRADLE SONG); 393(i) (STALHAM); 393(ii) (DUNSTAN).

9d. *Songs of Praise for Children*. Editors as for *Songs of Praise*. Publication: OUP, 1933.

    i. Original tunes composed and/or contributed by RVW: 87 (SINE NOMINE); 113 (WHITE GATES); 147 (RANDOLPH).

    ii. Tunes arranged by RVW and under his copyright: 37 (RESONET IN LAUDIBUS); 44 (FOREST GREEN); 45 (RODMELL); 68 (MONK'S GATE); 135 (HARDWICK).

10. *The Oxford Book of Carols*. Text editor, Percy Dearmer. Music editors, Martin Shaw and RVW. Publication: OUP, 1928.[16]

    a. Original tunes composed by RVW: 173 (The Golden Carol); 185 (Wither's Rocking Hymn); 186 (Snow in the Street); 196 (Blake's Cradle Song).

    b. Tunes arranged by RVW: 7 (Hereford Carol); 17 (All in the Morning); 24 (Sussex Carol); 31 (Gloucestershire Wassail); 36 (The Salutation Carol); 39 (This Endris Night); 43 (The Seven Virgins); 45 (Sussex Mummers' Carol); 47 (May Carol); 51 (The Sinners' Redemption); 53 (The Carnal and the Crane); 55 (The Miraculous Harvest); 57 (Dives and Lazarus); 61 (Down in Yon Forest); 68 (The Truth from Above); 77 (Song of the Crib); 79 (Quem Pastores Laudavere); 115 (Joseph and Mary); 131 (Coverdale's Carol); 132 (Psalm of Sion); 134 (If Ye Would Hear; with Martin Shaw); 138 (O Little Town); 142 (Children's Song of the Nativity).

11. *Hymns for Sunday School Anniversaries and Other Special Occasions*. Edited by G. W. Briggs, Percy Dearmer, Martin Shaw, and RVW. Fourteen hymns, with accompaniments. RVW contributed no. 12 (DOWN AMPNEY). Publication: OUP, 1930.

12. *Nine Carols for Male Voices*. For TTBB choir. 1. God Rest You Merry; 2. As Joseph Was a-Walking (The Cherry Tree Carol); 3. Mummers' Carol; 4. The First Nowell; 5. The Lord at First; 6. Coventry Carol; 7. I Saw Three Ships (bar. solo and chorus); 8. A Virgin Most Pure; 9. Dives and Lazarus. Publication: OUP, 1942.

B. Contributions by Vaughan Williams to Series Edited by Others

1. *Folk Songs from the Eastern Counties*. Book II of *Folk Songs of England*, ed. Cecil Sharp (Novello, 1908). Collected and set with piano accompaniment by RVW. Other arrangements were subsequently released for some of these songs; for details, see *CVW*, 40.

(a) From Essex: Bushes and Briars (collected 1903); Tarry Trowsers, A Bold Young Farmer, The Lost Lady Found, As I Walked Out [a.k.a. The Old Garden Gate],[17] The Lark in the Morning (all collected 1904).

(b) From Norfolk: On Board a Ninety-Eight, The Captain's Apprentice, Ward the Pirate, The Saucy Bold Robber, The Bold Princess Royal, The Lincolnshire Farmer, The Sheffield Apprentice (all collected 1905).

(c) From Cambridgeshire: Geordie, Harry the Tailor (both collected 1906).

2. *Church Songs.* Collected by Sabine Baring-Gould, music arranged by Henry Fleetwood Sheppard and RVW. The latter arranged hymns 1–8, 11–13, 16–17, 19–21, and 23–25. RVW used an arrangement by Cecil Sharp for no. 15. Publication: Society for the Promotion of Christian Knowledge, 1911.

3. *Folk Songs for Schools.* Arranged for unison singing with piano accompaniment. The following were collected and arranged by RVW: 1. The Jolly Plough Boy; 2. The Cuckoo and the Nightingale; 4. The Female Highwayman; 5. The Carter; 7. My Boy Billy; 11. The Painful Plough. The remainder were collected by H. E. D. Hammond and arranged by RVW: 3. Servant Man and Husbandman; 6. I Will Give My Love an Apple; 8. Down by the Riverside; 9. The Fox; 10. Farmyard Song. Publication: *Novello's School Songs*, ed. William McNaught, Book 232, Novello, 1912.

4. *Folk Songs of England,* vol. V (*Folk Songs from Sussex*), ed. Cecil J. Sharp. Collected by W. Percy Merrick, with piano accompaniments by RVW and Albert Robins. 1. Bold General Wolfe; 2. Low Down in the Broom; 3. The Thresherman and the Squire; 4. The Pretty Ploughboy; 5. O Who Is That That Raps at My Window?; 6. The Unquiet Grave (with violin accompaniment ad lib); 7. Captain Grant; 8. Farewell, Lads; 9. Come All You Worthy Christians; 10. The Turkish Lady; 11. The Seeds of Love; 12. The Maid of Islington; 13. Here's Adieu to All Judges and Juries; 14. Lovely Joan; 15. The Isle of France. Publication: Novello, 1912.

5. *Songtime.* Edited by Percy Dearmer and Martin Shaw. RVW contributed or arranged the following: 1. An Acre of Land (collected from Frank Bailey of Coombe Bisset, 1904); 2. Quem pastores (fifteenth-century German melody); 3. EAST HORNDEN (no. 595 in *The English Hymnal*); 4. SHIPSTON (no. 599); 5. ST. HUGH (no. 606). Publication: Curwen, 1915.

6. *Hymns for Today, Missionary and Devotional.* Edited by H. L. Hemmends, Jeremy Noel Thomas Howat, and Hilda Poulter. Contains two tunes attributed to RVW: 36 (MONK'S GATE); 79 (SINE NOMINE). Publication: Psalms and Hymns Trust, 1930.

7. *Twelve Traditional Country Dances.* Collected and described by Maud Karpeles, with piano arrangements by RVW in collaboration with Maud Karpeles. 1. Corn Rigs; 2. Morpeth Rant (arranged by RVW); 3. Soldier's Joy; 4. Roxburgh Castle (collected and arranged by Cecil Sharp); 5. The Sylph; 6. Long Eight (arranged by RVW); 7. Three around Three *or* Pleasures of the Town; 8. Steamboat; 9. Piper's Fancy (collected by Sharp, arranged by RVW and Maud Karpeles); 10. The Tempest; 11. The Self; 12. Kitty's Rambles. Publication: Novello, 1931.

8. *Folk Songs from Newfoundland.* Collected and arranged by Maud Karpeles, with piano accompaniments by RVW and others. Dedication: To Fred and Isabel Emerson of St. John's. RVW arranged the following:

a. Vol. I. Ballads: 1. Sweet William's Ghost; 2. The Cruel Mother; 3. The Gypsy Laddie; 7. The Bloody Gardener. Songs: 8. The Maiden's Lament; 9. Proud Nancy; 10. The Morning Dew.

b. Vol. II. Ballads: 1. The Bonny Banks of Virgie-O (The Bonny Banks o' Fordie); 2. Earl Brand; 3. Lord Akeman (Lord Bateman); 7. The Lover's Ghost. Songs: 8. She's like the Swallow; 9. Young Florio; 10. The Winter's Gone and Past; 11. The Cuckoo. Publication: OUP, 1934. Republished as *Fifteen Songs from Newfoundland* (OUP, 1968).

9. *Folk Songs*, Volume II. Compiled by Cyril Winn. A selection of thirty-three folk songs, arranged by Cecil Sharp, RVW, and others for voice and piano. RVW collected and arranged the following: 7. The Bold Princess Royal; 18. The Jolly Ploughboy; 32. Ward the Pirate. Publication: Novello, 1935.

10. *Nine English Folk Songs from the Southern Appalachian Mountains.* For voice and piano. Arrangements by RVW (ca. 1938) based on tunes in Cecil Sharp's *English Folk Songs from the Southern Appalachians* (ed. Maud Karpeles, OUP, 1952) and given to Maud Karpeles. 1. The Elfin Knight, or The Lovers' Tasks; 2. Lord Randal; 3. Lord Thomas and Fair Ellinor; 4. Fair Margaret and Sweet William; 5. Barbara Allen; 6. The Daemon Lover, or The House Carpenter; 7. The Rich Old Lady; 8. The Tree in the Wood; 9. The Ten Commandments, or The Twelve Apostles. Publication: OUP, 1967.

11. *A Yacre of Land.* Edited by Imogen Holst and Ursula Vaughan Williams. Folksongs from RVW's personal collection. Arranged for unison voices and piano, and for unaccompanied part singing, by Imogen Holst. Sixteen songs: 1. A Yacre of Land; 2. John Reilly; 3. The Week before Easter; 4. Willie Foster; 5. The Jolly Harin'; 6. Nine Joys of Mary; 7. Joseph and His Wedded Wife; 8. The Lord of Life; 9. Over the Hills and Mountains; 10. The Foxhunt; 11. Come All You Young Ploughboys; 12. A Bold Young Sailor; 13. The Pretty Ploughboy; 14. Seventeen Come Sunday; 15. It Was One Morning; 16. My Coffin Shall Be Black. Publication: OUP, 1961.

X. Juvenilia, Student Exercises, and Sketches and Fragments

A. Juvenilia

1. Selections from a sketchbook dated 5 June 1882.
   a. Overture to the Major.
   b. Pianoforte Sonata in F. "Respectfully dedicated to Miss Sophy Wedgewood."
   c. Chant du matin.
   d. Overture to the Ram Opera.
   e. "How Doth the Little Busy Bee."
   f. Sonata in Three Movements. Marked "op. 4."
   g. Overture to *The Galoshes of Happienes* [sic].
2. Various works, all approximately dated 1882.
   a. Chorale, op. 9.
   b. *Grand March des Bramas*, for piano duet, op. 10.
   c. Duet for two violins and piano.
   d. Song: "Here I Come, Creeping, Creeping, Everywhere" (Sarah Roberts Boyle).
   e. Sketches for a Nativity Scene.
3. Introduction for two violins, cello (?) and piano. Undated, ca. 1882–1889.
4. Andante in F for piano. Undated, ca. 1882–1889.
5. Minuet and trio. Piano score. Undated, ca. 1882–1889.
6. Piano arrangement of a string quartet. Undated, ca. 1882–1889.
7. Three Kyries. Composed at Charterhouse, June 1889.

B. Student Exercises and Minor Compositions (RCM)

1. Organ Overture. Christmas term, 1890.
2. Sonatina in E♭ for piano. Christmas term, 1890.
3. Finale of a string quartet. Spring 1891.
4. Passacaglia. For organ. Spring–Summer 1891.
5. Anthem: *I Heard a Voice from Heaven* (Revelation, 14:13). For tenor and chorus. Summer term 1891.
6. Multiple versions of a Gloria. Summer and Christmas terms 1891.
7. Theme with Variations. For piano. Christmas term 1891.
8. Tunes "For a Ballet." 1891. Possibly expanded and performed as "Scenes de Ballet" for orchestra, May 1899.[18]
9. Prelude, Minuet, and Adagio. For organ and cello. Undated; possibly 1891–1892.
10. *Super Flumina Babylonis* (Psalm 137). For mixed chorus (SATB) and string orchestra. Spring Term 1892.
11. *Fantasia à la valse.* For orchestra (short score), with arrangement for piano duet. 1892.
12. Five Valses for Orchestra. 1892.
13. Arrangement of Beethoven's op. 2, no. 2, second movement (Largo appassionato). For orchestra. Summer term, 1892.
14. *Happy Day at Gunby.* For violins, violoncellos, pianoforte, and organ. Includes passage marked "Old Country Dance." 1892.
15. Variations on a Ground Bass by Lully. For piano. 1892.
16. Andantino for Violin and Piano. Undated, ca. 1892–1895.
17. Moderato for Piano. Undated, ca. 1892–1895.
18. *Wedding Minuet.* For piano. Undated, ca. 1892–1895.
19. Adagio molto in E♭. For piano. Dated 4 October 1893.
20. Suite. For four hands on one piano. Four movements: I. Prelude; II. Minuet; III. Sarabande; IV. Gigue. 1893.
21. *Reminiscences of a Walk at Frankham.* For piano. Dated 28 August 1894.

C. Sketches and Fragments

1. Portion of Minuet and Trio. For string quartet. Spring–Summer 1891.
2. Incomplete arrangement of Beethoven's op. 7. For orchestra. Summer term 1892.
3. "Ach neige, du schmerzenreiche" (Johann von Goethe). Incomplete setting for voice and piano. Likely 1892–1895.
4. "Her Feet Are Set in a Rugged Way." Fair copy for voice and piano. Likely 1892–1895.
5. Sketch for "Prospice" (Robert Browning). Voice and piano. Likely 1892–1895.
6. Song sketch: "Break, Break, Break" (Tennyson). Likely 1892–1895.
7. Trio in C Major. For violin, cello, and piano. Draft of first movement completed 28 June 1895. Incomplete.
8. Sonata for Horn and Pianoforte. Four movements projected: I. Andante sostenuto— Allegro; II. Romanza; III. Scherzo and Trio; IV. Finale. Horn part only survives; brief passages from the Romanza, Scherzo, and Finale appear in piano score form. Undated, likely 1897–1902.
9. Sketch for a Prelude to *Orestes.* Short score. 1902.

10. Sketches and fragments in a sketchbook dated ca. 1897–1902.
    a. Rhapsody. Possibly a sketch for the *Symphonic Rhapsody*.
    b. Dramatic March. Possibly incorporated into *Heroic Elegy and Triumphal Epilogue* (**III.C.3**)
    c. Dirge for orchestra. Possibly incorporated into *Heroic Elegy and Triumphal Epilogue* (**III.C.3**).
    d. Fragments and sketches for a symphonic poem (or suite?): *Ozymandias*. Also in a second sketchbook dated ca. 1938. Includes parts for English horn and solo singer.
    e. Setting of *Dover Beach* (Matthew Arnold). No information known other than that it was composed by April 1900.
    f. Sketch for *Let Us Now Praise Famous Men* (different from **IV.D.3**).
    g. Sketch: "Viola piece."
    h. Sketch: "Ballet tune."
11. Sketch for *Aethiopia Saluting the Colours* (Walt Whitman). Undated, possibly ca. 1908. Includes parts for narrator, solo soprano, solo male voice, and chorus (marked "humming").
12. *The Future* (Matthew Arnold). For solo soprano, chorus, and orchestra. Incomplete vocal score. Undated, possibly ca. 1908. Extended and completed by Martin Yates. First performance: Usher Hall, Edinburgh, 8 November 2019.
13. Incomplete setting of "Come, O Thou Traveller Unknown" (Charles Wesley). Two verses. Undated; before 1914.
14. *Saraband—Helen* (Christopher Marlowe). Tenor solo, SATB chorus, and orchestra. Vocal score, some indications of orchestration. Undated and incomplete, ca. 1914.
15. Sketches and fragments in a sketchbook dated ca. 1938.
    a. Pages of a string quartet.
    b. Sketches for a Romance for Organ.
    c. Sketches for *Exsultate Jubilate*, for double choir.
    d. Sketches for *Ozymandias* (see **X.C.10.d**).
16. Sketches for a Concerto for Cello and Orchestra. Three projected movements: I. Rhapsody; II. Lento; III. Finale. Intended for Pablo Casals. Likely begun 1942–1943; additional work after 1953.
17. Sketches for a *Fantasia for Vibraphone*. Undated, likely ca. 1956–1958.
18. Sketch for *London Calling*. Mixed chorus and piano. Undated.
19. "David of the White Rock." Welsh folksong, arranged for voice and piano. Vocal score, words not set. Undated.
20. *Thomas the Rhymer,* an opera in three acts. Libretto by Ursula Vaughan Williams, based on the ballads *Thomas the Rhymer* and *Tam Lin*. Completed in piano and vocal score, but not revised. Left unfinished at the time of RVW's death.

Details on additional minor fragments, sketches, and notes are available in *CVW*, 10–11, 76, and 242.

Personalia

Allen, Hugh P. (1869–1946), organist, conductor, and administrator. Attended Christ's College, Cambridge, where he led the University Musical Club and met RVW. Later served as organist at Ely Cathedral and New College, Oxford (named Fellow in 1908), and conductor of the London Bach Choir (1907–1921). Appointed Professor of Music at Oxford and Director of the RCM in 1918; reformed and modernized the latter institution, appointing RVW to the faculty. Dedicatee of *Hugh the Drover*.

Barbirolli, John (1899–1970), conductor and cellist. Attended Trinity College of Music and the Royal Academy of Music, pursuing dual career as a performer and conductor. Led the Scottish Orchestra and the Northern Philharmonic Orchestra before succeeding Toscanini at the New York Philharmonic. Returned to England to lead the Hallé Orchestra (1943–1970). Active proponent of RVW's music; dedicatee of the Eighth Symphony.

Bliss, Arthur (1891–1975), composer, conductor, administrator, and author. Studied at Cambridge and the RCM before enlisting in the Great War. Moved briefly to the United States in 1923; upon returning to England, established himself as one of the leading composers of his generation, his idiom informed by neoclassicism and Elgarian Romanticism. Appointed BBC Director of Music in 1942, Master of the Queen's Music in 1953. Friend and trusted advisor to RVW.

Boult, Adrian (1889–1983), conductor. Attended Christ Church, Oxford (DMus, 1914) and the Leipzig Conservatory, studying under Arthur Nikisch. Joined RCM faculty in 1919, later serving as music director for the City of Birmingham Orchestra (1924–1930), the BBC Symphony Orchestra (1930–1950), and the London Philharmonic Orchestra (1950–1957). Among the foremost interpreters of RVW's symphonies; dedicatee of *Job*.

Boughton, Rutland (1878–1960), composer and writer. Briefly studied at the RCM, later teaching at the Midland Institute School of Music (Birmingham). Founded the Glastonbury Festival in 1914, drawing inspiration from Wagner's *Festspielhaus* at Bayreuth, Morrisonian socialism, and Arthurian legend. His opera *The Immortal Hour* (1914) enjoyed brief but enormous popular success when staged in London (1922).

Broadwood, Lucy (1859–1929), folklorist, singer, editor, and administrator. Co-editor (with J. A. Fuller Maitland) of *English County Songs* (1893); active collector of folk songs in Surrey and Sussex. Founding member of the Folk Song Society; later its honorary secretary (1904) and editor (1908). RVW regularly used melodies she collected in his own works; dedicatee of "Orpheus with His Lute" (1904).

Browne, William Denis (1888–1915), composer and critic. Studied at Clare College, Cambridge, completing MusB in 1912; served as critic for *The Times* and *New Statesman* before being killed in action during the Great War. Chorister in premiere of *The Wasps*; assisted RVW in reconstructing the score to *A London Symphony*.

Bruch, Max (1838–1920), composer, conductor, and teacher. Spent his early career as both a freelance and court composer; later held conducting posts in Berlin, Liverpool, and Breslau before leading composition classes at the Höchschule für Musik in Berlin (1890–1911). Tutored RVW between 1897 and 1898.

Butterworth, George S. K. (1885–1916), composer, dancer, and folk-song collector. Attended Trinity College, Oxford, serving as president of the University Music Club. Cofounder of the English Folk Dance Society; composer of numerous songs and instrumental works inspired by A. E. Housman's poetry. Killed in action while serving with the 13th Durham Light Infantry. Dedicatee (posthumously) of *A London Symphony*, having inspired RVW to write the work.

Child, Harold (1869–1945), author and critic. Cofounder and longtime leader writer for *The Times Literary Supplement* (London) (1902); also first assistant editor of the *Academy*, and dramatic critic for the *Observer* and *The Times* (London) (both from 1912). Librettist for *Hugh the Drover*; lyricist for *The New Commonwealth* and "Our Love Goes Out to English Skies." ·

Cohen, Harriet (1895–1967), English pianist. Graduate of the Royal Academy of Music, and a leading figure in the promotion of keyboard works by Bach and contemporary English composers. Dedicatee of RVW's Piano Concerto and his *Hymn Tune Prelude on "Song 13" by Orlando Gibbons*. Arranged RVW's *Charterhouse Suite* for piano and string orchestra.

Curle, Cordelia (née Fisher, 1879–1970), youngest sister of Adeline Vaughan Williams, known as "Cork" or "Boo." Exchanged near-daily correspondence with Adeline for decades; later friend and confidante of Ursula Vaughan Williams.

Dearmer, Percy (1867–1936), Anglican clergyman, scholar, and activist. Attended Christ Church, Oxford (1886–1889), later authoring the reformist tract *The Parson's Handbook* (1899). Recruited RVW as musical editor of *The English Hymnal*, *Songs of Praise*, and *The Oxford Book of Carols*, for which he himself served as literary editor.

Dent, Edward J. (1876–1957), musicologist, critic, and pedagogue. A Cambridge graduate, he was elected a fellow at King's College (1902), leaving to become a critic in London in 1918, but returning when appointed Professor of Music in 1926. A reform-minded educator with a gift for languages and wide-ranging musical tastes, he was a close colleague of and advisor to RVW.

Douglas, Roy (1907–2015), composer and arranger. Self-taught as a composer, with extensive original contributions to film and television. Served as RVW's regular copyist, consultant, and arranger from 1944 to 1958, later writing the memoir *Working with Vaughan Williams* (1972/1988).

Duncan, Isadora (1878–1927), American dancer. Trained in classical ballet; adopted a dancing style inspired by neoclassical design and reflecting natural movement.

Proposed a collaborative "choral ballet" with RVW and Gilbert Murray that ultimately foundered, but led to RVW's composition of a series of choruses for Greek plays.

Ellis, Francis Bevis ("F. B.," 1883–1916), composer, conductor and philanthropist. Attended Christ Church, Oxford (1901–1905), later organizing and funding a concert series showcasing the music of contemporary British composers, including RVW's *Phantasy Quintet* and *A London Symphony*. Killed in action while serving with the 10th Northumberland Fusiliers.

Falkner, (Donald) Keith (1900–91), bass-baritone singer, teacher, and administrator. Graduate of the RCM, returning as its Director (1960–1974); also served as Professor of Voice at Cornell University (1950–1960). Regular soloist in the LHMC and the Dorking *Passions* led by RVW; dedicatee of "Menelaus on the Beach at Pharos."

Farrer, Evangeline (née Knox, 1871–1968), administrator, teacher, and suffragist. Studied composition under Parry at the RCM before teaching music professionally. In Abinger, music tutor for the children of Thomas Cecil, Second Baron Farrer; later, his second wife. With Meggie Vaughan Williams, joint founder of the LHMC and its longtime President and Chair (1904–1947).

Farrer, Frances ("Fanny," 1895–1977), administrator and public servant. Attended Newnham College, Cambridge; founder member and first secretary of the Abinger Women's Institute (1920), rising through the WI ranks to become General Secretary (1929–1959). Honorary Secretary for the LHMC, 1923–1939.

Fisher, Adeline—see Vaughan Williams, Adeline.

Foss, Hubert (1899–1953), pianist, editor, and author. Joined OUP in 1921, serving as founding editor of its music department (1925–1941). Tireless champion of British composers; author of the first monograph study of RVW's music (1950).

Fuller Maitland, John A. (1856–1936), critic, editor, and music scholar. Attended Trinity College, Cambridge; later assistant editor and prolific contributor for Grove's *Dictionary*. Music critic for the *Pall Mall Gazette*, *The Guardian*, and most influentially, *The Times* (1889–1911). Co-editor with Lucy Broadwood of *English County Songs* (1893); also responsible for editions of *The Fitzwilliam Virginal Book* and the works of Henry Purcell. Early promoter of RVW's music.

Gatty, Nicholas (1874–1946), English composer, critic, conductor, and scholar. Contemporary of RVW's at the RCM, studying under Stanford, before attending Downing College, Cambridge. Specialized in opera composition; served as critic for several London newspapers and assistant editor for the second and third editions of Grove's *Dictionary*. Along with his brothers Ivor and René (Reginald) and sister, Margot, became close friends with both RVW and Adeline Vaughan Williams.

Gladstone, Francis Edward (1845–1928), organist, composer, conductor, and teacher. Articled pupil at Winchester Cathedral, later earning MusD at Cambridge (1879). Prolific composer of choral and organ music; Professor of Harmony at the RCM, where he provided RVW's earliest compositional instruction.

Gray, Alan (1855–1935), English organist and composer. Abandoned a legal career for one in music, graduating with MusB and doctorate from Cambridge. Musical director at Wellington College; later conductor of the Cambridge University Musical Society (1892–1912), organist of Trinity College (1892–1930), and editor for the Purcell Society. RVW's organ tutor at Cambridge; dedicatee of the Three Preludes Founded on Welsh Hymn-Tunes.

Gurney, Ivor (1890–1937), composer and poet. Studied under Stanford and RVW at the RCM. One of his generation's most gifted composers of English art song; authored the poetic anthologies *Severn and Somme* and *War's Embers*. Gassed and shot serving with the 2/5ᵗʰ Gloucester Regiment in the Great War, leading to severe post-traumatic stress disorder; institutionalized in 1922 until his death. RVW was one of his few contacts with the outside world during this time.

Haig Brown, William (1823–1907), headmaster of Charterhouse School. Fellow of Pembroke College, Cambridge, where he received a double first in classics and mathematics (1846); took holy orders in 1852. Appointed Headmaster of Charterhouse in 1863. Oversaw the school's relocation from Smithfield to Godalming (1872), earning him the title of "second founder." Headmaster during RVW's student tenure.

Holst, Gustav[us von] (1874–1934), composer, trombonist, and teacher. Studied under Stanford at the RCM, where he met RVW; later held trombonist positions in the Queen's Hall and Scottish Orchestras, and with the Carl Rosa Opera company. Longtime head of music at St. Paul's Girls School (Hammersmith) and director of music at Morley College (1907–1924). RVW's closest friend and most trusted critic; their compositional "field days" did much to develop their musical idioms.

Howells, Herbert (1892–1983), composer, organist, and teacher. Articled pupil at Gloucester Cathedral; studied under Stanford at the RCM, later serving as Professor of Composition, and as King Edward VII Professor of Music at the University of London. Precocious and prodigious composer, with outstanding contributions to Anglican church music. Dedicatee of *Hodie*.

Ireland, John (1879–1962), composer, teacher, and pianist. Contemporary of RVW at the RCM, studying piano with Frederic Cliffe and composition with Stanford; completed BMus at Durham University. One of the leading organists of his generation; excelled in small-scale compositions such as songs and character pieces for piano. Joined the RCM composition faculty at the same time as RVW.

Irving, Ernest (1878–1953), conductor and composer. Musical director for Ealing Film Studios from 1935 to 1953. Commissioned numerous film scores from RVW, and worked from his themes to create the score for *Bitter Springs*. Dedicatee of *Sinfonia Antartica*.

Jacob, Gordon (1895–1984), composer, teacher, and author. Studied under RVW at the RCM, later serving on the teaching staff (1924–1966) and writing several composition textbooks. RVW regularly solicited his opinions on musical matters; arranged several of RVW's works, most notably the *English Folk Songs Suite* (1924).

Karpeles, Maud (1885–1976), collector and scholar of English and North American folk music. Longtime assistant to Cecil Sharp; founding member of the board of the English Folk Dance Society. Amassed notable collections of folk music from Appalachia and Newfoundland. Close ally to RVW in matters regarding the EFDS.

Kennedy, Douglas (1893–1988), folklorist, dancer, and administrator. Succeeded Cecil Sharp as Director of the EFDS (1924–1961), overseeing the merger with the Folk-Song Society and the foundation of Cecil Sharp House. Longtime collaborator (if sometimes fractiously) with RVW in the affairs of the EFDS.

Kennedy, Michael (1926–2014), music critic and author. Joined the staff of *The Daily Telegraph* following naval service in WWII; began writing music columns in 1948 until his retirement in 2005. Notable for his biographies of Elgar, Richard Strauss, and Walton (among others), and for *The Works of Ralph Vaughan Williams*, the authorized study of the composer's music, strongly informed by his close relationship with RVW.

Keynes, Geoffrey (1887–1982), surgeon and literary scholar. Served in the RAMC during the Great War, becoming an expert on blood transfusion and writing a book on the subject (1922). Editor and bibliographer for authors ranging from John Donne to Jane Austen to Rupert Brooke; his work on William Blake was perhaps the most influential. Devised the scenario for *Job* in collaboration with Gwen Raverat and RVW.

Lambert, Constant (1905–1951), composer, conductor, and critic. Studied under RVW at the RCM; his music displays influences of neoclassicism, jazz, and contemporary French music. As conductor of the Camargo Society, played an influential role in influencing British ballet; his book *Music Ho!* (1934) was a perceptive and waspish assessment of contemporary British musical culture. Arranged RVW's *Job* for theatrical performance, conducting the stage premiere in 1931.

Leather, Ella Mary (1874–1928), accomplished ethnographer and author of *The Folklore of Herefordshire* (1912). Accompanied Vaughan Williams on multiple collecting excursions between 1908 and 1913; a co-edited selection of their findings was published as *Twelve Traditional Carols from Herefordshire* (1920).

Ley, Henry (1887–1962), organist and arranger. Studied at St. George's Chapel (Windsor) and the RCM under Parratt, later made choragus at Oxford and Professor of Organ at the RCM. Dedicatee of RVW's Prelude and Fugue in C Minor, and arranger of many of RVW's works for organ.

Maconchy, Elizabeth (1907–1994), English composer. Studied with RVW at the RCM and with K. B. Jirák in Prague. Best known for her chamber music and her opera *The Sofa* (1959), featuring a libretto by Ursula Vaughan Williams.

Maitland, Frederic (1850–1906), historian, lawyer, and scholar. Elected Reader in English law at Cambridge (1884), later Downing Professor of the Laws of England (1888), in which position he demonstrated strong reformist tendencies. Married Florence Fisher (1886), eldest sister of Adeline Vaughan Williams; it was through Maitland's family musicales that RVW and Adeline met.

Mathieson, Muir (1911–1975), Scottish conductor and film music director. Appointed music director for London Films (1934) after graduating from the RCM; responsible for persuading many eminent composers to write scores for feature films, including RVW, whose first cinematic score (for *49th Parallel*) came at Mathieson's behest.

Morris, Reginald Owen ("R. O.," 1886–1948), composer, teacher, and theorist who married Vaughan Williams's sister-in-law, Emmeline ("Jane") Fisher. Graduate of and later Professor of Counterpoint at the RCM and (briefly) the Curtis Institute. Author of the influential *Contrapuntal Technique in the Sixteenth Century* (1922), as well as several widely adopted textbooks on the subject.

Mukle, May (1880–1963), English cellist, active both as a soloist and as a chamber musician, and founder of the MM (Mainly Musicians) Club. Dedicatee of the *Six Studies in English Folk Song*.

Müller-Hartmann, Robert (1884–1950), German-born composer and editor. Lecturer in Music at the Hanseatic [Hamburg] University before emigrating to Dorking in 1937. Assisted RVW as copyist and translator. Dedicatee of the Partita for Double String Orchestra.

Mullinar, Michael (1895–1973), pianist and composer. Studied composition under RVW at the RCM. Later served as both copyist and *repetiteur* for read-throughs of major new works. Dedicatee of Symphony No. 6, and the intended soloist for the *Fantasia (quasi variazione) on the "Old 104th" Psalm Tune.*

Ord, Bernhard ("Boris," 1897–1961), organist and conductor. Organ scholar at Corpus Christi, Cambridge, and cofounder of the Cambridge University Madrigal Society; later elected fellow at King's (1923). Director of the Cambridge University Musical Society from 1936; directed the premiere of RVW's *Old King Cole* (1923) and a very successful Cambridge production of *The Pilgrim's Progress* (1954).

Parratt, Walter (1841–1924), organist, teacher, and composer. Served at St. George's Chapel, Windsor, before being named the inaugural Professor of Organ at the RCM (1883). Succeeded Parry as Heather Professor of Music at Oxford (1908), and served as Master of the King's Musick (1893–1924). Taught organ lessons to RVW, helping him gain the FRCO.

Parry, C. Hubert H. (1848–1918), composer, teacher, and scholar. Abandoned work as an underwriter for Lloyd's to pursue a music career, working as a subeditor for and contributor to Grove's *Dictionary.* Appointed Professor of Music History at the RCM (1883), where he also taught composition and served as Director (1895–1918). Also served as Heather Professor of Music at Oxford (1900–1908). RVW studied under him from 1891 to 1894.

Ravel, Maurice (1875–1937), French composer. Pioneering figure in impressionistic and post-tonal composition, having studied under Bériot and Fauré at the Paris Conservatoire; his works are renowned for their meticulous craftsmanship and striking timbres. Tutored RVW privately in Paris, 1907–1908.

Raverat, Gwendolyn (1885–1957), engraver, designer, and author. Leading figure in twentieth-century wood engraving. Second cousin to RVW; designed scenery and costumes for *Job,* collaborating on the scenario with Geoffrey Keynes and RVW.

Sargent, Malcolm (1895–1967), English conductor. Completed BMus and doctorate from Durham University. Joined the RCM faculty in 1923, later leading the Hallé Orchestra, Liverpool Symphony Orchestra, and BBC Symphony Orchestra, having directed the Henry Wood Promenade Concerts since 1947. Conducted first performances of *Hugh the Drover, Sir John in Love, Riders to the Sea,* and Symphony No. 9, among others.

Sharp, Cecil J. (1859–1924), folklorist and editor. Leading figure in the collection and promotion of English folk song and folk dance in the early twentieth century, beginning with *Folk Songs from Somerset* (1905–1909), and continuing with *English Folk-Song: Some Conclusions* (1907) and *The Morris Book* (with H. C. MacIlwaine, 1907–1913). Collected nearly 5000 tunes in the United Kingdom and United States over the course of his career.

Sharp, Evelyn (1869–1955), author, journalist, and suffragist. Sister of Cecil Sharp; founding member of the United Suffragists, and an active campaigner on behalf of women's voting rights. Librettist for *The Poisoned Kiss.*

Shaw, Martin (1876–1958), composer, organist, and scholar. A contemporary of RVW's at the RCM, he enjoyed a successful compositional career, particularly in the realms of theatrical and church music. Served as co-editor with RVW on the multiple editions of *Songs of Praise* and *The Oxford Book of Carols.*

Shove, Fredegond (née Maitland, 1889–1949), Georgian poet, daughter of Frederic and Florence Maitland, and Vaughan Williams's niece by marriage. RVW set four of her poems to music between 1922 and 1925.

Stanford, Charles Villiers (1852–1924), Anglo-Irish composer, scholar, organist, and conductor; among the most influential composition teachers in British history. Served as Professor of Composition at the RCM from its founding, as well as Professor of Music at Cambridge (1887–1924), and conductor for the Cambridge University Music Society, the Bach Choir (London), the Leeds Philharmonic Society, and the Leeds Triennial Festival. Prodigious composer in numerous genres; RVW studied under him between 1895 and 1897.

Stewart, Jean (1914–2002), English violist. Performed in the Leighton Quartet, Menges Quartet, and the Richards Piano Quintet, and often appeared at the Leith Hill Festival. Close friends with both RVW and Ursula Wood; dedicatee of RVW's String Quartet in A Minor.

Vaughan Williams, Adeline (née Fisher, 1870–1951), cellist, pianist, and RVW's first wife (1897). The fifth of eleven children; raised in Brockenhurst and Hove, and met RVW at Cambridge through her eldest sister, Florence, wife of Frederic Maitland. Assisted RVW as copyist, editor, critic, and corresponding secretary for almost forty years until rheumatoid arthritis made it impossible to continue. His earliest and staunchest supporter, dedicating herself to the advancement of his career.

Vaughan Williams, Ursula (née Lock, later Wood, 1911–2007), author, poet, and RVW's second wife (1953). Studied at the Old Vic in the early 1930s, marrying Michael Forrester Wood (1901–1942) in 1933. Began an affair with RVW shortly after their meeting in 1938, becoming his indispensable assistant, collaborator, and muse. Her books include *No Other Choice, The Fall of the Leaf, A Wandering Pilgrimage,* and the authorized biography of RVW. Authored texts used in *The Sons of Light, The Pilgrim's Progress, Silence and Music, Hodie,* and the *Four Last Songs.*

Waddington, Sidney Peine ("S. P.," 1869–1953), composer, pianist, and teacher. Studied at the RCM, and in Frankfurt and Vienna, later teaching harmony and counterpoint at the RCM. Served as *maestro al pianoforte* at Covent Garden; master of the opera class at the RCM. Dedicatee of *Sir John in Love.*

Walthew, Richard (1872–1951), composer and conductor. RVW's contemporary at the RCM, studying under Parry and Stanford; later Professor of Music at the Queen's College, Oxford. Served as conductor of the University College Musical Society and the South Place Orchestra (Finsbury).

Wedgwood, Ralph ("Randolph," 1874–1956), chief general manager of the London and North Eastern Railway, and chair of the Railway Executive Committee (1939–1941). Second cousin to RVW, with whom he was a contemporary and close friend at Trinity College and for many years after. Dedicatee of *A Sea Symphony* and *In the Fen Country.*

Williams, Grace (1906–1977), Welsh composer and teacher. Studied under RVW at the RCM, later with Egon Wellesz in Vienna. Taught at Camden School for Girls and Southlands College of Education, returning to Wales in 1947 to work for the

BBC and compose independently; her major contributions are to orchestral and choral music.

Williamson, Honorine (1909–1940), niece of R. O. and Emmeline Morris, and so RVW's niece by marriage. Served as the Vaughan Williams's housekeeper and Adeline's companion and assistant at both 13 Cheyne Walk and White Gates. Killed in London during the Blitz, only months after her marriage to trumpeter Bernard Brown.

Wilson, (James) Steuart (1889–1966), tenor and administrator. Leading tenor soloist during the 1920s and 1930s before taking on administrative roles at the Curtis Institute, the BBC, the Arts Council, and Covent Garden, where he facilitated the first performance of *The Pilgrim's Progress*. Dedicatee of the Four Hymns.

Wood, Charles (1866–1926), Irish-born teacher, composer, and organist. Studied with Parry and Stanford at the RCM, where he later taught harmony; also organ scholar and lecturer in harmony and counterpoint at Gonville and Caius College, Cambridge, achieving the rank of university lecturer in 1897. Appointed Professor of Music at Cambridge in 1924. Prolific composer, particularly of church music; instructed RVW in the MusB degree at Cambridge.

Wood, Henry J. (1869–1944), English conductor. Founder and director of the Promenade Concerts at the Queen's Hall and the Royal Albert Hall, now named in his honor. Notable champion of both contemporary and British composers. Dedicatee of RVW's *Serenade to Music*.

Wood, Ursula—see Vaughan Williams, Ursula.

APPENDIX D

Select Bibliography

This bibliography is selective and narrowly focused, concentrating on monographs and scholarly essays published after 1950 rather than reviews or general overviews within larger, non-specialized publications. Individual essays within edited volumes dedicated wholly or substantially to Vaughan Williams (including Adams and Wells 2003; Foreman 1998; Frogley 1996; Frogley and Thomson 2013; Norris and Neill 2004; and Rushton 2010) are not listed separately, though many are present within the endnotes. The bulk of Vaughan Williams's own essays and correspondence are available in Cobbe 2008 (and Cobbe, Hogg, and Coleman, n.d.), Douglas 1988, Manning 2008, Vaughan Williams 1987/ 1996, and Vaughan Williams and Holst 1959/1974. Those seeking a more comprehensive bibliography should consult Ross 2016 and Manning et al.

Adams, Byron, and Robin Wells, eds. *Vaughan Williams Essays* (Aldershot: Ashgate, 2003).

Alldritt, Keith. *Vaughan Williams: Composer, Radical, Patriot—A Biography* (Marlborough: Robert Hale, 2015; reprint with corrections, 2016).

Barone, Anthony. "Modernist Rifts in a Pastoral Landscape: Observations on the Manuscripts of Vaughan Williams's Fourth Symphony," *Musical Quarterly* 91, nos. 1–2 (Spring–Summer 2008): 60–88.

Beckerman, Michael. "The Composer as Pole Seeker: Reading Vaughan Williams's *Sinfonia Antartica*," *Current Musicology*, no. 69 (Spring 2000): 42–67.

Clark, A. A. Gordon, ed. *Leith Hill Musical Festival, 1905–1955: A Record of Fifty Years of Music-Making in Surrey* (Epsom: Pullingers, 1955).

Cobbe, Hugh, ed. *Letters of Ralph Vaughan Williams, 1895–1958* (Oxford: OUP, 2008).

Cobbe, Hugh, Katharine Hogg, and Colin Coleman, eds. *The Letters of Ralph Vaughan Williams*, The Vaughan Williams Charitable Trust, http://vaughanwilliams.uk.

Connock, Stephen. *The Edge of Beyond: Ralph Vaughan Williams in the First World War* (Tonbridge: Albion Music, 2021).

Connock, Stephen, ed. *Toward the Sun Rising: Ralph Vaughan Williams Remembered* (Tonbridge: Albion Music, 2018).

Connock, Stephen, Ursula Vaughan Williams, and Robin Wells, eds. *There Was a Time . . . Ralph Vaughan Williams: A Pictorial Journey from the Collection of Ursula Vaughan Williams* (Tonbridge: Albion Music, 2003).

Corke, Shirley, ed. *Music Won the Cause: 100 Years of the Leith Hill Musical Festival, 1905–2005* (Dorking: Leith Hill Musical Festival, 2005).

Day, James. *Vaughan Williams*, 3rd ed. (Oxford and New York: OUP, 1998).

Dickinson, A. E. F. *Vaughan Williams* (London: Faber & Faber, 1963).

Dineen, Frank. *Ralph's People: The Ingrave Secret* (Tonbridge: Albion Music, 2001).

Douglas, Roy. *Working with Vaughan Williams: The Correspondence of Ralph Vaughan Williams and Roy Douglas* (London: British Library, 1988).

Foreman, Lewis, ed. *Ralph Vaughan Williams in Perspective* (Tonbridge: Albion Music, 1998).

Foss, Hubert. *Ralph Vaughan Williams: A Study* (London: George G. Harrap, 1950).

Francis, John. "A Question of Chronology," *VWJ*, no. 74 (February 2019): 9–13.

Frogley, Alain. "H. G. Wells and Vaughan Williams's *A London Symphony*: Politics and Culture in Fin-de-Siècle England," in *Sundry Sorts of Music Books: Essays on the British Library Collections*, ed. Chris Banks, Arthur Searle, and Malcolm Turner (London: British Library, 1993), 299–308.

Frogley, Alain. "Tonality on the Town: Orchestrating the Metropolis in Vaughan Williams's *A London Symphony*," in *Tonality 1900–1950: Concept and Practice*, ed. Felix Wörner, Ullrich Scheideler, and Philip Rupprecht (Stuttgart: Franz Steiner Verlag, 2012), 187–202.

Frogley, Alain. "Vaughan Williams and Nazi Germany: The 1937 Hamburg Shakespeare Prize," in *Music as a Bridge: Musikalische Beziehungen zwischen England und Deutschland 1920–1950*, ed. Christa Brüstle and Guido Heldt (Hildesheim: Georg Olms Verlag, 2005), 113–32.

Frogley, Alain. "Vaughan Williams and Thomas Hardy: 'Tess' and the Slow Movement of the Ninth Symphony," *ML* 68, no. 1 (January 1987): 42–59.

Frogley, Alain. *Vaughan Williams's Ninth Symphony* (Oxford: OUP, 2001).

Frogley, Alain, ed. *Vaughan Williams Studies* (Cambridge: Cambridge University Press, 1996).

Frogley, Alain, and Aidan Thomson, eds. *The Cambridge Companion to Vaughan Williams* (Cambridge: Cambridge University Press, 2013).

Grimley, Daniel. "Landscape and Distance: Vaughan Williams, Modernism and the Symphonic Pastoral," in *British Music and Modernism, 1895–1960*, ed. Matthew Riley (Farnham: Ashgate, 2010), 147–74.

Grimley, Daniel. "Music, Ice, and the 'Geometry of Fear': The Landscapes of Vaughan Williams's *Sinfonia Antartica*," *MQ* 91, nos. 1–2 (Spring–Summer 2008): 116–50.

Harper-Scott, J. P. E. "Vaughan Williams's Antic Symphony," in *British Music and Modernism, 1895–1960*, ed. Matthew Riley (Farnham: Ashgate, 2010), 175–96.

Heffer, Simon. *Vaughan Williams* (London: Weidenfeld & Nicolson, 2000).

Hesse, Lutz-Werner. *Studien zum Schaffen des Komponisten Ralph Vaughan Williams* (Regensburg: G. Bosse, 1983).

Holmes, Paul. *Vaughan Williams* (London and New York: Omnibus Press, 1997).

Howes, Frank. *The Music of Ralph Vaughan Williams* (London: OUP, 1954).

Hurd, Michael. *Vaughan Williams* (London: Faber & Faber, 1970).

Kennedy, Michael. *The Works of Ralph Vaughan Williams*, 2nd ed. (London: OUP, 1964; 2nd ed., 1980; reprint, Oxford, 1992, 1995).

Kennedy, Michael. *A Catalogue of the Works of Ralph Vaughan Williams*, 2nd ed. (Oxford and New York: OUP, 1996; reprint, 1998).

Manning, David, ed. *Vaughan Williams on Music* (Oxford: OUP, 2008).

Manning, David, Paulina Piedzia Colón, Devora Geller, et al., eds. "Ralph Vaughan Williams: An Annotated Bibliography," *The Ralph Vaughan Williams Society*, https://rvwsociety.com/bibliography/.

Mellers, Wilfrid. *Vaughan Williams and the Vision of Albion* (London: Barrie & Jenkins, 1989).

Mitchell, Jon Ceander. *Ralph Vaughan Williams' Wind Works* (Galesville, MD: Meredith Music Publications, 2008).

Moore, Jerrold Northrop. *Vaughan Williams: A Life in Photographs* (Oxford and New York: OUP, 1992).

Neighbour, Oliver. "Ralph, Adeline, and Ursula Vaughan Williams: Some Facts and Speculation (with a Note about Tippett)," *ML* 89, no. 3 (2008): 337–45.

Newbery, Celia, ed. *Vaughan Williams in Dorking* (Dorking: Dorking & Leith Hill Preservation Society, 1979).

Norris, John, and Andrew Neill, eds. *A Special Flame: The Music of Elgar and Vaughan Williams* (Rickmansworth: Elgar Editions, 2004).

Ottaway, Hugh. *Vaughan Williams Symphonies* (London: BBC Books, 1972; reprint, 1987).

Ottaway, Hugh, and Alain Frogley. "Vaughan Williams, Ralph," in *Grove Music Online*, https://www.oxfordmusiconline.com.

Pakenham, Simona. *Vaughan Williams: A Discovery of His Music* (London: Macmillan, 1957).

Palmer, Roy, ed. *Bushes and Briars: Folk Songs Collected by Ralph Vaughan Williams*, 2nd ed. (Burnham-on-Sea: Llanerch Publishers, 1983).

Pike, Lionel. *Vaughan Williams and the Symphony* (London: Toccata Press, 2003).

Ross, Ryan. *Ralph Vaughan Williams: A Research and Information Guide* (New York and London: Routledge, 2016).

Rushton, Julian, ed. *Let Beauty Awake: Elgar, Vaughan Williams and Literature* (Rickmansworth: Elgar Editions, 2010).

Savage, Roger. *Masques, Mayings and Music-Dramas: Vaughan Williams and the Early Twentieth-Century Stage* (Woodbridge: Boydell Press, 2014).

Saylor, Eric. *English Pastoral Music: From Arcadia to Utopia, 1900–1955* (Urbana, Chicago, and Springfield: University of Illinois Press, 2017).

Schwartz, Elliot S. *The Symphonies of Ralph Vaughan Williams* (Amherst: University of Massachusetts Press, 1964).

Town, Stephen. *The Choral-Orchestral Works of Ralph Vaughan Williams: Autographs, Context, Discourse* (Lanham, MD: Lexington Books, 2020).

Various authors. "Dr. Ralph Vaughan Williams, O.M.," *RCMM* 55, no. 1 (February 1959): 2–56; reprinted as *Tributes to Vaughan Williams: 50 Years On* (London: RCM, 2009).

Various authors. *Tales of a Field Ambulance 1914–1918* (Southend-on-Sea: Borough Printing and Publishing, 1935).

Various authors. "Tributes to Vaughan Williams," *MT* 99, no. 1388 (October 1958): 535–39.

Vaughan Williams, Ralph. *National Music and Other Essays*, 2nd ed., ed. Michael Kennedy (Oxford: OUP, 1987; reprint, 1996).

Vaughan Williams, Ursula. *Paradise Remembered*, ed. Roger Buckley and Joyce Kennedy (Tonbridge: Albion Music, 2002).

Vaughan Williams, Ursula. *RVW: A Biography of Ralph Vaughan Williams* (London: OUP, 1964; reprint with corrections, 1988).

Vaughan Williams, Ursula, and Imogen Holst, eds. *Heirs and Rebels: Letters Written to Each Other and Occasional Writings on Music by Ralph Vaughan Williams and Gustav Holst* (London: OUP, 1959; reprint, New York, 1974).

Vaughan Williams, Ursula, and John E. Lunn, eds. *Ralph Vaughan Williams: A Pictorial Biography* (London: OUP, 1971).

Vignal, Marc. *Ralph Vaughan Williams* (Paris: bleu nuit éditeur, 2015).

Young, Percy M. *Vaughan Williams* (London: Dennis Dobson, 1953).

Notes

Preface

1 James Day, *Vaughan Williams,* 3rd ed. (Oxford and New York: OUP, 1998), ix.
2 Julian Horton, "The Later Symphonies," in *CCVW,* 226.

Chapter 1

1 Far more detail on Vaughan Williams's ancestry and childhood is available in *RVW,* 1–30.
2 Eric Saylor, *English Pastoral Music: From Arcadia to Utopia, 1900–1955* (Urbana, Chicago, and Springfield: University of Illinois Press, 2017), 153; see also Julian Onderdonk, "The Composer and Society: Family, Politics, Nation," in *CCVW,* 11–13, 15–19.
3 *RVW,* 13.
4 RVW to Margaret Keynes, 20 December 1953, *VWL* 2746.
5 RVW, "A Musical Autobiography," in *NME,* 177.
6 Stanley Godman, "Dr. R. Vaughan Williams," *Times* (London), 5 September 1958, 14.
7 RVW, "A Musical Autobiography," 179.
8 Ibid., 180.
9 Ibid., 180.
10 RVW, "Sir Hubert Parry," in *VWM,* 295.
11 RVW, "A Musical Autobiography," 182.
12 *HR,* 21.
13 RVW, "Sir Hubert Parry," in *VWM,* 296.
14 RVW, "A Musical Autobiography," 183.
15 RVW to T. S. Bull, 29 October 1952, *VWL* 4440; and RVW, "A Musical Autobiography," 178.
16 RVW, "The Teaching of Parry and Stanford," in *VWM,* 321.
17 RVW, "A Musical Autobiography," 185; see also Byron Adams, "Vaughan Williams's Musical Apprenticeship," in *CCVW,* 36.
18 Alan Gray to Walter Parratt, n.d., BL MS Mus. 1714/1/1, ff. 7–8; quoted in *RVW,* 41–42.
19 G. F. McCleary, "Dr. Ralph Vaughan Williams, O. M.," *RCMM* 55, no. 1 (Easter Term 1959): 14.
20 Gwen Raverat, *Period Piece: A Cambridge Childhood* (London: Faber and Faber, 1960), 273.
21 RVW, "A Musical Autobiography," 186.
22 McCleary, "Dr. Ralph Vaughan Williams," 14.
23 RVW, "A Musical Autobiography," 182–83.
24 McCleary, "Dr. Ralph Vaughan Williams," 14.
25 RVW, "A Musical Autobiography," 192.
26 Ibid., 184; and McCleary, "Dr. Ralph Vaughan Williams," 12–14. McCleary noted that RCM violin instructor Haydn Inwards, a member of the club, dissented from prevailing

opinions about Vaughan Williams's piece. "'You are all wrong,' he said, 'that is real good stuff.'"

27 *HR*, x; John Ireland, "Tributes to Vaughan Williams," *MT* 99, no. 1388 (October 1958): 535.
28 RVW to Ralph Wedgwood, ca. 1895, *VWL* 4449.
29 Ibid.
30 RVW, "Gustav Holst: A Great Composer," in *VWM*, 314.
31 *HR*, 21.
32 Recollections of Ralph Vaughan Williams by Claire Mackail, BL MS Mus. 1714/1/4, f. 75.
33 RVW, "A Musical Autobiography," 186.
34 RVW to Ralph Wedgwood, ca. June 1899, *VWL* 263. Throughout this book, contemporary values of past monetary amounts are calculated according to the Retail Price Index (RPI) for 2020, then converted from UK pounds sterling to the US dollar using the midmarket rate from 1 January 2020 ($1.00=£1.3265) as the exchange rate. See Measuring Worth Foundation, "Five Ways to Compute the Relative Value of a UK Pound Amount, 1270 to Present," *MeasuringWorth.com*, accessed 14 November 2021, https://www.measuringworth.com/calculators/ukcompare/; and "Historical Rate Tables," *XE.com*, accessed 14 November 2021, https://www.xe.com/currencytables/?from=USD&date=2020-01-01#table-section.
35 RVW, "A Musical Autobiography," 186.
36 Margot Parrington (née Gatty) to Ursula Vaughan Williams, n.d., BL MS Mus. 1714/1/25, ff. 12, 40.
37 Mary Bennett, "Dr. Ralph Vaughan Williams, O. M.," *RCMM* 55, no. 1 (February 1959): 19.
38 Oliver Neighbour's examination of the events surrounding Duckworth's death is essential reading; see "Ralph, Adeline, and Ursula Vaughan Williams: Some Facts and Speculation (with a Note about Tippett)," *ML* 89, no. 3 (August 2008): 337–45.
39 RVW, "A Musical Autobiography," 187.
40 Ibid.
41 Bruch's indulgence went only so far, however, as Vaughan Williams's use of parallel fifths inspired a response of "ach, die Quints, Quints! Nein, nein! You muss *not*. Quints, quints." See Rupert Erlebach, "Dr. Ralph Vaughan Williams, O. M.," *RCMM* 55, no. 1 (Easter Term 1959): 30. Erlebach does not name the Kapellmeister credited with this remark, but Byron Adams's identification of Bruch seems likely; see "Vaughan Williams's Musical Apprenticeship," in *CCVW*, 54n36.
42 Max Bruch to RVW, 5 February 1898, *VWL* 202.
43 Vaughan Williams secured at least one and possibly two other deputies during his tenure at St. Barnabas, reinforcing his claims of lack of interest in the job; see William Harris to Ursula Vaughan Williams, 29 July 1959, BL MS Mus. 1714/1/2, ff. 7–9; and RVW to Herbert Ellingford [ca. October 1930], *VWL* 892.
44 RVW to Ralph Wedgwood, May or June 1898, *VWL* 260.
45 Adeline Vaughan Williams to Ralph Wedgwood, 15 December 1899, *VWL* 280. Vaughan Williams's fair copy of the *Mass* was formally deposited in the Cambridge University Library on 4 May 1900.
46 Earlier sources suggested that the Vaughan Williamses moved to Barton Street in February 1899, but details in their correspondence point to 1900 as the correct date. See also John Francis, "A Question of Chronology," *VWJ*, no. 74 (February 2019): 9–13.
47 *RVW*, 57.
48 RVW to Ralph Wedgwood, ca. 7 February 1900, *VWL* 277.

49 "How to Play Brahms" was evidently revised and published as "Brahms and Tchaikovsky." All of his *Vocalist* articles are available in *VWM*, 17–30 and 125–63.

50 RVW to Ralph Wedgwood, [December 1900], *VWL* 126.

51 The entry in *NME* is the revised version of 1925. The original (1904) focuses more on the mechanics of conducting, includes an annotated bibliography, and features several other deviations from its successor.

52 Adeline Vaughan Williams to Ralph Wedgwood, 27 December [1901], *VWL* 107.

Chapter 2

1 In addition to the early works he withdrew or suppressed, he made sketches and drafts for several others that never came to fruition; see *CVW*, 10–11. One of these, a sonata for horn and piano, was mentioned by Robin Legge in a program note (1905), suggesting that it might have been completed at some point; see BL MS Mus. 1714/1/3, f. 118.

2 RVW, "A Musical Autobiography," 177.

3 RVW, "The Teaching of Parry and Stanford," in *VWM*, 316. Unfortunately for Vaughan Williams, Parry said "it was too much like *Siegfried* to be allowed to pass," but fortunately for posterity, it was spared destruction.

4 RVW, "A Musical Autobiography," 180; and McCleary, "Dr. Ralph Vaughan Williams," 12.

5 The publication date of Bell's book indicates that the year Kennedy assigned to the cycle is too early; 1896 or 1897 seems more likely. He also accounts only for "Lollipop's Song" and "Spinning Song," not the concluding "Rumpelstiltskin's Song." See *CVW*, 5.

6 RVW to Adrian Boult, [late 1920/early 1921?], *VWL* 715; and RVW to Stanley Godman, 23 November 1955, *VWL* 3813.

7 See Adeline Vaughan Williams to René Gatty, 30 May and 4 July 1898, *VWL* 295 and 297.

8 RVW to Gustav Holst, ca. October 1899, *VWL* 236.

9 Michael Kennedy to Ursula Vaughan Williams, 23 June 1965, BL MS Mus. 1714/1/2, f. 6.

10 Adeline Vaughan Williams to Ralph Wedgwood, 15 December [1899], *VWL* 280.

11 See Michael Vaillancourt, "Coming of Age: The Earliest Orchestral Music of Ralph Vaughan Williams," in *VWS*, 27.

12 The repeated claim that Michael Kennedy added the title "Prelude" to the first movement is incorrect. Though absent from the autograph score at the Yale University Library, the title *is* present on the MS held at the British Library (Add. MS 27572).

13 Julian Rushton, "Vaughan Williams: *Serenade in A Minor* (1898): Addendum to the Published Score," *VWJ*, no. 57 (June 2013): 17.

14 Alan Tongue, "A Significant Find," *VWJ*, no. 49 (October 2010): 14.

15 RVW to Ralph Wedgwood, ca. June 1899, *VWL* 263.

16 See *WVW*, 42; and *RVW*, 42, 58.

17 See *RVW*, 138.

18 RVW to Gustav Holst, ca. late 1898, *VWL* 231.

19 RVW to Ralph Wedgwood, ca. December 1900, *VWL* 126.

20 Adeline Vaughan Williams to Ralph Wedgwood, 1 December [1900], *VWL* 132.

21 RVW, "A Musical Autobiography," 188. Vaughan Williams's memory may be faulty, for he remembered approaching Elgar "about the year 1900," but a letter from Holst written in 1903 suggested that they ask Elgar for assistance together; see Gustav Holst to RVW, [March 1903], *VWL* 135.

22 RVW, "What Have We Learnt from Elgar?" *ML* 16, no. 1 (January 1935): 16; quoted in *NME*, 252.

23 RVW to Gustav Holst, [1901?], *VWL* 113.

24 *HR*, 9; and RVW, *Heroic Elegy and Triumphal Epilogue for Orchestra (1901)*, full score (London: Faber Music, 2008), v.

25 According to Adeline, Stanford was responsible for the title *Heroic Elegy*: "It sounds as if it had to do with the [Boer] war w^h isn't strictly true—but it fits very well." See Adeline Vaughan Williams to Ralph Wedgwood, 25 March [1901], *VWL* 178.

26 Alain Frogley, "History and Geography: The Early Orchestral Works and the First Three Symphonies," in *CCVW*, 86.

27 BL MS Mus. 1714/1/2, f. 77.

28 RVW to John Ireland, 5 October 1952, *VWL* 2479.

29 John Ireland to RVW, 29 August 1952, *VWL* 2464.

30 See also Adams, "Vaughan Williams's Musical Apprenticeship," in *CCVW*, 29–32.

31 RVW, "The Letter and the Spirit," in *NME*, 122.

32 RVW, "Some Conclusions," in *NME*, 70.

Chapter 3

1 RVW to Ralph Wedgwood, [early 1902], *VWL* 133. In 2020 terms, this means that each song cost approximately $7.36, and Vaughan Williams earned about $0.90 per copy. He later claimed that the royalties for "Linden Lea" brought in more money than anything else he ever wrote.

2 Vaughan Williams continued writing occasional prose pieces throughout his career; for an overview of major themes, see Aidan J. Thomson, "'Es klang so alt und war doch so neu': Vaughan Williams, Aesthetics, and History," in *British Musical Criticism and Intellectual Thought, 1850–1950*, ed. Jeremy Dibble and Julian Horton, 255–73 (Woodbridge: Boydell Press, 2018).

3 RVW, "A School of English Music," in *VWM*, 18.

4 RVW, "A Sermon to Vocalists," in *VWM*, 29.

5 See Julian Onderdonk, "Folksong Arrangements, Hymn Tunes and Church Music," in *CCVW*, 136–37; and Ceri Owen, "Vaughan Williams, Song, and the Idea of 'Englishness'" (DPhil dissertation, University of Oxford, 2014), 23–29. Owen additionally points out the ironic placement of "A School of English Music" in the same issue of *The Vocalist* in which "Linden Lea"—with its curious subtitle of "A Dorset Folk Song"—was first published.

6 Vaughan Williams had in fact been giving public lectures for some years, the earliest being one at the Hammersmith Kelmscott Club in February 1900, and extension lectures in Oxford sporadically in 1901. Details on his lectures generally and his Brentwood engagement in particular are available in Tony Kendall, "Through Bushes and Through Briars . . . Vaughan Williams's Earliest Folk-Song Collecting," in *VWP*, 50–58.

7 "Broadwood Concert," *Daily Graphic* (London), n.d., BL MS Mus. 1714/11/2/2.

8 *HR*, 14–15.

9 Gustav Holst to RVW, [March 1903], *VWL* 135.

10 *Burley Heath* and *The Solent* (see *CVW*, 19–20).

11 Edwin Evans, "Modern British Composers. VI," *Musical Standard* 20, no. 499 (25 July 1903): 53.

12 RVW, "Religious Folk Songs," in *WVW*, 33–34.

13 RVW, "A Musical Autobiography," 190.

14 Rowan Williams, "Sermon in Commemoration of the Fiftieth Anniversary of Vaughan Williams's Death," *VWJ*, no. 45 (June 2009): 14–15.

15 See John Bawden, "Vaughan Williams and the Hymnals—A New Perspective," *VWJ*, no. 29 (February 2004): 7–9.

16 RVW, "Some Reminiscences of *The English Hymnal*," in *VWM*, 116.

17 Bawden, "Vaughan Williams and the Hymnals," 11; see also Simon Wright, "Vaughan Williams and *The English Hymnal*," *Discovering Music: Early 20th Century*, British Library, https://www.bl.uk/20th-century-music/articles/vaughan-williams-and-the-english-hymnal.

18 "Mr. Vaughan Williams' Concert," *Manchester Courier*, 3 December 1904, in BL MS Mus. 1714/11/2/2.

19 For details on the division of responsibilities and the names of and sources for the tunes employed, see RVW, "*Pan's Anniversary*," in *VWM*, 333.

20 See Roger Savage, *Masques, Mayings and Music-Dramas* (Woodbridge: Boydell Press, 2014), 50–51; also six letters from RVW to F. W. Evans, March 1905, *VWL* 193–197 and 3986.

21 "At Shakespeare's Shrine," *Birmingham Weekly Mercury*, 29 April 1905, 28.

22 The current standard history of the LHMC (after 1950, the Leith Hill Musical Festival) provides much greater detail on the women's roles in its founding; see Shirley Corke, *Music Won the Cause: 100 Years of the Leith Hill Musical Festival, 1905–2005* (Dorking: Leith Hill Musical Festival, 2005), 11–17. See also *RVW*, 73–75.

23 Ralph Vaughan Williams, "Reminiscences of Fifty Years," in *Leith Hill Musical Festival, 1905–1955: A Record of Fifty Years of Music-Making in Surrey*, ed. A. A. Gordon Clark (Epsom: Pullingers, 1955), 36.

24 The "3 great electric light chimneys" refers to the now-closed Lots Road Power Station, located just north of Chelsea Harbour, between Battersea Bridge and Battersea Railway Bridge. RVW to Ralph Wedgwood, 12 November 1905, *VWL* 200.

25 The other two movements, now known as the *Norfolk Rhapsody No. 2 in D Minor* and the *Norfolk Rhapsody No. 3 in G Minor and Major*, had their first performances on 27 September 1907 in Cardiff (see *CVW*, 34–36). The score for the latter is lost, while two manuscript pages of the former are missing; however, Stephen Hogger completed an edited version of No. 2 (OUP, 2014).

26 RVW to Imogen Holst, [1948?], *VWL* 1766.

27 RVW to Ralph Wedgwood, [October 1907], *VWL* 154.

28 RVW to Ralph Wedgwood, 3 July 1907, *VWL* 4461.

29 RVW, "A Musical Autobiography," 188–89; a colloquial translation would be "it's no small thing." Left unexplained is why Delius would have addressed Vaughan Williams in French rather than English.

30 Ibid., 191.

31 Adams, "Vaughan Williams's Musical Apprenticeship," in *CCVW*, 38.

32 See ibid., 41.

33 RVW to M. D. Calvocoressi, [December 1907], *VWL* 156. See also "M. D. Calvocoressi," in *TSR*, 252–53.

34 RVW to M. D. Calvocoressi, [January 1908], *VWL* 160.

35 RVW, "A Musical Autobiography," 191.

36 RVW to M. D. Calvocoressi, [December 1907], *VWL* 156.

37 Ironically, the deciding vote may have been Stanford's, who served on the prize committee and allegedly disliked *Sita* intensely; see Michael Short, *Gustav Holst: The Man and His Music* (Hastings: Circaidy Gregory Press, 2014), 42.

Chapter 4

1 RVW, "The Folk-Song," in *NME*, 22.

2 Julian Onderdonk, "Vaughan Williams's Folksong Transcriptions: A Case of Idealization?" in *VWS*, 127.

3 For an overview of Vaughan Williams's collecting activities and techniques, see Roy Palmer, ed., *Bushes and Briars: Folk Songs Collected by Ralph Vaughan Williams* (Burnham-on-Sea: Llanerch Publishers, 1999), viii–xxii; first published as *Folk Songs Collected by Ralph Vaughan Williams* (London, J. M Dent, 1983). The English Folk Dance and Song Society also provides access to Vaughan Williams's folk song collections; see Vaughan Williams Memorial Library, "Ralph Vaughan Williams Folk Song Collection," the English Folk Dance and Song Society, https://www.vwml.org/archives-catalogue/rvw1 and https://www.vwml.org/archives-catalogue/RVW2.

4 More nuanced treatment may be found in Onderdonk, "Vaughan Williams's Folksong Transcriptions," in *VWS*, 124–38.

5 He also told Maud Karpeles, "If words are very stupid not worth printing them"; RVW to Maud Karpeles, [1927?], *VWL* 4799.

6 The editors added the subtitle "A Dorset Folk Song" to both "Linden Lea" and "Blackmwore by the Stour," further misrepresenting their origins.

7 *CVW*, 17.

8 See Julian Rushton, "'A Thing of Wonder': Triadic Magic in Early Vaughan Williams," in *Let Beauty Awake: Elgar, Vaughan Williams, and Literature*, ed. Julian Rushton (Rickmansworth: Elgar Editions, 2010), 127–32.

9 See the various reviews of this concert in BL MS Mus. 1714/11/2/2.

10 See Stephen Banfield, *Sensibility and English Song* (Cambridge: Cambridge University Press, 1985; reprint, single volume paperback, 1988), 78–80.

11 Rufus Hallmark, "Robert Louis Stevenson, Ralph Vaughan Williams and Their *Songs of Travel*," in *VWE*, 138.

12 Ibid., 133.

13 Sophie Fuller, "The Songs and Shorter Secular Choral Works," in *CCVW*, 114.

14 See Karen Leistra-Jones, "'When Once You Have Fallen into an Equable Stride': The Peripatetic in Vaughan Williams's *Songs of Travel*," *Journal of Musicological Research* 36, no. 4 (2016): 259–91; and Savage, *Masques, Mayings and Music-Dramas*, 304–58 passim.

15 See *CVW*, 25–26; Hallmark, "Robert Louis Stevenson, Ralph Vaughan Williams and Their *Songs of Travel*," in *VWE*, 135–36; and William Adams, "Elements of Form and Unity in *Songs of Travel*," *VWJ*, no. 25 (October 2002): 6–11.

16 Boosey and Hawkes released "The Vagabond," "Bright is the Ring of Words," and "The Roadside Fire" as Book I (1905), with "Let Beauty Awake," "Youth and Love," "In Dreams," and "The Infinite Shining Heavens" constituting Book II (1907).

17 See "Crescendo," *Star*, 3 December 1904, in BL MS Mus. 1714/11/2/2.

18 In fact, the first performance in Reading also featured a string quartet ad lib, although it was not present for the Bechstein Hall concert noted previously.

19 RVW to Martin Shaw, 19 November 1907, *VWL* 4322.

20 John Bawden, "The Music of the English Hymnal," in *Strengthen for Service: 100 Years of the English Hymnal 1906–2006*, ed. Alan Luff (Norwich: Canterbury Press, 2005), 136.

21 See *CVW*, 30–32, and RVW, "Some Reminiscences of the English Hymnal," in *VWM*, 116. "Mr. Anon" was also given credit for Vaughan Williams's four original tunes in the earliest printings of *The English Hymnal*.

22 Julian Onderdonk, "Hymn Tunes from Folk-Songs: Vaughan Williams and English Hymnody," in *VWE*, 109.

23 Savage, *Masques, Mayings and Music-Dramas*, 49.

24 See ibid., 48–55 and 58–59; see also RVW, "*Pan's Anniversary*," 333; and Deborah Heckert, *Composing History: National Identities and the English Masque Revival, 1860–1920* (Woodbridge: Boydell Press, 2018), esp. 33, 78, and 123.

25 Nathaniel Lew, "Editor's Preface," in Ralph Vaughan Williams, *Scenes Adapted from Bunyan's "Pilgrim's Progress*," ed. Nathaniel Lew (Wellington: Promethean Editions, 2008), 5; see also Lew, "'Words and Music That Are Forever England': *The Pilgrim's Progress* and the Pitfalls of Nostalgia," in *VWE*, 182.

26 This song was not present in the original Reigate production; see Lew, "Editor's Preface," 4.

27 RVW to Harold Child, ca. 15 July 1910, *VWL* 365.

28 See Lew, "'Words and Music That Are Forever England,'" 195–200.

29 RVW to Edwin Evans, ca. June 1903, *VWL* 134.

30 *CVW*, 19. Kennedy's reason for assigning the prospective collection two titles is unclear.

31 Paired as *Two Impressions for Orchestra*; see *CVW*, 23.

32 See Andrew Herbert, "Unfinished Business: The Evolution of the 'Solent' Theme," in *VWP*, 69–90; and RVW, *The Solent*, study score, ed. James Francis Brown (Oxford: Oxford University Press, 2013), v–vi.

33 See Vaillancourt, "Coming of Age," 42.

34 Ibid., 38–39.

35 The revised version was first performed by the Bournemouth Municipal Orchestra on 21 May 1914.

36 It also is identical to the opening phrase of the folk song "This is the Truth Sent from Above," but Vaughan Williams did not collect this until 1909.

37 Frogley, "History and Geography," in *CCVW*, 88.

38 "Concerts," *Times* (London), 15 December 1905, 11.

39 Kennedy refers to this revised pairing as *Two Short Pieces for String Quintet* under the entry for the original *Ballade and Scherzo* of 1904; see *CVW*, 22–23.

40 In fact, the actual second movement of the *Three Nocturnes*—like the others, for voice and orchestra—was a setting of Whitman's *Whispers of Heavenly Death*, the earliest result of Vaughan Williams's work with Ravel. For details, see RVW, *Nocturne: Whispers of Heavenly Death for Voice and Orchestra (1908)*, full score, introduction by Hugh Cobbe (London: Faber Music, 2013), v; and RVW, *Three Nocturnes for Voice and Orchestra*, full score, introduction by Hugh Cobbe (London: Faber Music, 2017), v.

41 For further detail, see Alain Frogley, "'O Farther Sail': Vaughan Williams and Whitman," in *Let Beauty Awake*, 85–89.

42 See Palmer, *Bushes and Briars*, 34.

43 Roger Savage, "'While the Moon Shines Gold': Vaughan Williams and Literature: an Overview," in *Let Beauty Awake*, 49. It also showcased much earthier qualities, about which Vaughan Williams (among many other British musicians) was less sanguine; see Byron Adams, "'No Armpits, Please, We're British': Whitman and English Music, 1884–1936,"

in *Walt Whitman and Modern Music: War, Desire, and the Trials of Nationhood*, ed. Lawrence Kramer (New York: Routledge, 2000), 25–42.

44 See Charles Edward McGuire, "Vaughan Williams and the English Music Festival: 1910," in *VWE*, 236–39.

45 Ibid., 238.

46 Anonymous, "Leeds Musical Festival," *MT* 48, no. 777 (1 November 1907): 737.

Chapter 5

1 The pageant was held from 10 through 16 June at Fulham Palace; Hugh Allen and William Barclay Squire were the other committee members. Vaughan Williams's role is unclear, but he likely recommended some of the hymns, and possibly arranged a handful of secular tunes (such as the Agincourt Song and "Robin Hood and the Tanner"). See C. R. Peers, ed., *The Book of the English Church Pageant* (London: Eyre and Spottiswoode, 1909), xv–xvi.

2 RVW to Ruth Charrington, [March 1910], *VWL* 320.

3 Two of the nocturnes were completed by Anthony Payne and published in 2017. See *CVW*, 41–42; and Hugh Cobbe, "Introduction," in RVW, *Three Nocturnes* (London: Faber Music, 2017), v–vi. *The Future* was extended, completed, and scored by Martin Yates, and was first performed in Edinburgh by the Royal Scottish National Orchestra on 8 November 2019.

4 RVW to Ralph Wedgwood, [20 March 1909], *VWL* 204.

5 "Nigel Finzi," in *TSR*, 143.

6 RVW to Roy Douglas, 17 June 1954, *VWL* 2830.

7 "Mary Bennett," in *TSR*, 93.

8 RVW to Ralph Wedgwood, [1909], *VWL* 123. He completed a full draft in 1907, but continued revising and scoring it for two more years; see RVW to Herbert Thompson, ca. September 1910, *VWL* 331.

9 Subsequent productions took place in 1883, 1885, 1887, and 1890 before triennial performances were established in 1894. For a full list of plays, see The Cambridge Greek Play Committee, "The Cambridge Greek Play," University of Cambridge, https://www.cambridgegreekplay.com/past-plays.

10 Quoted in Raymond Raikes to Ursula Vaughan Williams, 19 May 1969, BL MS Mus. 1714/1/3, f. 143.

11 Adeline Vaughan Williams to Gustav von Holst, 8 January 1901, *VWL* 127.

12 RVW to Harold Child, ca. 15 July 1910, *VWL* 365.

13 Uniquely in the Festival's history, it preceded an oratorio (Elgar's *The Dream of Gerontius*). See McGuire, "Vaughan Williams and the English Music Festival: 1910," in *VWE*, 247–48.

14 See Aidan Thomson, "Becoming a National Composer: Critical Reception to c. 1925," in *CCVW*, 65.

15 J. A. Fuller Maitland, "Music: The Three Choirs Festival," *Times* (London), 7 September 1910, 11.

16 RVW to Ernest Farrar, 31 December 1911, *VWL* 378.

17 Barry Still, *Two Hundred and Fifty Years of the Three Choirs Festival* (Gloucester: Three Choirs Festival Association, 1977), 22.

18 RVW to Ralph Wedgwood, [1910?], *VWL* 302.

19 Rebecca Clarke, transcription of an interview on WQXR radio (New York), October 1958, BL MS Mus. 1714/1/4, f. 32.

20 RVW to Beryl Reeves, [12 May 1910], *VWL* 364.

21　J. A. Fuller Maitland, "Leeds Musical Festival—*A Sea Symphony*," *Times* (London), 14 October 1910, 10.

22　Samuel Langford, "Dr. Vaughan Williams's *Sea Symphony*," *Manchester Guardian*, 13 October 1910, 9.

23　Parodies of Whitman's text reflecting the piece's performing challenges (by Frank Kidson and Mary Venables) are in BL MS Mus. 1714/1/4, ff. 14–19, 72.

24　RVW to Cecil Sharp, [May 1907?] *VWL* 151. See also Saylor, *English Pastoral Music*, 51–55.

25　See also RVW to Charles Sayle, 14 March 1920, *VWL* 463, fn. 3.

26　For far more detail, see Savage, *Masques, Mayings and Music-Dramas*, 165–221.

27　Many years later, he told Grace Williams "I never had a 'Grand Passion' for Isadora purely business like relations—But I liked her very much—a real humorous American, & she easily threw off her 'high falutin'." See RVW to Grace Williams, [mid-1930s?], *VWL* 3863; and John Francis, "Gathering Dreams," *VWJ*, no. 71 (February 2018): 3–10.

28　Though not always as a composer; see Aidan Thomson, "Becoming a National Composer," in *CCVW*, 59–63.

29　Arthur Bliss, *As I Remember*, rev. ed. (London: Thames Publishing, 1989), 26.

30　Hubert Parry to Meggie Vaughan Williams, 19 May 1911, *VWL* 370.

31　Maurice Ravel to RVW, 5 August 1912; quoted in *RVW*, 103.

32　*RVW*, 105.

33　RVW, "Who Wants the English Composer?" in *VWM*, 40–41.

34　Ibid., 41–42.

35　RVW to Ernest Farrar, 8 July 1911, *VWL* 373.

36　See Jeremy Dibble, "Parry, Stanford and Vaughan Williams: the creation of tradition," in *VWP*, 37–38; also "Gordon Jacob," in *TSR*, 282. A decade later, Stanford did congratulate Vaughan Williams on leading the *St. Matthew Passion* with the Bach Choir; see Charles Villiers Stanford to RVW, 8 March 1923, *VWL* 508.

37　See *CVW*, 59–67.

38　A graduate of Christ Church, Oxford, and friend of both Butterworth and Hugh Allen, Ellis (1883–1916) was an amateur composer who used his family fortune to sponsor and promote performances of new English music.

39　See BL MS Mus. 1714/1/4, ff. 97–99.

40　J. C. Trewin, *Benson and the Bensonians* (London: Barrie and Rockliff, 1960), 193.

41　Ibid., 194. Vaughan Williams did not write incidental music for *Twelfth Night* at this time, as the play was not programmed in spring 1913; the piece listed in *CVW*, 74 refers to a production by Tom Harrison intended for a 1939 performance in Walliswood (Surrey). See Tom Harrison, "Twelfth Night," BL MS Mus. 1714/1/12, f. 53.

42　RVW, "A Musical Autobiography," 193. For more on Butterworth's role in shaping the work, see Phillip Brookes, "The Strange Case of *A London Symphony* and What George Butterworth Actually Did," *VWJ*, no. 78 (June 2020): 3–9.

43　RVW, "*A London Symphony*," in *VWM*, 339–40.

44　R. O. Morris to Adeline Vaughan Williams, n.d. (Sunday), BL MS Mus. 1714/1/5, f. 21.

45　"Mr F. B. Ellis's Concerts," *Sunday Times* (London), 29 March 1914, n.p., BL MS Mus. 1714/11/2/1.

46　George Butterworth to RVW, 28 March 1914, *VWL* 395; E. J. Dent to RVW, 31 March 1914, BL MS Mus. 1714/1/5, f. 20; Steuart Wilson to RVW, 28 March 1914, BL MS Mus. 1714/1/5, f. 24.

47　Gustav Holst to RVW, 29 March 1914, *VWL* 3958.

48 RVW to E. J. Dent, ca. 1 April 1914, *VWL* 396.
49 RVW to Evangeline Farrer, 25 May 1914, *VWL* 4393.

Chapter 6

1 See Adams, "Vaughan Williams's Musical Apprenticeship," in *CCVW*, 44–53; and Rushton, "Triadic Magic," in *Let Beauty Awake*, 119–34.
2 RVW to Athelstan Riley, 11 February 1914, *VWL* 392.
3 See Adams, "Vaughan Williams's Musical Apprenticeship," in *CCVW*, 39.
4 Clarke, interview on WQXR radio (New York), f. 31.
5 "London and Suburban Concerts," *MT* 50, no. 802 (1 December 1909): 797; E. H., "London Concerts," *Musical News* 37, no. 977 (20 November 1909): 472; "Music: Aeolian Hall," *Times* (London), 16 November 1909, 14.
6 RVW to E. J. Dent, [January 1910?], *VWL* 307.
7 See Christopher Mark, "Chamber Music and Works for Soloist with Orchestra," in *CCVW*, 181–82; and Adams, "Vaughan Williams's Musical Apprenticeship," in *CCVW*, 47.
8 See *CVW*, 44–45.
9 Examples of his approach to Shakespeare may be found in Byron Adams, "'Music in the Air': Vaughan Williams, Shakespeare, and the Construction of an Elizabethan Tradition," in *Let Beauty Awake: Elgar, Vaughan Williams and Literature*, ed. Julian Rushton (London: Elgar Editions, 2010), 103–7.
10 RVW to Hubert Foss, 25 March 1938, *VWL* 1284.
11 "Is My Team Ploughing?" and "Clun" both predate Vaughan Williams's study with Ravel, though were very likely revised afterwards.
12 Ernest Newman, however, was unconvinced; see "Concerning 'A Shropshire Lad' and Other Matters," *MT* 59, no. 907 (1 September 1918): 393–98.
13 See Adams, "Vaughan Williams's Musical Apprenticeship," in *CCVW*, 41.
14 Anon, "'The Wasps' at Cambridge," *Times* (London), 27 November 1909, 12.
15 Additional quotations came from Mendelssohn, Offenbach, and Lehár in the Dances for the Sons of Carcinus, which conclude with original melodies mimicking folk dances. See Eric Saylor, "Music for Stage and Film," in *CCVW*, 167.
16 Frogley, "History and Geography," in *CCVW*, 90.
17 But see also Anthony Pople, "Vaughan Williams, Tallis, and the Phantasy Principle," in *VWS*, 48–50.
18 See ibid., 47–80; and Rushton, "Triadic Magic," in *Let Beauty Awake*, 124–26.
19 Effective treatments and assessments of this practice include Pople, "Vaughan Williams, Tallis, and the Phantasy Principle," in *VWS*, 50–55; Frogley, "History and Geography," in *CCVW*, 90–92; and Allan Atlas, "On the Structure and Proportions of Vaughan Williams's *Fantasia on a Theme by Thomas Tallis*," *JRMA* 135, no. 1 (May 2010): 135–39. The rehearsal mark refers to the Faber edition of 2010.
20 See Atlas, "On the Structure and Proportions," 118, 141–43; and "All Performances of Ralph Vaughan Williams: *Fantasia on a Theme by Thomas Tallis* at BBC Proms," Proms: The World's Greatest Classical Music Festival, the BBC, last modified 2021, https://www.bbc.co.uk/proms/events/works/b4ebdd9b-361c-3642-a1bb-8398f432bf51.
21 Hugh Ottaway, *Vaughan Williams Symphonies*, BBC Music Guides (London: BBC Books, 1972; reprint, 1987), 12.

22 See Stephen Town, "'Full of Fresh Thoughts': Vaughan Williams, Whitman and the Genesis of *A Sea Symphony*," in *VWE*, 84–99; and Herbert, "Unfinished Business," in *VWP*, 75–90.

23 Frogley, "History and Geography," in *CCVW*, 95.

24 McGuire, "Vaughan Williams and the English Music Festival: 1910," in *VWE*, 247. Delius's setting of Whitman in the similarly expansive *Sea-Drift* may explain why Vaughan Williams shared an early draft of *A Sea Symphony* with him.

25 RVW to Herbert Thompson, [September 1910], *VWL* 331.

26 See Frogley, "History and Geography," in *CCVW*, 93–94.

27 Daniel Grimley, "Music, Ice, and the 'Geometry of Fear': The Landscapes of Vaughan Williams's *Sinfonia Antartica*," *MQ* 91, nos. 1–2 (Spring–Summer 2008): 128–29.

28 McGuire, "Vaughan Williams and the English Music Festival," 240; see also Eric Saylor, "Political Visions, National Identities, and the Sea Itself: Stanford and Vaughan Williams in 1910," in *The Sea in the British Musical Imagination*, ed. Eric Saylor and Christopher M. Scheer (Woodbridge: Boydell Press, 2015), 205–16.

29 "Greek Choruses and English Music," *Standard*, 27 May 1912, n.p.

30 See RVW to Gilbert Murray, 6 November 1911, *VWL* 374.

31 See A. E. F. Dickinson, *Vaughan Williams* (London: Faber & Faber, 1963), 172–74.

32 RVW to Cecil Sharp, [July 1913], *VWL* 338; and *RVW*, 108–9.

33 See Onderdonk, "Folksong Arrangements," in *CCVW*, 138–45; and *CVW*, 38–39, 56, 59, 61–66.

34 RVW to Harold Child, [summer 1910], *VWL* 4925; and *CVW*, 53–54, where Kennedy suggests that the piece was withdrawn and recast after the war as the *English Folk Songs Suite*.

35 See Cecil Sharp, RVW, and Lucy Broadwood, "Carols," in *Journal of the Folk-Song Society* 2, no. 7 (1905): 115–39; RVW to Cecil Sharp, [1911], *VWL* 305.

36 See Ella Mary Leather, Lucy Broadwood, A. G. Gilchrist, et al., "Carols from Herefordshire," *Journal of the Folk-Song Society* 4, no. 14 (June 1910): 3–51; Simona Pakenham, "Vaughan Williams and Ella Mary Leather," *VWJ*, no. 9 (June 1997): 10–11; and Andrew King, "Resources in the Vaughan Williams Memorial Library: The Ella Mary Leather Manuscript Collection," *Folk Music Journal* 9, no. 5 (2010): 749–812.

37 "Three Choirs Festival," *Times* (London), 13 September 1912, 6. The *Fantasia on English Folk Song* met similar criticism; see *WVW*, 92–93; and Thomson, "Becoming a National Composer," in *CCVW*, 62.

38 "Occasional Notes," *MT* 46, no. 754 (1 December 1905): 791.

39 See David Maw, "'Phantasy Mania': Quest for a National Style," in *Essays on the History of English Music in Honour of John Caldwell*, ed. Emma Hornby and David Maw (Woodbridge: Boydell Press, 2010), 117.

40 "Concert of Chamber Music," *Times* (London) (24 March 1914), 10.

41 One unusual detail about the chimes stands out. The Westminster Chimes employ five different phrases in two successive cycles: phrase 1 for the quarter hour, phrases 2 + 3 for the half, 4 + 5 +1 for the three-quarter, and 2 + 3 + 4 + 5 for the hour. Though the chimes sound the half hour in the first movement, they strike the first three phrases of the *hour* cycle—eliding the fourth—when they return in the finale, rather than the three phrases of the three-quarter-hour cycle. That the composer had lived within earshot of Big Ben for several years (and thus would have known the sequence very well) suggests that was not an error, but a deliberately truncated version of the hour chime, strengthening the implications of existential crisis or impending doom that scholars like Alain Frogley have

associated with the final movement. (My thanks to Hugh Cobbe for alerting me to this detail.)

42 RVW, "*A London Symphony*," in *VWM*, 339–40. See also Madelon Coates to Percy Scholes, 28 August 1924, *VWL* 568.

43 RVW to Olin Downes, 24 January 1941, *VWL* 3844. Vaughan Williams authorized this program (originally written by Coates's wife) believing it a one-off for an American audience, but did his best to suppress it upon learning of its wider circulation.

44 Katharine Eggar, "Ralph Vaughan Williams: Some Reflections on His Work," *Music Student* 12 (1919–1920): 515; but see also Alain Frogley, "Vaughan Williams and Thomas Hardy: 'Tess' and the Slow Movement of the Ninth Symphony," *ML* 68, no. 1 (January 1987): 42–43.

45 Quoted in *CVW*, 71–72.

46 See Alain Frogley, "H. G. Wells and Vaughan Williams's *A London Symphony*: Politics and Culture in Fin-de-Siècle England," in *Sundry Sorts of Music Books: Essays on the British Library Collections*, ed. Chris Banks, Arthur Searle, and Malcolm Turner (London: British Library, 1993), 299–308.

47 For details on the revisions, see *CVW*, 69–71.

48 See Alain Frogley, "Tonality on the Town: Orchestrating the Metropolis in Vaughan Williams's *A London* Symphony," in *Tonality 1900–1950: Concept and Practice*, ed. Felix Wörner, Ullrich Scheideler and Philip Rupprecht (Stuttgart: Franz Steiner Verlag, 2012), 194–200.

Chapter 7

1 Ursula Vaughan Williams said the score was posted to Breitkopf and Härtel in Leipzig for engraving (see *RVW*, 113). In a letter to Michael Kennedy, however, Vaughan Williams said that he sent it to conductor Fritz Busch to consider for performance; see RVW to Michael Kennedy, 20 August 1957, *VWL* 3539. The latter seems more likely, because Ursula's claim that he could not pay to have the score copied prior to posting is contradicted by a letter indicating he recruited Cecil Coles for this exact job. Coles enlisted before he could do it, but Vaughan Williams advanced him the money with the understanding that he would credit it against future work; see RVW to Edward Dent, [September 1914], *VWL* 348. The work's second performance took place in Harrogate on 12 August; if so, presumably the conductor (Julian Clifford) used the short score, as it seems unlikely that Vaughan Williams would have posted the full score to Germany *after* the war broke out. Finally, Stephen Lloyd dismisses Vaughan Williams's claim that Butterworth helped with the reconstruction (he had already enlisted), while Adeline's participation—hitherto unacknowledged—was confirmed in a letter from RVW to Dent, ca. 12 October 1914, *VWL* 413; also Stephen Lloyd, "Vaughan Williams's *A London Symphony*: The Original Version and Early Performances and Recordings," in *VWP*, 92–95; and Brookes, "The Strange Case of *A London Symphony*," 6–8.

2 See RVW to Clive Carey, 8 August 1915, *VWL* 4833.

3 In October 1916, he was formally admonished for "losing by neglect his cap badge" in the field and had to pay for a replacement (see "Casualty Form—Active Service," UK National Archives, WO 374/75055), and later fulminated that his officer training involved "a good deal of stupid ceremonial—<u>white gloves</u>!! (on ceremonial parades) (N.B. I believe there is a war on)." RVW to Gustav Holst, 4 August 1917, *VWL* 432.

4 Harry Steggles, "Dr. Ralph Vaughan Williams, O. M.," in *RCMM* 55, no. 1 (February 1959): 21.

5 Various authors, *Tales of a Field Ambulance, 1914–1918* (Southend-on-Sea: Borough Printing and Publishing, 1935), 47.

6 RVW to Gustav Holst, late June 1916, *VWL* 353.

7 RVW to Gustav Holst, 21 October 1916, *VWL* 426.

8 Harry Steggles, "Dr. Ralph Vaughan Williams, O. M.," 24.

9 John Tindall Robinson to Ursula Vaughan Williams, 21 October 1959, BL MS Mus. 1714/1/5, ff. 93–94.

10 A. J. Moore to John Brown (OUP), 27 July 1959, BL MS Mus. 1714/1/5, f. 74.

11 See "W. A. Marshall (War Memory No. 1)," in *TSR*, 296.

12 "E. R. Winship (War Memory No. 4)," in *TSR*, 336.

13 Major Stanley Smith to the Secretary, War Office, 19 October 1920, UK National Archives, WO 374/75055.

14 Quoted in *WVW*, 147.

15 Various authors, "Dr. Ralph Vaughan Williams, O. M.," *RCMM* 55, no. 1 (February 1959): 50.

16 See RVW, "A Musical Autobiography," 192.

17 See "Nicola LeFanu," in *TSR*, 181–82.

18 "Michael Mullinar," in *TSR*, 308.

19 See Jennifer Doctor, "'Working for Her Own Salvation': Vaughan Williams as a Teacher of Elizabeth Maconchy, Grace Williams, and Ina Boyle," in *VWP*, 181–201.

20 "Belinda Norman-Butler," in *TSR*, 193.

21 RVW, "A Musical Autobiography," 187.

22 RVW to George McCleary, undated letter [early 1920s], *VWL* 4698.

23 Alfred Kalisch, "British Music Society's Congress," *MT* 61, no. 928 (1 June 1920): 389.

24 Mary Buxton to Ursula Vaughan Williams, 19 February 1961, BL MS Mus. 1714/1/5, f. 209. He accepted the Bach Choir's offer with the proviso that he stay on with the Handel Society until a suitable replacement could be found; Eugène Goossens eventually took over the Handel Society's directorship.

25 RVW, "The Letter and the Spirit," in *NME*, 122.

26 Ibid., 128.

27 RVW to Vally Lasker, [June 1921], *VWL* 4888.

28 Oscar Thompson, "American and British Works Given First Performances at Norfolk, Conn.," *Musical America* (17 June 1922): 5.

29 RVW to Gustav Holst, [5 June 1922], *VWL* 226.

30 Adeline Vaughan Williams to Cordelia Curle, 14 July 1922, *VWL* 502.

31 Karl Straube to RVW, 5 December 1923, *VWL* 537. At the request of the publisher (Curwen), Straube sent a 5000-mark note as a token gesture of payment, since hyperinflation had rendered the currency worthless (the exchange rate at the time was somewhere between fifteen and twenty-five trillion marks to the pound).

Chapter 8

1 *RVW*, 132.

2 Saylor, *English Pastoral Music*, 155.

3 See Henry R. Clayton to Cecil Sharp, 16 April 1919, quoted in *WVW*, 151. The unsuccessful work in question may be "A Farmer's Son So Sweet"; see *CVW*, 90.

4 RVW to Laurence Taylor, 2 October 1955, *VWL* 3199.

5 RVW to Louis Fleury, 10 March 1920, *VWL* 460.

6 RVW to Harriet Cohen, 16 October 1933, *VWL* 1102.

7 See Stephen Lloyd, *Constant Lambert* (Woodbridge: Boydell Press, 2014), 137n61 and 141n84.

8 Given the context, it may be notable that Dorothy Longman was the violinist at the premiere; see Chapter 13 of the present volume, esp. 162–63.

9 For an overview, see Saylor, *English Pastoral Music*, 9–23.

10 Ibid., 115.

11 Ibid., 83–92.

12 Daniel M. Grimley, "Landscape and Distance: Vaughan Williams, Modernism and the Symphonic Pastoral," in *British Music and Modernism, 1895–1960*, ed. Matthew Riley (Farnham: Ashgate, 2010), 174.

13 Ibid., 151–59.

14 See Herbert Howells, "Vaughan Williams's 'Pastoral' Symphony," *ML* 3, no. 2 (April 1922): 125.

15 See Frank Howes, *The Music of Ralph Vaughan Williams* (London: OUP, 1954), 23; Stephen Connock, "The Edge of Beyond," *VWJ*, no. 16 (October 1999): 3; and Saylor, *English Pastoral Music*, 90.

16 RVW to Donald Tovey, 3 March 1927, *VWL* 468.

17 RVW to Rutland Boughton, 21(?) May 1951, *VWL* 2245.

18 See Saylor, *English Pastoral Music*, 147–55.

19 RVW, "A Musical Autobiography," 189–90.

20 Quoted in *WVW*, 160.

21 See Onderdonk, "Folksong Arrangements," in *CCVW*, 154–55.

Chapter 9

1 Gustav Holst to RVW, 9 March 1923, *VWL* 3960.

2 Dorothy Longman to RVW, 8 April 1923, *VWL* 4596.

3 RVW to Bernhard Ord, 15 April 1923, *VWL* 515.

4 According to one source, the CUMS Orchestra may have been fortified at the last minute by some ringers from the London Philharmonic Orchestra, but I have not been able to corroborate this claim; see J. G. S., "Old King Cole . . . (Mrs. Vulliamy's memories of the Ballet reported to J. G. S. 19.9.62)," BL MS Mus. 1714/1/6, ff. 114–16; see also *CVW*, 95.

5 RVW to John Burnaby, [ca. 10 June 1923], *VWL* 517.

6 See *VWW*, 27.

7 He allegedly began composing *Sancta Civitas* while writing his essay "The Letter and the Spirit" in 1920; see *RVW*, 163.

8 Cecil Armstrong Gibbs to Ursula Vaughan Williams, 9 September 1958, BL MS Mus. 1714/1/6, f. 119.

9 RVW to Martin Shaw, 3 January 1924, *VWL* 4083.

10 RVW to Thomas Marshall, 16 September 1924, *VWL* 558.

11 RVW to E. J. Dent, [September 1924], *VWL* 557.

12 [Robin Legge], "Hugh the Drover," *Daily Telegraph* (London), 15 July 1924, 16.

13 See Edward Sackville-West, "Hugh the Drover," *Spectator*, 10 July 1924, 90–91; and H. C. Colles, "Hugh the Drover," *Times* (London), 15 July 1924, 12.

14 Bobby Longman to RVW, 19 July 1924, BL MS Mus. 1714/1/6, f. 167.

15 See Pamela Blevins, *Ivor Gurney and Marion Scott: Song of Pain and Beauty* (Woodbridge: Boydell Press, 2008), 216.

16 Adeline Vaughan Williams to Cordelia Curle, 19 May 1925, *VWL* 587; and Hubert Foss, "The International Music Festival, Prague, 1925," *MT* 66, no 989 (1 July 1925): 606–7.

17 RVW to Gustav Holst, ca. 1 November 1925, *VWL* 589.

18 Gustav Holst to RVW, 11 November 1925, *VWL* 3961.

19 Although the memo lacks an addressee, Holst clearly refers to it in a subsequent letter; see Gustav Holst to RVW, [ca. May or June 1926], *VWL* 3903.

20 RVW, "Memorandum on the General Strike," [May 1926], *VWL* 794.

21 RVW to Rutland Boughton, 9 July 1952, *VWL* 2448.

22 RVW to Rutland Boughton, 9 December 1956, *VWL* 3451.

23 Ralph Vaughan Williams, *Sancta Civitas* (London: Curwen, 1925), ii; copy held in the Royal College of Music Library, 45.E.10.

24 Richard Capell(?), "London Concerts," *Daily Telegraph* (London), 10 June 1926, 16; Leigh Henry, "London Letter," *Chesterian* 8, no. 56 (July–August 1926): 278; and H. C. Colles, "The Bach Choir," *Times* (London), 10 June 1926, 14.

25 Harold Child to RVW, 9 June 1926, *VWL* 606.

26 Quoted in *WVW*, 195.

27 RVW to Frederic Wilkinson, 11 August 1937, *VWL* 1203.

28 See Adeline Vaughan Williams to Marion Scott, 3 November 1922, *VWL* 3241; also *RVW*, 169.

29 It had, however, received a BBC radio broadcast on 8 August 1926, and at least one concert performance (in Bradford, West Yorkshire, on 20 March 1927) prior to the one identified in *CVW*, 116. I am grateful to John Francis for drawing my attention to this detail.

30 RVW to Evelyn Sharp, [early August 1927], *VWL* 618.

31 See RVW to Hubert Foss, [ca. 1 October 1928], *VWL* 635.

32 RVW to Adrian Boult, 14 October 1928, *VWL* 636.

33 RVW to S. P. Waddington, [early 1929], *VWL* 4560.

34 RVW to Grace Williams, [1931], *VWL* 3879; for a list of texts used in the libretto, see *CVW*, 122, 124.

35 RVW to Myra Hess, 5 October 1939, *VWL* 1596.

36 Robert de Ropp, *Warrior's Way* (London: George Allen & Unwin, 1979), 49.

37 See RVW, "The Late Mr. Frank Kidson" and "Lucy Broadwood: An Appreciation," in *VWM*, 221–22 and 223–25.

38 An annex for Vaughan Williams's mother was later added; see Rosamund Carr to Ursula Vaughan Williams, n.d., BL MS Mus. 1714/1/9, f. 19.

Chapter 10

1 See *CVW*, 93–94; and J. G. S., "Old King Cole . . . ," BL MS Mus. 1714/1/6, ff. 115–16.

2 See *CVW*, 114–16 for more details on the scenario and its revisions.

3 See Eric Saylor, "Dramatic Applications of Folksong in Vaughan Williams's Operas *Hugh the Drover* and *Sir John in Love*," *JRMA* 134, no. 1 (2009): 45–46. Ernest Newman, Edward Sackville-West, and H. C. Colles were some of the most prominent figures taking issue with the opera.

4 RVW to Harold Child, ca. 15 July 1910, *VWL* 365; and RVW to Harold Child, [1912?], *VWL* 4944. It also seems likely that Vaughan Williams was thinking about England's most

successful example of ballad opera, John Gay's *The Beggar's Opera*, which also featured an array of folk and popular tunes amid a distinctively English setting.

5 RVW to Harold Child, ca. 15 July 1910, *VWL* 365. See also Savage, *Masques, Mayings, and Music-Dramas*, 304–58, in which he argues that the work represents a latter-day reinterpretation of the older English mumming drama.

6 RVW to Harold Child, ca. 15 July 1910, *VWL* 365.

7 A more extended synopsis is available in RVW, *Hugh the Drover*, vocal score, Curwen Edition (London: Faber Music, 1990), viii–ix.

8 This title is most commonly used, but the program for the premiere simply identifies it as "Suite." The published score of 1924 identifies it as *Folk Song Suite*, while *CVW* provides the title "*English Folk Songs*. Suite for military band." See *VWW*, 42, 45; and *CVW*, 96.

9 See *VWW*, 44.

10 *RVW*, 152; see also *CVW*, 97; and *VWW*, 29–41.

11 See *VWW*, 57.

12 The concerto also borrowed the finale's main theme from Act II of *Hugh the Drover*, and may have been inspired in part by the solos he wrote for *Old King Cole*; see *CVW*, 109 and *WVW*, 163.

13 RVW to Alexander Kaye Butterworth, 2 December 1917, *VWL* 435. See also Mark, "Chamber Music and Works for Soloist with Orchestra," in *CCVW*, 187–88.

14 See RVW to Cedric Glover, [April 1924], *VWL* 786; also Hugh Allen to RVW, 14 May 1924, BL MS Mus. 1714/1/6, f. 164.

15 RVW, "Bach, the Great Bourgeois," in *NME*, 171; see also "The Mass in B Minor in English," in *NME*, 199–201.

16 RVW, "Preface to *The English Hymnal*," in *VWM*, 32.

17 "Martin Shaw," in *TSR*, 310.

18 Francis Cornford, "Dr. Ralph Vaughan Williams, O. M.," *RCMM* 55, no. 1 (Easter Term 1959): 10.

19 RVW to Joan Shaw, 19 October [1941?], *VWL* 4515.

20 See Lucy Broadwood to RVW, [ca. 1 November 1928], *VWL* 638; and RVW to Lucy Broadwood, 30 October 1928, *VWL* 637.

21 RVW to George Parker, 25 June 1952, *VWL* 2439.

22 Frogley, "O Farther Sail," in *Let Beauty Awake*, 91. All three Whitman songs feature a different ground bass.

23 Contrary to repeated claims, the score for "The Soldier" was not destroyed: both it and "Good-Bye" are in BL MS Mus. 157, ff. 5–8. "The Soldier" was originally numbered fourth in the series and "Good-Bye" seventh, the ordering of which means that "The Sigh That Heaves the Grasses" was fifth (see *CVW*, 116–17).

24 This interpretation may reflect art imitating life, as Vaughan Williams was allegedly leading on a woman who was infatuated with him, and "used to go & see her rather a lot then, to work himself up into the terrific state he needed to be in to be able to write it—but he never went far enough to get actually involved" (Ursula Vaughan Williams to Michael Kennedy, quoted in Byron Adams, "'No Armpits, Please, We're British,'" in *Walt Whitman and Modern Music*, 41n34. Kennedy claimed that the woman was an RCM student, but without supporting evidence; see "Fluctuations in the Response to the Music of Ralph Vaughan Williams," in *CCVW*, 278.

25 *CVW*, 107.

26 See Harold Owen and John Bell, eds., *Wilfred Owen: Collected Letters* (London: OUP, 1967), 429; Charles McGuire, "'An Englishman and a Democrat':Vaughan Williams, Large Choral Works, and the British Festival Tradition," in *CCVW*, 128; and Day, *Vaughan Williams*, 130–31.

27 The resultant effect resembles that of the "Farben" movement from Arnold Schoenberg's *Five Pieces for Orchestra* (1912), though there is no evidence Vaughan Williams had this in mind.

28 H. C. Colles, "Vaughan Williams and Handel," *Times* (London), 12 June 1926, 12.

29 See Savage, *Masques, Mayings and Music Dramas*, 222–74, esp. 223–31.

30 See ibid., 240n34; and *CVW*, 122–24.

31 See Saylor, "Dramatic Applications of Folksong," 62–80.

32 *CVW*, 122–24; and RVW to Penelope Spencer, January 1929, *VWL* 656. The two operas also shared one other trait:Vaughan Williams's decision to adapt them into cantatas—titled *A Cotswold Romance* and *In Windsor Forest*, respectively—as a means of keeping their music in circulation, given the uncertainty of future stage productions.

Chapter 11

1 Ruth Dyson, quoted in *VWD*, 6.

2 De Ropp, *Warrior's Way*, 54–55.

3 E. J. N. Polkinhorne to RVW, April 1929, BL MS Mus. 1714/1/7, f. 114.

4 "Account of the Executors," 22 June 1939, BL MS Mus. 1714/1/10, f. 9.

5 RVW to Diana Awdry, 11 February 1930, *VWL* 843.

6 Geoffrey Keynes, "Blake's *Job* on the Stage," in *Blake Studies: Essays on His Life and Work*, 2d ed. (Oxford: Clarendon Press, 1971), 192. Vaughan Williams accepted Diaghilev's rejection with equanimity, as he thought the scenario misfit the "decadent & frivolous attitude of the [Ballets Russes] towards everything—can you imagine *Job* sandwiched in between 'Les Biches' and 'Cimarosiana'—& that dreadful pseudo-cultured audience saying to each other 'my dear have you seen God at the Russian Ballet.'" RVW to Gwen Raverat, [October 1927], *VWL* 814.

7 "Norwich Musical Festival," *Times* (London), 24 October 1930, 12.

8 Further financial support came from Keynes's father and a colleague at St. Bart's Hospital, Sir Thomas Dunhill (not to be confused with the composer of the same name).

9 A. H. Fox-Strangways, "The Camargo Society," *Observer*, 12 July 1931, n.p.

10 RVW, "Reminiscences of Fifty Years," in *Leith Hill Musical Festival*, 40.

11 *VWD*, 18, and Michael Kennedy, "R.V.W. & J. S. B.," *VWJ*, no. 18 (June 2000): 4.

12 RVW to Adrian Boult, 19 August 1934, *VWL* 1280.

13 RVW to Imogen Holst, 3 March 1935, *VWL* 249.

14 David Manning, "The Public Figure: Vaughan Williams as Writer and Activist," in *CCVW*, 244.

15 RVW to Adrian Boult, 7 February 1933, *VWL* 1044.

16 RVW to Edward Elgar, 19 February 1934, *VWL* 1191.

17 Carice Blake to RVW, 25 April 1934, *VWL* 1237.

18 RVW to Imogen and Isobel Holst, 25 May 1934, *VWL* 1242.

19 Adeline Vaughan Williams to Cordelia Curle, [22 June 1934], *VWL* 4625.

20 RVW to Bobby Longman, [December 1937], *VWL* 645.

21 RVW to Maud Karpeles, 14 October [1934?], *VWL* 4828.

22 RVW to Harriet Cohen, [September 1933], *VWL* 1352.

23 RVW to Adrian Boult, [8 April 1933?], *VWL* 1234; and RVW to Grace Williams, n.d., *VWL* 3841. His comment to Boult was made in the context of conducting Bach's *St. Matthew Passion*.

24 RVW to the Master of the Worshipful Company of Musicians, 13 July 1934, *VWL* 4592.

25 Rosamund Carr said that Adeline "*always* face-washed (Uncle R's expression) every single bit of music he wrote, large or small. She went through it correcting & suggesting & cleaning up. He used to bring it into her page by page before he parted with it or while he was considering it. Always always always" (Rosamund Carr to Ursula Vaughan Williams, n.d., BL MS Mus. 1714/1/9, ff. 16–19).

26 RVW to Arthur Bliss, 6 November 1934, *VWL* 1325.

27 Adeline Vaughan Williams to Cordelia Curle, 8 April 1935, *VWL* 315.

28 Maud Karpeles to RVW, 15 April 1935, BL MS Mus. 1714/1/9, ff. 126–28; Elizabeth Trevelyan to RVW, BL MS Mus. 1714/1/9, ff. 138–39; and H. C. Colles, "B.B.C. Orchestra—Vaughan Williams's New Symphony," *Times* (London), 11 April 1935, 12.

29 Arnold Bax to RVW, n.d., BL MS Mus. 1714/1/9, f. 115.

30 Edmund Rubbra to RVW, 17 April 1935, BL MS Mus. 1714/1/9, f. 123; H. Balfour Gardiner to RVW, 12 April 1935, *VWL* 4610; Arthur Benjamin to RVW, 21 April 1935, BL MS Mus. 1714/1/9, ff. 113–14.

31 Adeline Vaughan Williams to Rosamund Carr, n.d., BL MS Mus. 1714/1/9, ff. 13–14.

32 RVW to Bobby Longman, [December 1937], *VWL* 645.

33 See RVW to Imogen Holst, 7 June 1935, *VWL* 727.

34 RVW to Lord Farrer, 7 June 1935, *VWL* 4389.

35 Adeline's brother Herbert Fisher received the same honor two years later, as did Vaughan Williams's friends Gilbert Murray and G. E. Moore in 1941 and 1951, respectively.

36 RVW to Gerald Finzi, 8 June 1935, *VWL* 731; RVW to Boris Ord, 7 June 1935, *VWL* 721.

37 RVW to Diana Awdry, 4 August 1935, *VWL* 762.

38 RVW to Alexander Butterworth, 23 August 1935, *VWL* 3809. He eventually left £1000 to the Butterworth Trust in his will; see BL MS Mus. 1714/9/1, f.17.

39 See RVW to Peter Montgomery, ca. June 1930, *VWL* 891; and RVW to Lord Kennet, 20 May 1941, *VWL* 1537 for extended meditations by the composer on this subject.

40 Eric Saylor, "Music for Stage and Film," in *CCVW*, 161.

41 RVW to Evelyn Sharp, 22 May 1936, *VWL* 945.

42 RVW, "Tribute to Elgar," Elgar Centenary Programme (BBC), May 1957, *VWL* 3488.

43 Adeline Vaughan Williams to Rosamond Carr, February 1936, BL MS Mus. 1714/1/9, f. 162.

44 *RVW*, 212.

Chapter 12

1 See Duncan Hinnells, "Vaughan Williams's Piano Concerto: The First Seventy Years," in *VWP*, 122–27.

2 The *Benedicite*, Three Choral Hymns, and *The Hundredth Psalm* are treated at length in Howes, *The Music of Ralph Vaughan Williams*, 154–63.

3 RVW to Gustav Holst, 20 March 1932, *VWL* 999.

4 Ibid.

5   Byron Adams, "Scripture, Church, and Culture: Biblical Texts in the Works of Ralph Vaughan Williams," in *VWS*, 114–15.

6   For extended treatment of this phenomenon in *Job*, see Alison Sanders McFarland, "A Deconstruction of William Blake's Vision: Vaughan Williams and *Job*," in *VWE*, 29–53, with a comparison of the multiple scenarios on 45–50.

7   See Heckert, *Composing History*, 202–5.

8   McFarland, "A Deconstruction of William Blake's Vision," in *VWE*, 44; also Saylor, "Music for Stage and Film," in *CCVW*, 164.

9   See Adeline Vaughan Williams to Cordelia Curle, n.d., BL MS Mus. 1714/1/33, f. 115; also Adeline Vaughan Williams to Cordelia Curle, [October 1948], *VWL* 4683.

10 Harriet Cohen's account of its origin is available in *A Bundle of Time: The Memoirs of Harriet Cohen* (London: Faber & Faber, 1969), 158–59.

11 See RVW to Harriet Cohen, 16 October 1933, *VWL* 1102.

12 See *CVW*, 145 for details.

13 See John Francis, "Ralph Vaughan Williams and Henry Ley," *VWJ*, no. 63 (June 2015): 12; and Henry Ley, "VW," in BL MS Mus. 1714/1/4, f. 36.

14 Quoted in Simon Wright, "Harriet Cohen: Alluring Woman, Great Pianist Devoted to Bach," *OUPblog* (29 August 2013), https://blog.oup.com/2013/08/harriet-cohen-alluring-woman-great-pianist-devoted-to-bach/.

15 See Hinnells, "Vaughan Williams's Piano Concerto," in *VWP*, 134n36. Her inability to play it well and unwillingness to let others try greatly annoyed Vaughan Williams; see Simona Pakenham, "Music in Wartime," *VWJ*, no. 22 (October 2001): 26.

16 See RVW to Harriet Cohen, 22 July 1933, *VWL* 1063.

17 Sorting out the Concerto's various revisions and arrangements has proven difficult, especially if the carte blanche Vaughan Williams extended to Cooper, Boult, and Cohen to alter passages is taken into consideration. See Hinnells, "Vaughan Williams's Piano Concerto," in *VWP*, 150–54.

18 See Mark, "Chamber Music," in *CCVW*, 189–91.

19 As with the Fourth Symphony, Vaughan Williams felt ambivalent about the Concerto; see RVW to Harriet Cohen, 14 October 1942, *VWL* 1704.

20 Howes, *The Music of Ralph Vaughan Williams*, 30–31.

21 John Warrack to Ursula Vaughan Williams, 6 September [no year], BL MS Mus. 1719/1/9, f. 150; and *RVW*, 190. Ursula Vaughan Williams's claim is bolstered by the composer's own comments; see RVW to Olin Downes, 25 September 1943, *VWL* 3846. If true, the piece in *The Times* may have been the Second Symphony of Vladimir Dukelsky, better known as Vernon Duke; see Anthony Barone, "Modernist Rifts in a Pastoral Landscape: Observations on the Manuscripts of Vaughan Williams's Fourth Symphony," *MQ* 91, nos. 1–2 (Spring–Summer 2008): 64.

22 Ottaway, *Vaughan Williams Symphonies*, 29.

23 For an excellent overview of this issue, see Ryan Ross, "'Blaspheming Beethoven?' The Altered BACH Motive in Vaughan Williams's Fourth Symphony," *Acta Musicologica* 91, no. 2 (2019): 126–45.

24 RVW to Olin Downes, 25 September 1943, *VWL* 3846. In this, he meant the intervals were identical, not the pitches; but see also Ross, "Blaspheming Beethoven?," 133–34.

25 RVW, "A Musical Autobiography," 181, 183.

26 RVW, "Some Thoughts on Beethoven's Choral Symphony," in *NME*, 83, 84, 92.

27 RVW, "A Musical Autobiography," 181.

28 Quoted in *WVW*, 246.

29 Ottaway, *Vaughan Williams Symphonies*, 31.

30 Lionel Pike, *Vaughan Williams and the Symphony* (London: Toccata Press, 2003), 141.

31 For a much closer analysis, see Ross, "Blaspheming Beethoven?," 132–41.

32 Ibid., 138.

33 See Arthur Benjamin to RVW, 21 April 1935, BL MS Mus. 1714/1/9, ff. 113–14.

34 Barone, "Modernist Rifts in a Pastoral Landscape," 86n20.

35 RVW to Evelyn Sharp, 18 August 1927, *VWL* 619; see also *WVW*, 198–200.

36 Ursula Vaughan Williams was responsible for this revision; see Stephen Connock, "'It Will Be Alright in the End': The Complex Evolution of the Libretto," *VWJ*, no. 26 (February 2003): 4–6.

37 Gerald Cockshott, notes on working with Vaughan Williams, 1945, BL MS Mus. 1714/1/32, f. 71.

38 Quoted in RVW, *Dona Nobis Pacem*, full score (London: OUP, 1971), iv.

39 Charles McGuire, "'An Englishman and a Democrat,'" in *CCVW*, 129.

Chapter 13

1 RVW to Douglas Kennedy, 18 December 1937, *VWL* 4928.

2 Henry Wood to RVW, 25 January 1938, *VWL* 1275.

3 RVW to Douglas Kennedy, 16 January 1938, *VWL* 4929.

4 *RVW*, 219.

5 Ibid., also "Ursula Vaughan Williams," in *TSR*, 219. This sort of behavior in taxis was not new for Vaughan Williams; see Oliver Neighbour, "Ralph, Adeline, and Ursula Vaughan Williams," 341n23.

6 "Ursula Vaughan Williams," in *TSR*, 219.

7 RVW to Ursula Wood, 4 October 1938, *VWL* 1378.

8 RVW to Ursula Wood, 26 June 1938, *VWL* 1329.

9 The link between the Hornsteins and Müller-Hartmanns went beyond friendship: Yanya Hornstein had an ongoing affair with the Müller-Hartmanns' daughter, Susanne, while Genia and Robert were themselves having an affair; Genia's daughter, Eva, was also Robert's. See Steven K. White, ed., *Dear Müller-Hartmann: Letters from Ralph Vaughan Williams to Robert Müller-Hartmann*, 2d ed. (privately published, 2009), 21.

10 For expanded treatment of this episode, see Alain Frogley, "Vaughan Williams and Nazi Germany: the 1937 Hamburg Shakespeare Prize," in *Music as a Bridge: Musikalische Beziehungen zwischen England und Deutschland 1920–1950*, ed. Christa Brüstle and Guido Heldt (Hildesheim: Georg Olms Verlag, 2005), 113–32.

11 RVW to Hermann Fiedler, July 1937, *VWL* 643.

12 See Julian Budden to Ursula Vaughan Williams, 6 August 1985, BL MS Mus. 1714/1/11, f. 32.

13 Frogley, "Vaughan Williams and Nazi Germany," in *Music as a Bridge*, 119; and RVW to Laurence Binyon, 9 July 1938, *VWL* 3615.

14 Katharine Atholl, Sidney M. Berry, Muirhead Bone, et al., "Persecution of the Jews," *Times* (London), 22 November 1938, 10.

15 RVW to Maud Karpeles, 20 December 1938, *VWL* 4860.

16 RVW to an unidentified correspondent (possibly Alan Bush?), 4 January 1939, *VWL* 4549.

17 RVW to [Anne Wynne?] Thackeray, 31 August 1940, *VWL* 4711.

18 RVW to Iris Lemare, 4 October 1940, *VWL* 1442.

19 RVW to Ursula Wood, [October 1939], *VWL* 684.

20 RVW to Elisabeth Lutyens, 6 November 1939, *VWL* 1621.

21 *VWD*, 14–17.

22 It later became the opening number of the compilation *Five Wartime Hymns* (1942), which also included Vaughan Williams's hymn *A Call to the Free Nations* (1941).

23 This work is mistakenly dated 1913 in *CVW*, 74.

24 RVW to Granville Bantock, 21 August 1940, *VWL* 1430. Copies of the letter went to leading figures in musical composition, education, and criticism, including Adrian Boult, Hugh Allen, William Walton, H. C. Colles, and Constant Lambert.

25 Hugh Cobbe, "Vaughan Williams, Germany, and the German Tradition: A View from the Letters," in *VWS*, 94.

26 RVW to Ferdinand Rauter, 16 August 1942, *VWL* 1680; for his letter to Strasser, see *VWL* 512.

27 Ferdinand Rauter to RVW, 26 September 1942, *VWL* 1692.

28 RVW to Arnold Barter, 1 November [1943?], *VWL* 1818. See also RVW, "Nationalism and Internationalism," in *NME*, 154–59.

29 RVW to Bobby Longman, 2 June 1940, *VWL* 1423.

30 See, for instance, RVW to Ursula Wood, 7 October 1939, *VWL* 1598.

31 RVW to Ursula Wood, [after October 1940], *VWL* 1499.

32 RVW, "The Composer in Wartime," in *VWM*, 85.

33 Nancy Bush and Lewis Foreman, *Alan Bush: Music, Politics and Life* (London: Thames, 2000), 40.

34 RVW to the BBC Director General, 9 March 1941, *VWL* 1526.

35 RVW to Gerald Cockshott, 19 October [early 1940s], *VWL* 4745; and RVW to Fritz Hart, 14 August [1941], *VWL* 1575.

36 RVW to Gerald Finzi, 10 December 1941, *VWL* 1599.

37 He also submitted a work that Norman Peterkin referred to "Epithalamium [sic]–Ballet–Edmund Spenser (the spelling is that of V.W. not mine)," likely the version of *The Bridal Day* completed in 1939. See Norman Peterkin to Humphrey Milford, 24 April 1942, *VWL* 1641.

38 RVW to Harold Child, 11 May 1942, *VWL* 4881.

39 *RVW*, 248.

40 RVW to Ursula Wood, [August 1942?], *VWL* 1741.

41 Notable examples exist in letters to Jean Stewart, Diana Awdry, and Grace Williams, the latter after she left the RCM. The terms "niece" and "nymph" were also used by Adeline and by the subjects themselves. Comments made to Stewart suggest there may have been a closer relationship between them than generally assumed, although Stewart, who was close friends with Wood, said that Wood "made it clear that he was her property and I mustn't come near. I wasn't attempting to, really" ("Jean Stewart," in *TSR*, 211).

42 Neighbour, "Ralph, Adeline, and Ursula Vaughan Williams," 338.

43 Robert Longman, "Ralph and Dorothy," BL MS Mus. 1714/1/26, f. 11. Longman added that he found a cache of Vaughan Williams's letters to Dorothy after her death, and destroyed them without reading them. Another collection of letters from Vaughan Williams to Fanny Farrer are privately held by her family, who have not released details as to their content.

44 Longman, "Ralph and Dorothy," f. 12.

45 De Ropp, *Warrior's Way*, 51–52. De Ropp further asserted that Adeline was infertile, which he thought might explain her behavior.

46 "Jean Stewart," *TSR*, 211, and Neighbour, "Ralph, Adeline, and Ursula Vaughan Williams," 342n24.

47 Neighbour, "Ralph, Adeline, and Ursula Vaughan Williams," 338.

48 See ibid.

49 RVW to Arnold Goldsborough, 19 October 1942, *VWL* 1709.

50 RVW to Herbert Howells, 17 December 1942, *VWL* 1737.

51 Jean Stewart to RVW, 18 February 1943, *VWL* 1752.

52 RVW to Elizabeth Trevelyan, 23 June 1943, *VWL* 1789.

53 Adrian Boult to RVW, 27 June 1943, *VWL* 1791.

Chapter 14

1 This work was written for Alan Bush, intended to open a pageant designed as part of a larger Festival for Music of the People held at the Royal Albert Hall. Vaughan Williams initially balked at participating in such an overtly political event—the festival counted Paul Robeson among its participants, and featured the debut of Benjamin Britten's *Ballad of Heroes*—but agreed to write the short *Flourish* in lieu of a larger contribution.

2 Vaughan Williams did not anticipate that the RPS, which commissioned this work, would agree to his expansive orchestral demands ("I expect the Society will not see the fun of this"), but they had no objections. The piece was likely meant for the coronation of Edward VIII, but was used instead for that of George VI. Though the reduced version was apparently intended for a performance in Dorking, Vaughan Williams did not want the RPS to find out "or they will try to do me on the cheap." See RVW to Keith Douglas, 23 August 1936, *VWL* 4720; and RVW to Alan Frank, ca. January 1937, *VWL* 554.

3 The complicated details of this work, which includes the Overture, the Folk Dance Medley, and the single-movement March Suite Founded on English Folk Tunes, are available in *VWW*, 101–7; and Lewis Foreman, "Music for an EFDS Masque," liner notes for *Ralph Vaughan Williams: The Blue Bird & Variations for Orchestra etc.*, Dutton CDLX 7351, 2018, compact disc.

4 Vaughan Williams cut about 15 percent of the original play, but left what remained almost entirely unaltered; see Walter Aaron Clark, "Vaughan Williams and the 'Night Side of Nature': Octatonicism in *Riders to the Sea*," in *VWE*, 56.

5 Saylor, *English Pastoral Music*, 87.

6 Clark, "Vaughan Williams and the 'Night Side of Nature,'" in *VWE*, 64.

7 RVW to Gerald Finzi, 25 July 1937, *VWL* 1190.

8 Kennedy, "Fluctuations in the response . . . ," in *CCVW*, 283.

9 A chart comparing the layouts of *The Bridal Day* and *Epithalamion* is available in A. E. F. Dickinson, *Vaughan Williams* (London: Faber & Faber, 1963), 468–69.

10 The strings were enlarged to a full complement in *Epithalamion* to better balance the chorus.

11 Ursula Vaughan Williams, preface to RVW, *Epithalamion*, full score (Oxford: OUP, 1990), iii.

12 Howes, *The Music of Ralph Vaughan Williams*, 234.

13 See RVW, "A Musical Autobiography," 189; and RVW, "The Evolution of the Folk-Song (continued)," in *NME*, 41–42.

14 Many variants of the tune and text exist; Vaughan Williams apparently collected one in Norfolk in 1905 set to the text "The Murder of Maria Martin in the Red Barn" (see *WVW*, 278, and *CVW*, 35), and published another version taken from a phonograph recording made by Ella Mary Leather in 1907; see *Journal of the Folk-Song Society* 4 (1910): 47–48.

15 "Shrubsole," originally published in 1943; see *NME*, 202–4.

16 *CVW*, 166.

17 Vaughan Williams also apparently arranged three movements from his *Viola Suite* on this occasion for a quartet of pipes and piano, but the location of this score is unknown; see RVW to Margaret James, 22 July 1939, *VWL* 1576.

18 RVW to Canon G. W. Briggs, 1 February 1940, *VWL* 4100; see also RVW to Adrian Boult, ca. 2 September 1940, *VWL* 1434.

19 The first two were published as part of the compilation *Five Wartime Hymns* (1942), which also featured contributions from Martin Shaw and Ivor Atkins. Both had been independently released prior to this collection (in 1939 and 1940, respectively).

20 RVW, "The Composer in Wartime," in *VWM*, 84–85.

21 Vaughan Williams also arranged *A Folk Dance Medley* and the somewhat misnamed single-movement *March Suite Founded on English Folk Tunes* for the BBC Military Band; see *VWW*, 101–7.

22 RVW, "Composing for the Films," in *NME*, 106. Mathieson remembered the meeting rather differently; see Jeffrey Richards, "Vaughan Williams and British Wartime Cinema," in *VWS*, 141.

23 RVW, "Composing for the Films," 159, 161.

24 Richards, "Vaughan Williams and British Wartime Cinema," in *VWS*, 142.

25 The broader impact of Vaughan Williams's wartime film music is covered in ibid., 147–60.

26 Details on the *Twelfth Night* production and Vaughan Williams's role in it are available from Tom Harrison, "Twelfth Night," BL MS Mus. 1714/1/12, f. 53; the tunes themselves are found in BL Add MS. 69451, with a list on f. 30. The *Richard II* score differed from the one used for Stratford in 1913.

27 A reduced version of this production was released by Christopher Palmer on the Hyperion label in 1991 and reissued in 2008 as *A Bunyan Sequence*, with drastic cuts made to the original script in order to make the whole fit onto one CD, although the vast majority of the music was preserved. A full recording of the original BBC performance was released by Albion Records in 2015 (ABLCD023/024). The full script is available, retyped for a 1959 revival at the Camden Theatre (also broadcast by the BBC), in BL MS Mus. 1714/2/2, ff. 37–71.

28 See Neighbour, "Ralph, Adeline, and Ursula Vaughan Williams," 338.

29 See *CVW*, 162. Other pageant contributors included John Ticehurst—who wrote all of the music for Act I—William Cole, Mary Couper, David Moule-Evans, and Julian Gardiner. More detail on this unusual work is available in *VWD*, 9–11; and Saylor, *English Pastoral Music*, 131–35.

30 A list of these is available in *CVW*, 206–7.

31 Samuel Hynes, *A War Imagined: The First World War and English Culture* (New York: Collier Books, 1990), 283.

32 Ottaway, *Vaughan Williams Symphonies*, 36.

33 Pike, *Vaughan Williams and the Symphony*, 157.

34 Ottaway, *Vaughan Williams Symphonies*, 37.
35 Eggar, "Ralph Vaughan Williams: Some Reflections on His Work," 515.
36 RVW, "What Have We Learnt from Elgar?" in *NME*, 251.

Chapter 15

1 For a more complete account of the piece's genesis and early performance, see RVW to Victor Hely-Hutchinson, 14 May 1945, *VWL* 1889. The title was changed to *A Song of Thanksgiving* in 1952.
2 RVW to Fritz Hart, 13 August [1944?], *VWL* 1925.
3 See correspondence from Adeline Vaughan Williams, BL MS Mus. 1714/1/15, ff. 43–54; and from R. O. Morris to Ursula Wood, BL MS Mus. 1714/1/26, ff. 128–29.
4 Adeline Vaughan Williams to Ursula Wood, [1943?], BL MS Mus. 1714/1/15, f. 62.
5 RVW to Elizabeth Trevelyan, 1 August 1944, *VWL* 1924.
6 RVW to Ralph Wedgwood, [spring 1947?], *VWL* 1780.
7 Unusually, *Thanksgiving for Victory* was recorded before its public debut, which took place in September 1945; see *CVW*, 177; and Lewis Foreman, "*A Song of Thanksgiving*: Vaughan Williams Celebrates the End of the Second World War," *VWJ*, no. 22 (October 2001): 23–24.
8 See Daniel Goldmark, "Music, Film, and Vaughan Williams," in *VWE*, 228n10.
9 RVW to Robert Müller-Hartmann, 2 January 1945, *VWL* 1857; and Adeline Vaughan Williams to Cordelia Curle, [1946?], BL MS Mus. 1714/1/16, f. 72.
10 Norman Peterkin, OUP file note, 20 November 1945, *VWL* 2020; and Hubert Foss to RVW, 10 December 1945, BL MS Mus. 1714/1/16, f. 100.
11 For additional details from the composer on his preparation of the piece, see "The Mass in B Minor in English: A Programme Note," in *NME*, 199–201; and BL MS Mus. 1714/1/28, ff. 1–41.
12 RVW to Henry Wood, 5 February 1944, *VWL* 1862. He indicated elsewhere that he meant this work both "as music and as film accompaniment"; RVW to Gerald Cockshott, 3 June [1946?], *VWL* 4746.
13 See RVW to Alan Frank, 9 April 1946, *VWL* 2032, esp. n.1.
14 RVW to Michael Mullinar, 20 February [1946], *VWL* 3680. The year is speculative, but since Vaughan Williams began composing the piece in 1944, it seems unlikely that it would have advanced enough for consideration by early 1945.
15 *RVW*, 267–68.
16 See RVW to Harriet Cohen, 24 August 1946, *VWL* 2058.
17 See Hinnells, "Vaughan Williams's Piano Concerto," in *VWP*, 138–41.
18 Ernest Irving to RVW, 9 December 1946, *VWL* 2142.
19 RVW to Michael Kennedy, 29 August 1946, *VWL* 2091.
20 RVW to Roy Douglas, 13 February 1947, *VWL* 2155.
21 More specifics on Douglas's activities are available in his memoir, *Working with Vaughan Williams* (London: British Library, 1988).
22 Ernest Irving to RVW, 20 January 1948, *VWL* 2542.
23 As it happened, Boult's first recording of the piece included both the original and revised versions of that movement. See RVW to Bruce Flegg, 19 January 1950, *VWL* 1974.
24 RVW to Margery Cullen, 8 March 1950, *VWL* 1982.

25 Howard Ferguson to Oliver Neighbour, 4 January 1994, quoted in Neighbour, "The Place of the Eighth among Vaughan Williams's Symphonies," in *VWS*, 224. "The Big Three" refers to the meeting of Winston Churchill, Franklin Roosevelt, and Joseph Stalin at Yalta in 1945 to begin planning the shape of the postwar world.

26 *RVW*, 284–85.

27 RVW to Alan Frank, 8 July 1948, *VWL* 4106.

28 RVW to Geoffrey Keynes, 17 November [likely 1945], *VWL* 2019.

29 RVW to Alan Frank, 16 December 1948, *VWL* 2936.

30 RVW to Ernest Irving, 29 June 1949, *VWL* 3174. Not until very late in the process did the composer settle on *Sinfonia Antartica* (with one "c") as the title.

31 Douglas, *Working with Vaughan Williams*, 27.

32 *RVW*, 308.

33 RVW to Elizabeth Trevelyan, 21 May 1951, *VWL* 2243.

34 RVW to Victor Sheppard, 8 June 1951, *VWL* 2252.

Chapter 16

1 Two divergent analyses of this movement may be found in Caireann Shannon, "The Oboe Concerto: First Movement Themes and Motifs," *VWJ*, no. 34 (October 2005): 8–10; and Mark, "Chamber Music," in *CCVW*, 192.

2 *WVW*, 285.

3 See Mark, "Chamber Music," in *CCVW*, 194.

4 Passages from "Indian Music 3" and "Nazis on the Run" resemble the melody, but neither matches exactly. Additionally, the final movement sports the subtitle "Greetings from Joan to Jean," featuring music Vaughan Williams had planned to use for an unrealized film about Joan of Arc.

5 Adrian Boult to RVW, 17 August 1943, *VWL* 1800.

6 RVW to Victor Hely-Hutchinson, 14 May 1945, *VWL* 1889.

7 This latter portion of the work was popular enough to be released independently in multiple arrangements; see *CVW*, 177–78.

8 Though Vaughan Williams provided suggestions as to how the problems might be overcome; see *CVW*, 177.

9 The LHMC was renamed the LHMF in 1950; see Corke, *Music Won the Cause*, 14.

10 *CVW*, 184.

11 Vaughan Williams was quite proud of this work, but thought that the reference to its cinematic origins kept it from being taken seriously, telling Frank Howes "if I had called it 'Sinfonia Flamenca' it would probably have had as much fuss made about it by the Press and public as my [Symphony] No. 6." This complaint may explain why he used the title *Sinfonia Antartica* when reimagining his music from *Scott of the Antarctic*; see RVW to Frank Howes, 4 June 1952, *VWL* 4469.

12 See RVW to Alan Frank, 15 January 1948, *VWL* 2540, in which Vaughan Williams notes specifically that the last movement of the *Partita* is new, implying that the first movement was only renamed.

13 Kennedy suggests that the Intermezzo's main melody alludes to Hall's signature tune, "Here's to the Next Time"; see *WVW*, 358.

14 See RVW to Frank Howes, 4 June 1952, *VWL* 4469; also Pike, *Vaughan Williams and the Symphony*, 221.

15 Jaclyn Howerton, "'Doing His Bit': Ralph Vaughan Williams's Music for British Wartime Propaganda Films" (PhD diss., University of California–Riverside, 2019), 169–84.
16 Michael Kennedy, "Conducting RVW," *VWJ*, no. 24 (June 2002): 4.
17 RVW to Alan Frank, 25 March 1948, *VWL* 2584.
18 RVW to Michael Kennedy, 22 January 1956, *VWL* 3259.
19 William Shakespeare, *The Tempest*, Act IV. sc. 1, in *The Annotated Shakespeare*, ed. A. L. Rowse (New York: Greenwich House, 1988), 2433.
20 Oliver Neighbour, "The Place of the Eighth," in *VWS*, 224.
21 See Julian Horton, "The Later Symphonies," in *CCVW*, 209–10; and Pike, *Vaughan Williams and the Symphony*, 202–19.
22 Constant Lambert, *Music Ho!* (New York: October House, 1967), 146; and *CVW*, 182, although Vaughan Williams referred to Lambert's quotation in conjunction with the Scherzo's saxophone solo.
23 *CVW*, 182.
24 Horton, "The Later Symphonies," in *CCVW*, 213.
25 *CVW*, 182.
26 Deryck Cooke, *The Language of Music* (London: OUP, 1959), 252–53. See also Adams, "'Music in the Air,'" 105–7.
27 See Manning, "The Public Figure," in *CCVW*, 238; and Lorna Gibson, "Ralph Vaughan Williams and the Women's Institute," *VWJ*, no. 30 (June 2004): 7–8.
28 *CVW*, 189.
29 Ravenscroft's melody was no. 178 in *The English Hymnal*, but with a different text ("Disposer supreme, and Judge of the earth") translated by Isaac Williams from Latin verses by Jean-Baptiste de Santeuil.
30 *RVW*, 194.
31 *CVW*, 190; see also Michael Kennedy, liner notes to *The Film Music of Ralph Vaughan Williams*, vol. 3, the Philharmonia Orchestra conducted by Rumon Gamba, recorded 2006. Chandos CHAN 10529(3), 2009, compact disc.
32 A full listing of the numbers from *Scott*, including material not present in *CVW*, is available in Christopher J. Parker, "The Music for 'Scott of the Antarctic,'" *VWJ*, no. 21 (June 2001): 11–14.
33 Adeline Vaughan Williams to Cordelia Curle, "Monday" (n.d.; possibly late 1946?), BL MS Mus. 1714/1/16, f. 76.
34 *CVW*, 188–89.
35 See also "William Llewellyn," in *TSR*, 185.
36 See Nathaniel Lew, "Editor's Preface," in RVW, *The Mayor of Casterbridge* (Wellington: Promethean Editions, 2011), 4–6.
37 Details on the complicated road to securing the first production—and its connection to the Festival of Britain—may be found in Nathaniel Lew, *Tonic to the Nation: Making English Music in the Festival of Britain* (London: Routledge, 2017), 86–90.
38 RVW to E. J. Dent, 17 May 1951, *CVW*, 204. Vaughan Williams and Dent's extensive post-premiere correspondence on the work may be found in *CVW*, 196–206.
39 RVW to Steuart Wilson, 12 August 1948, *VWL* 2785.
40 RVW to Hubert Foss, 17 May 1951, *VWL* 2236; and RVW to Rutland Boughton, 21 May 1951, *VWL* 2245.
41 Dyneley Hussey, "Vaughan Williams' *The Pilgrim's Progress*," *Foyer* 1 (Autumn 1951): 16.
42 See Lew, "'Words and Music That Are Forever England,'" in *VWE*, 185.

Chapter 17

1 See Neighbour, "Ralph, Adeline, and Ursula Vaughan Williams," 339–40.

2 Ursula Wood to Beryl Lock, 5 August 1951, BL MS Mus. 1714/1/19, f. 70v. This equates to just over $8500 in 2020. In earnings records, the money was listed as a salary for Wood's secretarial duties; see, for example, BL MS Mus. 1714/1/21, f. 133.

3 *RVW*, 313.

4 *RVW*, 316.

5 "Larry Adler," *TSR*, 241–42.

6 RVW to Hubert Foss, 17 March 1952, *VWL* 2383.

7 "Dr. Vaughan Williams," *Times* (London), 11 October 1952, 7.

8 Herbert Howells, "Speech at I. S. M. Dinner," 6 October 1952, BL MS Mus. 1714/1/20, f. 34.

9 See *WVW*, 287.

10 Ernest Irving to RVW, n.d., BL MS Mus. 1714/1/20, f. 146.

11 "Sallie Ashe and Ruth Jenkins" and "Nigel Finzi," in *TSR*, 82–83, 147; see also Elias Canetti, *Party in the Blitz* (London: Harvill Press, 2005), 231–32, 245.

12 Ralph Vaughan Williams, "Gloriana," *Times* (London), 18 June 1953, 9.

13 Ursula Vaughan Williams to Mary Sheppard, 13 July 1953, *VWL* 4339.

14 *RVW*, 355.

15 RVW, "Martin Shaw," in *VWM*, 275.

16 See RVW, "Howland Medal Lecture," in *VWM*, 99–109.

17 RVW to Cedric Glover, 4 November 1954, *VWL* 2883; and RVW to Michael Kennedy, 17 January 1955, *VWL* 2988.

18 RVW to Albert Sturgess, 9 June 1955, *VWL* 3094. His performance fees for the financial year ending 31 March 1955 came to £15,341 18s 11d ($545,854.75 in 2020), and constituted the bulk of his income; see "Statement of Earnings," BL MS Mus. 1714/1/21, ff. 133–37.

19 Vaughan Williams outlined the objects and desired aims for support in a memo to the Trust Committee, 29 October 1956, *VWL* 3445; for the official document itself, see BL MS Mus. 1714/1/22, ff. 104–9.

20 See RVW to Iris Lemare, 21 May 1955, *VWL* 3090, n.2; see also RVW to *The Times* (London), 17 August 1955, *VWL* 3184 for his subsequent efforts to preserve the Lemare-Macnaghten series after they had both retired.

21 RVW to Tom Whitestone, 9 October 1956, *VWL* 3432.

22 See Joy Finzi to RVW, 28 September 1956, *VWL* 3424.

23 RVW to Michael Kennedy, 6 March 1958, *VWL* 3327.

24 Johann Sebastian Bach, *St. Matthew Passion*, Leith Hill Musical Festival Chorus and Orchestra, cond. Ralph Vaughan Williams, recorded 5 March 1958, Pearl GEMS 0079, 2000, compact disc.

25 Ursula Vaughan Williams claimed that it was phlebitis that kept him from going to King's Lynn (*RVW*, 397), but revealed the actual reason to the Kennedys; see Ursula Vaughan Williams to Michael and Eslyn Kennedy, 27 July 1958, *VWL* 3272.

26 See Ursula Vaughan Williams to Jean Stewart, 28 August 1958, *VWL* 5098. A second funeral service followed at Dorking's St. Martin's Parish Church on 28 September.

27 For the funeral program, see "Westminster Abbey: Commemoration and Funeral Service of Ralph Vaughan Williams, O.M., M.A., D.Mus.," Charterhouse Library (Godalming), ACC/0259/47; see also "Dr. Ralph Vaughan Williams: Abbey Commemoration," *Times* (London), 20 September 1958, 8.

28 "Rutland Boughton," in *TSR*, 249.

Chapter 18

1 His most famous statement on the subject came in his twenty-six-word contribution to an obituary article about Arnold Schoenberg published in *ML*: "Schoenberg meant nothing to me—but as he apparently meant a lot to a lot of other people I daresay it is all my own fault" (*VWM*, 173).

2 RVW to Cecil Armstrong Gibbs, 15 December 1949, *VWL* 2124.

3 Leon Forrester to RVW; 13, 22, and 25 June 1956; BL MS Mus. 1714/1/22, ff. 72–74.

4 *An Oxford Elegy* received its public premiere in June 1952, but had already been performed privately three years earlier.

5 See Ernest Irving to RVW, 9 January 1953, *VWL* 2608.

6 See also Grimley, "Music, Ice, and the 'Geometry of Fear,'" 128–34.

7 See ibid., 125–26; for a slightly broader perspective, see Ryan Ross, "Is It Symphonic? Some Thoughts on the Critical Reception of Vaughan Williams's *Sinfonia Antartica*," *VWJ*, no. 69 (June 2017): 6–9.

8 See, for instance, Christopher J. Parker, "The Music for 'Scott of the Antarctic,'" *VWJ* 21 (June 2001): 11–14.

9 In movement order, these included excerpts from Percy Shelley's *Prometheus Unbound*—used also in the *Six Choral Songs* (1940)—Psalm 104; Samuel Taylor Coleridge's *Hymn before Sunrise, in the Vale of Chamouni*; John Donne's *The Sun Rising*; and Scott's last journal.

10 See Michael Beckerman, "The Composer as Pole Seeker: Reading Vaughan Williams's *Sinfonia Antartica*," *Current Musicology*, no. 69 (Spring 2000): 49–51.

11 *RVW*, 279.

12 Robert Falcon Scott, *Scott's Last Expedition* (New York: Dodd, Mead and Co., 1913), 416; quoted in Beckerman, "The Composer as Pole Seeker," 48.

13 *RVW*, 279.

14 See also Grimley, "Music, Ice, and the 'Geometry of Fear,'" 136–41.

15 *WVW*, 325.

16 Vaughan Williams correctly predicted that some people would erroneously sing the equal-note version of the tune instead; see RVW to Robin Ivison, 16 May 1957, *VWL* 3516.

17 *CVW*, 216.

18 Simona Pakenham, *Ralph Vaughan Williams*, 170. The harshest critique came from Donald Mitchell, "Contemporary Chronicle," *Musical Opinion* 78, no. 931 (April 1955): 409–11.

19 "Christopher ('Kiffer') Finzi," in *TSR*, 139.

20 See also John Cook, "The First Nowell," *VWJ*, no. 64 (October 2015): 15–16.

21 RVW to Eila Mackenzie, [late 1954], *VWL* 3924.

22 It has never been sung or recorded elsewhere, but the text and three measures of the MS are reprinted in Clark, *Leith Hill Musical Festival 1905–1955*, 6–7.

23 See *CVW*, 221; and Douglas, *Working with Vaughan Williams*, 82–85.

24 Felix Aprahamian, "R.V.W. in D Minor," *Sunday Times* (London), 6 May 1956, 12.

25 Michael Kennedy, "Preface," in RVW, *Symphony No. 8 in D Minor*, ed. David Lloyd-Jones, study score (Oxford: OUP, 2016), v. See also this same volume, xiii–xvi, or *CVW*, 221–25 for Vaughan Williams's full program note.

26 See *CVW*, 223. For details on the transformation of fourths, see Eric Saylor, "Valdedictory *Variazioni*: Form and Function in the First Movement of Vaughan Williams's Symphony No. 8," *MT* 153, no. 1919 (Summer 2012): 68–71.

27 See Neighbour, "The Place of the Eighth," in *VWS*, 228–29; and Saylor, "Valedictory *Variazioni*," 66–68.

28 Vaughan Williams confirmed the chorale's presence to Paul Henry Lang; see Neighbour, "The Place of the Eighth," in *VWS*, 228–32.

29 RVW, "Some Thoughts on Beethoven's Choral Symphony," in *NME*, 88.

30 Herbert, "Unfinished Business," in *VWP*, 80–81. Muir Mathieson later adapted two concert suites from the film score; see *CVW*, 226–27.

31 The Psalm numbering is from the King James Version (KJV).

32 See *VWW*, 139–43. Vaughan Williams evidently included parts for celesta and glockenspiel, even though these would not have been allowed under the rules of the competition, suggesting that he was thinking of the piece's future prospects. Subsequent transcriptions were made for orchestra (Gordon Jacob, 1960) and wind band (Donald Hunsberger, 1988, published 1998).

33 RVW to Anthony Scott, 30 July 1955, *VWL* 3106; *CVW*, 231; see also "Jeremy Dale Roberts," in *TSR*, 112. Ursula Vaughan Williams suggests the inspiration for the flugelhorn came during a trip to Austria in 1957 (*RVW*, 381), but earlier sketches reveal its presence.

34 See Douglas, *Working with Vaughan Williams*, 90–91, 96.

35 See *CVW*, 231–36; *WVW*, 342–43; and Robin Barber, "Malcolm Sargent, Vaughan Williams and the Ninth Symphony," *VWJ*, no. 24 (June 2002): 8–9.

36 *WVW*, 343.

37 RVW to Alan Frank, 15 February 1958, *VWL* 3375.

38 The definitive treatment of this topic is Alain Frogley, *Vaughan Williams's Ninth Symphony* (OUP, 2001), particularly chap. 7.

39 *CVW*, 233.

40 See Frogley, "Vaughan Williams and Thomas Hardy," 42–59.

41 RVW, "A Musical Autobiography," 191.

42 Pike, *Vaughan Williams and the Symphony*, 335; see also 301–3.

43 *RVW*, 386.

44 Final revisions were likely not finished, however, as dynamics are all but absent.

45 Renée Chérie Clark, "A Critical Appraisal of the *Four Last Songs*," in *VWE*, 157–59, 171.

46 James Day, *Vaughan Williams*, 116–17.

Appendix B

1 *CVW* indicates that the first performance of the reconstructed score (the original having been lost) was at the Winter Gardens, Bournemouth, 11 February 1915. That concert was actually the third performance of that version; the first took place in Harrogate, 12 August 1914, and a second in Edinburgh, 30 November 1914.

2 An orchestral arrangement of this work was recorded in 2017 as *Little March Suite* by Martin Yates and the Royal Scottish National Orchestra (Dutton DCLX 7351).

3 The work was originally titled "Mass." Its modification to *A Cambridge Mass* was offered by Alan Tongue upon its revival in order to distinguish it from the Mass in G Minor (see **IV.C.9**)

4 The composer indicates that the text includes passages from Richard Taverner's version of the Bible (1539). However, the few textual passages deviating from the KJV do not correspond with Taverner's, suggesting that such modifications were Vaughan Williams's own.

5 This movement was originally composed in 1911.

6 Other versions exist for four soloists (SATB) with chorus and orchestra, full chorus and orchestra, or orchestra alone.

7 Alternative version for women's voices: Here, Queen Uncrown'd.

8 A suite for small orchestra was arranged from this work by Roy Douglas, featuring the following five movements: I. To the Ploughboy and May Song; II. The Green Meadow and An Acre of Land; III. The Spring of Thyme and The Lark in the Morning; IV. The Cuckoo; V. Wassail Song and Children's Christmas Song.

9 Although these are technically arrangements, they are very freely treated and clearly conceived of as a group, and so are included here rather than in **VIII**.

10 A note on the score reads, in part, "This service is designed for college chapels and other churches where there is, besides the choir, a large body of voices who also wish for a share in the musical settings of the service. The part allotted to these voices is entirely in unison or octaves."

11 This final song was not discovered until after the composer's death, and added to the cycle posthumously.

12 Contrary to *CVW*, it was not destroyed; an MS copy may be found in BL MS Mus. 157, ff. 5–6.

13 Only seven of the eight songs were performed at the premiere, as well as at several subsequent performances, but which ones are unknown (only nos. 5 and 8 are specifically mentioned in reviews). The original numbering was also different. The first three songs were organized as above, and the remainder as follows: 4. The Soldier; 5. The Sigh That Heaves the Grasses; 6. In the Morning; 7. Good-Bye; 8. Fancy's Knell; 9. With Rue My Heart Is Laden.

14 This performance predates the one indicated in *CVW*.

15 Sine Nomine, Down Ampney, Randolph, and Salve Festa Dies were all first published in *The English Hymnal* (see **IX.A.2a**).

16 Further arrangements from this collection are available in *The Oxford Book of Carols for Schools* (50 carols arranged for unison singing; OUP, 1956) and *English Traditional Carols* (21 carols from the *OBC* arranged for sopranos or trebles and altos in two, three, and four parts, some with descant; OUP, 1954).

17 This is a variant of the tune featuring this name referred to in Chapter 4, which RVW collected from the same singer in 1903.

18 See *VWL* 261 for context.

General Index

Index of Works